C000146839

International Review of Strategic Management

VOLUME 4 1993

MEMBERS OF THE EDITORIAL BOARD

International Review of Strategic Management

VOLUME 4 1993

Edited by

D. E. Hussey

Harbridge Consulting Group Ltd

JOHN WILEY & SONS

CHICHESTER · NEW YORK · BRISBANE · TORONTO · SINGAPORE

International Review of Strategic Management ISSN 1047–7918

Published annually by John Wiley & Sons

Library of Congress Cataloging-in-Publication Data

is available 90–641036

British Library Cataloguing in Publication Data

International review of strategic management—vol 4 (1993)—
658

ISBN 0-471-93968-4

Typeset in 11/12pt Palatino by Mathematical Composition Setters Ltd, Salisbury, Wiltshire
Printed and bound in Great Britain by Biddles, Ltd, Guildford, and King's Lynn

CONTENTS

PART THREE: OTHER TOPICS

ABOUT THE CONTRIBUTORS

H. IGOR ANSOFF is one of the best known authorities in the field of strategic management. His early book, *Corporate Strategy* (McGraw-Hill, New York, 1965), was the major influence in the development of a strategic approach to planning. In the early 1970s he made another contribution, in the development of the concept of strategic management. More recently, he has developed an approach to strategy which takes account of the level of environmental turbulence: his chapter in this book continues his work on this concept. He is professor at United States International University, San Diego, and President of Ansoff Associates. Among his many honorary appointments is membership of the editorial board of the *International Review of Strategic Management*.

DAVID ASCH is Dean and Director of studies at the School of Management at the Open University. He has written widely on strategic management and his books include *Strategic Management* (Macmillan, 1987) and *Readings in Strategic Management* (Macmillan, 1989), both prepared with Cliff Bowman. His current research includes strategic change in organizations and the development of the UK domestic electrical appliance industry.

CHARLES CARROLL is currently completing his doctoral studies in strategic management at the University of Illinois. His interdisciplinary approach to research places particular emphasis on the evolution of collectives of firms and the impact of those collectives on industry dynamics. This research applies network analysis to patterns of cooperation and competition among firms. Analytic methods are also developed to assess the core competence of firms and model the dynamics of mobility barriers.

COLIN COULSON-THOMAS counsels and advises organizations on an international basis. He is Chairman and Chief Executive of Adaptation Ltd, and has undertaken a comprehensive programme of surveys of best practice on behalf of professional associations and business clients. He is an authority on the achievement of corporate transformation and strategic business development. The most recent of his 30 books and reports is *Creating the Global Company* (McGraw-Hill, Maidenhead, 1992).

KENNETH DAVID is Associate Professor of Anthropology and International Business at Michigan State University. He holds a BA (Honours) from Wesleyan University of Connecticut, an MA and PhD from the University of Chicago, and an MBA from Michigan State. He works on a global basis. His research from 1968 to 1974 was on variations of rural socio-cultural structure in Sri Lanka. Since 1981 he has focused on international business research, particularly on cultural and power issues that often inhibit implementation of a coherent strategy. He co-authored the second and third editions of *The Cultural Environment of International Business* (Cincinnati, South Western, 1984 and 1991), and *Investing in Developing Countries: A Guide for Executives* (Lexington Press, 1986). In addition he has written many articles and contributed chapters to other publications.

GARY HAMEL is Associate Professor in Strategy and International Management at the London Business School. In addition to the article in this book, he co-authored another landmark article, The Core Competence of Organizations, *Harvard Business Review*, May/June 1990.

DAVID HUSSEY has had many years of experience in corporate planning, as a practitioner in industry from 1964 to 1975, and as a consultant since 1976. Prior to moving into corporate planning, he was engaged in industrial development work in a developing country. He is a vice-president of a well-known US consultancy and managing director of its European operations, and is the author of several books on the subject of strategic management, including *Corporate Planning: Theory and Practice* (Pergamon, 1974), which won the John Player management author of the year award. He was one of the founders of the Society for Strategic Planning, and has been associated with the official journal of the society, *Long Range Planning*, since its foundation. He is a member of the editorial board of *Strategic Directions*, and is a director of the Japanese Society of Strategic Management. He is editor of the *Journal of Strategic Change*, which was launched in 1992.

AKIRA ICHIKAWA has had 27 years of business experience, including corporate planning, new business development, and personnel affairs. In addition he has had 7 years of academic experience teaching strategic management, corporate culture, business development, and total quality control. He is actively engaged in writing, and in lecturing to business firms. He is Professor of Fuji Junior College Management Research Institute, and senior managing director of the Japanese Society of Strategic Management. His many works include *Handbook of Corporate Philosophy and Long-Term Vision*, *Strategic Management of Growing Companies*, and *Practice of Strategic TQC for Middle Managers*. All of these are in Japanese.

FRANZ-FRIEDRICH NEUBAUER is Professor of Multinational Strategy and Planning at IMD in Lausanne, and adjunct professor of Business at the Pennsylvania State University at Harrisburg, USA. He holds a doctorate from the University of Würzburg and an MBA (Dipl Kfm) from the University of Frankfurt. He has extensive management consulting experience with multinational companies in the area of strategic planning, and is the author of a number of books on business policy and strategic planning. He is a member of the editorial board of this book series.

JOHN NICHOLLS graduated as an engineer from Imperial College, London, and started his career with Alcan in Canada, for whom he worked for 10 years before being awarded a Ford Foundation Doctoral Fellowship to study at Stanford University, where he received his MBA and PhD. Before setting up his present consultancy, John Nicholls Associates, he was a Director of the British Institute of Management with the task of re-establishing their Division of Management Education and Training. His book *Creating a Committed Workforce* was published by the Institute of Personnel Management and McGraw-Hill in 1987.

J. R. M. PANDIAN is at the University of St. Andrews.

JAGDISH PARIKH (PhD in management, MBA, ITP, Harvard Business School, BA Economics, BComm., Bombay) is managing director of Lemuir group of companies, Bombay. He is a member of the governing boards of three major institutions: the Harvard Business School Alumni Association, the Asian Institute of Management, Philippines, and the Indian Institute of Management. His research interests are intuition, corporate visioning and transformative management.

C. K. PRAHALAD is Professor of Corporate Strategy at the University of Michigan. He is internationally known as an authority on the strategy management of large, diversified global corporations. Written with Yves Doz, his book the *The Multinational Mission* (Free Press, New York, 1987) was one of the first substantial works on global strategy.

W. KEITH SCHILIT is an accomplished author, consultant, entrepreneur and lecturer. He is the author of three recent books on venture capital and emerging growth ventures, and is engaged on a fourth book on 'hypergrowth' companies. He is head of the consulting firm Catalyst Ventures of Tampa, Florida, and is on the faculty of the University of South Florida.

HARBIR SINGH is an Associate Professor of Management at the Wharton School. He did his doctoral work at the University of Michigan, Ann Arbor, receiving a PhD in 1984. His research addresses the impact of Board characteristics on top management decisions, the role of acquisitions in corporate strategy, and choices between joint venture and internal development as alternative modes of corporate growth. More recently, his work has addressed cultural conflict in the management of acquisitions and joint ventures. His work has been published in the *Strategic Management Journal*, the *Journal of Management Studies*, the *Academy of Management Review* and the *Journal of International Business Studies*. He serves on the editorial boards of the *Strategic Management Journal* and *Organisation Science*. His current research and teaching interests address predictors of effective corporate revitalization. At Wharton Dr Singh is Research Director at the Sol Snider Center for Entrepreneurial Management.

KAREN SODERBERG is an associate director at management consultants Harbridge Consulting Group Ltd., where her work focuses primarily on the areas of organizational change and business and individual performance improvement. She is currently developing new thinking in the areas of leadership, coaching and empowerment. Her recent projects have included working with client teams to address problems and opportunities posed by global and matrix management, self-directed work team structures and strategic alliances. Previously at Arthur D. Little Inc. she received a Presidential Merit Award for outstanding leadership of two international client engagements. She holds a BA degree in management and legal studies from Bowdoin College and an MBA degree from the Johnson Graduate School of Management, Cornell University. She also studied politics in a Swedish graduate programme and was a Rotary International Graduate Scholar at the Scandinavian Institute of Maritime and Petroleum Law, Oslo University, Norway. She is fluent in Swedish, and proficient in Norwegian and German.

PATRICK A. SULLIVAN is Associate Professor of Strategic Management at the US International University in San Diego, where he received his doctoral degree in the strategic management programme. Prior to his present position, he has spent a long and distinguished career in a civil service organization which serves infrastructural needs of the US Navy.

HOWARD THOMAS is the Dean of the College of Commerce and Business Administration, the James F. Towey Professor of Strategic Management and Policy, and the Director of the Office of International and Strategic Management at the University of Illinois at Urbana-Champaign. He has held permanent and visiting appointments at universities in the UK, Australia, and a number of other North American Universities. He has written numerous books and articles, and is on the editorial boards of seven journals. He was awarded the designation of University Senior Scholar in 1986 and Outstanding Educator, Executive MBA Program 1986, 1988 and 1989. He received the Excellence-in-Teaching award from the Commerce Alumni Association in 1990. He became Acting Dean at the University of Illinois at Urbana-Champaign in 1991 and permanent Dean in 1992.

INTRODUCTION

This is the fourth volume of the *International Review of Strategic Management*, and continues to follow the objective of the series, which is to produce an annual critical review of developments and best practice in strategic management. Over the years this will accumulate to a significant reference source. Each book contains its own index, as well as a cumulative contents list for the series. It is intended to produce a special index to cover all volumes with the fifth volume, which will be published in 1994.

As we move towards the year 2000 it is possible to observe new nuances of meaning about the way organizations should manage. The importance of the human factor in strategic management is being increasingly recognized, and terms like *performance management*, *empowerment*, *leadership* and *vision* are spread across the new writings on the subject. This does not mean that the issues raised have never been discussed before, but that there is a line of thinking that is drawing more of them together.

In part this is due to the ever increasing complexity of many businesses, as they strive to succeed in a business environment which is changing and moving. Hussey (1991) examined much of the research on the major trends affecting management, and divided them into trigger factors and organizational response trends. Although the analysis revealed many factors that affect strategy formulation, there were at least as many that in some way affected the people aspects of strategic management.

As situations become more difficult and complex, the need for good leadership increases. In this context leadership has to include both the setting of an appropriate direction for the organization, and the ability to communicate this, to motivate the organization, and to manage in such a way that the organization journeys successfully to the chosen destination. The personal characteristics of a good leader are bound up with the ability to make good strategic decisions. Although good leadership may sometimes overcome the deficiencies of a strategy, and sometimes a powerful strategy may strengthen poor leadership, the best results can only come when both are in balance.

For these reasons it was felt that this volume of the *Review* should take leadership as its theme. However, it soon became apparent that to look only at transformational or visionary leadership without also giving some consideration to modern thinking about vision was only to do part of the job.

An element in the whole strategic management process, which seems to be much more to the fore in modern writing, is the development of a vision for the organization by top management. This does not necessarily have to come out of the head of only one person, although sometimes it may. The vision is the view which goes beyond the life span of the corporate plans, which identifies the future nature and philosophy of the organization. The quality of the vision is tied in directly with the quality of leadership, and of course a good system of planning cannot compensate for a lack of leadership. We will return to both vision and leadership later. The word 'vision' has many meanings. In this context it combines things like 'foresight', 'a vivid concept or mental picture', 'imaginative perception', 'a pleasing imaginative plan for, or anticipation of, future events'. (All taken from Kirkpatrick, 1983.)

The dictionary, through some of the other meanings, also reveals the pitfalls in the concept of vision, such as 'a revelation ... in sleep', or a visionary 'given to reverie or fantasy', and 'out of touch with reality, impractical'. My own description of visions gone wrong comes through word association: 'vision ... dream ... nightmare'. Like so much else in strategic management, the chief executive has to get it right.

Vision and leadership are not new concepts, although the ideas around them may be. Ansoff (1965) contained a chapter about a system of objectives. Drucker (1955) and Levitt (1960), both wrote on issues which would not be out of place in a modern discussion on vision.

We have three contributions which are related to the idea of vision. Gary Hamel and C. K. Prahalad's landmark article on strategic intent is reprinted from the *Harvard Business Review*. Colin Coulson-Thomas conducted three surveys which looked at the process of setting vision, and found that many organizations were naïve in the way they approached it. His chapter, which originally appeared in that excellent journal *Long Range Planning*, offers useful advice on the process. This theme is continued in Jagdish Parikh and Fred Neubauer's chapter on corporate visioning, which also makes a neat bridge to subsequent chapters on leadership. Indeed, it was Fred, who is an editorial board member, who suggested leadership as a theme for this book.

John Nicholls has been exploring leadership for at least a decade. He provides two contributions, an article which explores the various concepts of leadership, which first appeared in the *Journal of General Management*, and a new preface to that article, especially written for the *Review*, which includes his latest thinking. Karen Soderberg offers concepts of leadership based on research and empirical experience. Her chapter is complemented by one from Japan, by Akira Ichikawa. A second Japanese article has been written by Masaharu Saruya, but translation delays mean that it will appear in the next volume. I should like to thank Gen-Ichi Nakamura, another editorial board member, for finding these authors for me, and for organizing the translation of their work. This is only one of many contributions which he has made to the *Review*. The role of his two co-translators,

Dae-Ryong Choi and Kumiko Yokoi, should also not pass unnoticed, and their help in giving us access to Japanese thinkers is very much appreciated.

In discussing the theme articles first, I have omitted to mention the first chapter of this book. This is the state of the art review, which this year follows a slightly different pattern from past practice. The first three volumes contained general overviews, contributed by authors from Japan, the United States of America and the United Kingdom. This strategy provided very different perspectives. In this book Howard Thomas, another active supporter of the *Review*, Charles Carroll and J. R. M. Pandian have written a far-reaching review of the role of analytic models in corporate strategy. This makes a significant contribution to our knowledge on this subject, and I was very pleased to receive it.

Four of our five general contributions in the last section of the book are not too far away from the theme. Igor Ansoff and Patrick Sullivan have chosen this series to present the results of an eight-year-long empirical research programme on success behaviours in a variety of organizations. This relates to the environmental turbulence model, which regular readers may recall Igor wrote about in volume 2 of this series.

David Asch provides a case study on the management of strategic change in a high-technology environment, which itself is a major leadership challenge. The chapter provides a case study of Rank Xerox UK.

Kenneth David and Harbir Singh contribute a chapter on cultural compatability and risk in acquisitions, which is full of original thinking. My own chapter gives some thinking on effective management development. The models offered have a direct connection with strategic management.

The article by W. Keith Schilit is based on research into the relationship of risk and returns in investments. This type of article is new to the *Review*, but is very much within its planned scope.

I should like to thank the many contributors to this book for all the effort that they have put in. It is the excellence of the contributions which determines whether a series such as this can meet its ambitious objectives. Thanks are also due to the editorial board members, not only those I have already mentioned, but the whole team whose advice and active help plays a major part in shaping the series.

REFERENCES

Ansoff, H. I. (1965) *Corporate Strategy*, McGraw-Hill, New York.

Drucker, P. F. (1955) *The Practice of Management*. Heinemann, London.

Hussy, D. E. (1991) Strategic management for the 1990s. In D. E. Hussey, (ed.), *International Review of Strategic Management*, 2.2. Wiley, Chichester.

Kirkpatrick, E. M. (ed.) (1983) *Chambers Twentieth Century Dictionary*, New Edition. Chambers, Edinburgh.

Levitt, T. (1960) Marketing myopia, *Harvard Business Review*, July–August.

Part One

STATE OF THE ART REVIEW

1

THE ROLE OF ANALYTIC MODELS IN STRATEGIC MANAGEMENT

Charles Carroll, J. R. M. Pandian and Howard Thomas

University of Illinois at Urbana-Champaign

THE ROLE OF ANALYTIC MODELS IN STRATEGIC MANAGEMENT

Decision-makers charged with the strategic management of organizations are often confronted with unstructured, ambiguous situations. Top level managers faced most directly by the open-system nature of the organization must stay aware of the complex web of interdependence that unites the organization's diverse set of stakeholders (e.g. managers themselves, shareholders, labor, suppliers, buyers, rivals, government agencies, special interest groups, society at large). The scope and ambiguity of managerial tasks may be overwhelming at times.

Managers lack the cognitive capacity to consider all environmental events and possible responses simultaneously (i.e. in parallel), and they lack the time to consider them serially. Managers must adopt a pragmatic, heuristic approach to making decisions under these conditions. Models can be extremely valuable for reducing the complexity of a problem (Day, DeSarbo, and Oliva, 1987). This could make it easier for practitioners to diagnose and frame problems/ opportunities (Thomas, 1988, 1990; Myers and de B. Wijnholds, 1990). They may assist managers making decisions in the grey areas where there is no policy guidance (Snyder, 1988) or when rational thought is clouded by confusion and imprecision (Barnett and Tress, 1990).

Models can also provide a language to facilitate the articulation of ideas (Day, DeSarbo, and Oliva, 1987). The Boston Consulting Group (BCG) portfolio matrix illustrates this point; terms such as 'cash cows,' 'stars,' 'problem children,' and

International Review of Strategic Management, volume 4.
Edited by D. E. Hussey

'dogs' have become a part of popular business jargon. These two benefits (simplification and communication) are the impetus behind a number of group-oriented decision aids (Alavi, 1991).

However, Rhodes (1989) points out that the ability to simplify a problem may be both a virtue and a vice. Organizations may be thought of as open systems that may have subsystems nested within them. Models may help managers make some sense of the systems. The *caveat emptor* is that models do reflect a particular point of view, and they only provide a limited representation.

Their simplicity predisposes them to biases. At the same time, their simplicity allows the generation of possible solutions when more comprehensive algorithmic approaches are intractable. While there are certain situations which may invalidate the use of heuristics, there exist a wide range of conditions under which heuristics perform quite well (Weist, 1966). If this were not true, heuristics would not be expected to evolve and persist as they do.

Biases are inevitable in human thought, regardless of the nature of the decision aid. As with any heuristic approach, when analytic models are used as simplifying heuristics, decision-makers will become predisposed to certain types of errors. For example, Stevens and Martin (1989) argue that the use of inadequate internal decision models may have contributed to the decline in the competitiveness of US firms. Even if relatively adequate models are used, the output must be interpreted appropriately by managers if it is to be useful (New, Lockett, and Boaden, 1991).

However, models need not (and should not) act as constraints. When used appropriately, analytic models may stimulate thought and (re)direct thinking. They may help focus attention and overcome blind spots (Porter, 1980; Zajac and Bazerman, 1991). When evaluating alternative strategies, models may force managers to carefully consider aspects, positive and negative, that they might otherwise gloss over (Treleven and Schweikhart, 1988). For instance, managers often fail to consider the changes that would be required in implementing a new strategy (Judson, 1991).

For example, critical variables (parameters) in a decision model can be systematically varied to explore the impact of changes in technology, shifts in demographic characteristics, fluctuations in the economy, etc. (Michman, 1987; Shalliker, 1987). Managers can compare a number of strategic alternatives by examining the strengths and weaknesses of each alternative under a variety of plausible scenarios. This 'what if' or sensitivity analysis approach for evaluating strategic options can be used to prioritize alternatives for future consideration and possible implementation (Utsey, 1987; Leviton, 1989).

Perhaps more important than providing a vocabulary for discussion, the use of models may serve as a catalyst for dialogue among decision-makers. This dialogue may actually be more beneficial than the output of the models. It may provide a forum for debating world views, problem formulations, available options, likely scenarios, and may facilitate the exposure of previously implicit assumptions (Thomas, 1988, 1990).

Decision aids may play in iterative cycles of problem formulation, alternative generation, and alternative evaluation (Thomas, 1988, 1990). Tracing the formulation/generation/selection processes over time may reflect the generation of, and movement through, a decision tree using a branch and bound heuristic. Analytic models may be used to identify and frame problems by identifying critical events in the environment or providing benchmarks for assessing competitive position. Each framing of a problem would generate a node in the tree.

Within each framing of the problem, models may be used to trigger debates and insights in the alternative generation process. These would be reflected as branches representing alternative solutions stemming from a node reflecting the initial state or framing of the problem used by the managers. The forecasted consequences may provide new insights (the next node). More dramatically, the insights may spark the reframing of the entire problem. Managers would, thereby, branch to a new subtree. (Decision trees containing a number of problem reformulations may be considered as 'supertrees' that are analogous to supergames in game theory.) After evaluating the alternatives (branches) that were generated, managers may prune away branches that are expected to be less fruitful in order to conserve decision-making time and energy.

As thinking and debate moves managers down each bounded set of branches, another generation of new insights may be triggered. Hence, new branches would be illuminated. The iterative cycle of problem diagnosis, alternative generation, and alternative evaluation would continue until an acceptable solution is obtained. Bear in mind that the threshold for what is acceptable may change dramatically as deadlines approach. Terminal nodes that were 'put on hold' may be revisited if superior results are not found by experimenting with alternative branches or subtrees.

This cyclical process of narrowing and expanding the scope of a problem is illustrated in the use of Chatterjee, Eliashberg, Gatignon, and Lodish's (1988) TESTER model. TESTER is a Bayesian model which incorporates continuous distributions of uncertain outcomes to minimize the amount of information that must be obtained from each manager. That is, it reduces the scope of the problem. By making several simplified passes at the problem rather than trying to handle everything at once, managers may process information more efficiently and effectively. Managers who have used the model reported that the interactive process proved useful for triggering questions that, in turn, led to new insights into the problem. That is, it subsequently broadened the scope of the problem by generating new branches in the decision tree.

A common misconception about analytical models is that they provide answers. It is easy to reach incorrect conclusions by relying solely on the output of analytical models. Models would be better thought of as decision aids or tools that may assist managers (Edmister, 1988; Jasany, 1989; O'Neill, 1991; Thomas, 1988, 1990).

Thus far, we have only considered the role of analytic models in developing, evaluating, and selecting strategy. Issues of implementation have only been discussed as criteria for evaluating strategic options. Analytic models may also play a role in the implementation process itself by providing a means of communicating the strategic vision to others. Models can be expressed as simulations or games (Gatignon, 1987). These types of models allow top management to convey the underlying logic and anticipated impact of a proposed strategic plan to middle management in a quick and effective manner (*Supervision*, 1989). Models may also be used to institutionalize aspects of a particular strategy. The models may then be used as part of an educational process as managers and other employees are trained to implement various aspects of a particular strategy (Saeed and Linstrom, 1988; Peterson, 1991). Performance on such simulations has even been used in hiring processes to screen potential managers (Faria, 1989).

More generally, many firms use simulations to hone the skills and improve the performance of their employees (Broadwell, 1987; Faria, 1989). Business schools have successfully used simulations and games to train executive MBAs (Gooding and Keys, 1990) and other students. The use of this approach in universities and management training programs is quite widespread and its application appears to be growing (Faria, 1989).

APPLICATIONS OF ANALYTIC MODELS

Analytic models have been used as aids in an extremely wide range of problems faced by managers. They have been applied to problems throughout the value chain from the utilization of natural resources, the flow of materials through stages of processing, transactions between suppliers and buyers throughout the chain, and ultimately, interactions with the end consumer. They also have addressed issues of organizational design and structure.

A taxonomy may be useful for outlining the role of analytic models in strategic management. First, analytic models may be categorized based on the unit of analysis. For the purposes of this taxonomy, a dichotomy will be imposed between models addressing lower level (strategic business unit (SBU) and functional) issues and those addressing higher level (corporate) issues. Within the former group (i.e. SBU and functional models), there are those models which focus primarily on supply-side or demand-side issues while others focus more broadly on competition among rivals. The dichotomy between lower and higher level issues and the subsequent division of the lower level issues effectively yields four categories describing the use of analytic models in strategic management: (a) supply-side, (b) demand-side, (c) general competition, and (d) corporate.

Second, while some simple models describe patterns observed in data, others have been derived from theoretical debate. Of course, an empirical/theoretical distinction does not yield a perfect dichotomy; the development of models generally involves both data-driven and theory-driven insights. This dichotomy

		Empirical	Theoretical
Strategic business unit (SBU)	Supply-side	Scale effects Experience effects Site selection	Operations research Product innovation Choice of technology Harvesting resources Purchasing resources Manufacturing systems Flow and inventory Distribution
	Demand-side	Consumer choice Market response Product diffusion Market share	Market segmentation Product differentiation Optimal pricing
	Competition	PIMS database Strategic groups	Game theory Spatial competition Innovation competition
Corporate		Diversification Scope effects Control systems	Diversification Scope effects Portfolio analysis

Figure 1.1 The role of analytic models used in strategic management categorized by level (SBU–corporate) and origin (empirical–theoretical)

is imposed to reflect the origin of the models and the relative emphasis on theoretical versus empirical influences in subsequent development.

These distinctions are the basis for a 4×2 taxonomy that captures the primary influences addressed by analytic models in strategic management in recent years (see Figure 1.1). While the categories are neither mutually exclusive nor exhaustive, the taxonomy does provide a sound, structural framework for discussing the role of analytic models.

Supply-Side Models

Models that assist managers in developing and providing goods or services are categorized as supply-side models in this taxonomy. Those which were derived empirically will be discussed first. Those with stronger conceptual roots will then be considered.

Empirical

Two areas of empirically driven modeling reflect observed relationships between the unit cost of production and two factors—scale and experience effects. A third branch of supply-side modeling, namely, data-driven models of site selection, will also be discussed.

Scale effects

A variety of methods have been used to develop models which reflect the negative relationship between scale and unit cost. Economies of scale have been observed in the railroad (Kim, 1987), major home appliance (Tellis, 1989) and local public education (Callan and Santerre, 1990) industries. However, diseconomies of scale have been identified in other industries such as municipal police departments (Gyimah-Brempong, 1987). Not only are there inconsistencies across industries, there seem to be inconsistencies within industries. Within an industry, differences in returns to scale may be associated with specific generic strategies (Goldberg, Hanweck, Keenan, and Young, 1991; Kim and Ben-Zion, 1989) and technologies (Krautmann and Solow, 1988). Scale effects may also be specific to functional areas (Cho, 1988; van Dalen, Koerts, and Thurik, 1990) and even to projects within an area (Banker and Kemerer, 1989).

Banker and Kemerer (1989) outline a method to identify the most productive scale-size (MPSS) for software development projects. Data envelopment analysis has also been used to study the positive and negative effects of scale on unit cost. Results suggest that the optimal scale varies across application environments.

While economies of scale may exist up to very large plant sizes, technological constraints may limit the maximum feasible scale. Lieberman (1987a) proposes a 'scale frontier' model to reflect this imposed upper bound. The model provides a good fit to data reflecting the size of new plants built in the chemical processing industries.

Taken together, these findings suggest that there is no simple rule of thumb that managers should follow when making scale decisions. However, analytic models may be quite helpful for managers who need to make strategic decisions regarding the scale of various aspects of their operations.

Experience/learning effects

Another well known branch of empirically driven modeling is the examination of the effects of experience on unit cost. The unit cost of production is an exponential function of the cumulative number of units produced. Experience curve models have been used to adjust forecasts of average unit costs (LeFrois, 1987). This information has been used to evaluate the cost of alternatives involving new products or processes (Pogue, 1990). It may be useful in evaluating pricing strategies for new products given the rate at which learning is expected to diffuse across rival firms (Lieberman, 1987b). It has also been recommended for governmental use in defense contracting to aid buyers in assessing fair prices and evaluating alternative systems (Anton and Yao, 1987).

A number of innovative methods have been proposed for assessing experience effects. Harrison and Ketz (1989) suggest that users lacking a strong background in management science may find successive linear programming (SLP) easier to use than alternative methods involving the implementation of sophisticated algorithms in mathematical programming solutions. The SLP method only requires access to a linear programming package.

Naim and Towill (1990) use algorithms based on the least squared error (LSE) via the Taylor series expansion method. In their article, emphasis is placed on combining a continuous trend and a cyclical component in this time-series approach. The method performed well in modeling efficiency in the electricity supply industry.

Learning or experience may influence a number of factors in addition to unit cost. Harrison and Ketz (1989) examine the impact of learning effects on the amount of labor required per unit of production. The impact of learning effects on labor can be especially significant in the implementation of new processes. This has obvious implications for managers making strategic decisions regarding process innovations, the adoption of new technologies and in the use of flexible manufacturing systems (Pattison and Teplitz, 1989).

Towill (1990, p. 25) expands the scope of concern further and argues that forecasting the effects of experience is 'an important industrial requirement for many purposes, including costing, process capacity planning, manpower planning, batch sizing and delivery date projections.'

Site selection

Decisions regarding the location of facilities may be critical in manufacturing industries. Demand-side issues of location selection include transportation and labor costs, employee morale, and public relations (Azani and Khorramshahgol, 1990). The impact of location on competition among rivals (i.e. spatial competition) will be addressed in the category of conceptually driven models of competition.

General Motors Corp. developed a system of mathematical models to aid managers in selecting sites to support products overseas (Breitman and Lucas, 1987). The model, Production Location Analysis Network System (PLANETS), lets the user define the environment and the assumptions. PLANETS automatically checks the feasibility of possible scenarios, then generates mathematical models and their solutions. It even provides interpretations and generates a report. After 80 actual applications, the authors report that the model made it possible to consider more scenarios in less time and with greater reliability. Further, it has resulted in an estimated $1 billion in cost savings.

Site selection is obviously a critical aspect of management in service industries. In the hotel industry, La Quinta Motor Inns developed a regression model and incorporated it into a spreadsheet decision model for site selection to minimize the risk of choosing unprofitable sites (Kimes and Fitzsimmons, 1990). In the tourism industry, the LOCAT model generates an overall attractiveness index for sites based on (a) accessibility, (b) uniqueness, (c) catchment population, and (d) the probability of patronage (Moutinho and Paton, 1991). It is suggested that the model may help managers avoid serious errors in site selection.

Theoretical

Theoretically driven models of supply-side issues in strategic management are derived from the areas of operations research and production management in general. Specific applications include the choice of technology, plant layout, the flow of materials through production processes, managing inventory, and quality assessment.

Overview of operations research and production management
A number of studies of US firms have identified a strong need to integrate manufacturing strategy with overall corporate strategy and with strategy in other functional areas such as research and development (R&D), marketing, and after-sales service (Armistead and Clark, 1991; Lindberg, 1990; Marucheck, Pannesi, and Anderson, 1990; Skinner, 1978). Not surprisingly, manufacturing now plays a crucial role in strategic management in many firms (Marucheck, Pannesi, and Anderson, 1990; Reitsperger and Daniel, 1990; Swamidass and Newell, 1987; Vickery, 1991). Further, it has been found that the relative influence of manufacturing in strategic management is positively related to the performance of the firm (Swamidass and Newell, 1987; Vickery, 1991). Operations research has even been touted as a universal language for business strategy (Wagner, 1988).

A survey of journal articles suggests that the use of analytic models is one of the dominant approaches in operations management research (Amoako-Gyampah and Meredith, 1989). Academicians are not alone in their reliance on such models. A survey of the 500 largest US industrial firms reveals that simulation, linear programming, and regression analysis (primarily in quality control) are heavily used. Network models experienced moderate use (primarily in the planning and control stage of projects). Game theory, queuing theory, and dynamic programming were hardly used.

While the use of analytic models has been widely accepted in operations research, Wagner (1988, pp. 801–802) notes three philosophical criticisms raised by others. First, decisions driven by formal models will be predictable, and rivals will be able to anticipate the responses of the firm. A cloud of ambiguity may be preferred to precision and predictability. Second, the cold and calculating nature of formal model building may 'alter our social ethics or undermine reverence for human value.' Third, 'a model, like Frankenstein's monster, can get out of control and overpower its own creator.' Wagner plays down the validity of these criticisms and looks forward to continued progress in this area of research.

There certainly seems to be a need for analytic models as managers will be faced with increasingly complex decisions such as those related to flexible manufacturing systems (Singhal, Fine, Meredith, and Suri, 1987). Models may play a major role in every phase of system development from the initial choice of technology, to the design of the physical system, to scheduling and control systems, to steady-state operation.

In addition to the rising complexity of manufacturing problems, there is an increase in the adoption of time-based approaches to competition (Azzone, Masella, and Bertele, 1991; Stalk and Hout, 1990). Even if a time-based strategy is not explicitly pursued, managers are often caught in last-minute crises that demand rapid decisions. Surl (1988) recommends the use of a rapid modeling technique that is based on four propositions. First, it is better to have a rough model immediately than to have a refined model later. Second, there is greater interdepartmental linkage to corporate strategy if the decision support tools do not require extensive training. Third, managers should focus efforts on better planning rather than better scheduling. Fourth, intuition and existing knowledge can play a greater role when decision tools are interactive. The method yields rough-cut models that lack precision, but are fast and easy to use.

Such models facilitate the consideration of manufacturing issues in the formulation of strategy. Hence, the use of models may facilitate the development of strategy that integrates issues from manufacturing with those from other functional areas and those at the corporate level.

Product innovation

In many high-tech firms R&D expenditures may be as much as 10% of sales, and the cost may rise to 20% to 30% of sales in the future (Kuwahara and Takeda, 1990). A critical task for managers in such firms is to control cost by evaluating projects and allocating resources wisely.

There is an increasing awareness that R&D should be integrated with marketing and manufacturing functions. Analytic models may help managers incorporate consumer preferences for product characteristics in the idea generation and evaluation phases of R&D projects (Muramatsu, Ichimura, and Ishii, 1990). Computer simulations have been used to analyze preference patterns for product characteristics and predict market share for two or more competing products as well as the likely market penetration for a given configuration of product characteristics (Winokur and Venkitaraman, 1991). Another simulation (Vepsalainen and Lauro, 1988) utilizing customer preferences also incorporated the relative technological strengths of rivals and respective R&D budgets to predict the return on R&D investment and the potential for sustainable competitive advantage. Managers may use the results of such computer simulations to guide efforts in the early stages of product development and in establishing priorities for R&D funding.

Other methods have been developed for evaluating ongoing R&D projects. Bard (1990) developed a model that takes as its input (a) a set of R&D projects, (b) a set of objectives, (c) likelihood measures linking effort on projects to success, (d) budget and performance constraints, and (e) a utility function based on the possible range of outcomes. Using a probabilistic goal program approach, a heuristic is used to identify the best funding scheme.

A mathematical model used by managers in the electronics industry to evaluate the cost-effectiveness of R&D projects takes into account the phase of research, the product's life cycle, and factors affecting future growth (Kuwahara and Takeda, 1990). Given a set of objectives, several variations of figure of merit are given; the most useful figure-of-merit approach was research-contributed-to-profit method. This model may be used to obtain an overall evaluation of current R&D. Also, long range planning data could be used in strategic R&D planning to evaluate prestart and ongoing projects.

Finally, implicit in the evaluation of R&D projects is that it might be appropriate to cut some of the less promising projects. Aggarwal and Soenen (1989) propose a model that uses an extended version of the net present value rule for exit calculations. An economic profile of the effect of premature termination of a project can be graphed for the life cycle of the project. Managers may use this to quantify the economic consequences and risks associated with dropping a project at various stages. Such information could be useful for managers who must decide if a project should be terminated because of technological changes, governmental actions, or the need to maintain strategic flexibility in situations of environmental uncertainty.

Process innovation and choice of technology

Technological innovations may play a profound role in rivalry among firms (Schumpeter, 1934). For example, Aivazian, Callen, Chan and Mountain (1987) found that the growth in productivity in the US natural gas transmission industry (1953–1979) was greatly influenced by technological innovations. Innovations have influenced productivity as much, and often more than, the influence of economies of scale.

If innovations offer a competitive advantage, it is reasonable to expect rivals to attempt to mimic successfully implemented technological innovations. Often, the barriers preventing imitation are not sufficient to deter entry into the emerging, technology-based strategic group of innovating firms.

Tombak (1990) used game theory to model rivalry among firms when viable innovations (i.e. those which increase revenues and/or decrease costs) are accessible to a number of similar firms in an oligopolistic industry. Results of the model support the Schumpeterian hypothesis that firms would compete to be first mover in implementing such innovations. Consequently, innovations would be adopted in 'swarms' within industries. Data on the adoption of flexible manufacturing systems in machine-tool, automobile, aerospace, heavy machinery, and electronics industries supported the prediction that implementations would occur in swarms.

This suggests that the choice of technology can play a crucial role in strategic management. The degree to which an innovation can 'create winners and losers' depends on how managers respond to the innovation's impact on competition (Porter, 1980; Schroeder, 1990). The difficulty managers face is that it is not always clear what that impact will be and when it will manifest itself. Empirical evidence (Schroeder, 1990) suggests that (a) the time it takes for an innovation to have an effect will vary across industry segments, (b) the effects may be asymmetric across strategic groups of firms, (c) the effects of a given innovation will be influenced by subsequent development of that innovation, the emergence of complementary technologies, and diffusion of the innovation within the target market. Further, the best use of a given innovation may vary across strategic groups of firms as differences in strategic postures may drive differences in implementation.

Many technology-choice models focus on differences in cost. For example, Bemis and DeAngelis (1990) evaluate the cost-effectiveness of alternative methods of electricity production using a Lotus 1-2-3 spreadsheet. Booth (1991) used a time-state-preference valuation model to study the impact of technology choices on a firm's risk, and consequently, its cost of capital. A Cobb–Douglas production function was used to compare fixed and flexible methods of production. The trade-off between fixed-cost and variable-cost has been examined in a dynamic, stochastic model reflecting demand uncertainty (Cohen and Halperin, 1986). DePorter and Craig (1989) use linear programming to evaluate technological alternatives for office automation based on shadow costs. Kostreva (1990) uses a differential game model to examine cost-reduction of new technologies in service industries; the solution concept is a memoryless closed-loop Nash equilibrium which is computed by numerical approximation.

While the relative cost of operation is important in evaluating alternatives, overly simplistic decision-making aids may mislead managers. For instance, it is often implicitly assumed that the most profitable alternative will be the one with the greatest cost savings and that revenues will be unaffected by the choice of technology. The extensive use of investment practices that neglect the impact of technology investment on profitability and focus solely on cost may have limited the level of such investments in the US relative to Japan and Europe (Stevens and Martin, 1989). Park, Park, and Ntuen (1990) attribute the slow adoption of advanced manufacturing systems to the tendency of managers to underestimate or even fail to consider strategic factors in their decisions. Consequently, they propose a method to help managers consider strategic implications along with the more traditional economic concerns.

Putrus (1991) also offers a method of evaluating alternative technologies based on intangible benefits (e.g. quicker introduction of new products). The user is prompted to construct decision models reflecting the goals of the business. Criteria for selection are defined and weighed, and manufacturing options are compared. The role of the model is clearly to aid managers in making their own decisions. It relies on the experience and discretion of business managers and does not require detailed information. Parsaei and Wilhelm (1989) and Soni, Parsaei, and Liles (1990) also recommend using intangible benefits in evaluating alternative technologies. Ordinal scale measures are used to weigh intangible benefits in a linear additive modeling approach.

It bears repeating that the ability of technology to 'create winners and losers' depends on how managers respond to the effects of the technology (Porter, 1980; Schroeder, 1990). Analytic models can suggest the impact that external factors could have on the profitability of the alternative technology choices. Results of models could be used to stimulate debate when planning a strategic response to innovations.

Gaimon (1989) uses game theory to demonstrate how constraints imposed by external forces may influence a firm when a new technology significantly lowers the firm's unit operating cost. Such external constraints may force irreversible commitments. Due to labor union contracts, for example, a firm may be obligated to maintain its entire workforce regardless of its competitor's behavior. The results of the model suggest that if one or both firms have such constraints, profits will be lower for both firms. The implication for managers is that they should consider constraints that they may be under when evaluating technological alternatives. Further, they also need to consider constraints that their rivals may face, as the actions of their rivals will influence their profitability.

Runge (1987) uses a 3-stage model to examine how environmental consequences and governmental restrictions may influence the choice of agricultural technology. Relative to lower income segments of the population, higher income segments generally assign more value to environmental quality than to agricultural production. This pattern influences both the development and regulation of agricultural technology and has serious implications for both domestic and international policies. Again, the use of analytic models may aid managers (and policy-makers) by illustrating the impact of factors that might otherwise be overlooked.

Implicit in the modeling of technology choices is that innovations cause changes in the nature of competition over time. Yet there are relatively few models that consider time. Amit and Ilan (1990) include the rate of product diffusion in the target market when developing a technology switching policy. Roth, Gaimon, and Krajewski (1991) take a dynamic perspective when evaluating the choice of flexible manufacturing technology with respect to the effects of technology in the marketplace and the rate of organizational learning.

Harvesting available resources

Firms may have direct access to resources either through ownership or relatively open access. Some resources, as in forestry and fishing industries, can be replenished, although the process does take time. Other resources, such as minerals and fossil fuels, cannot be replenished. With this in mind, the harvesting of these resources must be managed prudently for the sake of long-run profits, if not for the growing importance of ethical and environmental concerns. The model may indicate previously unrecognized limits and help managers to identify optimal harvest rates (Hof and Baltic, 1991).

A variety of methods have been used to identify optimal harvesting policies for replenishing resources. The management of forestry resources has been modeled using an ordinary linear programming model (Eriksson and Bjorheden, 1989), a nonlinear partial differential equation solved by numerical methods (Morck, Schwartz, and Stangeland, 1989), and a multilevel optimization approach (Hof and Baltic, 1991). In the UK, the Sea-Fishing Industry Authority has used computer simulations to guide fleet-management policy given expected changes in the structure of the fleet, fish prices, and fish stocks (Shalliker, 1987). The optimal production policy for aquatic animals (e.g. shrimp) in controlled environments ('farms' as opposed to the open sea) has been modeled using mixed-integer linear programming (Shaftel and Wilson, 1990). The model incorporated price structure as well as technological choices regarding seed type, feed and feeding techniques, and water quality.

Optimal strategies for the extraction of nonreplenishing resources have also been examined using a variety of methods. An intelligent decision-support system incorporates management's rules of thumb into an optimization-based system that is used to aid managers in determining optimal phosphate-mining strategies (Klingman and Phillips, 1988). The model has benefited management by increasing the availability of information in a timely manner. It also allows extensive use of 'what-if' analysis.

A model based on a stochastic dynamic programming algorithm is used to help managers of an offshore oil field achieve quarterly production goals (Findlay, Kobbacy, and Goodman, 1989). The management problem is complicated by the existence of governmental regulations. Natural gas often accompanies crude oil in the extraction process. Given that natural gas has a much lower value than crude oil, there is an economic incentive to burn this gas off as waste. Environmental restrictions limit the amount of natural gas that can be flared to waste. Consequently, firms are forced to process the natural gas. This may slow down the production of crude oil. The model helps managers to determine the optimal production rate as well as the probability and cost of not achieving the quarterly goal.

Purchasing resources from suppliers

Evaluating and selecting suppliers may be a critical and time-consuming aspect of doing business especially when a just-in-time strategy is pursued. Willis and Huston (1990) propose a model to assist in this process. It incorporates financial, service, and technical dimensions.

When dealing with existing suppliers, models may help to establish purchasing strategies. Buffa and Munn (1990) propose a consolidation algorithm for grouping of items to reduce total logistics cost of replenishing materials. Reyniers (1990) derives an algorithm based on the theory of high-low search in order to minimize the costs of oversupply and undersupply when demand uncertainty exists.

Models have been developed to adjust purchasing strategies when supplier prices are expected to increase (Dompere, 1989; Jordan, 1987; Markowski, 1990). Purchasing decisions may also be influenced by the anticipation of periodic disruptions in the market. The impact of random disruptions in the petroleum market is examined in determining optimal purchasing and stockpiling strategies for the Strategic Petroleum Reserve (Murphy, Toman, and Weiss, 1989). Disruptions in the market were modeled as a stationary Markov process. Infinite-horizon dynamic programming techniques were used to solve the problem.

Negotiations between buyers and suppliers have been modeled using game theory (Anandalingam, 1987; Bard, 1987). Limited contract enforcement has also been examined, and strategic renegotiation is contrasted against renegotiation in response to surprise events under conditions of uncertainty (Huberman and Kahn, 1988). Analytic models have been used to study issues in competitive bidding (King and Mercer, 1988, 1991), including conditions of blind bidding (Blumenthal, 1988) and withdrawable winning bids (Rothkopf, 1991).

Layout of manufacturing systems

Perhaps one of the most widely used approaches to managing resources is manufacturing resource planning (MRP II). In 1988, MRP II was used by 70% of the Fortune 500 companies (Baron, 1988). A variety of other approaches have been developed to model the layout of manufacturing facilities and the flow of materials through the system.

Sophisticated manufacturing techniques (e.g. computer-integrated manufacturing) often require high-level control of production processes and operation. The use of cellular manufacturing techniques can simplify the planning and control of the system. Vig, Dooley, and Starr (1989) suggest that physical experimentation with prototype cellular systems is often too costly and disruptive. A discrete event computer simulation is offered as an alternative method of predicting the behavior of cells. Simulations can be used to evaluate alternative design or operational strategies.

The layout of manufacturing systems need not remain constant throughout the life cycle of a manufacturing system. Montreuil and Venkatadri (1991) present a method for designing dynamic layouts that can accommodate anticipated phases of expansion and decline. The method estimates probable scenarios of the system requirements for the mature phase. These scenarios are used to strategically design the layout for the mature phase. Finally, the model works backwards to interpolate intermediate layouts until it reaches the initial facilities plan.

Flow of materials and inventory

Decisions regarding production scheduling and inventories may play an important role when competing for a group of customers. Bergmann (1989) used a computer simulation to explore the impact of inventory and scheduling heuristics on profits within an oligopoly. The structure of a firm's production costs and consumer behavior are considered in predicting which inventory and scheduling heuristics would prevail.

Scheduling and inventory models may be used to evaluate alternative methods of handling material. Models have been used to study the flow of materials before those materials even get through the door. Bagchi and Davis (1988) use a simulation to evaluate alternative ways of receiving materials from suppliers. The simulation can be used for quick analysis of consolidation schemes. Empirical results indicate that direct shipments from vendors are almost always more expensive and are associated with longer delivery times.

There are a number of models tracing the flow of pieces of work or jobs through a linear sequence of operations (i.e. flow-shop environments). Gavish and Johnson (1990) propose a fully polynomial approximation scheme for single product scheduling. To coordinate the flow of several streams of resources, Bean, Birge, Mittenthal, and Noon (1991) developed heuristics to approximate optimal continuous match ups in automobile manufacturing.

Delays may occur between or within stages of production. Langston (1987) examined the effects of transportation delays between operations. Delays within operations may be critical as stages of production may move jobs through at different rates. The impact of congestion at bottlenecks should be considered (Hum and Sarin, 1991; Spearman, 1991).

With the advent of flexible manufacturing systems, scheduling problems can play a critical role in manufacturing strategy. Ahluwalia and Ji (1991) propose a distributed decision-making approach to scheduling large and complex manufacturing systems. A central processor can be used to monitor and coordinate a network of nodes (machines or tools), each of which contains its own computer for control and communications purposes. When the manufacturing system is operating normally, a linear programming model is used for scheduling. In the event of malfunctions in one or more of the nodes, a nonlinear programming model is used to reschedule jobs.

Inventories planning may be a critical aspect of managing operations. A number of models have been developed to assist managers in this decision-making process. Gupta and Houshyar (1990) offer a mathematical model that considers the number of material handler trips when considering the use of in-stage buffers and central buffers for bulk storage. The optimal solution is that which minimizes total system cost.

Inventory planning may be complicated somewhat by changes in demand. Mathematical models have been used to assist decision-makers under conditions of deteriorating products in declining markets (Aggarwal and Bahari-Kashani,

1991), seasonal demand (Gardner and McKenzie, 1989), and under demand uncertainty (Hsu and El-Najdawi, 1991).

Concepts of zero inventory, just-in-time (JIT), and Kanban have been popularized in the manufacturing community. Two mathematical models have been used to ascertain if these methods would be suitable for a given facility. Zangwill (1987) attempts to identify beforehand which facilities can operate without inventory. Such predictions could be used to simplify strategic decisions regarding facility design, site location, and space utilization. Suri and de Treville (1986) assess the appropriateness of a JIT approach by examining the information value of disruptions in production due to lack of inventory. If learning does not occur as a function of disruption, then JIT may not be appropriate for that manufacturing system.

One of the major concerns in scheduling and inventory planning is the cost of tardy jobs or backlogs. De, Ghosh, and Wells (1990) test the performance of four different approaches to minimize the total weighted tardiness (and earliness) of jobs: (a) a 0–1 quadratic programming formulation, (b) branch and bound schemes with recursion, (c) dynamic programming algorithms, and (d) a simple heuristic based on the 0–1 programming approach. The dynamic programming algorithms consistently outperformed the other exact algorithms considered, and the heuristic yielded close-to-optimal solutions in negligible time.

Daniels and Sarin (1989) treat job processing time as a controllable variable that can be influenced through the allocation of resources (e.g. overtime, additional personnel). Results of the model suggest means of developing the trade-off curve between the number of tardy jobs and the total amount of resources allocated. This approach should help managers in scheduling jobs by indicating strategies for resource allocation that lead to the most profitable level of customer service in terms of the number of tardy jobs.

A final issue affecting the flow of materials through a manufacturing system is quality inspection. Porteus (1990) examines the relationship between process quality and lot size. An inspection delay time is measured in units produced after an inspection is made and before the results are known. A method is presented for determining the optimal production and inspection lot sizes given the inspection delay.

Chakravarty and Shtub (1987) develop two mathematical models for designing inspection systems. Both models consider inspection-related costs; one model additionally considers setup and inventory carrying costs. McDowell (1987) developed a model examining the cost of sampling control strategies. The model focuses on (a) fixed and variable sampling costs, (b) the separation of the upper and lower specification limits, and (c) measurement errors on the optimal sampling policy.

Distribution

The link between production and distribution is addressed by Cohen and Lee

(1988). A comprehensive framework is described for modeling the links between decisions and performance throughout the material-production-distribution supply chain. A series of linked, approximate submodels and a heuristic optimization procedure have been developed along with a supporting software package. This approach predicts the performance of a firm in terms of (a) the cost of products, (b) the level of customer service provided, and (c) the flexibility and responsiveness of the production/distribution system.

Analytic models have been used extensively in solving vehicle routing problems (Anily and Federguen, 1990; Campbell, 1990; Campos, Corberan, and Mota, 1991). The general form of the problem is that materials at one or more depots must be shipped to a set of geographically dispersed retailers using vehicles of known capacity. Models are used to develop efficient routes, schedules, numbers of terminals, etc. in order to minimize costs. Costs may be decomposed into inventory, transportation, and terminal costs. An additional time-window constraint can be imposed by considering earliest and latest acceptable dates of delivery (Koskosidis and Powell, 1990).

Demand-Side Models

Models that assist managers in predicting and perhaps influencing the actions of consumers are categorized as demand-side models in this taxonomy. The discussion will address empirically driven models (e.g. models of market share, market response, and consumer choice) and conceptually driven models (e.g. models of market segmentation, product differentiation, and optimal pricing).

Empirical

Three of the main areas of empirically driven modeling relevant to strategic management are (a) consumer choice, (b) market responses to marketing instruments, and (c) market share.

Consumer choice

There are a number of analytic models that reflect empirical observations of consumers' behavior when choosing products. One of the most popular approaches to discrete choices is the use of logit models (Anderson, de Palma, and Thisse, 1988; Buckley, 1988). Such models can represent decisions as series of hierarchically nested choices in decision trees.

An alternative method of inferring hierarchical models of consumer choice is based on a nonparametric classification algorithm for identifying the if-then rules linking predictor variables to discrete choices. Currim, Meyer, and Le (1988) developed this 'concept learning system' to estimate the decision trees used by individuals without recourse to prior assumptions regarding tree form.

Models have been used to predict how consumers will behave when their choices are constrained (Kahn, Moore, and Glazer, 1987) or substitutions are possible (Delmas and Gadrey, 1987). Empirical results suggest that consumers use prior knowledge to guide their choices (d'Astous and Rouzies, 1987). In the absence of such knowledge, consumers must assume some risk in making choices. Hales and Shams (1991) found that consumers often adopt a 'cautious incremental consumption' strategy rather than searching for indirect sources of information. The risk to the consumer need not be unidimensional. Schlee (1990) uses a two-period model to determine how consumer choices are influenced by risk aversion in consumers when risk is multivariate in nature. This approach does not require restrictions on the multivariate distribution of risk.

Market response

Market-response models are used to forecast the impact that environmental events or strategic interventions may have on a firm's performance (e.g. sales, market share). These forecasts may help managers to determine (a) which events in the environment need to be responded to and (b) how effective various responses or interventions are likely to be (Leone, 1987).

In forecasting market response to environmental events, Fletcher and Latham (1990) use cones to model the effect that an entrant will have on the market share held by various incumbents. The impact of changes in governmental regulations is modeled by Rea (1987) to assess the impact of banning the use of sex as a discriminating variable in pricing annuities in insurance markets. Brueggeman and Thibodeau (1987) also developed two models to predict the effects of the Tax Reform Act of 1986 on the multifamily housing and commercial (office) real estate markets. Results of models such as these can help managers to allocate their time and effort by prioritizing environmental events for further attention.

Of course, market-response models need not be used in such a reactive manner. They may be applied in a more proactive style in forecasting the impact of strategic initiatives. For example, market-response models have been used to identify opportunities in long-distance passenger rail service in Australia (Johnson and Nelson, 1991).

Market-response models have been used to assess a variety of strategic interventions. American Airlines and United Airlines took advantage of their information systems (Sabre and Covia, respectively) in implementing pricing strategies when competing against People Express. These information systems allowed American and United to make hundreds of thousands of pricing changes daily, thereby influencing buying patterns *vis-à-vis* People Express (Francett, 1990).

Other applications of market-response models assess (a) the impact of coupon promotions on market share (Neslin, 1990), (b) the effects of advertising pulsing policies on sales (Arsham, 1987; Sasieni, 1989), (c) the effectiveness of salesforce efforts (Cravens, Moncrief, Lamb, and Dielman, 1990; Gatignon and Hanssens, 1987), and (d) the benefits of various strategies for managing customer complaints (Fornell and Wernerfelt, 1987).

Some of the methods used in forecasting market responses are (a) an aggregate version of the multinomial logit choice model using stated preference data (Johnson and Nelson, 1991), (b) meta-analysis (Vanhonacker, Lehmann, and Sultan, 1990), (c) an elimination by aspect model using a general maximum likelihood routine (Fader and McAlister, 1990), and (d) an econometric and time series analysis using an autoregressive moving average (ARMA) model (Franses, 1991).

As this area of modeling is data-driven, Arinze (1990) notes that successful implementation of market-response models as decision aids may hinge on managerial agreement on the nature and sources of data used. For any given problem, managers need to consider the overall relevance of the model and how the model should be fitted or calibrated to that specific situation. While some minimal level of agreement among managers is necessary, perfect consensus on these issues is not a must. The models may be quite useful in fueling the debate among managers as they try to make sense of and adapt to changes in their environment. The ensuing dialogue may be more valuable than the output of the model. Ultimately, the mark of a good model is that it helps managers move towards effective strategic actions. The usefulness of analytic models should be evaluated in that context.

Product diffusion

Projecting demand for a new product may be rather difficult. Demand is expected to be low initially, then to rise over time if the product is successful. It may be difficult for managers to make accurate forecasts of market penetration. Diffusion rates may vary across products and need not be constant for a given product.

Depending on how innovative the new product really is, the problem of forecasting demand may be framed as introducing a substitute product into a known market or as opening up an entirely new market. Assuming that many products may fall somewhere in between these two extremes, substitution effects may be combined with diffusion effects to forecast dynamic sales behavior for new products. Norton and Bass (1987) used a model combining these two effects to explain the rise and fall of demand for successive generations of two categories of integrated circuits.

It is generally assumed that diffusion of a new product is influenced by two means of communication: mass media and word of mouth (Mahajan, Muller, and Bass, 1990). Horsky and Mate (1988) use a nonzero sum Markovian game to model the effects that these two forms of communication have on competition between two firms with new products. To establish optimal advertising policies, dynamic programming is used to solve this stochastic closed-loop problem. Results suggest that the magnitude of the first-mover advantage is positively related to the intensity of word of mouth. The first-mover advantage can be nullified by a follower that enters with a superior product which receives more enthusiastic support from consumers.

The intensity of the word-of-mouth effect may be influenced by the degree to which consumers are risk-averse. Relatively risk-averse consumers may delay purchasing the new product until they obtain information from early adopters. Oren and Schwartz (1988) suggest that late consumers may adjust their prior uncertainties about the product in a Bayesian manner. In a decision-theoretic approach, consumers maximize their expected utility when choosing between current and new products.

Interactions among consumers may entail more than just the exchange of information. Consumers may transfer the product itself. Computer software piracy is an issue of some concern as it is assumed to reduce the profits of the firm and/or raise the price levied on paying customers. Conner and Rumelt (1991) model the effects of software protection policies on the diffusion of software. Results suggest that, under some conditions, allowing piracy to go unchecked may actually increase the firm's profits and reduce selling prices to paying consumers. This illustrates the usefulness of models in identifying counter-intuitive phenomena that managers might otherwise overlook.

Issues in market-response modeling may be linked to those in product diffusion by examining the interplay between market responses to pricing and diffusion trajectories. Gottardi and Copolla (1988) developed a model in which the number and type of *potential* adopters (consumers) is allowed to vary. Price influences the *current* number of adopters, and the current number of adopters influences the rate of diffusion. Faster diffusion rates allow the firm to move faster down the experience curve, resulting in cost reductions. (See the discussion of experience effects in the empirically driven, supply-side category.) Cost reductions make further price reductions feasible, and the chain reaction may be started again. Logically, the process is limited as the experience curve levels off and/or the market becomes saturated. The analytic model may serve as a guide for pricing strategies as the product moves toward maturity in its lifecycle.

Any number of external factors could affect the rate of diffusion when a product is introduced into a market. Infrastructure has played a critical role in the videocassette recorder (VCR) market (Redmond, 1991). Contingent purchasing behavior necessitates the simultaneous consideration of diffusion rates of more than one product (Bayus, 1987). For example, the diffusion rate of compact disks (CDs) is linked to the diffusion rate of CD players, and computer software sales are linked to computer hardware sales. Small, outside influences may have dramatic and enduring consequences for market responses for a given product (Redmond, 1991). Models may be used to play out scenarios of likely events, thereby giving managers a better intuitive feel for how factors in the environment might affect the demand for their new product over time.

Market share

Kumar and Heath (1990) compared a range of market-share models using weekly scanner data. They examined full, reduced, and naïve forms of three types of market-share models: linear, multiplicative, and attraction specifications. Overall, attraction models made the best predictions. Attraction models were superior when models were fully specified, while linear models were superior when important variables were omitted (reduced form). Results suggest that naïve models generally did not perform well.

While the market-share attraction models may provide superior performance, it may be difficult for managers to get an intuitive feel for the results. To help managers interpret the findings, the structure underlying asymmetric cross-elasticities can be visually represented in 'competitive maps' using 3-mode factor analysis (Cooper, 1988). These maps can be used to identify competitive threats among brands as well as where major opportunities may lie.

It has been suggested that the need to accurately model market share stems from the (presumed) link between market share and performance (Oral and Kettani, 1989). In a study of three industries (plastics, paper, and industrial equipment) using Standard & Poor's COMPUSTAT database, a significant positive correlation between market share and profitability was found, but only in one of the industries (plastics) (Markell, Strickland, and Neeley, 1988). A positive correlation between market share and return on investment (ROI) was observed in the PIMS database (Hall, 1987). However, Hall cautioned that correlation does not necessarily imply causation.

Counter examples to the positive correlation have been found. Schwalbach (1991) examined the PIMS database and found that ROI decreased for values of market share beyond a critical point (between 65% and 70%). In industries characterized by boom-bust cycles in demand, sacrificing market share is positively related to long-term profitability (Anterasian and Graham, 1989). Waterson (1990) noted that, when customers have different ideas about what constitutes an ideal product, supplying some customers will be more costly than supplying others. Therefore, while it may be possible to set higher prices in those cases, the increased prices may not fully compensate the added cost under the given demand framework. Hence, profits may be negatively related to market share.

Hall (1987) notes that despite frequent references in the literature to this presumably causal relationship, there has been little theoretical examination of when market share should directly influence profitability. The bivariate correlation between profitability (ROI) and market share may be due to other factors that simultaneously influence these two variables such as (a) economies of scale and scope, (b) market power, (c) experience, and (d) quality of management (Boulding and Staelin, 1990; Hall, 1987; Jacobson, 1988). It appears that increasing market share will only result in rises in profitability under fairly limited circumstances (Boulding and Staelin, 1990; Hall, 1987).

Research on the link between market share and profitability illustrates one of the hazards of data-driven models. 'Shotgun research' or 'fishing expeditions' are virtually guaranteed to unearth a number of patterns in the data. This is certainly informative and there is a need of this type of research during early phases of research. However, the patterns found in the data may be interpreted in innumerable ways. As richer data sets are developed and more sophisticated analyses are performed, some of the early interpretations may be ruled out. This phenomenon is not unique to the empirically driven models. Theoretically driven models go through evolutionary processes of their own. Unfortunately, while the models are evolving, managers may place their faith in versions of models that may misdirect their strategy.

To create a competitive advantage, managers often must take chances. If managers only stick with the tried and true methods, they will confine themselves to strategies that everyone else is already aware of. As managers push back the frontiers of business, models may suggest plausible strategies. The *caveat emptor* is that these models may or may not accurately describe the data that will emerge as the firm pursues the new strategy. Models should not be taken on blind faith, but should be used as fodder for debate.

Theoretical

Theoretically driven issues of relevance to strategic management include models of market segmentation, product differentiation, product innovation, and optimal pricing.

Market segmentation

There are of course a range of approaches to defining market segments. Grover and Srinivasan (1987) define market segments based on groups of consumers with homogeneous preferences in terms of choices within a class of products and develop a model of brand switching in which the likelihood of switching is proportional to the market shares of the brands. In this way, competitive market structure is determined by the possibly overlapping groups of brands. Market segmentation and market structuring then become opposite sides of the same analysis.

Market segmentation uses a set of variables to divide consumers into groups, and then assess demand or responsiveness within those groups. In a relatively direct approach, the likelihood of response may be used as an integral part of segment definition itself. Li (1987) defined segments using two dimensions. A traditional descriptive approach to defining segments was combined with a statistical modeling approach to predict the likelihood of response. Flodhammar (1988) used information from sales representatives to get data on the quality of customer relations for potential as well as current customers. Kannan and Wright (1991) draw on consumer choice modeling techniques by using a nested logit approach to segment consumers based on their decision trees. Segments of 'switchers' can be identified by decision trees which predispose them to be responsive to marketing programs. If segments defined by demand or responsiveness can be selectively targeted, promotional campaigns could be conducted more efficiently than if segments were defined based on less direct measures (e.g. sex, age, marital status).

Laughlin and Taylor (1991) criticize models of industrial market segmentation for ignoring managerial requirements and implementation issues (e.g the costs of modifying products to the end use) when defining segments. These issues are addressed in a model which incorporates controllable marketing variables.

Models can be useful in simplifying the complexity of markets. Kale and Sudharshan (1987) suggest that segmentation within countries is becoming critical for survival in global competition. Managers must select which countries to enter and which segments to target within each country. An analytic framework is offered to help managers segment the world marketplace into cross-national segments that reduce the total number of marketing mixes a firm has to offer.

Sophisticated market segmentation often incorporates a number of potentially overlapping variables. The work of managers may be simplified if redundancies in the data can be reduced without sacrificing too much unique information in the process. Hosseini, Harmon, and Zwick (1991) present an information theoretic framework for multivariate market segmentation.

Product differentiation

In a review of the product differentiation literature, Waterson (1989) suggests that the field has made considerable progress over the past two decades. One of the primary gains has been in the distinction between horizontal and vertical product differentiation. In horizontal differentiation, products are distinguished by unique attributes or differences in emphasis on shared dimensions. That is, one product may be high on dimension A and low on dimension B, while another product may be low on A and high on B. In vertical differentiation, two products emphasize the same desirable dimensions but one is superior to (e.g. of higher quality than) the other. The implication is that all consumers will agree on the ranking of vertically differentiated products, but rankings of horizontally differentiated products will differ across market segments due to differences in taste (Cremer and Thisse, 1991).

Cremer and Thisse (1991) suggest that Hotelling-type (1929) models of horizontal product differentiation could be considered as special cases of a vertical product differentiation model. The two types of models generate equilibria that are identical in a well-defined sense. Some recently published models of vertical product differentiation will be discussed initially; a discussion of models of horizontal differentiation will then follow.

Vertical differentiation. Models of vertical product differentiation have been used to demonstrate that monopolists will always find it more profitable to sell more than one quality of a product and charge different prices based on quality

(Chander and Leruth, 1989). This follows from the observation that few if any top-quality goods will be purchased at the price associated with being top quality. To maximize profits, the monopolist must produce lower quality products and sell them at commensurate prices.

Approaching the price–quality interplay from another angle, an analytic model was used to demonstrate that price regulation may stifle differentiation based on quality (Thomas, 1989). Results suggest that price flexibility can encourage quality competition.

Models of imperfect quality discrimination have been developed to reflect distortion at both ends of the quality continuum (Beard and Ekelund, 1991). Srinagesh and Bradburd (1989) develop a model in which the standard assumption (consumers with higher total utility also have higher marginal utility for quality) is violated. This model is used to argue that quality distortions should be considered relative to consumer groups rather than at some fixed level of quality. Distortions occur for the consumer group that derives the lowest utility of quality. The level of quality purchased by this group determines precisely where distortions will occur on the continuum.

Horizontal differentiation. Many models of horizontal product differentiation take a Hotelling (1929) perspective. For example, Neven (1987) developed a two-stage model in which firms (a) enter an industry sequentially, and then (b) compete on price. Results suggest that early entrants tend to locate symmetrically around the center, forcing later entrants to locate closer to the boundaries. Simultaneous entry generally does not result in such an even distribution of firms across the product range, as firms tend to locate more densely in the center. The model illustrates that fixed costs can act as an entry barrier thereby fostering the development of natural monopoly, duopoly, and triopoly.

Chaplin and Nalebuff (1986) used a two-stage model (location choice, then price competition) to study the effects of cost asymmetries on product differentiation. It is suggested that low-cost entrants seeking to capture the whole market should imitate the incumbent's product (i.e. locate near the incumbent in the product space). On the other hand, high-cost firms may wish to locate near the boundaries in an attempt to avoid competition with low-cost rivals.

A model of spatial product differentiation has been used to infer the impact of a firm straddling two apparently separate markets. As the actions of the straddling firm are influenced by actions of rivals in both markets, firms in the two markets experience an indirect competition that may impose discipline on pricing. Due to the indirect competition, the presence of one straddling firm may affect conduct in the market as much as the entrance of several (nonstraddling) firms.

Shaked and Sutton (1990) note that product differentiation models generally admit many equilibria. Concentration equilibria may be modeled in which a small number of firms each offer a large number of products, and fragmented equilibria can be modeled in which a large number of firms each produce one product. Unfortunately, the models are greatly influenced by factors that are difficult to assess empirically. The parameters of such models can be modified to correspond to empirically observable market characteristics. These models may then be used to generate testable predictions about relationships between market size and market structure.

Optimal pricing

It is fairly obvious that factors such as the threat of entry or experience effects generally drive prices lower (Mesak, 1990), but in the complexity of real world decisions, one might ask, 'How low is low?' Many optimal pricing models can be made quite accessible to managers through the use of templates in Lotus 1-2-3. Weil (1987) illustrates the use of Lotus data tables and templates for calculating the optimal price for a product line as well as break even points given changes in fixed costs.

Optimal pricing models may be invaluable to managers confronted with arrays of factors which may influence pricing in opposite directions. Analytic models may illuminate how these factors interact to influence pricing. Conflicting influences in the computer software industry illustrate this point. As noted in the section on product diffusion (demand-side, empirically driven models), 'piracy' or copying poses a major problem for managers. Nascimento and Vanhonacker (1988) note that setting high initial prices for software provides high margins, but it may encourage copying. On the other hand, setting a low initial price may reduce the incentive to copy, but it results in low margins. This may be problematic given R&D expenditures and the relatively short life cycle of software products. A mathematical model generates optimal price trajectories given two diffusion rates (sales and copying) and utilizes control theory methodology. Results suggest that copy protection is appropriate only if marginal costs are low and the diffusion rate of sales is much faster than that of copying. When copy protection is not used, skimming pricing strategies are optimal.

If managers rely heavily on economies of scope to keep their firm profitable, they may find it necessary to bundle products. Hanson and Martin (1990) propose a method for optimal bundle pricing. This is considered as a mixed integer linear problem using disjunctive programming. In addition to identifying the optimal price for a given bundle, the model may be used to select items for bundling. However, due to the combinatorial nature of the problem, item selection becomes computationally problematic as the number of possible items becomes large.

Optimal pricing models can be used to design multi-tier pricing schemes. For example, discount fares for early purchase of airline tickets take advantage of reductions in price sensitivity as the date of a flight approaches (Pfeifer, 1989). In the UK railroad industry, travel passes are offered in the form of 'railcards' (offering a discount from the full fare) and 'travelcards' (allowing unlimited travel within a time period). Carbojo (1988) developed a model that forecasts profits and consumer surplus, given a variety of objectives (e.g. profit maximization).

Pricing models overlap with market-response models when they are used to predict the effects of changes in prices. Price promotions may be used to attract 'deal-responsive' consumers. Theoretical predictions and empirical findings suggest that the probability of price promotions tends to increase as the number of brands increases within a brand category, (Raju, Srinivasan, and Lal, 1990).

Fraser and Ginter (1988) model patterns of competition when there are so many firms that there will be at least one firm offering a deal at any time. When two or more firms offer deals simultaneously, dealing wars result and the brand with the best deal attracts the deal-responsive customers. In a later article (Fraser and Ginter, 1991), these authors present a probabilistic strategy that would enable all premium brands in the market to obtain nonnegative profits without active cooperation. Among the findings, it is concluded that deal values should be either large or small; intermediate deal values do not attract a sufficient proportion of the deal-sensitive consumers to offset the revenue loss due to reduced prices.

While price promotion models suggest avoiding overlapping the actions of rivals when reducing prices, the best strategy for a firm that wishes to raise prices is to immediately follow the pricing action of its last competitor. This is expected to maximize profits over the entire period (Mesak and Clelland, 1988).

Competition Models

While many of the supply-side and demand-side models consider competition between rivals, they have a relatively limited focus. Models considered in this category (competition models) take a somewhat broader perspective. Again, empirically driven and conceptually/theoretically driven models will be discussed separately.

Empirical

PIMS database

Empirically driven models of competition are generally based on patterns of managerially controllable variables that are linked to performance (e.g. profitability, risk). Data of this nature are used in their simplest form to establish benchmarks as measures of relative performance. The Profit Impact of Market Strategy (PIMS) database (Buzzell and Gale, 1987) has been used to establish par ROI scores (Gale and Branch, 1987), relative measures of productivity in the marketing area (Hawkins, Best, and Lillis, 1987), and other multidimensional measures of performance (Gale and Branch, 1987).

Internationally, there have been several attempts to replicate findings from PIMS studies using data from Europe and Japan. Yip (1991) reported that relationships found in the US and Canada (PIMS) were in the opposite direction to those found in Europe. Campbell (1988) found that while markets in Japan tended to be less concentrated than those in PIMS, the relationship between market share and the safety of market leaders was similar.

In a very different approach, Kotabe, Duhan, Smith, and Wilson (1991) asked Japanese managers for their perceptions of a set of 28 PIMS principles related to strategic actions, performance, and the environment. Responses from 205 Japanese managers suggested that most of the PIMS principles applied in Japan. However, ratings obtained from Japanese executives regarding the veracity of many of the principles differed from ratings obtained from US executives.

A number of relationships have been identified using bivariate correlations and multiple regression techniques. Examples of this in the past five years of publications include links between strategy and shareholder wealth (Gale and Swire, 1988) and, more specifically, between quality-based strategies and profitability (Band, 1989; Jacobson and Aaker, 1987).

Hagerty, Carman, and Russell (1988) used the PIMS database to estimate elasticities and noted that problems in the data can result in large measurement errors for some variables. However, it was suggested that reasonable estimates can be obtained and managers can use their own judgement and other data to adjust those estimates.

Jacobson, Buzzell, and Boulding (1990) summarize some of the debates in the literature regarding the validity of findings from the PIMS database. It is concluded that strategic factors do account for much of the variance in profitability (ROI), however unobservable factors affect, and are affected by, those strategic factors.

Data-driven researches using the PIMS and other databases (e.g. COMPUSTAT, Federal Trade Commission's (FTC) Line-of-Business database) have not gone without criticism. Marshall and Buzzell (1990) address criticisms based on sample composition, measurement methodologies, and underlying data structures of the PIMS and FTC databases. Analyses were done independently on the two data sets using descriptive statistics and a simple regression model of profitability. Results from the two data sets tended to be comparable.

Strategic groups

Firms within an industry tend to vary in terms of resources, abilities, goals, and strategies used to reach their goals (Fiegenbaum, McGee, and Thomas, 1988). This heterogeneity among firms complicates the process of industry forecasting. A strategic groups approach may simplify industry analysis and forecasting by identifying groups of firms that tend to (a) respond to events in similar ways and (b) view firms within the same group as closer rivals than firms in other groups (Porter, 1980).

While much of the modeling in this area has a strong data-driven flavor, a variety of theoretical perspectives have influenced the stream of research: industrial/organizational (I/O) economics (Porter, 1980), population ecology (Boeker, 1991; Mascarenhas, 1989), environmental adaption (Mascarenhas, 1989), and strategic choice (Mascarenhas, 1989; Tang and Thomas, 1991). Theoretical pluralism is recommended, as each perspective provides unique information about the phenomenon (Mascarenhas, 1989; Porac, Thomas, and Baden-Fuller, 1989; Porac, Thomas, and Carroll, in press; Thomas and Porac, April 1991; Thomas and Carroll, 1991).

Different criteria have been used within the analyses to identify groups. Some simplistic approaches consider only one variable such as size (Porter, 1979). More comprehensive approaches have used arrays of financial statement variables from data sets such as COMPUSTAT (Cool and Schendel, 1987; Fiegenbaum, Sudharshan, and Thomas, 1990; Baird, Sudharshan, and Thomas, 1988), data extracted from industry-specific reports (Feigenbaum and Thomas, 1990), survey data reflecting managerial perceptions of their environment (Fombrun and Zajac, 1987) and other strategic issues that are not reflected in published data sets (De Bondt, Sleuwaegen, and Veugelers, 1988; Lewis and Thomas, 1990).

In addition to differences in types of variables used to define groups, a variety of methods have been used to examine the data: cluster analysis (Amel and Rhoades, 1988; Carroll, Lewis, and Thomas, 1992; Fombrun and Zajac, 1987; Lewis and Thomas, 1990), multidimensional scaling (Pegels and Sekar, 1989), and network analysis (Nohria and Garcia-Pont, 1991). Given a set of strategy variables and sample of firms, these methods essentially break a sample of firms into groups based on statistical measures of proximity.

The set of strategic variables that define the groups may be industry-specific (Cool and Schendel, 1987, 1988; Mascarenhas and Aaker, 1989). Further, the composition and distinguishing features of strategic groups may change over time within an industry (Baird, Sudharshan, and Thomas, 1988; De Bondt, Sleuwaegen, and Veugelers, 1988; Fiegenbaum, Sudharshan, and Thomas, 1987, 1990; Fiegenbaum and Thomas, 1990; Kumar, Thomas, and Fiegenbaum, 1990). It is not always clear *a priori* which variables will be most influential.

An alternative to empirically observing industry structure (strategic groupings) is to impose a relatively theory-driven structure onto the industry. In such an approach, firms are assigned to preconceived categories (groups) within a conceptual typology, such as Porter's (1980) generic strategies (Ashmos and McDaniel, 1991), Miles and Snow's (1978) typology (Zahra, 1987), or Hrebiniak and Joyce's (1985) typology (Lawless and Finch, 1989).

As noted, one of the primary benefits of considering strategic groups is that it may simplify industry level forecasting by identifying firms that are likely to behave in similar ways. However, strategic groupings may have implications for industry structure. Hence, it may also enrich the analysis of rivals' behaviors as it provides information regarding the nature and intensity of competition among firms. For example, the threat of entry would be reduced if mobility barriers limit movement from one strategic group to another. These barriers may be asymmetric (Hatten and Hatten, 1987; Mascarenhas and Aaker, 1989; Kumar, 1990), and the nature of the barriers may change over time due to changes in technology, government regulations, or other forces influencing industry evolution (Fiegenbaum, Sudharshan, and Thomas, 1987; Geroski and Murfin, 1991; Hatten and Hatten, 1987; May, 1987). This is consistent with the proposition that the features distinguishing groups may change over time.

Profitability. Assume that firms can move freely from one group to another and managers are motivated to direct their firms into more profitable groups. As more firms enter a group, the effects of competition drive down profits. Hence, supranormal profits should not be sustainable. Maintaining the assumption that managers are motivated to direct their firms into more profitable groups, if sustainable differences in the performance of groups is observed, then mobility barriers must be present.

This reasoning started a stream of studies searching for sustainable performance differences between strategic groups. Given that the concept of strategic groups is based on heterogeneity of goals and strategies to obtain them, a single measure of performance (e.g. ROI) may not be appropriate for all of the groups. Some firms (groups) may focus on market share, others on risk, etc. Studies have used multiple measures of performance to reflect those differences (Carroll, Lewis, and Thomas, 1992; Cool and Schendel, 1987; Fiegenbaum and Thomas, 1990; Lewis and Thomas, 1990).

Given that these studies were based on differences in (a) industries with idiosyncratic structures, (b) strategic variables, (c) methods of examining those variables, and (d) measures of performance, it is not surprising that some studies found performance differences across strategic groups while other studies found no differences (Thomas and Venkatraman, 1988). The assertion that a firm's performance depends on its strategic group membership has been used by some researchers as a critical test of the validity and usefulness of the strategic groups concept (Barney and Hoskisson, 1990). However, this is logically inconsistent with the intuition behind strategic groups and mobility barriers. Syllogistically, assuming a 'rational man' perspective, if movement between groups is free (P), then profits will be normal (Q). From that premise it is valid to assume that if sustainable differences in the performance of groups are observed (not Q), then mobility barriers must be present—movement is not free (not P). It is not valid to assume that if profits are normal (Q), then mobility barriers do not exist—movement is free (P); nor is it valid to conclude that strategic groups do not exist.

Perhaps the relationship between strategic groups and performance can be best explained through reasoning by analogy. Recall the discussion of product differentiation. Vertical differentiation (differences based on quality) generally makes differences in prices possible. Horizontal differentiation (differences based on attribute mixes that appeal to differences in taste) may or may not be associated with price differences depending on structural characteristics.

Now, instead of products positioned in product attribute space, consider firms positioned in resource space. Horizontal differentiation refers to strategic groupings based on asset configurations, skills, etc. Vertical differentiation refers to differences in competence or execution ability (Lawless, Bergh, and Wilsted, 1989; Porter, 1980). While vertical differences in competence will generally make differences in profitability profitable, horizontal differences based on resources (strategic group membership) may or may not allow differences depending on a number of structural factors. Failing to find profitability differences among strategic groups is like failing to find price differences among horizontally differentiated products. The concepts have useful implications for strategists beyond predicting price or profitability (Carroll, Lewis, and Thomas, 1992; Lewis and Thomas, 1990; McGee and Thomas, 1986).

In a market, it is easy to imagine products that are both horizontally and vertically differentiated. Differences in price may be found both within and between product categories. Similarly, in an industry, the profitability of a firm may be influenced both by strategy and by the ability to execute the strategy, and it has been shown that performance of firms varies both within and between strategic groups (Cool and Schendel, 1988). It would be unlikely to find performance differences across groups in industries in which (a) a variety of strategies (asset configurations) are equally profitable, or (b) initial differences in profitability existed, but mobility barriers are not sufficient to deter entry. Even if initial profitability differences were sustainable due to mobility barriers, differences in competence within groups could create sufficient variance in performance to swamp the effects across groups. That is, within-group variance may be greater than between-group variance.

The existence or relevance of the strategic group should not be determined solely by whether or not performance differences are found across groups (Kumar, 1987). Strategic groupings may be quite useful in identifying structural patterns of competition within industries (Lewis and Thomas, 1990). That is, which firms are perceived as close rivals with relatively high degrees of interdependence (Porter, 1980). Perhaps the best way to move forward in modeling strategic groups is to adopt some of the philosophy from a network analysis perspective (Burt, 1982; Rogers, 1987). To understand the relationship between the attributes of firms and performance, it may help to consider how those attributes are related to the structural positioning of firms and how that structural positioning influences profitability (Hergert, 1988). The relationship between a firm's attributes and its performance should vary over time as the variables (attributes) defining strategic groups and mobility variables change. The enduring relationship should be the link between structural positioning (i.e. how the firm fits into patterns of interactions in the industry) and performance. This suggests that future models might be more useful if they added a more direct focus on relational data and analyses (e.g. patterns of competition and cooperation within and between groups) in conjunction with attribute-based approaches (Knoke and Kuklinski, 1982; Porac, Thomas, and Carroll, in press; Thomas and Carroll, October 1991).

Theoretical

Game theory

Game theory is widely used for modeling phenomena in business (Shapiro, 1989; Thakor, 1991; Wang and Parlar, 1989) and a variety of other fields (e.g. anthropology, biology, psychology, sociology). Applying game theory to rivalry among firms makes it possible to project the consequences (equilibrium sets) associated with alternative strategies: (a) cooperative versus competitive strategies (Nielsen, 1988), (b) threats of withdrawal from cooperation (Cave, 1987), (c) preemption and threats of retaliation (Brams and Kilgour, 1987), etc. A time-dependent supergame can be used to model cumulative effects of actions within a dynamic oligopoly (Friedman, 1990). Predictions of consequences may be extended further by considering cyclically stable sets as an alternative solution concept to a Nash equilibrium (Gilboa and Matsui, 1991).

Yet, many authors are quick to note that game theory does not predict behavior; it merely suggests what might happen under certain scenarios (Rubinstein, 1991; di Benedetto, 1987). One of the problems is that game theory must use overly simplistic models to remain tractable; it therefore must ignore variables that may have an impact on interactions among firms and subsequent outcomes (di Benedetto, 1987).

This is not to suggest that game theory is not without merit. Dynamics within an oligopoly may lead to a wide variety of outcomes (Fisher, 1989). Taking a game theory approach may help simplify the dimensions of the competitive marketplace and impose some structure on what might otherwise appear to managers as a complex, amorphous problem (Kerin and Harvey, 1987). It may help prune the set of possible strategies to be considered by identifying the best outcome, and then trace backwards to identify the strategies that would be most likely to obtain it (Maital, 1991). Further, models in game theory may help managers to draw on their existing knowledge by providing a means of formalizing anecdotes (Fisher, 1989) and folk theorems (Friedman, 1990).

Perhaps the greatest contribution from game theory models is the explicit recognition that actors mutually influence each other's decisions. Viewing conflict from the opponent's perspective is a crucial part of understanding industry dynamics (Maital, 1991). Often managers have blind spots when considering patterns of mutual influence among rivals, and game theory models may help identify perceptual gaps (Zajac and Bazerman, 1991). The mark of a good game theory model is that it helps frame the perceptions of real life social phenomena using the factors that decision-makers perceive as relevant (Fisher, 1989; Maital, 1991; Rubinstein, 1991).

Shubik (1987) suggests that there are at least three types of game theories. The first is 'high church game theory.' This refers to the highly mathematical orientation that focuses on systems of axioms and formal proofs. The second is 'low church game theory.' This branch is more applied in that it addresses specific, real world problems and produces actual calculation. Finally, the third form is referred to as 'conversational game theory' which gives advice on how to think strategically. Dasgupta (1989) suggests that approaches to game theory can be placed along a dimension ranging from an evolutionary perspective at one extreme and a prescriptive perspective on the other, and the development of future models will probably fall somewhere between those extremes.

Spatial competition

Spatial competition is a branch of game theory modeling (Tang and Thomas, 1991). Hotelling (1929) developed the first model of spatial competition. The approach has been applied to positioning in geographic space and product characteristic space (Braid, 1989; Thisse and Vives, 1988). Models in this section will deal with geographic positioning. Models which focus specifically on competition in product space are discussed earlier in the chapter along with other models of product differentiation in the theoretical, demand-side category of models.

ReVelle and Serra (1991) consider the placement of new facilities with the goal of maximizing market share. In a dynamic oligopoly, a firm which enters the market after the initial sites are established may select a location in order to capture a large portion of an incumbent's market. Hence, incumbents may wish to relocate in order to regain some of their market. Cournot and Stackelberg strategies are modeled using a zero–one linear programming approach. The model is extended to an oligopoly market.

Braid (1989) developed a model of optimal locations when residential locations are uniformly distributed along one side of a river, employment locations are distributed uniformly along the other side, and multiple bridges link the two sides. The model examines the optimal number and location of those bridges. The model could also be applied to the optimal location of facilities when the consumers meet there as pairs (e.g. restaurants, tennis court). A third interpretation of the model is related to product differentiation as it identifies optimal positioning in product space when two consumers (e.g. spouses) make joint purchasing decisions.

While Braid (1989) alternates the interpretation of the model as reflecting competition in either geographic or product attribute space, some models consider positioning in both geographic and product attribute space simultaneously. Ben-Akiva, de Palma, and Thisse (1989) develop such a model to handle spatial competition with differentiated products. It is assumed that the behavior of consumers will be influenced by the trade-off between brand preference and convenience. For the consumer, transportation costs (in geographic space) are assumed to be linear, while deviations from the preferred brand (in product attribute space) follow a quadratic cost function. Results suggest that the likelihood of firms clustering in the geographic center are greater when (a) consumers are heterogeneous with respect to tastes, (b) transportation costs are low, (c) market size is small, and (d) the number of firms is small.

Innovation-based competition

A branch of modeling that is obviously related to product differentiation is product innovation. Managing the innovation process may be a critical aspect of competition for some firms. Kumar and Sudharshan (1988) present a model of competitive responses to the introduction of a new product (e.g. price reductions for existing products). This model may be used to help managers of the innovating firm to forecast their own advertising and distribution expenditures given the likely responses of rivals.

Models may also guide decisions based on regulatory review time and patent life as well as the rate of generic competition (Grabowski and Vernon, 1987). Lippman and McCardle (1988) use game theory to model innovation-based competition in winner-take-all patent races between two firms. Their model is used to demonstrate that the equilibria set is influenced by the length of time required for research. For example, when projects take an intermediate length of time for research, the equilibrium is such that followers can essentially force leaders to withdraw from the patent race.

Corporate Models

Porter (1987) examined 33 US firms over a 37-year period (1950–1986). On the average, the firms diversified into 80 new industries and 27 entirely new fields. In this sample, 70% of these entries were made via acquisition, 22% through internal development, and 8% through joint ventures. Eventually, these firms divested over 50% of the acquisitions in different industries and over 60% of the acquisitions in entirely different fields. While it would be imprudent to generalize beyond this sample, this study does reflect some of the interesting dimensions examined in models of strategic management at the corporate level: (a) organizational form and mode of entry (e.g. joint venture, acquisition, internal development), (b) type of diversity (e.g related versus unrelated diversification), and (c) managing a portfolio of SBUs (e.g. resource allocation, divestment). Again, these are divided into empirically-driven and theoretically-driven categories.

Empirical

Diversification

After decades of research, data-driven modeling in diversification has yielded equivocal sets of results (Duhaime and Stimpert, 1990; Hill and Hanson, 1991). It is difficult to find patterns that can be generalized beyond a specific sample of firms, a given time period, or even across different operationalizations of the same constructs. Even within a given sample, Chatterjee and Wernerfelt (1991) found that their model fitted high-performance firms better than low-performance firms. The summary presented here is not an attempt to sort through the tangled pattern of relationships in the literature. Discussion will focus on some of the salient dimensions explored over the last five years of publication. It is hoped that this will maintain the focus on the role of analytic models in strategic management and avoid digressing too far into what is generally viewed as a perplexing set of substantive issues.

Firms may diversify along a number of dimensions. Some of Rumelt's (1974) categories have been used in studies searching for causes and consequences of diversity. The most commonly used distinction contrasts related and unrelated diversifiers (Blackburn, Lang, and Johnson, 1990; Chatterjee and Wernerfelt, 1991; Keats, 1990; Plaut and Ilan, 1987). Other categories in Rumelt's typology, such as single and dominant forms, have also been used (Keats, 1990), and geographic diversity has received some attention, reflecting the trend toward global competition (Madura and Whyte, 1990; Tang and Yu, 1990). Other forms of organizing have been examined internationally. For example, in Korea, 'business groups' essentially operate as broadly diversified entities with characteristics similar to conglomerates with vertical integration (Chang and Choi, 1988).

Along with different types of diversity reflected in content-oriented models, there are many ways to diversify reflected in what might be thought of as process-oriented models. When searching for the relative advantages of various methods of diversifying, the most common pairings pit internal development against merger/acquisition (M&A) (Chatterjee, 1990; Hitt, Hoskisson, and Ireland, 1990; Porter, 1987). Models also examine firms diversifying through joint venture (Porter, 1987; Tang and Yu, 1990). For geographic diversification, foreign direct investment, exclusive licensing, and multiple licensing are also considered (Tang and Yu, 1990).

Empirical models have examined forces that might push diversification: environmental turbulence (Keats and Hitt, 1988), risk aversion (*Asian Finance*, 1990; Hill and Hansen, 1991; Hitt, Hoskisson, and Ireland, 1990; Plaut and Ilan, 1987), the need to stabilize cash flows (Madura and Whyte, 1990). At the opposite extreme of the push argument, diversification may be fueled (and directed) by excess resources. Slack could be in the form of internal funds, physical resources, knowledge, and other intangible resources (Chatterjee, 1990; Chatterjee and

Wernerfelt, 1991). Similarly, firms may attempt to capitalize on economies of scale and experience effects (Plaut and Ilan, 1987), or they may seek to create synergies in sales, operating, investment, or management dimensions (Mahajan and Wind, 1988; Porter, 1987).

Models have also examined forces that might pull firms to diversify. Firms may diversify along certain dimensions (e.g. related, unrelated, vertical, geographic) in order to capitalize on opportunities. Goals may be related to accounting-based measures of profitability (Chang and Choi, 1988; Mahajan and Wind, 1988) or stock market measure of performance (Blackburn, Lang, and Johnson, 1990; Chatterjee, 1990; Keats, 1990). Other industries may offer superior growth and investment opportunities (*Asian Finance*, 1990).

These represent only a few of the possible reasons for firms to diversify. Interviews with top executives of Fortune 500 firms suggest that there may be many more. In fact, executives may think about diversification strategies in styles that are not captured by existing models. Concepts of relatedness may rest on idiosyncratic dimensions that cannot be captured using the (currently) dominant methods of research.

Given the confusion resulting from decades of equivocal findings, the one point that seems clear is that the nature of diversity, the process of diversification, and the associated driving forces should not be treated as unidimensional constructs with simple linear relationships connecting them. There is reason to believe that each of the constructs may be multidimensional in nature (Keats, 1990), and the relationships among them may be moderated in complex ways by variables inside and/or outside the firm (Blackburn, Lang, and Johnson, 1990).

Scope effects

One of the basic assumptions in the diversification literature is that there are some advantages to a broader range of products. In a study of 1400 business units sampled from the PIMS database, it was found that the breadth of the product line (scope) was positively related to profitability and market share, but it was not related to production costs (Kekre and Srinivasan, 1990).

Since it probably makes a difference what things are being combined within the scope, it is not surprising that the links between scope and production costs vary across industries. Economies of scope have been identified in petroleum refining (Shoesmith, 1988) and banking industries (Kim and Ben-Zion, 1989). However, relationships went in the opposite direction (i.e. diseconomies of scope) in the water utility (Hayes, 1987), gas and electric utilities (Sing, 1987), and railroad industries (Kim, 1987). Finally, there was no relationship found between scope and production costs in the securities industry (Goldberg, Hanweck, Keenan, and Young, 1991) and a municipal police department (Gyimah-Brempong, 1987).

In addition to varying across industries, scope effects may vary across firms and over time within a given industry (Hayes, 1987). Even when (dis)economies of scope are identified, it is important that managers consider why the relationship exists. For instance, a plausible explanation for the diseconomies of scope found in the gas and electric utilities industries is that firms with broader scope endeavor to provide a higher quality of service and, therefore, incur higher production costs.

The most widely used method of assessing economies of scope seems to be a multiproduct translog cost function (Goldberg *et al.*, 1991; Gyimah-Brempong, 1987; Kim, 1987; Shoesmith, 1988). CAPM has also been used (Chang, 1988).

Control systems

Models in this category address the influence of corporate–SBU relationships on performance. Two prominent dimensions used in the models are (a) the degree of autonomy granted the SBU (Datta and Grant, 1990; Goold and Campbell, 1987; Govindarajan, 1988; Gupta, 1987; Keren and Levhari, 1989), and (b) the relative emphasis of financial versus behavioral controls (Goold and Campbell, 1987; Govindarajan, 1988; Govindarajan and Fisher, 1990; Gupta, 1987). Findings consistently suggest that the performance of the firm will suffer if the method of control is not tailored to the needs of the firm (Datta and Grant, 1990; Govindarajan, 1988; Govindarajan and Fisher, 1990; Gupta, 1987; Nwachukwu and Tsalikis, 1990–91). Firms pursuing a differentiation strategy tend to perform better if they allow their SBUs a high degree of autonomy and emphasize behavioral controls. In contrast, firms pursuing a low-cost strategy tend to perform better if they adopt financial controls and grant SBUs less autonomy.

Carroll (1988) proposed that it is not necessary for corporations to use the same style of control for all of their SBUs. SBUs within a conglomerate may be pursuing different strategies and should be managed with different control systems. Interestingly, Datta (1991) found that differences in control systems between parent and acquired firms did not affect post-acquisition performance. However, differences in top management styles lowered performance. These patterns held regardless of the degree of autonomy granted to the acquired firm.

Theoretical

Diversification

Diversification has been approached from a number of theoretical stances. Taking a resource-dependency perspective, firms diversify to reduce their external dependencies, thereby reducing the threat of external control (Pfeffer and Salancik, 1978). This is often used to explain vertical integration. This perspective does not constrain thinking to defensive orientations. Firms may diversify as part of a strategy to gain external control over rivals. This could lead to acquisitions in directions that might appear unrelated to the diversifying firm's core business. However, the dominant logic or unifying thread may be defined in terms of interactions in multipoint competition.

While the resource-dependency view of the firm focuses on threats arising from the need for resources, the resource-based view of the firm focuses on opportunities derived from stocks of resources. The resource-based view proposes that firms diversify to utilize excess resources or to generate synergies (Farjoun, 1991). Slack resources and potential synergies would generally push firms toward related diversification. Financial resources would be the exception in that they could be applied to unrelated diversification as well.

A transaction costs approach suggests that diversification is driven by efficiency (Williamson, 1975). Firms will diversify when administrative costs are less than transaction costs (i.e. when organizations are more efficient than markets). This has been one of the dominant perspectives used in explaining geographic diversification of multinational enterprises (Tallman, 1991).

Given the equivocal nature of the empirical research linking diversification to performance, it is not clear that diversification is always in the best interest of the shareholder, yet it continues to occur. Agency theory has been applied to diversification to issues when it is unclear that the interests of the stockholders coincide with those of the managers. Aron (1988) used results from a mathematical model to suggest that diversification is the optimal response to the moral hazard problem that owners face. Allen and Cebenoyan (1991) suggest that managerial incentives may drive diversification in spite of the potentially negative impact on stockholder wealth. Their empirical findings were consistent with this view of agency conflict in that positive bidder returns were found only for those firms in which managers had substantial stockholdings and the stockholders were highly concentrated.

Selection and bargaining. If diversification is achieved through acquisitions and/or mergers, managers must be careful in targeting firms. Kroll and Caples (1987) suggest that portfolio models (e.g. the McKinsey model, the BCG model) lack the necessary precision for selecting firms, while traditional financial performance measures lack analytical breadth. It is suggested that these techniques can be supplemented through the use of an arbitrage pricing model (an extension of the capital asset pricing model—CAPM) to assess the economic sensitivities of acquisition candidates.

Linear goal programming (LGP) has been suggested as another means of identifying suitable candidates for mergers, acquisitions, and join ventures (Dean and Schniederjans, 1991; Schniederjans and Fowler, 1989). This approach makes it possible to consider a large volume of accounting, finance, marketing, and management factors. Further it allows managers to incorporate synergistic relationships in the model. When managers consider entering a variety of industries, this approach may help identify each industry's strengths and weaknesses through the careful interpretation of dual solution values and sensitivity analysis coefficients.

Once a firm has been selected for merger or acquisition, a bargaining process begins in which the manager of the acquiring firm is uncertain about the minimum price the stockholders of the target firm will accept. The problem is complicated further in that the bargaining process generally involves a series of offers, and the minimum acceptable price may change during that time. Roy (1989) developed a model to generate optimal offer strategies when there is uncertainty about the minimum acceptable offer. This uncertainty is represented as a probability distribution, and it is assumed that the market is efficient.

Scope effects

Economies of scope may be obtained through the sharing of (often fixed) inputs in the production of goods or services (Grosskopf and Yaisawarng, 1990). The existence of economies of scope may lead to counter-intuitive interpretations which managers might easily overlook in the absence of analytic models. For example, under certain circumstances, profits are maximized for the firm if it loses money on one product (Ladd, 1988). The existence of economies of scope may complicate decisions regarding optimal production and pricing. Ladd's model is useful in generating decision rules for production and pricing as a function of the firm's resources (fixed and fully utilized versus underutilized) and its goals (profit-maximizing versus revenue-maximizing).

In operations research, Kekre (1987) demonstrated the impact of increasing product mix while maintaining the same machine load. The model suggests that the resulting increase in the heterogeneity of parts causes an increase in the optimal batch size, and hence longer production runs. As runs and queue times increase, lead times and work-in-progress inventories increase. This reduces the performance of the cell. However, the marginal rate of deterioration of performance gets smaller as group size gets larger.

In a similar vein, Cohen and Moon (1991) developed a model for assigning product lines and volumes to a set of capacitated plants. The model incorporates both economies of scope and scale in the assignment process along with the costs associated with inbound supply and outbound distribution flows. The problem of assigning product lines and volumes to plants is solved using a concave mixed-integer mathematical program. Such models may help managers to evaluate the trade-offs between receiving, production, and distribution costs. This has clear implications for firms that have diversified (or are considering diversifying) based on similar processes; it is possible, but not certain, that synergies could be obtained through the sharing of facilities. The complexity of the problem is of such depth that analytic models may certainly be of use to managers.

Models of economies of scope have also been applied to the sharing of administrative costs for local public services (Grosskopf and Yaisawarng, 1990). While economies of scope may exist under some conditions, Brueckner and Lee (1991) point out that the joint provision of public goods is inherently accompanied by a loss of efficiency as it becomes impossible to independently adjust the sizes of the consumption group to accommodate the congestion properties of each public good. The proposed model examines the trade-off between cost-complementarity gains and efficiency losses in joint provision. The likelihood that the costs outweigh the gains increases as congestion differences increase.

Firms producing a range of products may find it advantageous to bundle some of their product lines. Wilson, Weiss, and John (1990) use a mathematical model to examine competition among firms selling industrial systems when some of the firms offer complete (bundled) systems while specialist firms offer individual components that consumers can 'mix and match' to create complete systems. The model evaluates three options for firms that are currently bundling their components, namely, (a) continue selling complete systems, (b) sell the system as unbundled components, or (c) reduce the scope by producing only a subset of components. The model is useful in describing several managerial heuristics. The tendency to unbundle products is shown to be related to the diffusion of technology across rivals and the evolution of standards; firms are more likely to unbundle their products as their industry matures. The primary incentive for unbundling arises from the potential growth in the size of the market.

To assess the impact of economies of scope on market structure, Eaton and Lemche (1991) used a two-good partial-equilibrium model to assess interactions among three types of firms: those producing product A only, those producing product B only, those producing both A and B. Results indicated that equilibrium market structure is determined by cost as well as demand conditions, and it is unlikely that markets will form with more types of firms than products.

Portfolios of business units

Given the mammoth proportions of conglomerates today, corporate managers may find it difficult to get a clear picture of the overall strategic position of the firm. It is generally helpful to divide corporations into strategic business units (SBUs) representing relatively independent elements of the corporation (Bhattacharya, 1987). While these SBUs often require a certain degree of autonomy in formulating and implementing strategy, there is some need to coordinate them at the corporate level. Portfolio analysis offers a means of getting an overarching view of SBUs with respect to a few salient dimensions. Generally, graphic representations provide managers with an intuitive feel for the firm's current position. It also allows projections of the firm's future position and representations of desired positions. This can help managers identify problems that need to be remedied and opportunities that could be capitalized on (Turnbull, 1990).

Studies of executives in Fortune 1000 firms found that three of the perceived benefits of portfolio analysis include: (a) increased capacity for performing the strategic management task, (b) improvements in the quality of corporate and business strategies, and (c) greater discrimination in the allocation of corporate resources (Asch, 1987). For instance, after implementing its value-based portfolio management system Dexter Corp. stopped investing in business segments with high-growth potential until the segment showed actual improvements in performance. Dexter Corp. also sold segments at book value to its employees if those segments had negative value or if an offer was made in excess of foreseeable valuation (Chakravarthy, Loomis, and Vrabel, 1988).

In addition to facilitating analyses, the models have inspired a vocabulary that has gained popular use. SBUs are often described as 'cash cows,' 'stars,' 'problem children,' and 'dogs,' while strategies may be described in terms of 'harvest,' 'build,' 'hold,' and 'divest.' This underscores one of the main tenets of this chapter; the usefulness of analytic models may lie more in the discussions they generate than in the output they produce.

Marshall and Tomkins (1988) developed a computer model based on the Boston Consulting Group (BCG) matrix. The model located discounted cash flow values on the matrix in an attempt to move the advise associated with the model to a more precise form. Discounted cash flows were also used to modify the McKinsey matrix to examine the impact that SBUs may have on the stock price of the firm. Reimann (1987, 1989, 1990) uses discounted cash flows in assessing the riskiness of SBUs. By adjusting the cash flows for their relative uncertainty, the method avoids the task of assigning unique hurdle rates to each SBU.

Proctor and Hassard (1990) also propose a modification to the McKinsey matrix method. A third dimension is added to reflect environmental turbulence. Given a relatively stable environment, the modified approach provides the same recommendations as the BCG and McKinsey models.

The use of portfolio models may be helpful in reducing the complexity of managing a diverse set of firms, but in simplifying the problem the method ignores a wide range of strategic issues (Clarke and Brennan, 1990). Naugle and Davies (1987) suggest that by viewing corporations as collections of (existing) SBUs, focus is shifted away from functional skills which may provide the impetus for developing new businesses. It is recommended that managers move beyond identifying competitive advantages of SBUs to identifying, developing, and monitoring functional skills.

A portfolio approach has been offered as a means of identifying the potential for synergies among SBUs. Clarke and Brennan (1990) use four portfolios simultaneously to represent relationships among SBUs in terms of products, resources, customers, and technology. This approach may stimulate insights regarding the management of synergies through cultural and structural means.

CONCLUSION

Earlier models with relatively narrow applications (e.g. portfolio matrices developed by the Boston Consulting Group and General Electric) are being replaced by more sophisticated models designed to help managers integrate more pieces of the strategy puzzle. There has been a concerted effort to make user-friendly models that reduce and integrate more complex sets of inputs into easily digested sets of output (Hussein, 1987). With the technological advances in computers and the increasing reliance on information as a strategic weapon, managers will be expected to do more complex modeling with fewer staff during the next decade (Berman and Kautz, 1990).

This trend is exemplified by a software package (Compete!) offered by Manageware for IBM-compatible personal computers (Berman and Kautz, 1990). Analyses include, among other things, manpower planning, single-unit forecasting, competitive shareholder value, market analysis, and manufacturing strategy. It can analyze large data sets and is capable of modeling the microeconomics of an entire industry. Compete! is even capable of performing backward what-if analyses as part of a goal-seeking function.

However, it is important to bear in mind that models are merely tools; their effectiveness depends on the craftsmanship of the decision-makers using them. In a very pragmatic sense, the mark of any good tool is that it helps the craftsman to get the job done. As the sophistication and the number of bells and whistles attached to models increases, it is important to remember that a good model is one that it helps managers move the organization towards effective strategic actions.

REFERENCES

Aggarwal, R. and Soenen, L. A. (1989) Project exit value as a measure of flexibility and risk exposure. *Engineering Economist*, 35 (1). 39–54.

Aggarwal, V. and Bahari-Kashani, H. (1991) Synchronized production policies for deteriorating items in a declining market. *IIE Transactions*, 23 (2). 185–197.

Ahluwalia, R. S. and Ji, P. (1991) A distributed approach to job scheduling in a flexible manufacturing system. *Computers and Industrial Engineering*, 20 (1). 95–103.

Aivazian, V. A., Callen, J. L., Chan, M. W. L. and Mountain, D. C. (1987) Economies of scale versus technological change in the natural gas transmission industry. *Review of Economics and Statistics (Netherlands)*, 69 (3). 556–561.

Alavi, M. (1991) Group decision support systems: A key to business team productivity. *Journal of Information Systems Management*, 8 (3). 36–41.

Allen, L. and Cebenoyan, A. S. (1991) Bank acquisitions and ownership structure: Theory and evidence. *Journal of Banking and Finance (Netherlands)*, 15 (2). 425–448.

Amel, D. F. and Rhoades, S. A. (1988) Strategic groups in banking. *Review of Economics and Statistics (Netherlands)*, 70 (4). 685–689.

Amit, R. and Ilan, Y. (1990) The choice of manufacturing technology in the presence of dynamic demand and experience effects. *IIE Transactions*, 22 (2). 100–111.

Amoako-Gyampah, K. and Meredith, J. R. (1989) The operations management research agenda: An update. *Journal of Operations Management*, 8 (3). 250–262.

Anandalingam, G. (1987) Asymmetric players and bargaining for profit shares in natural resource development. *Management Science*, 33 (8). 1048–1057.

Anderson, S. P., de Palma, A. and Thisse, J.-F. (1988) A representative consumer theory of the logit model. *International Economic Review*, 29 (3). 461–466.

Anily, S. and Federgruen, A. (1990) One warehouse multiple retailer systems with vehicle routing costs. *Management Science*, 36 (1). 92–114.

Anterasian, C. and Graham, J. L. (1989) When it's good management to sacrifice market share. *Journal of Business Research*, 19 (3). 187–213.

Anton, J. J. and Yao, D. A. (1987) Second sourcing and the experience curve: Price competition in defense procurement. *Rand Journal of Economics*, 18 (1). 57–76.

Arinze, B. (1990) Market planning with computer models: A case study in the software industry. *Industrial Marketing Management*, 19 (2). 117–129.

Armistead, C. and Clark, G. (1991) A framework for formulating after-sales support strategy. *International Journal of Operations and Production Management*, 11 (3). 111–124.

Aron, D. J. (1988) Ability, moral hazard, firm size, and diversification. *Rand Journal of Economics*, 19 (1). 72–87.

Arsham, H. (1987) A stochastic model of optimal advertising pulsing policy. *Computers and Operations Research (UK)*, 14 (3). 231–239.

Asch, D. (1987) Techniques for formulating corporate strategy. *Management Accounting (UK)*, 65 (8). 28–29.

Ashmos, D. P. and McDaniel, R. R. Jr, (1991) Physician participation in hospital strategic decision making: The effect of hospital strategy and decision content. *Health Services Research*, 26 (3). 375–401.

Asian Finance (1990) Mergers and acquisitions: The rules of the game. 16 (1). 15–16.

Azani, H. and Khorramshahgol, R. (1990) Analytic Delphi Method (ADM): A strategic decision making model applied to location planning. *Engineering Costs and Production Economics (Netherlands)*, 20 (1). 23–28.

Azzone, G., Masella, C. and Bertele, U. (1991) Design of performance measures for time-based companies. *International Journal of Operations and Production Management*, 11 (3). 77–85.

Bagchi, P. K. and Davis, F. W. Jr (1988) Some insights into inbound freight consolidation. *International Journal of Physical Distribution and Materials Management (UK)*, 18 (6). 27–33.

Baird, I. S., Sudharshan, D. and Thomas, H. (1988) Addressing temporal change in strategic groups analysis: A three-mode factor analysis approach. *Journal of Management*, 14 (3). 425–439.

Band, W. (1989) Quality is king for marketers. *Sales and Marketing Management in Canada (Canada)*, 30 (3). 6–8.

Banker, R. D. and Kemerer, C. F. (1989) Scale economies in new software development. *IEEE Transactions on Software Engineering*, 15 (10). 1199–1205.

Bard, J. F. (1987) Developing competitive strategies for buyer-supplier negotiations. *Management Science*, 33 (9). 1181–1191.

Bard, J. F. (1990) Using multicriteria methods in the early stages of new product development. *Journal of the Operational Research Society (UK)*, 41 (8). 755–766.

Barnett, A. and Tress, H. (1990) Misapplications reviews: Rain men. *Interfaces*, 20 (2). 42–47.

Barney, J. B. and Hoskisson, R. E. (1990) Strategic groups: Untested assertions and research proposals. *Managerial and Decision Economics (UK)*, 11 (3). 187–198.

Baron, R. C. (1988) Leap over the ROI barriers to CIM. *Automation*, 35 (7). 50–52.

Bayus, B. L. (1987) Forecasting sales of new contingent products: An application to the compact disc market. *Journal of Product Innovation Management*, 4 (4). 243–255.

Bean, J. C., Birge, J. R., Mittenthal, J. and Noon, C. E. (1991) Matchup scheduling with multiple resources, release dates and disruptions. *Operations Research*, 39 (3). 470–483.

Beard, T. R. and Ekelund, R. B. Jr (1991) Quality choice and price discrimination: A note on Dupuit's Conjecture. *Southern Economic Journal*, 57 (4). 1155–1163.

Bemis, G. R. and DeAngelis, M. (1990) Levelized cost of electricity generation technologies. *Contemporary Policy Issues*, 8 (3). 200–214.

Ben-Akiva, M., de Palma, A. and Thisse, J.-F. (1989) Spatial competition with differentiated products. *Regional Science and Urban Economics (Netherlands)*, 19 (1). 5–19.

Bergmann, B. R. (1989) A microsimulated model of inventories in interfirm competition. *Engineering Costs and Production Economics (Netherlands)*, 15. 9–15.

Berman, S. J. and Kautz, R. F. (1990) Compete! A sophisticated tool that facilitates strategic analysis. *Planning Review*, 18 (4). 35–39.

Bhattacharya, K. (1987) Strategic budgets. *Management Accounting (UK)*, 65 (11). 39.

Blackburn, V. L., Lang, J. R. and Johnson, K. H. (1990) Mergers and shareholder returns: The roles of acquiring firm's ownership and diversification strategy. *Journal of Management*, 16(4). 769–782.

Blumenthal, M. A. (1988) Auctions with constrained information: Blind bidding for motion pictures. *Review of Economics and Statistics (Netherlands)*, 70 (2). 191–198.

Boeker, W. (1991) Organizational strategy: An ecological perspective. *Academy of Management Journal*, 34 (3). 613–635.

Booth, L. (1991) The influence of production technology on risk and the cost of capital. *Journal of Financial and Quantitative Analysis*, 26 (1). 109–127.

Boulding, W. and Staelin, R. (1990) Environment, market share, and market power. *Management Science*, 36 (10). 1160–1177.

Braid, R. M. (1989) The optimal locations of multiple bridges, connecting facilities, or product varieties. *Journal of Regional Science*, 29 (1). 63–70.

Brams, S. J. and Kilgour, D. M. (1987) Optimal threats. *Operations Research*, 35 (4). 524–536.

Breitman, R. L. and Lucas, J. M. (1987) PLANETS: A modeling system for business planning. *Interfaces*, 17 (1). 94–106.

Broadwell, L. (1987) Business games: They're more than child's play. *Successful Meetings*, 36 (7). 36–39.

Brueckner, J. K. and Lee, K. (1991) Economies of scope and multiproduct clubs. *Public Finance Quarterly*, 19 (2). 193–208.

Brueggeman, W. B. and Thibodeau, T. G. (1987) Real estate returns and market responses to 1986 tax reform. *Real Estate Review*, 17 (1). 69–75.

Buckley, P. G. (1988) Nested multinomial logit analysis of scanner data for a hierarchical choice model. *Journal of Business Research*, 17 (2). 133–154.

Buffa, F. P. and Munn, J. R. (1990) Multi-item grouping algorithm yielding near-optimal logistics cost. *Decision Sciences*, 21 (1). 14–34.

Burt, R. (1982) Toward a structural theory of action. In R. Burt (Ed.), *Toward a Structural Theory of Action: Network Models of Social Structure, Perception and Action*, (pp. 1–16). New York, Academic Press.

Buzzell, R. D. and Gale, B. T. (1987) *The PIMS principles*. New York, Free Press.

Callan, S. J. and Santerre, R. E. (1990) The production characteristics of local public education: A multiple product and input analysis. *Southern Economic Journal*, 57 (2). 468–480.

Campbell, J. F. (1990) Designing logistics systems by analyzing transportation, inventory and terminal cost tradeoffs. *Journal of Business Logistics*, 11 (1). 159–179.

Campbell, N. C. G. (1988) Market-share patterns and market leadership in Japan. *International Studies of Management and Organization*, 18 (1). 50–66.

Campos, V., Corberan, A. and Mota, E. (1991) Polyhedral results for a vehicle routing problem. *European Journal of Operational Research (Netherlands)*, 52 (1). 75–85.

Carbajo, J. C. (1988) The economics of travel passes: Non-uniform pricing in transport. *Journal of Transport Economics and Policy (UK)*, 22 (2). 153–173.

Carroll, C., Lewis, P. and Thomas, H. (April, 1992) Using strategic groups to analyse effective competitive strategies in the retailing industry. *Long Range Planning*, 25 (2).

Carroll, S. J. (1988) Handling the need for consistency and the need for contingency in the management of compensation. *Human Resource Planning*, 11 (3). 191–196.

Cave, J. (1987) Long-term competition in a dynamic game: The cold fish war. *Rand Journal of Economics*, 18 (4). 596–610.

Chakravarthy, B., Loomis, W. and Vrabel, J. (1988) Dexter Corporation's value-based strategic planning system. *Planning Review*, 16 (1). 34–41.

Chakravarty A. K. and Shtub, A. (1987) Strategic allocation of inspection effort in a serial, multi-product production system. *IIE Transactions*, 19 (1). 13–22.

Chander, P. and Leruth, L. (1989) The optimal product mix for a monopolist in the presence of congestion effects: A model and some results. *International Journal of Industrial Organization (Netherlands)*, 7 (4). 437–449.

Chang, P. (1988) Economies of scope, synergy, and the CAPM. *Journal of Financial Research*, 11 (3). 255–263.

Chang, S. J. and Choi, U. (1988) Strategy, structure and performance of Korean business groups: A transactions cost approach. *Journal of Industrial Economics (UK)*, 37 (2). 141–158.

Chaplin, A. S. and Nalebuff, B. J. (1986) Multi-dimensional product differentiation and price competition. *Oxford Economic Papers (UK) (Supplement)*, 38. 129–145.

Chatterjee, R., Eliashberg, J., Gatignon, H. and Lodish, L. M. (1988) A practical Bayesian approach to selection of optimal market testing strategies. *Journal of Marketing Research*, 25 (4). 363–375.

Chatterjee, S. (1990) Excess resources, utilization costs, and mode of entry. *Academy of Management Journal*, 33 (4). 780–800.

Chatterjee, S. and Wernerfelt, B. (1991) The link between resources and type of diversification: Theory and evidence. *Strategic Management Journal (UK)*, 12 (1). 33–48.

Cho, D. (1988) Some evidence of scale economies in workers' compensation insurance. *Journal of Risk and Insurance*, 55 (2). 324–330.

Clarke, C. J. and Brennan, K. (1990) Building synergy in the diversified business. *Long Range Planning (UK)*, 23 (2). 9–16.

Cohen, M. A. and Halperin, R. M. (1986) Optimal technology choice in a dynamic-stochastic environment. *Journal of Operations Management*, 6 (3/4). 317–331.

Cohen, M. A. and Lee, H. L. (1988) Strategic analysis of integrated production-distribution systems: Models and methods. *Operations Research*, 36 (2). 216–228.

Cohen, M. A. and Moon, S. (1991) An integrated plant loading model with economies of scale and scope. *European Journal of Operational Research (Netherlands)*, 50 (3). 266–279.

Conner, K. R. and Rumelt, R. P. (1991) Software piracy: An analysis of protection strategies. *Management Science*, 37 (2). 125–139.

Cool, K. O. and Schendel, D. (1987) Strategic group formation and performance: The case of the U.S. pharmaceutical industry, 1963–1982. *Management Science,* 33 (9). 1102–1124.

Cool, K. and Schendel, D. (1988) Performance differences among strategic group members. *Strategic Management Journal (UK),* 9 (3). 207–223.

Cooper, L. G. (1988) Competitive maps: The structure underlying asymmetric cross elasticities. *Management Science,* 34 (6). 707–723.

Cravens, D. W., Moncrief, W. C., Lamb, C. W. Jr, and Dielman, T. (1990) Sequential modeling approach for redeploying selling effort in field salesforces. *Journal of Business Research.* 20 (3). 217–233.

Cremer, H. and Thisse, J.-F. (1991) Location models of horizontal differentiation: A special case of vertical differentiation models. *Journal of Industrial Economics (UK),* 39 (4). 383–390.

Currim, I. S., Meyer, R. J., and Le, N. T. (1988) Disaggregate tree-structured modeling of consumer choice data. *Journal of Marketing Research,* 25 (3). 253–265.

d'Astous, A. and Rouzies, D. (1987) Selection and implementation of processing strategies in consumer evaluative judgment and choice. *International Journal of Research in Marketing (Netherlands),* 4 (2). 99–110.

Daniels, R. L. and Sarin, R. K. (1989) Single machine scheduling with controllable processing times and number of jobs tardy. *Operations Research,* 37 (6). 981–984.

Dasgupta, P. (1989) Applying game theory: Some theoretical considerations. *European Economic Review (Netherlands),* 33 (2, 3). 619–624.

Datta, D. K. (1991) Organizational fit and acquisition performance: Effects of post-acquisition integration. *Strategic Management Journal (UK),* 12 (4). 281–297.

Datta, D. K. and Grant, J. H. (1990) Relationships between type of acquisition, the autonomy given to the acquired firm, and acquisition success: An empirical analysis. *Journal of Management,* 16 (1). 29–44.

Day, D. L., DeSarbo, W. S. and Oliva, T. A. (1987) Strategy maps: A spatial representation of intra-industry competitive strategy. *Management Science,* 33 (12). 1534–1551.

De Bondt, R., Sleuwaegen, L. and Veugelers, R. (1988) Innovative strategic groups in multinational industries. *European Economic Review (Netherlands),* 32 (4). 905–925.

De, P., Ghosh, J. B. and Wells, C. E. (1990) CON due-date determination and sequencing. *Computers and Operations Research (UK),* 17 (4). 333–342.

Dean, B. V. and Schniederjans, M. J. (1991) A multiple objective selection methodology for strategic industry selection analysis. *IEEE Transactions on Engineering Management,* 38 (1). 53–62.

Delmas, B. and Gadrey, J. (1987) On the substitution of goods and services. *Service Industries Journal (UK),* 7 (4). 12–25.

DePorter, E. L. and Craig, K. J. (1989) Linear programming as a tool for office automation planning. *Computers and Industrial Engineering,* 17 (1–4). 421–424.

di Benedetto, C. A. (1987) Modeling rationality in marketing decision-making with game theory. *Journal of the Academy of Marketing Science,* 15 (4). 22–32.

Dompere, K. K. (1989) The internal structure and the functional representation of capital-adjustment costs. *Engineering Costs and Production Economics (Netherlands),* 18 (2). 105–115.

Duhaime, I. M. and Stimpert, J. L. (January, 1990) One more time: A look at the factors influencing performance. Working paper.

Eaton, B. C. and Lemche, S. Q. (1991) The Geometry of supply, demand, and competitive market structure with economies of scope. *American Economic Review*, 81 (4). 901–911.

Edmister, R. O. (1988) Combining human credit analysis and numerical credit scoring for business failure prediction. *Akron Business and Economic Review*, 19 (3). 6–14.

Eriksson, L. O. and Bjorheden, R. (6, 1989) Optimal storing, transport and processing for a forest-fuel supplier. *European Journal of Operational Research (Netherlands)*, 43 (1). 26–33.

Fader, P. S. and McAlister, L. (1990) An elimination by aspects model of consumer response to promotion calibrated on UPC scanner data. *Journal of Marketing Research*, 27 (3). 322–332.

Faria, A. J. (1989) Business gaming: Current usage levels. *Journal of Management Development (UK)*, 8 (2). 58–65.

Farjoun, M. (1991) Beyond industry boundaries: Human expertise, diversification, and related industries. Unpublished doctoral dissertation, Northwestern University, Evanston, IL.

Fiegenbaum, A., McGee, J. and Thomas, H. (1988) Exploring the linkage between strategic groups and competitive strategy. *International Studies of Management and Organization*, 18 (1). 6–25.

Fiegenbaum, A., Sudharshan, D. and Thomas, H. (1987) The concept of stable strategic time periods in strategic group research. *Managerial and Decision Economics (UK)*, 8 (2). 139–148.

Fiegenbaum, A., Sudharshan, D. and Thomas, H. (1990) Strategic time periods and strategic groups research: Concepts and an empirical example. *Journal of Management Studies (UK)*, 27 (2). 133–148.

Fiegenbaum, A. and Thomas, H. (1990) Strategic groups and performance: The U.S. insurance industry, 1970–84. *Strategic Management Journal (UK)*, 11 (3) 197–215.

Findlay, P. L., Kobbacy, K. A. H. and Goodman, D. J. (1989) Optimization of the daily production rates for an offshore oilfield. *Journal of the Operational Research Society (UK)*, 40 (12). 1079–1088.

Fisher, F. M. (1989) Games economists play: A noncooperative view. *Rand Journal of Economics*, 20 (1) 113–124.

Fletcher, J. and Latham, J. (1990) The use of cones to determine the market shares of service establishments in a single market. *Service Industries Journal (UK)*, 10 (4). 722–736.

Flodhammar, A. (1988) A sales force approach to industrial marketing segmentation. *Quarterly Review of Marketing (UK)*, 13 (2). 5–9.

Fombrun, C. J. and Zajac, E. J. (1987) Structural and perceptual influences on intraindustry stratification. *Academy of Management Journal*, 30 (1). 33–50.

Fornell, C. and Wernerfelt, B. (1987) Defensive marketing strategy by customer complaint management: A theoretical analysis. *Journal of Marketing Research*, 24 (4). 337–346.

Francett, B. (1990) Using pricing to change buying patterns. *Computerworld*, 24 (44). 116–117.

Franses, P. H. (1991) Primary demand for beer in The Netherlands: An application of ARMAX model specification. *Journal of Marketing Research*, 28 (2). 240–245.

Fraser, C. and Ginter, J. L. (1988) Competitive dealing strategy and deal value escalation. *Management Science*, 34 (11). 1315–1323.

Fraser, C. and Ginter, J. (1991) A probabilistic dealing strategy. *Decision Sciences*, 22 (1). 91–103.

Friedman, J. W. (1990) A modification of the Folk Theorem to apply to time-dependent supergames. *Oxford Economic Papers (UK)*, 42 (2). 317–335.

Gaimon, C. (1989) Dynamic game results of the acquisition of new technology. *Operations Research*, 37 (3). 410–425.

Gale, B. T. and Branch, B. (1987) 'Allocating' capital more effectively. *Sloan Management Review*, 29(1). 21–31.

Gale, B. T. and Swire, D. J. (1988) Business strategies that create wealth. *Planning Review*, 16 (2). 6–13, 47.

Gardner, E. S., Jr and McKenzie, E. (1989) Seasonal exponential smoothing with damped trends. *Management Science*, 35 (3). 372–376.

Gatignon, H. (1987) Strategic studies in Markstrat. *Journal of Business Research*, 15 (6). 469–480.

Gatignon, H. and Hanssens, D. M. (1987) Modeling marketing interactions with application to salesforce effectiveness. *Journal of Marketing Research*, 24 (3). 247–257.

Gavish, B. and Johnson, R. E. (1990) A fully polynomial approximation scheme for single-product scheduling in a finite capacity facility. *Operations Research*, 38 (1). 70–83.

Geroski, P. A. and Murfin, A. (1991) Entry and industry evolution: the UK car industry, 1958–83. *Applied Economics (UK)*, 23 (4B). 799–809.

Gilboa, I. and Matsui, A. (1991) Social stability and equilibrium. *Econometrica*, 59 (3). 859–867.

Goldberg, L. G., Hanweck, G. A., Keenan, M. and Young, A. (1991) Economies of scale and scope in the securities industry. *Journal of Banking and Finance (Netherlands)*, 15 (1). 91–107.

Gooding, C. and Keys, B. (1990) Introducing executive MBA programmes with management games. *Journal of Management Development (UK)*, 9 (2). 53–60.

Goold, M. and Campbell, A. (1987) Managing diversity: Strategy and control in diversified British companies. *Long Range Planning (UK)*, 20 (5). 42–52.

Gottardi, G. and Copolla, L. (1988) Estimating capital cost dynamics of new technologies. *AACE Transactions*, J.2.1–J.2.8.

Govindarajan, V. (1988) A contingency approach to strategy implementation at the business-unit level: Integrating administrative mechanism with strategy. *Academy of Management Journal*, 31 (4). 828–853.

Govindarajan, V. and Fisher, J. (1990) Strategy, control systems, and resource sharing: Effects on business-unit performance. *Academy of Management Journal*, 33 (2). 259–285.

Grabowski, H. G. and Vernon, J. M. (1987) Pioneers, imitators, and generics—A simulation model of Schumpeterian competition. *Quarterly Journal of Economics*, 102 (3). 491–525.

Grosskopf, S. and Yaisawarng, S. (1990) Economies of scope in the provision of local public services. *National Tax Journal*, 43 (1). 61–74.

Grover, R. and Srinivasan, V. (1987) A simultaneous approach to market segmentation and market structuring. *Journal of Marketing Research*, 24 (2). 139–153.

Gupta, A. K. (1987) SBU strategies, corporate-SBU relations, and SBU effectiveness in strategy implementation. *Academy of Management Journal*, 30 (3). 477–500.

Gupta, T. and Houshyar, A. (1990) Consideration of instage and central buffers in two-stage production system. *Computers and Industrial Engineering*. 19 (1–4). 427–431.

Gyimah-Brempong, K. (1987) Economies of scale in municipal police departments: The case of Florida. *Review of Economics and Statistics (Netherlands)*, 69 (2). 352–356.

Hagerty, M. R., Carman, J. M. and Russell, G. J. (1988) Estimating elasticities with PIMS data: Methodological issues and substantive implications. *Journal of Marketing Research*, 25 (1) 1–9.

Hales, C. and Shams, H. (1991) Cautious incremental consumption: A neglected consumer risk reduction strategy. *European Journal of Marketing*, 25 (7). 7–21.

Hall, G. (1987) When does market-share matter? *Journal of Economic Studies (UK)*, 14 (3). 41–54.

Hanson, W. and Martin, R. K. (1990) Optimal bundle pricing. *Management Science*, 36 (2). 155–174.

Harrison, T. P. and Ketz, J. E. (1989) Modeling learning effects via successive linear programming. *European Journal of Operational Research (Netherlands)*, 40 (1). 78–84.

Hatten, K. J. and Hatten, M. L. (1987) Strategic groups, asymmetrical mobility barriers and contestability. *Strategic Management Journal (UK)*, 8 (4). 329–342.

Hawkins, D. I., Best, R. J. and Lillis, C. M. (1987) The nature and measurement of marketing productivity in consumer durables industries: A firm level analysis. *Journal of the Academy of Marketing Science*, 15 (4). 1–8.

Hayes, K. (1987) Cost structure of the water utility industry. *Applied Economics (UK)*, 19 (3). 417–425.

Hergert, M. (1988) Causes and consequences of strategic grouping in U.S. manufacturing industries. *International Studies of Management and Organization*, 18 (1). 26–49.

Hill, C. W. L. and Hansen, G. S. (1991) A longitudinal study of the cause and consequences of changes in diversification in the U.S. pharmaceutical industry 1977–1986. *Strategic Management Journal (UK)*, 12 (3). 187–199.

Hitt, M. A., Hoskisson, R. E. and Ireland, R. D. (1990) Mergers and acquisitions and managerial commitment to innovation in M-Form firms. *Strategic Management Journal (UK)*, 11. 29–47.

Hof, J. and Baltic, T. (1991) A multilevel analysis of production capabilities of the National Forest System. *Operations Research*, 39 (4). 543–552.

Horsky, D. and Mate, K. (1988) Dynamic advertising strategies of competing durable good producers. *Marketing Science*. 7 (4). 356–367.

Hosseini, J. C., Harmon, R. R. and Zwick, M. (1991) An information theoretic framework for exploratory multivariate market segmentation research. *Decision Sciences*, 22 (3). 663–677.

Hotelling, H. (1929) Stability in competition. *Economic Journal*, 39. 41–57.

Hrebiniak, L. G. and Joyce, W. F. (1985) Organizational adaptation: Strategic choice and environmental determinism. *Administrative Science Quarterly*, 30 (3). 336–349.

Hsu, J. I. S. and El-Najdawi, M. K. (1991) Integrating safety stock and lot-sizing policies for multi-stage inventory systems under uncertainty. *Journal of Business Logistics*, 12 (2). 221–238.

Huberman, G. and Kahn, C. (1988) Limited contract enforcement and strategic renegotiation. *American Economic Review*, 78 (3). 471–484.

Hum, S. H. and Sarin, R. K. (1991) Simultaneous product-mix planning, lot sizing and scheduling at bottleneck facilities. *Operations Research*, 39 (2). 296–307.

Hussein, R. T. (1987) A critical review of strategic planning models. *Quarterly Review of Marketing (UK)*, 12 (3, 4). 16–21.

Jacobson, R. (1988) Distinguishing among competing theories of the market share effect. *Journal of Marketing*, 52 (4). 68–80.

Jacobson, R. and Aaker, D. A. (1987) The strategic role of product quality. *Journal of Marketing*, 51 (4). 31–44.

Jacobson, R., Buzzell, R. D. and Boulding, W. (1990) Unobservable effects and business performance; Comments; Reply. *Marketing Science*, 9 (1). 74–95.

Jasany, L. C. (1989) Simulation software update: Kudos and caveats. *Automation*, 36 (2). 27–29.

Johnson, L. W. and Nelson, C. J. (1991) Market response to changes in attributes of a long-distance passenger rail service. *Managerial and Decision Economics (UK)*, 12 (1). 43–55.

Jordan, P. C. (1987) Purchasing decisions considering future price increases: An empirical approach. *Journal of Purchasing and Materials Management*, 23 (1). 25–30.

Judson, A. S. (1991) Invest in a high-yield strategic plan. *Journal of Business Strategy*, 12 (4). 34–39.

Kahn, B., Moore, W. L. and Glazer, R. (1987) Experiments in constrained choice. *Journal of Consumer Research*, 14 (1). 96–113.

Kale, S. H. and Sudharshan, D. (1987) A strategic approach to international segmentation. *International Marketing Review (UK)*, 4 (2). 60–70.

Kannan, P. K. and Wright, G. P. (1991) Modeling and testing structured markets: A nested logit approach. *Marketing Science*, 10 (1). 58–82.

Keats, B. W. (1990) Diversification and business economic performance revisited: Issues of measurement and causality. *Journal of Management*, 16 (1). 61–72.

Keats, B. W. and Hitt, M. A. (1988) A causal model of linkages among environmental dimensions, macro organizational characteristics, and performance. *Academy of Management Journal*, 31 (3). 570–598.

Kekre, S. (1987) Performance of a manufacturing cell with increased product mix. *IIE Transactions*, 19 (3). 329–339.

Kekre, S. and Srinivasan, K. (1990) Broader product line: A necessity to achieve success? *Management Science*, 36 (10). 1216–1231.

Keren, M. and Levhari, D. (1989) Decentralization, aggregation, control loss and costs in a hierarchical model of the firm. *Journal of Economic Behavior and Organization (Netherlands)*, 11 (2). 213–236.

Kerin, R. A. and Harvey, M. G. (1987) Strategic marketing thinking: A game perspective. *Journal of Business and Industrial Marketing*, 2 (2). 47–54.

Kim, H. Y. (1987) Economies of scale and scope in multiproduct firms: Evidence from US railroads. *Applied Economics (UK)*, 19 (6). 733–741.

Kim, M. and Ben-Zion U. (1989) The structure of technology in a multioutput branch banking firm. *Journal of Business and Economic Statistics*, 7 (4). 489–496.

Kimes, S. E. and Fitzsimmons, J. A. (1990) Selecting profitable hotel sites at La Quinta Motor Inns. *Interfaces*, 20 (2). 12–20.

King, M. and Mercer, A. (1988) Recurrent competitive bidding. *European Journal of Operational Research (Netherlands)*, 33 (1). 2–16.

King, M. and Mercer, A. (1991) Distributions in competitive bidding. *Journal of the Operational Research Society (UK)*, 42 (2). 151–155.

Klingman, D. and Phillips, N. (1988) Integer programming for optimal phosphate-mining strategies. *Journal of the Operational Research Society (UK)*, 39 (9). 805–810.

Knoke, D. and Kuklinski, J. H. (1982) *Network Analysis*. Sage University Paper series on

Quantitative Application in the Social Sciences (series no. 07-028). Beverly Hills, CA: Sage Publications.

Koskosidis, Y. A. and Powell, W. B. (1990) Application of optimization based models on vehicle routing and scheduling problems with time window constraints. *Journal of Business Logistics*, 11 (2). 101–128.

Kostreva, M. M. (1990) Strategic analysis for a technological service industry: A differential game model. *Journal of the Operational Research Society (UK)*, 41 (7). 573–582.

Kotabe, M., Duhan, D. F., Smith, D. K., Jr and Wilson, R. D. (1991) The perceived veracity of PIMS strategy principles in Japan: An empirical inquiry. *Journal of Marketing*, 55 (1). 26–41.

Krautmann, A. C. and Solow, J. L. (1988) Economies of scale in nuclear power generation. *Southern Economic Journal*, 55 (1). 70–85.

Kroll, M. and Caples, S. (1987) Managing acquisitions of strategic business units with the aid of the arbitrage pricing model. *Academy of Management Review*, 12 (4). 676–685.

Kumar, K. R. (1987) The relationship between mixed strategies and strategic groups. *Managerial and Decision Economics (UK)*, 8 (3). 235–242.

Kumar, K. R. and Sudharshan, D. (1988) Defensive marketing strategies: An equilibrium analysis based on decoupled response function models. *Management Science*. 34 (7). 805–815.

Kumar, K. R., Thomas, H. and Fiegenbaum, A. (1990) Strategic groupings as competitive benchmarks for formulating future competitive strategy: A modeling approach. *Managerial and Decision Economics (UK)*, 11 (2). 99–109.

Kumar, N. (1990) Mobility barriers and profitability of multinational and local enterprises in Indian Manufacturing. *Journal of Industrial Economics (UK)*, 38 (4). 449–463.

Kumar, V. and Heath, T. B. (1990) A comparative study of market share models using disaggregate data. *International Journal of Forecasting (Netherlands)*, 6 (2). 163–174.

Kuwahara, Y. and Takeda, Y. (1990) A managerial approach to research and development cost-effectiveness evaluation. *IEEE Transactions on Engineering Management*, 37 (2). 134–138.

Ladd, G. W. (1988) Costs and goals of the multiproduct firm. *Managerial and Decision Economics (UK)*, 9 (4). 279–281.

Langston, M. A. (1987) Interstage transportation planning in the deterministic flow-shop environment. *Operations Research*, 35 (4). 556–564.

Laughlin, J. L. and Taylor, C. R. (1991) An approach to industrial market segmentation. *Industrial Marketing Management*, 20 (2). 127–136.

Lawless, M. W. and Finch, L. K. (1989) Choice and determinism: A test of Hrebiniak and Joyce's Framework on Strategy-Environment Fit. *Strategic Management Journal (UK)*, 10 (4). 351–365.

Lawless, M. W., Bergh, D. D. and Wilsted, W. D. (1989) Performance variations among strategic group members: An examination of individual firm capability. *Journal of Management*, 15 (4). 649–661.

LeFrois, R. T. (1987) Understanding experience curves for unit product costing. *Cost Engineering*, 29 (11). 16–19.

Leone, R. P. (1987) Forecasting the effect of an environmental change on market performance: An intervention time-series approach. *International Journal of Forecasting (Netherlands)*, 3 (3–4). 463–478.

Leviton, L. C. (1989) Can organizations benefit from worksite health promotion?. *Health Services Research*, 24 (2). 159–189.

Lewis, P. and Thomas, H. (1990) The linkage between strategy, strategic groups, and performance in the U.K. retail grocery industry. *Strategic Management Journal (UK)*, 11 (5). 385–397.

Li, R. P. (1987) The hunt for direct marketing success. *Direct Marketing*, 49 (11). 38–42.

Lieberman, M. B. (1987a) Market growth, economies of scale, and plant size in the chemical processing industries. *Journal of Industrial Economics (UK)*, 36 (2). 175–191.

Lieberman, M. B. (1987b) The learning curve, diffusion, and competitive strategy. *Strategic Management Journal (UK)*, 8 (5). 441–452.

Lindberg, P. (1990) Strategic manufacturing management: A proactive approach. *International Journal of Operations and Production Management (UK)*, 10 (2). 94–106.

Lippman, S. A. and McCardle, K. F. (1988) Preemption in R&D races. *European Economic Review (Netherlands)*, 32 (8). 1661–1669.

Madura, J. and Whyte, A. M. (1990) Diversification benefits of direct foreign investment. *Management International Review (Germany)*, 30 (1). 73–85.

Mahajan, V., Muller, E. and Bass, F. M. (1990) New product diffusion models in marketing: A review and directions for research. *Journal of Marketing*, 54 (1). 1–26.

Mahajan, V. and Wind, Y. (1988) Business synergy does not always pay off. *Long Range Planning (UK)*, 21 (1). 59–65.

Maital, S. (1991) Thinking ahead backward. *Across the Board*, 28 (6). 7–9.

Markell, S. J., Strickland, T. H. and Neeley, S. E. (1988) Explaining profitability: Dispelling the market share fog. *Journal of Business Research*, 16 (3). 189–196.

Markowski, E. P. (1990) Criteria for evaluating purchase quantity decisions in response to future price increases. *European Journal of Operational Research (Netherlands)*, 47 (3). 364–370.

Marshall, C. T. and Buzzell, R. D. (1990) PIMS and the FTC line-of-business data: A comparison. *Strategic Management Journal (UK)*, 11 (4). 269–282.

Marshall, P. and Tomkins, C. (1988) Incorporating discounted cash flow contours onto a BCG portfolio matrix using limit pricing. *Managerial and Decision Economics (UK)*, 9 (2). 119–126.

Marucheck, A., Pannesi, R. and Anderson, C. (1990) An exploratory study of the manufacturing strategy process in practice. *Journal of Operations Management*, 9 (1). 101–123.

Mascarenhas, B. (1989) Strategic group dynamics. *Academy of Management Journal*, 32 (2). 333–352.

Mascarenhas, B. and Aaker, D. A. (1989) Mobility barriers and strategic groups. *Strategic Management Journal (UK)*, 10 (5). 475–485.

May, T. (1987) When barriers are irrelevant or undefended: Non-bank banks cash in. *Business Horizons*, 30 (4). 51–55.

McDowell, E. D. (1987) The economic design of sampling control strategies for a class of industrial process. *IIE Transactions*, 19 (3). 289–295.

McGee, J. and Thomas, H. (1986) Strategic groups: A useful linkage between industry structure and strategic management. *Strategic Management Journal*, 7. 141–160.

Mesak, H. I. (1990) Impact of anticipated competitive entry and cost experience on optimal strategic pricing of technological innovations. *Computers and Operations Research (UK)*, 17 (1). 27–37.

Mesak, H. I. and Clelland, R. C. (1988) Optimum conservative price increase decisions in a competitive market. *Decision Sciences*, 19 (4). 920–929.

Michman, R. D. (1987) Linking futuristics with marketing planning, forecasting, and strategy. *Journal of Business and Industrial Marketing*, 2 (2). 61–67.

Miles, R. E. and Snow, C. C. (1978) *Organizational Strategy, Structure and Process*. New York, McGraw-Hill.

Montreuil, B. and Venkatadri, U. (1991) Strategic interpolative design of dynamic manufacturing systems layouts. *Management Science*, 37 (6). 682–694.

Morck, R., Schwartz, E. and Stangeland, D. (1989) The valuation of forestry resources under stochastic prices and inventories. *Journal of Financial and Quantitative Analysis*, 24 (4). 473–487.

Moutinho, L. and Paton, R. (1991) Site selection analysis in tourism: The LOCAT model. *Service Industries Journal (UK)*, 11 (1). 1–10.

Muramatsu, R., Ichimura, T. and Ishii, K. (1990) An analysis of needs assessment and information behaviour in product development based on the fusion model. *Technovation (Netherlands)*, 10 (5). 305–315.

Murphy, F. H., Toman, M. A. and Weiss, H. J. (1989) A dynamic Nash game model of oil market disruption and strategic stockpiling. *Operations Research*, 37 (6). 958–971.

Myers, T. and de B. Wijnholds, H. (1990) Marketing privatized public services: A model to identify roles and opportunities. *Journal of Professional Services Marketing*, 5 (2). 39–60.

Naim, M. M. and Towill, D. R (1990) An engineering approach to LSE modelling of experience curves in the electricity supply industry. *International Journal of Forecasting (Netherlands)*, 6 (4). 549–556.

Nascimento, F. and Vanhonacker, W. R. (1988) Optimal strategic pricing of reproducible consumer products. *Management Science*, 34 (8). 921–937.

Naugle, D. G. and Davies, G. A. (1987) Strategic-skill pools and competitive advantage. *Business Horizons*, 30 (6). 35–42.

Neslin, S. A. (1990) A market response model for coupon promotions. *Marketing Science*, 9 (2). 125–145.

Neven, D. J. (1987) Endogenous sequential entry in a spatial model. *International Journal of Industrial Organization (Netherlands)*, 5 (4). 419–434.

New, S. J., Lockett, A. G. and Boaden, R. J. (1991) Using simulation in capacity planning. *Journal of the Operational Research Society (UK)*, 42 (4). 271–279.

Nielsen, R. P. (1988) Cooperative strategy. *Strategic Management Journal (UK)*, 9 (5). 475–492.

Nohria, N. and Garcia-Pont, C. (1991) Global strategic linkages and industry structure. *Strategic Management Journal (UK)*, 12. 105–124.

Norton, J. A. and Bass, F. M. (1987) A diffusion theory model of adoption and substitution for successive generations of high-technology products. *Management Science*, 33 (9). 1069–1086.

Nwachukwu, O. C. and Tsalikis, J. (Spring 1990–1991) Environmental heterogeneity, strategy-making, structure and small business performance: A path analytic model. *Journal of Applied Business Research*, 7 (2). 38–44.

O'Neill, B. (1991) Comments on Brown and Rosenthal's reexamination. *Econometrica*. 59 (2). 503–507.

Oral, M. and Kettani, O. (1989) A mathematical programming model for market share prediction. *International Journal of Forecasting (Netherlands)*, 5 (1). 59–68.

Oren, S. S. and Schwartz, R. G. (1988) Diffusion of new products in risk-sensitive markets. *Journal of Forecasting (UK)*, 7 (4). 273–287.

Park, Y. H., Park, E. H. and Ntuen, C. A. (1990) Investment decisions: An integrated economic and strategic approach. *Computers and Industrial Engineering*, 19 (1–4). 534–538.

Parsaei, H. R. and Wilhelm, M. R. (1989) A justification methodology for automated manufacturing technologies. *Computers and Industrial Engineering*, 16 (3). 363–373.

Pattison, D. D. and Teplitz, C. J. (1989) Are learning curves still relevant? *Management Accounting*, 70 (8). 37–40.

Pegels, C. C. and Sekar, C. (1989) Determining strategic groups using multidimensional scaling. *Interfaces*, 19 (3). 47–57.

Peterson, C. (1991) This profit model makes each branch a company. *Savings Institutions*, 112 (2). 30–31.

Pfeffer J. and Salancik G. R. (1978) *The External Control of Organizations: A Resource Dependence Perspective*. New York, Harper and Son.

Pfeifer, P. E. (1989) The airline discount fare allocation problem. *Decision Sciences*, 20 (1). 149–157.

Plaut, S. E. and Ilan, Y. (1987) The optimal degree of diversification in 'high-tech' firms. *R&D Management (UK)*, 17 (3). 201–206.

Pogue, G. (1990) Case study in strategic management accounting (Part 5). *Management Accounting (UK)*, 68 (5). 64–66.

Porac, J. F., Thomas, H. and Baden-Fuller, C. (1989) Competitive groups as cognitive communities: The case of Scottish knitwear manufacturers. *Journal of Management Studies*, 26 (4). 397–416.

Porac, J., Thomas, H. and Carroll, C. (in press) The subjective organization of the Scottish knitwear industry. *Proceedings of the Strategic Processes Research Conference*, Oslo, Norway. Oxford, Basil Blackwell.

Porter, M. E. (1979) The structure within industries and companies' performance. *Review of Economics and Statistics*, 61. 214–219.

Porter, M. E. (1980) *Competitive strategy: Techniques for Analyzing Industries and Competitors*. New York, Free Press.

Porter, M. E. (1987) From competitive advantage to corporate strategy. *Harvard Business Review*, 65 (3). 43–59.

Porteus, E. L. (1990) The impact of inspection delay on process and inspection lot sizing. *Management Science*, 36 (8). 999–1007.

Proctor, R. A. and Hassard, J. S. (1990) Towards a new model for product portfolio analysis. *Management Decision (UK)*, 28 (3). 14–17.

Putrus, R. (1991) Accounting for intangibles in integrated manufacturing. *Financial and Accounting Systems*, 7 (1). 30–35.

Raju, J. S., Srinivasan, V. and Lal, R. (1990) The effects of brand loyalty on competitive price promotional strategies. *Management Science*, 36 (3). 276–304.

Rea, S. A. Jr (1987) The market response to the elimination of sex-based annuities. *Southern Economic Journal*, 54 (1). 55–63.

Redmond, W. H. (1991) When technologies compete: The role of externalities in nonlinear market response. *Journal of Product Innovation Management*, 8 (3). 170–183.

Reimann, B. C. (1987) Stock price and business success: What is the relationship? *Journal of Business Strategy*, 8 (1). 38–49.

Reimann, B. C. (1989) Creating value to keep the raiders at bay. *Long Range Planning (UK)*, 22 (3). 18–27.

Reimann, B. C. (1990) Why bother with risk adjusted hurdle rates? *Long Range Planning (UK)*, 23 (3). 57–65.

Reitsperger, W. D. and Daniel, S. J. (1990) Dynamic manufacturing: A comparison of attitudes in the U.S.A. and Japan. *Management International Review (Germany)*, 30 (3). 203–216.

ReVelle, C. and Serra, D. (1991) The maximum capture problem including relocation. *INFOR*, 29 (2). 130–138.

Reyniers, D. (1990) A high-low search algorithm for a newsboy problem with delayed information feedback. *Operations Research*, 38 (5). 838–846.

Rhodes, D. J. (1989) Models of manufacturing systems in different operational contexts. *Engineering Costs and Production Economics (Netherlands)*, 16 (3). 161–169.

Rogers, E. M. (1987) Progress, problems, and prospects for network research: Investigating relationships in the age of electronic communication technologies. *Social Networks*, 9. 285–310.

Roth, A. V., Gaimon, C. and Krajewski, L. (1991) Optimal acquisition of FMS technology subject to technological progress. *Decision Sciences*, 22 (2). 308–334.

Rothkopf, M. H. (1991) On auctions with withdrawable winning bids. *Marketing Science*, 10 (1). 40–57.

Roy, A. (1989) Optimal offer strategies in mergers and acquisitions. *Decision Sciences*, 20 (3). 591–601.

Rubinstein, A. (1991) Comments on the interpretation of game theory. *Econometrica*, 59 (4). 909–924.

Rumelt, R. (1974) *Strategy, Structure, and Economic Performance*. Cambridge MA, Harvard Business School Press.

Runge, C. F. (1987) Induced agricultural innovation and environmental quality: The case of groundwater regulation. *Land Economics*, 63 (3). 249–258.

Saeed, S. and Linstrom, K. (1988) Employees learn economics to understand their role in company's survival. *Industrial Engineering*, 20 (8). 52–53.

Sasieni, M. W. (1989) Optimal advertising strategies. *Marketing Science*, 8 (4). 358–370.

Schlee, E. E. (1990) Multivariate risk aversion and consumer choice. *International Economic Review*, 31 (3). 737–745.

Schniederjans, M. J. and Fowler, K. L. (1989) Strategic acquisition management: A multi-objective synergistic approach. *Journal of the Operational Research Society (UK)*, 40 (4). 333–345.

Schroeder, D. M. (1990) A dynamic perspective on the impact of process innovation upon competitive strategies. *Strategic Management Journal (UK)*, 11 (1). 25–41.

Schumpeter, J. A. (1934) *The Theory of Economic Development*. Cambridge, MA. Harvard University Press.

Schwalbach, J. (1991) Profitability and market share: A reflection on the functional relationship. *Strategic Management Journal (UK)*, 12 (4). 299–306.

Shaftel, T. L. and Wilson, B. M. (1990) A mixed-integer linear programming decision model for aquaculture. *Managerial & Decision Economics (UK)*, 11 (1). 31–38.

Shaked, A. and Sutton, J. (1990) Multiproduct firms and market structure. *Rand Journal of Economics*, 21 (1). 45–62.

Shalliker, J. (1987) Fleet structures model: Predictive modelling of the UK sea-fishing fleet. *Journal of the Operational Research Society (UK)*, 38 (11). 1007–1014.

Shapiro, C. (1989) The theory of business strategy. *Rand Journal of Economics*, 20 (1). 125–137.

Shoesmith, G. L. (1988) Economies of scale and scope in petroleum refining. *Applied Economics (UK)*, 20 (12). 1643–1652.

Shubik, M. (1987) What is an application and when is theory a waste of time? *Management Science*, 33 (12). 1511–1522.

Sing, M. (1987) Are combination gas and electric utilities multiproduct natural monopolies? *Review of Economics & Statistics (Netherlands)*, 69 (3). 392–398.

Singhal, K., Fine, C. H., Meredith, J. R. and Suri, R. (1987) Research and models for automated manufacturing. *Interfaces*, 17 (6). 5–14.

Skinner, W. (1978) *Manufacturing in the Corporate Strategy*. New York, John Wiley & Sons.

Snyder, C. L., Jr (1988) Loan pricing: Making the most of new information technologies. *Journal of Commercial Bank Lending*, 70 (6). 19–27.

Soni, R. G., Parsaei, H. R. and Liles, D. H. (1990) A methodology for evaluating computer integrated manufacturing technologies. *Computers & Industrial Engineering*, 19 (1–4). 210–214.

Spearman, M. L. (1991) An analytic congestion model for closed production systems with IFR processing times. *Management Science*, 37 (8). 1015–1029.

Srinagesh, P. and Bradburd, R. M. (1989) Quality distortion by a discriminating monopolist. *American Economic Review*, 79 (1). 96–105.

Stalk, G., Jr and Hout, T. M. (1990) *Competing against Time*. New York, Free Press.

Stevens, K. C. and Martin, L. R. (1989) The decline of U.S. competitiveness: Could internal decision models be to blame? *Advanced Management Journal*, 54 (1). 32–36.

Supervision (1988) Game solves key corporate problem. 49 (12). 12–13.

Suri, R. and de Treville, S. (1986) Getting from 'Just-in-Case' to 'Just-in-Time': Insights from a simple model. *Journal of Operations Management*, 6 (3/4). 295–304.

Surl, R. (1988) RMT puts manufacturing at the helm. *Manufacturing Engineering*, 100 (2). 41–44.

Swamidass, P. M. and Newell, W. T. (1987) Manufacturing strategy, environmental uncertainty and performance: A path analytic model. *Management Science*, 33 (4). 509–524.

Tallman, S. B. (1991) Strategic management models and resource-based strategies among MNEs in a host market. *Strategic Management Journal (UK)*, 12. 69–82.

Tang, M.-J. and Thomas, H. (1991) Strategic groups, spatial competition, and stochastic processes. *Managerial and Decision Economics*.

Tang, M.-J. and Yu, C.-M. J. (1990) Foreign market entry: Production-related strategies. *Management Science*, 36 (4). 476–489.

Tellis, G. J. (1989) The impact of corporate size and strategy on competitive pricing. *Strategic Management Journal (UK)*, 10 (6). 569–585.

Thakor, A. V. (1991) Game theory in finance. *Financial Management*, 20 (1). 71–94.

Thisse, J.-F. and Vives, X. (1988) On the strategic choice of spatial price policy. *American Economic Review*, 78 (1). 122–137.

Thomas, H. (1988) Policy dialogue in strategic planning: Talking our way through ambiguity and change. In L. R. Pondy, R. J. Boland, Jr and H. Thomas (Eds), *Managing Ambiguity and Change* (pp. 51–77). New York, John Wiley & Sons.

Thomas, H. (1990) Implementing decision analysis: Problems and opportunities. In I. Horowitz (Ed.), *Organization and Decision Theory* (pp. 213–245). Boston, Kluwer Academic Publishers.

Thomas, H. and Carroll, C. (October, 1991) *Theoretical and empirical links between strategic groups, cognitive communities, and networks of interacting firms*. Paper presented at the University of Minnesota Strategy Processes Conference, Minneapolis, MN.

Thomas, H. and Porac, J. F. (April, 1991) *Competitive structures of industries: A cognitive modelling approach*. Final research report of project R000231110.

Thomas, H. and Venkatraman, N. (1988) Research on strategic groups: Progress and prognosis. *Journal of Management Studies (UK)*, 25 (6). 537–555.

Thomas, J. M. (1989) An empirical investigation of product differentiation and pricing strategy: An application to the household goods motor carrier industry. *Southern Economic Journal*, 56 (1). 64–79.

Tombak, M. M. (1990) A strategic analysis of flexible manufacturing systems. *European Journal of Operational Research (Netherlands)*, 47 (2). 225–238.

Towill, D. R. (1990) Forecasting learning curves. *International Journal of Forecasting (Netherlands)*, 6 (1). 25–38.

Treleven, M. and Schweikhart, S. B. (1988) A risk/benefit analysis of sourcing strategies: Single vs. multiple sourcing. *Journal of Operations Management*, 7 (3, 4). 93–114.

Turnbull, P. W. (1990) A review of portfolio planning models for industrial marketing and purchasing management. *European Journal of Marketing (UK)*, 24 (3). 7–22.

Utsey, M. F. (1987) Profit potential as a martingale process. *Journal of Business Research*, 15 (6). 531–544.

van Dalen, J., Koerts, J. and Thurik, A. R. (1990) The measurement of labour productivity in wholesaling. *International Journal of Research in Marketing (Netherlands)*, 7 (1). 21–34.

Vanhonacker, W. R., Lehmann, D. R. and Sultan, F. (1990) Combining related and sparse data in linear regression models. *Journal of Business & Economic Statistics*, 8 (3). 327–335.

Vepsalainen, A. P. J. and Lauro, G. L. (1988) Analysis of R&D portfolio strategies for contract competition. *IEEE Transactions on Engineering Management*, 35 (3). 181–186.

Vickery, S. K. (1991) A theory of production competence revisited. *Decision Sciences*, 22 (3). 635–643.

Vig, M., Dooley, K. and Starr, P. (1989) Simulating cell activities in the CIM environment. *Manufacturing Engineering*, 102 (1). 65–68.

Wagner, H. M. (1988) Operations research: A global language for business strategy. *Operations Research*, 36 (5). 797–803.

Wang, Q. and Parlar, M. (1989) Static game theory models and their applications in management science. *European Journal of Operational Research (Netherlands)*, 42 (1). 1–21.

Waterson, M. (1989) Models of product differentiation. *Bulletin of Economic Research (UK)*, 41 (1). 1–27.

Waterson, M. (1990) Product differentiation and profitability: An asymmetric model. *Journal of Industrial Economics (UK)*, 39 (2). 113–130.

Weil, J. J. (1987) Using Lotus for pricing and break-even strategies. *Journal of Accountancy*, 164 (1). 112–120.

Weist, J. D. (1966) Heuristic programs for decision-making. *Harvard Business Review*, 44 (5). 129–143.

Williamson, O. E. (1975) *Markets and Hierarchies: Analysis and Antitrust Implications*. New York, The Free Press.

Willis, T. H. and Huston, C. R. (1990) Vendor requirements and evaluation in a just-in-time environment. *International Journal of Operations and Production Management (UK)*, 10 (4). 41–50.

Wilson, L. O., Weiss, A. M. and John, G. (1990) Unbundling of industrial systems. *Journal of Marketing Research*, 27 (2). 123–138.

Winokur, D. F. and Venkitaraman, R. (1991) Simulator software avoids costly market tests. *Marketing News*, 25 (5). 28.

Yip, G. S. (1991) A performance comparison of continental and national businesses in Europe. *International Marketing Review*, 8 (2). 31–39.

Zahra, S. A. (1987) Corporate strategic types, environmental perceptions, managerial philosophies, and goals: An empirical study. *Akron Business & Economic Review*, 18 (2). 64–77.

Zajac, E. J. and Bazerman, M. H. (1991) Blind spots in industry and competitor analysis: implications of interfirm (mis)perceptions for strategic decisions. *Academy of Management Review*, 16 (1). 37–56.

Zangwill, W. I. (1987) Eliminating inventory in a series facility production system. *Management Science*, 33 (9). 1150–1164.

Part Two

VISION AND LEADERSHIP

2

STRATEGIC INTENT

Gary Hamel

Associate Professor in Strategy and International Management, London Business School

and C. K. Prahalad

Professor of Corporate Strategy, University of Michigan

To revitalize corporate performance, we need a whole new model of strategy.

Today managers in many industries are working hard to match the competitive advantages of their new global rivals. They are moving manufacturing offshore in search of lower labor costs, rationalizing product lines to capture global scale economies, instituting quality circles and just-in-time production, and adopting Japanese human resource practices. When competitiveness still seems out of reach, they form strategic alliances—often with the very companies that upset the competitive balance in the first place.

Important as these initiatives are, few of them go beyond mere imitation. Too many companies are expending enormous energy simply to reproduce the cost and quality advantages their global competitors already enjoy. Imitation may be the sincerest form of flattery, but it will not lead to competitive revitalization. Strategies based on imitation are transparent to competitors who have already mastered them. Moreover, successful competitors rarely stand still. So it is not surprising that many executives feel trapped in a seemingly endless game of catch-up—regularly surprised by the new accomplishments of their rivals.

For these executives and their companies, regaining competitiveness will mean rethinking many of the basic concepts of strategy (among the first to apply

International Review of Strategic Management, volume 4.
Edited by D. E. Hussey. Published 1993 by John Wiley & Sons Ltd
Reprinted by permission of *Harvard Business Review*, 'Strategic intent', by Gary Hamel and C. K. Prahalad, Issue May/June 1989.

the concept of strategy to management were Ansoff, 1965, and Andrews, 1971). As 'strategy' has blossomed, the competitiveness of Western companies has withered. This may be coincidence, but we think not. We believe that the application of concepts such as 'strategic fit' (between resources and opportunities), 'generic strategies' (low cost vs differentiation vs focus), and the 'strategy hierarchy' (goals, strategies, and tactics) have often abetted the process of competitive decline. The new global competitors approach strategy from a

A company's strategic orthodoxies are more dangerous than its well-financed rivals.

perspective that is fundamentally different from that which underpins Western management thought. Against such competitors, marginal adjustments to current orthodoxies are no more likely to produce competitive revitalization than are marginal improvements in operating efficiency. (The insert, 'Remaking Strategy,' describes our research and summarizes the two contrasting approaches to strategy we see in large, multinational companies.)

Few Western companies have an enviable track record anticipating the moves of new global competitors. Why? The explanation begins with the way most companies have approached competitor analysis. Typically, competitor analysis focuses on the existing resources (human, technical, and financial) of present competitors. The only companies seen as a threat are those with the resources to erode margins and market share in the next planning period. Resourcefulness, the pace at which new competitive advantages are being built, rarely enters in.

In this respect, traditional competitor analysis is like a snapshot of a moving car. By itself, the photograph yields little information about the car's speed or direction—whether the driver is out for a quiet Sunday drive or warming up for the Grand Prix. Yet many managers have learned through painful experience that a business's initial resource endowment (whether bountiful or meager) is an unreliable predictor of future global success.

Think back. In 1970, few Japanese companies possessed the resource base, manufacturing volume, or technical prowess of US and European industry leaders. Komatsu was less than 35% as large as Caterpillar (measured by sales), was scarcely represented outside Japan, and relied on just one product line—small bulldozers—for most of its revenue. Honda was smaller than American Motors and had not yet begun to export cars to the United States.

Traditional competitor analysis is like a snapshot of a moving car.

Canon's first halting steps in the reprographics business looked pitifully small compared with the $4 billion Xerox powerhouse.

If Western managers had extended their competitor analysis to include these companies, it would merely have underlined how dramatic the resource discrepancies between them were. Yet by 1985, Komatsu was a $2.8 billion company with a product scope encompassing a broad range of earth-moving equipment, industrial robots, and semiconductors. Honda manufactured almost as many cars worldwide in 1987 as Chrysler. Canon had matched Xerox's global unit market share.

The lesson is clear: assessing the current tactical advantages of known competitors will not help you understand the resolution, stamina, and inventiveness of potential competitors. Sun-tzu, a Chinese military strategist, made the point 3000 years ago: 'All men can see the tactics whereby I conquer,' he wrote, 'but what none can see is the strategy out of which great victory is evolved.'

Companies that have risen to global leadership over the past 20 years invariably began with ambitions that were out of all proportion to their resources and capabilities. But they created an obsession with winning at all levels of the organization and then sustained that obsession over the 10- to 20-year quest for global leadership. We term this obsession 'strategic intent.'

On the one hand, strategic intent envisions a desired leadership position and establishes the criterion the organization will use to chart its progress. Komatsu set out to 'Encircle Caterpillar.' Canon sought to 'Beat Xerox.' Honda strove to become a second Ford—an automotive pioneer. All are expressions of strategic intent.

At the same time, strategic intent is more than simply unfettered ambition. (Many companies possess an ambitious strategic intent yet fall short of their goals.) The concept also encompasses an active management process that includes: focusing the organization's attention on the essence of winning; motivating people by communicating the value of the target; leaving room for individual and team contributions; sustaining enthusiasm by providing new operational definitions as circumstances change; and using intent consistently to guide resource allocations.

Strategic intent captures the essence of winning. The Apollo program—landing a man on the moon ahead of the Soviets—was as competitively focused as Komatsu's drive against Caterpillar. The space program became the scorecard for America's technology race with the USSR. In the turbulent information technology industry, it was hard to pick a single competitor as a target, so NEC's strategic intent, set in the early 1970s, was to acquire the technologies that would put it in the best position to exploit the convergence of computing and telecommunications. Other industry observers foresaw this convergence, but only NEC made convergence the guiding theme for subsequent strategic decisions by adopting 'computing and communications' as its intent. For Coca-Cola, strategic intent has been to put a Coke within 'arm's reach' of every consumer in the world.

Strategic intent is stable over time. In battles for global leadership, one of the most critical tasks is to lengthen the organization's attention span. Strategic intent provides consistency to short-term action, while leaving room for reinterpretation as new opportunities emerge. At Komatsu, encircling Caterpillar encompassed a succession of medium-term programs aimed at exploiting specific weaknesses in Caterpillar or building particular competitive advantages. When Caterpillar threatened Komatsu in Japan, for example, Komatsu responded by first improving quality, then driving down costs, then cultivating export markets, and then underwriting new product development.

REMAKING STRATEGY

Over the last ten years, our research on global competition, international alliances, and multinational management has brought us into close contact with senior managers in America, Europe, and Japan. As we tried to unravel the reasons for success and surrender in global markets, we became more and more suspicious that executives in Western and Far Eastern companies often operated with very different conceptions of competitive strategy. Understanding these differences, we thought, might help explain the conduct and outcome of competitive battles as well as supplement traditional explanations for Japan's ascendance and the West's decline.

We began by mapping the implicit strategy models of managers who had participated in our research. Then we built detailed histories of selected competitive battles. We searched for evidence of divergent views of strategy, competitive advantage, and the role of top management.

Two contrasting models of strategy emerged. One, which most Western managers will recognize, centers on the problem of maintaining strategic fit. The other centers on the problem of leveraging resources. The two are not mutually exclusive, but they represent a significant difference in emphasis—an emphasis that deeply affects how competitive battles get played out over time.

Both models recognize the problem of competing in a hostile environment with limited resources. But while the emphasis in the first is on trimming ambitions to match available resources, the emphasis in the second is on leveraging resources to reach seemingly unattainable goals.

Both models recognize that relative competitive advantage determines relative profitability. The first emphasizes the search for advantages that are inherently sustainable, the second emphasizes the need to accelerate organizational learning to outpace competitors in building new advantages.

Both models recognize the difficulty of competing against larger competitors. But while the first leads to a search for niches (or simply dissuades the company from challenging an entrenched competitor), the second produces a quest for new rules that can devalue the incumbent's advantages.

Both models recognize that balance in the scope of an organization's activities reduces risk. The first seeks to reduce financial risk by building a balanced portfolio of cash-generating and cash-consuming businesses. The second seeks to reduce competitive risk by ensuring a well-balanced and sufficiently broad portfolio of advantages.

Both models recognize the need to disaggregate the organization in a way that allows top management to differentiate among the investment needs of various planning units. In the first model, resources are allocated to product-market units in which relatedness is defined by common products, channels, and customers. Each business is assumed to own all the critical skills it needs to execute its strategy, successfully. In the second, investments are made in core competences (microprocessor controls or electronic imaging, for example) as well as in product-market units. By tracking these investments across businesses, top management works to assure that the plans of individual strategic units don't undermine future developments by default.

Both models recognize the need for consistency in action across organizational levels. In the first, consistency between corporate and business levels is largely a matter of conforming to financial objectives. Consistency between business and functional levels comes by tightly restricting the means the business uses to achieve its strategy—establishing standard operating procedures, defining the served market, adhering to accepted industry practices. In the second model, business-corporate consistency comes from allegiance to a particular strategic intent. Business-functional consistency comes from allegiance to intermediate-term goals, or challenges, with lower level employees encouraged to invent how those goals will be achieved.

Strategic intent sets a target that deserves personal effort and commitment. Ask the chairmen of many American corporations how they measure their contributions to their companies' success and you're likely to get an answer expressed in terms of shareholder wealth. In a company that possesses a strategic intent, top management is more likely to talk in terms of global market leadership. Market share leadership typically yields shareholder wealth, to be sure. But the two goals do not have the same motivational impact. It is hard to imagine middle managers, let alone blue-collar employees, waking up each day with the sole thought of creating more shareholder wealth. But mightn't they feel different given the challenge to 'Beat Benz'—the rallying cry at one Japanese auto producer? Strategic intent gives employees the only goal that is worthy of commitment: to unseat the best or remain the best, worldwide.

Many companies are more familiar with strategic planning than they are with strategic intent. The planning process typically acts as a 'feasibility sieve.' Strategies are accepted or rejected on the basis of whether managers can be precise about the 'how' as well as the 'what' of their plans. Are the milestones clear? Do we have the necessary skills and resources? How will competitors react? Has the market been thoroughly researched? In one form or another, the admonition 'Be realistic!' is given to line managers at almost every turn.

But can you *plan* for global leadership? Did Komatsu, Canon, and Honda have detailed, 20-year 'strategies' for attacking Western markets? Are Japanese and Korean managers better planners than their Western counterparts? No. As valuable as strategic planning is, global leadership is an objective that lies outside the range of planning. We know of few companies with highly developed planning systems that have managed to set a strategic intent. As tests of strategic fit become more stringent, goals that cannot be planned for fall by the wayside. Yet companies that are afraid to commit to goals that lie outside the range of planning are unlikely to become global leaders.

Although strategic planning is billed as a way of becoming more future oriented, most managers, when pressed, will admit that their strategic plans reveal more about today's problems than tomorrow's opportunities. With a fresh set of problems confronting managers at the beginning of every planning cycle, focus often shifts dramatically from year to year. And with the pace of change accelerating in most industries, the predictive horizon is becoming shorter and shorter. So plans do little more than project the present forward incrementally. The goal of strategic intent is to fold the future back into the present. The important question is not 'How will next year be different from this year?' but 'What must we do differently next year to get closer to our strategic intent?' Only with a carefully articulated and adhered-to strategic intent will a succession of year-on-year plans sum up to global leadership.

Just as you cannot plan a 10- to 20-year quest for global leadership, the chance of falling into a leadership position by accident is also remote. We don't believe that global leadership comes from an undirected process of intrapreneurship. Nor is it the product of a skunkworks or other techniques for internal venturing. Behind such programs lies a nihilistic assumption: the organization is so hidebound, so orthodox ridden that the only way to innovate is to put a few bright people in a dark room, pour in some money, and hope that something wonderful will happen. In this 'Silicon Valley' approach to innovation, the only role for top managers is to retrofit their corporate strategy to the entrepreneurial successes that emerge from below. Here the value added of top management is low indeed.

Sadly, this view of innovation may be consistent with the reality in many large companies (Burgelman, 1983). On the one hand, top management lacks any particular point of view about desirable ends beyond satisfying shareholders and keeping raiders at bay. On the other, the planning format, reward criteria, definition of served market, and belief in accepted industry practice all work together to tightly constrain the range of available means. As a result, innovation is necessarily an isolated activity. Growth depends more on the inventive capacity of individuals and small teams than on the ability of top management to aggregate the efforts of multiple teams towards an ambitious strategic intent.

Planners ask 'How will next year be different?' Winners ask 'What must we do differently?'

In companies that overcame resource constraints to build leadership positions, we see a different relationship between means and ends. While strategic intent is clear about ends, it is flexible as to means—it leaves room for improvisation. Achieving strategic intent requires enormous creativity with respect to means: witness Fujitsu's use of strategic alliances in Europe to attack IBM. But this creativity comes in the service of a clearly prescribed end. Creativity is unbridled, but not uncorralled, because top management establishes the criterion against which employees can pretest the logic of their initiatives. Middle managers must do more than deliver on promised financial targets; they must also deliver on the broad direction implicit in their organization's strategic intent.

Strategic intent implies a sizable stretch for an organization. Current capabilities and resources will not suffice. This forces the organization to be more inventive, to make the most of limited resources. Whereas the traditional view of strategy focuses on the degree of fit between existing resources and current opportunities, strategic intent creates an extreme misfit between resources and ambitions. Top management then challenges the organization to close the gap by systematically building new advantages. For Canon this meant first understanding Xerox's patents, then licensing technology to create a product that would yield early market experience, then gearing up internal R&D efforts, then licensing its own technology to other manufacturers to fund further R&D, then entering market segments in Japan and Europe where Xerox was weak, and so on.

In this respect, strategic intent is like a marathon run in 400-meter sprints. No one knows what the terrain will look like at mile 26, so the role of top management is to focus the organization's attention on the ground to be covered in the next 400 meters. In several companies, management did this by presenting the organization with a series of corporate challenges, each specifying the next hill in the race to achieve strategic intent. One year the challenge might be quality, the next total customer care, the next entry into new markets, the next a rejuvenated product line. As this example indicates, corporate challenges are a way to stage the acquisition of new competitive advantages, a way to identify the focal point for employees' efforts in the near to medium term. As with strategic intent, top management is specific about the ends (reducing product development times by 75%, for example) but less prescriptive about the means.

Like strategic intent, challenges stretch the organization. To preempt Xerox in the personal copier business, Canon set its engineers a target price of $1000 for a home copier. At the time, Canon's least expensive copier sold for several thousand dollars. Trying to reduce the cost of existing models would not have given Canon the radical price-performance improvement it needed to delay or deter Xerox's entry into personal copiers. Instead, Canon engineers were challenged to reinvent the copier—a challenge they met by substituting a disposable cartridge for the complex image-transfer mechanism used in other copiers.

Corporate challenges come from analyzing competitors as well as from the foreseeable pattern of industry evolution. Together these reveal potential competitive openings and identify the new skills the organization will need to take the initiative away from better positioned players. The exhibit, 'Building Competitive Advantage at Komatsu,' illustrates the way challenges helped that company achieve its intent.

For a challenge to be effective, individuals and teams throughout the organization must understand it and see its implications for their own jobs. Companies that set corporate challenges to create new competitive advantages (as Ford and IBM did with quality improvement) quickly discover that engaging the entire organization requires top management to:

Create a sense of urgency, or quasi crisis, by amplifying weak signals in the environment that point up the need to improve, instead of allowing inaction

The 'Silicon Valley' approach to innovation: put a few bright people in a dark room, pour in money, and hope.

to precipitate a real crisis. (Komatsu, for example, budgeted on the basis of worst case exchange rates that overvalued the yen.)

Develop a competitor focus at every level through widespread use of competitive intelligence. Every employee should be able to benchmark his or her efforts against best-in-class competitors so that the challenge becomes personal. (For example, Ford showed production-line workers videotapes of operations at Mazda's most efficient plant.)

Provide employees with the skills they need to work effectively—training in statistical tools, problem solving, value engineering, and team building, for example.

Give the organization time to digest one challenge before launching another. When competing initiatives overload the organization, middle managers often try to protect their people from the whipsaw of shifting priorities. But this 'wait and see if they're serious this time' attitude ultimately destroys the credibility of corporate challenges.

Establish clear milestones and review mechanisms to track progress and ensure that internal recognition and rewards reinforce desired behavior. The goal is to make the challenge inescapable for everyone in the company.

It is important to distinguish between the process of managing corporate challenges and the advantages that the process creates. Whatever the actual challenge may be—quality, cost, value engineering, or something else—there is the same need to engage employees intellectually and emotionally in the development of new skills. In each case, the challenge will take root only if senior executives and lower level employees feel a reciprocal responsibility for competitiveness.

We believe workers in many companies have been asked to take a disproportionate share of the blame for competitive failure. In one US company, for example, management had sought a 40% wage-package concession from hourly employees to bring labor costs into line with Far Eastern competitors. The result was a long strike and, ultimately, a 10% wage concession from employees on the line. However, direct labor costs in manufacturing accounted for less than 15% of total value added. The company thus succeeded in demoralizing its entire blue-collar work force for the sake of a 1.5% reduction in total costs. Ironically, further analysis showed that their competitors' most significant cost savings came not from lower hourly wages but from better work methods invented by employees. You can imagine how eager the US workers were to make similar contributions after the strike and concessions. Contrast this situation with what happened at Nissan when the yen strengthened: top management took a big pay cut and then asked middle managers and line employees to sacrifice relatively less.

Reciprocal responsibility means shared gain and shared pain. In too many companies, the pain of revitalization falls almost exclusively on the employees least responsible for the enterprise's decline. Too often, workers are asked to commit to corporate goals without any matching commitment from top management—be it employment security, gain sharing, or an ability to influence the direction of the business. This one-sided approach to regaining competitiveness keeps many companies from harnessing the intellectual horsepower of their employees.

Creating a sense of reciprocal responsibility is crucial because competitiveness ultimately depends on the pace at which a company embeds new advantages deep within its organization, not on its stock of advantages at any given time. Thus we need to expand the concept of competitive advantage beyond the scorecard many managers now use: Are my costs lower? Will my product command a price premium?

Few competitive advantages are long lasting. Uncovering a new competitive advantage is a bit like getting a hot tip on a stock: the first person to act on the insight makes more money than the last. When the experience curve was young, a company that built capacity ahead of competitors, dropped prices to fill plants, and reduced costs as volume rose went to the bank. The first mover traded on the fact that competitors undervalued market share—they didn't price to capture additional share because they didn't understand how market share leadership could be translated into lower costs and better margins. But there is no more undervalued market share when each of 20 semiconductor companies builds enough capacity to serve 10% of the world market.

Keeping score of existing advantages is not the same as building new advantages. The essence of strategy lies in creating tomorrow's competitive advantages faster than competitors mimic the ones you possess today. In the 1960s, Japanese producers relied on labor and capital cost advantages. As Western manufacturers began to move production offshore, Japanese companies accelerated their investment in process technology and created scale and quality advantages. Then as their US and European competitors rationalized manufacturing, they added another string to their bow by accelerating the rate of product development. Then they built global brands. Then they deskilled competitors through alliances and outsourcing deals. The moral? An organization's capacity to improve existing skills and learn new ones is the most defensible competitive advantage of all.

Table 2.1 Building competitive advantage at Komatsu

Corporate Challenge	Protect Komatsu's home market against Caterpillar		Reduce costs while maintaining quality		Make Komatsu an international enterprise and build export markets		Respond to external shocks that threaten markets		Create new products and markets	
Programs	early 1960s	Licensing deals with Cummins Engine, International Harvester, and Bucyrus-Erie to acquire technology and establish benchmarks	1965	CD (Cost Down) program	early 1960s	Develop Eastern bloc countries	1975	V-10 program to reduce costs by 10% while maintaining quality; reduce parts by 20%; rationalize manufacturing system	late 1970s	Accelerate product development to expand line
			1966	Total CD program	1967	Komatsu Europe marketing subsidiary established			1979	Future and Frontiers program to identify new businesses based on society's needs and company's know-how
	1961	Project A (for Ace) to advance the product quality of Komatsu's small- and			1970	Komatsu America established	1977	V 180 program to budget companywide for 180 yen to the dollar when exchange rate was 240		
					1972	Project B to improve the durability and			1981	EPOCHS program to

	medium-sized bulldozers above Caterpillar's				reliability and to reduce costs of large bulldozers	1979	Project E to establish teams to redouble cost and quality efforts in response to oil crisis		reconcile greater product variety with improved production efficiencies
1962	Quality Circles companywide to provide training for all employees			1972	Project C to improve payloaders				
				1972	Project D to improve hydraulic excavators				
				1974	Establish presales and service department to assist newly industrializing countries in construction projects				

To achieve a strategic intent, a company must usually take on larger, better financed competitors. That means carefully managing competitors engagements so that scarce resources are conserved. Managers cannot do that simply by playing the same game better—making marginal improvements to competitors' technology and business practices. Instead, they must fundamentally change the game in ways that disadvantage incumbents—devising novel approaches to market entry, advantage building, and competitive warfare. For smart competitors, the goal is not competitive imitation but competitive innovation, the art of containing competitive risks within manageable proportions.

Four approaches to competitive innovation are evident in the global expansion of Japanese companies. These are: building layers of advantage, searching for loose bricks, changing the terms of engagement, and competing through collaboration.

The wider a company's portfolio of advantages, the less risk it faces in competitive battles. New global competitors have built such portfolios by steadily expanding their arsenals of competitive weapons. They have moved inexorably from less defensible advantages such as low wage costs to more defensible advantages like global brands. The Japanese color television industry illustrates this layering process.

By 1967, Japan had become the largest producer of black-and-white television sets. By 1970, it was closing the gap in color televisions. Japanese manufacturers used their competitive advantage—at that time, primarily, low labor costs—to build a base in the private-label business, then moved quickly to establish

To keep the pressure on, Komatsu set its budgets on the basis of an even stronger yen.

world-scale plants. This investment gave them additional layers of advantage—quality and reliability—as well as further cost reductions from process improvements. At the same time, they recognized that these cost-based advantages were vulnerable to changes in labor costs, process and product technology, exchange rates, and trade policy. So throughout the 1970s, they also invested heavily in building channels and brands, thus creating another layer of advantage, a global franchise. In the late 1970s, they enlarged the scope of their products and businesses to amortize these grand investments, and by 1980 all the major players—Matsushita, Sharp, Toshiba, Hitachi, Sanyo—had established related sets of businesses that could support global marketing investments. More recently, they have been investing in regional manufacturing and design centers to tailor their products more closely to national markets.

These manufacturers thought of the various sources of competitive advantage as mutually desirable layers, not mutually exclusive choices. What some call competitive suicide—pursuing both cost and differentiation—is exactly what many competitors strive for (e.g. see Porter, 1980). Using flexible manufacturing technologies and better marketing intelligence, they are moving away from standardized 'world products' to products like Mazda's mini-van, developed in California expressly for the US, market.

Another approach to competitive innovation—searching for loose bricks—exploits the benefits of surprise, which is just as useful in business battles as it is in war. Particularly in the early stages of a war for global markets, successful new competitors work to stay below the response threshold of their larger, more powerful rivals. Staking out underdefended territory is one way to do this.

To find loose bricks, managers must have few orthodoxies about how to break into a market or challenge a competitor. For example, in one large US multinational, we asked several country managers to describe what a Japanese competitor was doing in the local market. The first executive said, 'They're coming at us in the low end. Japanese companies always come in at the bottom.' The second speaker found the comment interesting but disagreed: 'They don't offer any low-end products in my market, but they have some exciting stuff at the top end. We really should reverse engineer that thing.' Another colleague told still another story. 'They haven't taken any business away from me,' he said, 'but they've just made me a great offer to supply components.' In each country, their Japanese competitor had found a different loose brick.

The search for loose bricks begins with a careful analysis of the competitor's conventional wisdom: How does the company define its 'served market'? What activities are most profitable? Which geographic markets are too troublesome to enter? The objective is not to find a corner of the industry (or niche) where larger competitors seldom tread but to build a base of attack just outside the market territory that industry leaders currently occupy. The goal is an uncontested profit sanctuary, which could be a particular product segment (the 'low end' in motorcycles), a slice of the value chain (components in the computer industry), or a particular geographic market (Eastern Europe).

Honda was building a core competence in engines. Its US rivals saw only 50cc motorcycles.

When Honda took on leaders in the motorcycle industry, for example, it began with products that were just outside the conventional definition of the leaders' product-market domains. As a result, it could build a base of operations in underdefended territory and then use that base to launch an expanded attack. What many competitors failed to see was Honda's strategic intent and its growing competence in engines and power trains. Yet even as Honda was selling 50cc motorcycles in the United States, it was already racing larger bikes in Europe—assembling the design skills and technology it would need for a systematic expansion across the entire spectrum of motor-related businesses.

Honda's progress in creating a core competence in engines should have warned competitors that it might enter a series of seemingly unrelated industries—automobiles, lawn mowers, marine engines, generators. But with each company fixated on its own market, the threat of Honda's horizontal diversification went unnoticed. Today companies like Matsushita and Toshiba are similarly poised to move in unexpected ways across industry boundaries. In protecting loose bricks, companies must extend their peripheral vision by tracking and anticipating the migration of global competitors across product segments, businesses, national markets, value-added stages, and distribution channels.

Changing the terms of engagement—refusing to accept the front runner's definition of industry and segment boundaries—represents still another form of competitive innovation. Canon's entry into the copier business illustrates this approach.

During the 1970s, both Kodak and IBM tried to match Xerox's business system in terms of segmentation, products, distribution, service, and pricing. As a result, Xerox had no trouble decoding the new entrants' intentions and developing countermoves. IBM eventually withdrew from the copier business, while Kodak remains a distant second in the large copier market that Xerox still dominates.

Canon, on the other hand, changed the terms of competitive engagement. While Xerox built a wide range of copiers, Canon standardized machines and components to reduce costs. Canon chose to distribute through office-product dealers rather than try to match Xerox's huge direct sales force. It also avoided the need to create a national service network by designing reliability and serviceability into its product and then delegating service responsibility to the dealers. Canon copiers were sold rather than leased, freeing Canon from the burden of financing the lease base. Finally, instead of selling to the heads of corporate duplicating departments, Canon appealed to secretaries and department managers who wanted distributed copying. At each stage, Canon neatly sidestepped a potential barrier to entry.

Canon's experience suggests that there is an important distinction between barriers to entry and barriers to imitation. Competitors that tried to match Xerox's business system had to pay the same entry costs—the barriers to imitation were high. But Canon dramatically reduced the barriers to entry by changing the rules of the game.

Changing the rules also short-circuited Xerox's ability to retaliate quickly against its new rival. Confronted with the need to rethink its business strategy and organization, Xerox was paralyzed for a time. Xerox managers realized that the faster they downsized the product line, developed new channels, and improved reliability, the faster they would erode the company's traditional profit base. What might have been seen as critical success factors—Xerox's national sales force and service network, its large installed base of leased machines, and its reliance on service revenues—instead became barriers to retaliation. In this sense, competitive innovation is like judo: the goal is to use a larger competitor's weight against it. And that happens not by matching the leader's capabilities but by developing contrasting capabilities of one's own.

Competitive innovation works on the premise that a successful competitor is likely to be wedded to a 'recipe' for success. That's why the most effective weapon new competitors possess is probably a clean sheet of paper. And why an incumbent's greatest vulnerability is its belief in accepted practice.

Through licensing, outsourcing agreements, and joint ventures, it is sometimes possible to win without fighting. For example, Fujitsu's alliances in Europe with Siemens and STC (Britain's largest computer maker) and in the United States with Amdahl yield manufacturing volume and access to Western markets. In the early 1980s, Matsushita established a joint venture with Thorn (in the United Kingdom), Telefunken (in Germany), and Thomson (in France), which allowed it to quickly multiply the forces arrayed against Philips in the battle for leadership in the European VCR business. In fighting larger global rivals by proxy, Japanese companies have adopted a maxim as old as human conflict itself: my enemy's enemy is my friend.

Hijacking the development efforts of potential rivals is another goal of competitive collaboration. In the consumer electronics war, Japanese competitors attacked traditional businesses like TVs and hi-fis while volunteering to manufacture 'next generation' products like VCRs, camcorders, and compact disc players for Western rivals. They hoped their rivals would ratchet down development spending, and in most cases that is precisely what happened. But companies that abandoned their own development efforts seldom reemerged as serious competitors in subsequent new product battles.

Collaboration can also be used to calibrate competitors' strengths and weaknesses. Toyota's joint venture with GM, and Mazda's with Ford, give these automakers an invaluable vantage point for assessing the progress their US rivals have made in cost reduction, quality, and technology. They can also learn

---

Competitive innovation is like judo: upset your rivals by using their size against them.

---

how GM and Ford compete—when they will fight and when they won't. Of course, the reverse is also true: Ford and GM have an equal opportunity to learn from their partner-competitors.

The route to competitive revitalization we have been mapping implies a new view of strategy. Strategic intent assures consistency in resource allocation over the long term. Clearly articulated corporate challenges focus the efforts of individuals in the medium term. Finally, competitive innovation helps reduce competitive risk in the short term. This consistency in the long term, focus in the medium term, and inventiveness and involvement in the short term provide the key to leveraging limited resources in pursuit of ambitious goals. But just as there is a process of winning, so there is a process of surrender. Revitalization requires understanding that process too.

Given their technological leadership and access to large regional markets, how did US and European companies lose their apparent birthright to dominate global industries? There is no simple answer. Few companies recognize the value of documenting failure. Fewer still search their own managerial orthodoxies for the seeds for competitive surrender. But we believe there is a pathology of surrender (summarized in 'The Process of Surrender') that gives some important clues.

It is not very comforting to think that the essence of Western strategic thought can be reduced to eight rules for excellence, seven S's, five competitive forces, four product life-cycle stages, three generic strategies, and innumerable two-by-two matrices. (Strategic frameworks for resource allocation in diversified companies are summarized in Hofer and Schendel, 1978.)

The process of surrender.

In the battles for global leadership that have taken place during the last two decades, we have seen a pattern of competitive attack and retrenchment that was remarkably similar across industries. We call this the process of surrender.

The process started with unseen intent. Not possessing long-term, competitor-focused goals themselves, Western companies did not ascribe such intentions to their rivals. They also calculated the threat posed by potential competitors in terms of their existing resources rather than their resourcefulness. This led to systematic underestimation of smaller rivals who were fast gaining technology through licensing arrangements, acquiring market understanding from downstream OEM partners, and improving product quality and manufacturing productivity through company-wide employee involvement programs. Oblivious of the strategic intent and intangible advantages of their rivals, American and European businesses were caught off guard.

Adding to the competitive surprise was the fact that the new entrants typically attacked the periphery of a market (Honda in small motorcycles, Yamaha in grand pianos, Toshiba in small black-and-white televisions) before going head-to-head with incumbents. Incumbents often misread these attacks, seeing them as part of a niche strategy and not as a search for 'loose bricks.' Unconventional market entry strategies (minority holdings in less developed countries, use of nontraditional channels, extensive corporate advertising) were ignored or dismissed as quirky. For example, managers we spoke with said Japanese companies' position in the European computer industry was nonexistent. In terms of brand share that's nearly true, but the Japanese control as much as one-third of the manufacturing value added in the hardware sales of European-based computer businesses. Similarly, German auto producers claimed to feel unconcerned over the proclivity of Japanese producers to move upmarket. But with its low-end models under tremendous pressure from Japanese producers, Porsche has now announced that it will no longer make 'entry level' cars.

Western managers often misinterpreted their rivals' tactics. They believed that Japanese and Korean companies were competing solely on the basis of cost and

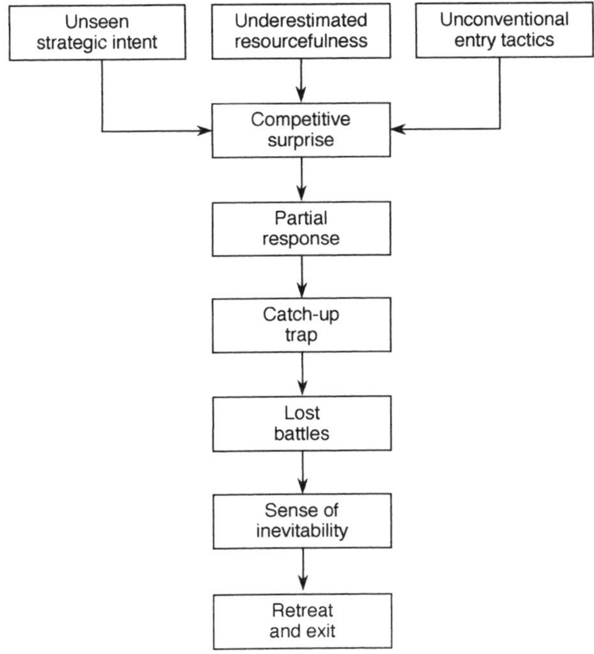

Figure 2.1 When does surrender become inevitable?

quality. This typically produced a partial response to those competitors' initiatives: moving manufacturing offshore, outsourcing, or instituting a quality program. Seldom was the full extent of the competitive threat appreciated—the multiple layers of advantage, the expansion across related product segments, the development of global brand positions. Imitating the currently visible tactics of rivals put Western businesses into a perpetual catch-up trap. One by one, companies lost battles and came to see surrender as inevitable. Surrender was not inevitable, of course, but the attack was staged in a way that disguised ultimate intentions and sidestepped direct confrontation.

Yet for the past 20 years, 'advances' in strategy have taken the form of ever more typologies, heuristics, and laundry lists, often with dubious empirical bases. Moreover, even reasonable concepts like the product life cycle, experience curve, product portfolios, and generic strategies often have toxic side effects: They reduce the number of strategic options management is willing to consider. They create a preference for selling businesses rather than defending them. They yield predictable strategies that rivals easily decode.

Strategy 'recipes' limit opportunities for competitive innovation. A company may have 40 businesses and only four strategies—invest, hold, harvest, or divest. Too often strategy is seen as a positioning exercise in which options are tested by how they fit the existing industry structure. But current industry structure reflects the strengths of the industry leader; and playing by the leader's rules is usually competitive suicide.

Armed with concepts like segmentation, the value chain, competitor benchmarking, strategic groups, and mobility barriers, many managers have become better and better at drawing industry maps. But while they have been busy map making, their competitors have been moving entire continents. The strategist's goal is not to find a niche within the existing industry space but to create new space that is uniquely suited to the company's own strengths, space that is off the map.

This is particularly true now that industry boundaries are becoming more and more unstable. In industries such as financial services and communications, rapidly changing technology, deregulation, and globalization have undermined the value of traditional industry analysis. Map-making skills are worth little in the epicenter of an earthquake. But an industry in upheaval presents opportunities for ambitious companies to redraw the map in their favor, so long as they can think outside traditional industry boundaries.

Playing by the industry leader's rules is competitive suicide.

Concepts like 'mature' and 'declining' are largely definitional. What most executives mean when they label a business mature is that sales growth has stagnated in their current geographic markets for existing products sold through existing channels. In such cases, it's not the industry that is mature, but the executives' conception of the industry. Asked if the piano business was mature, a senior executive in Yamaha replied, 'Only if we can't take any market share from anybody anywhere in the world and still make money. And anyway we're not in the "piano" business, we're in the "keyboard" business.' Year after year, Sony has revitalized its radio and tape recorder businesses, despite the fact that other manufacturers long ago abandoned these businesses as mature.

A narrow concept of maturity can foreclose a company from a broad stream of future opportunities. In the 1970s, several US companies thought that consumer electronics had become a mature industry. What could possibly top the color TV? they asked themselves. RCA and GE, distracted by opportunities in more 'attractive' industries like mainframe computers, left Japanese producers with a virtual monopoly in VCRs, camcorders, and compact disc players. Ironically, the TV business, once thought mature, is on the verge of a dramatic renaissance. A \$20-billion-a-year business will be created when high-definition television is launched in the United States. But the pioneers of television may capture only a small part of this bonanza.

Most of the tools of strategic analysis are focused domestically. Few force managers to consider global opportunities and threats. For example, portfolio planning portrays top management's investment options as an array of businesses rather than as an array of geographic markets. The result is predictable: as businesses come under attack from foreign competitors, the company attempts to abandon them and enter others in which the forces of global competition are not yet so strong. In the short term, this may be an appropriate response to waning competitiveness, but there are fewer and fewer businesses in which a domestic-oriented company can find refuge. We seldom hear such companies asking: Can we move into emerging markets overseas ahead of our global rivals and prolong the profitability of this business? Can we counterattack in our global competitors' home markets and slow the pace of their expansion? A senior executive in one successful global company made a telling comment: 'We're glad to find a competitor managing by the portfolio concept—we can almost predict how much share we'll have to take away to put the business on the CEO's "sell list."'

Companies can also be overcommitted to organizational recipes, such as strategic business units and the decentralization an SBU structure implies. Decentralization is seductive because it places the responsibility for success or failure squarely on the shoulders of line managers. Each business is assumed to have all the resources it needs to execute its strategies successfully, and in this no-excuses environment, it is hard for top management to fail. But desirable as clear lines of responsibility and accountability are, competitive revitalization requires positive value added from top management.

Few companies with a strong SBU orientation have built successful global distribution and brand positions. Investments in a global brand franchise typically transcend the resources and risk propensity of a single business. While some Western companies have had global brand positions for 30 or 40 years or more (Heinz, Siemens, IBM, Ford, and Kodak, for example), it is hard to identify any American or European company that has created a new global brand

---

Can you name one global corporate brand developed by a US company in the last twenty years?

---

franchise in the last 10 to 15 years. Yet Japanese companies have created a score or more—NEC, Fujitsu, Panasonic (Matsushita), Toshiba, Sony, Seiko, Epson, Canon, Minolta, and Honda, among them.

General Electric's situation is typical. In many of its businesses, this American giant has been almost unknown in Europe and Asia. GE made no coordinated effort to build a global corporate franchise. Any GE business with international ambitions had to bear the burden of establishing its credibility and credentials in the new market alone. Not surprisingly, some once-strong GE businesses opted out of the difficult task of building a global brand position. In contrast, smaller Korean companies like Samsung, Daewoo, and Lucky Gold Star are busy building global-brand umbrellas that will ease market entry for a whole range of businesses. The underlying principle is simple: economies of scope may be as important as economies of scale in entering global markets. But capturing economies of scope demands interbusiness coordination that only top management can provide.

We believe that inflexible SBU-type organizations have also contributed to the deskilling of some companies. For a single SBU, incapable of sustaining investment in a core competence such as semiconductors, optical media, or combustion engines, the only way to remain competitive is to purchase key components from potential (often Japanese or Korean) competitors. For an SBU defined in product-market terms, competitiveness means offering an end product that is competitive in price and performance. But that gives an SBU manager little incentive to distinguish between external sourcing that achieves 'product embodied' competitiveness and internal development that yields deeply embedded organizational competences that can be exploited across multiple businesses. Where upstream component manufacturing activities are seen as cost centers with cost-plus transfer pricing, additional investment in the core activity may seem a less profitable use of capital than investment in downstream activities. To make matters worse, internal accounting data may not reflect the competitive value of retaining control over core competence.

Together a shared global corporate brand franchise and shared core competence act as mortar in many Japanese companies. Lacking this mortar, a company's businesses are truly loose bricks—easily knocked out by global competitors that steadily invest in core competences. Such competitors can coopt domestically oriented companies into long-term sourcing dependence and capture the economies of scope of global brand investment through interbusiness coordination.

Last in decentralization's list of dangers is the standard of managerial performance typically used in SBU organizations. In many companies, business unit managers are rewarded solely on the basis of their performance against return on investment targets. Unfortunately, that often leads to denominator management because executives soon discover that reductions in investment and head count—the denominator—'improve' the financial ratios by which they are measured more easily than growth in the numerator—revenues. It also fosters a hair-trigger sensitivity to industry downturns that can be very costly. Managers who are quick to reduce investment and dismiss workers find it takes much longer to regain lost skills and catch up on investment when the industry turns upward again. As a result, they lose market share in every business cycle. Particularly in industries where there is fierce competition for the best people and where competitors invest relentlessly, denominator management creates a retrenchment ratchet.

The concept of the general manager as a movable peg reinforces the problem of denomination management. Business schools are guilty here because they have perpetuated the notion that a manager with net present value calculations in one hand and portfolio planning in the other can manage any business anywhere.

In many diversified companies, top management evaluates line managers on numbers alone because no other basis for dialogue exists. Managers move so many times as part of their 'career development' that they often do not understand the nuances of the businesses they are managing. At GE, for example, one fast-track manager heading an important new venture had moved across five businesses in five years. His series of quick successes finally came to an end when he confronted a Japanese competitor whose managers had been plodding along in the same business for more than a decade.

Regardless of ability and effort, fast-track managers are unlikely to develop the deep business knowledge they need to discuss technology options, competitors' strategies, and global opportunities substantively. Invariably, therefore, discussions gravitate to 'the numbers,' while the value added of managers is limited to the financial and planning savvy they carry from job to job. Knowledge of the company's internal planning and accounting systems substitutes for substantive knowledge of the business, making competitive innovation unlikely.

When managers know that their assignments have a two- to three-year time frame, they feel great pressure to create a good track record fast. This pressure often takes one of two forms. Either the manager does not commit to goals whose time line extends beyond his or her expected tenure. Or ambitious goals are adopted and squeezed into an unrealistically short time frame. Aiming to be number one in a business is the essence of strategic intent; but imposing a three to four-year horizon on the effort simply invites disaster. Acquisitions are made with little attention to the problems of integration. The organization becomes overloaded with initiatives. Collaborative ventures are formed without adequate attention to competitive consequences.

Almost every strategic management theory and nearly every corporate planning system is premised on a strategy hierarchy in which corporate goals guide business unit strategies and business unit strategies guide functional tactics (e.g. see Lorange and Vancil, 1977). In this hierarchy, senior management makes strategy and lower levels execute it. The dichotomy between formulation and implementation is familiar and widely accepted. But the strategy hierarchy undermines competitiveness by fostering an elitist view of management that tends to disenfranchise most of the organization. Employees fail to identify with corporate goals or involve themselves deeply in the work of becoming more competitive.

The strategy hierarchy isn't the only explanation for an elitist view of management, of course. The myths that grow up around successful top managers—'Lee Iacocca saved Chrysler,' 'De Benedetti rescued Olivetti,' 'John Sculley turned Apple around'—perpetuate it. So does the turbulent business environment. Middle managers buffeted by circumstances that seem to be beyond their control desperately want to believe that top management has all the answers. And top management, in turn, hesitates to admit it does not for fear of demoralizing lower level employees.

The result of all this is often a code of silence in which the full extent of a company's competitiveness problem is not widely shared. We interviewed business unit managers in one company, for example, who were extremely anxious because top management wasn't talking openly about the competitive challenges the company faced. They assumed the lack of communication indicated a lack of awareness on their senior managers' part. But when asked whether they were open with their own employees, these same managers replied that while they could face up to the problems, the people below them could not. Indeed, the only time the workforce heard about the company's competitiveness problems was during wage negotiations when problems were used to extract concessions.

Unfortunately, a threat that everyone perceives but no one talks about creates more anxiety than a threat that has been clearly identified and made the focal point for the problem-solving efforts of the entire company. That is one reason honesty and humility on the part of top management may be the first prerequisite of revitalization. Another reason is the need to make participation more than a buzzword.

Programs such as quality circles and total customer service often fall short of expectations because management does not recognize that successful implementation requires more than administrative structures. Difficulties in embedding new capabilities are typically put down to 'communication' problems, with the unstated assumption that if only downward communication were more effective—'if only middle management would get the message straight'—the new program would quickly take root. The need for upward communication is often ignored, or assumed to mean nothing more than feedback. In contrast, Japanese companies win, not because they have smarter managers, but because they have developed ways to harness the 'wisdom of the anthill.' They realize that top managers are a bit like the astronauts who circle the earth in the space shuttle. It may be the astronauts who get all the glory, but everyone knows that the real intelligence behind the mission is located firmly on the ground.

Top managers are like astronauts—to perform well, they need the intelligence that's back on the ground.

Where strategy formulation is an elitist activity it is also difficult to produce truly creative strategies. For one thing, there are not enough heads and points of view in divisional or corporate planning departments to challenge conventional wisdom. For another, creative strategies seldom emerge from the annual planning ritual. The starting point for next year's strategy is almost always this year's strategy. Improvements are incremental. The company sticks to the segments and territories it knows, even though the real opportunities may be elsewhere. The impetus for Canon's pioneering entry into the personal copier business came from an overseas sales subsidiary—not from planners in Japan.

The goal of the strategy hierarchy remains valid—to ensure consistency up and down the organization. But this consistency is better derived from a clearly

---

Investors aren't hopelessly short-term. They're justifiably skeptical of top management.

---

articulated strategic intent than from inflexibly applied top-down plans. In the 1990s, the challenge will be to enfranchise employees to invent the means to accomplish ambitious ends.

We seldom found cautious administrators among the top managements of companies that came from behind to challenge incumbents for global leadership. But in studying organizations that had surrendered, we invariably found senior managers who, for whatever reason, lacked the courage to commit their companies to heroic goals—goals that lay beyond the reach of planning and existing resources. The conservative goals they set failed to generate pressure and enthusiasm for competitive innovation or give the organization much useful guidance. Financial targets and vague mission statements just cannot provide the consistent direction that is a prerequisite for winning a global competitive war.

This kind of conservatism is usually blamed on the financial markets. But we believe that in most cases investors' so-called short-term orientation simply reflects their lack of confidence in the ability of senior managers to conceive and deliver stretch goals. The chairman of one company complained bitterly that even after improving return on capital employed to over 40% (by ruthlessly divesting lackluster businesses and downsizing others), the stock market held the company to an 8:1 price/earnings ratio. Of course the market's message was clear: 'We don't trust you. You've shown no ability to achieve profitable growth. Just cut out the slack, manage the denominators, and perhaps you'll be taken over by a company that can use your resources more creatively.' Very little in the track record of most large Western companies warrants the confidence of the stock market. Investors aren't hopelessly short-term, they're justifiably skeptical.

We believe that top management's caution reflects a lack of confidence in its own ability to involve the entire organization in revitalization—as opposed to simply raising financial targets. Developing faith in the organization's ability to deliver on tough goals, motivating it to do so, focusing its attention long enough to internalize new capabilities—this is the real challenge for top management. Only by rising to this challenge will senior managers gain the courage they need to commit themselves and their companies to global leadership.

REFERENCES

Andrews, Kenneth R. (1971) *The Concept of Corporate Strategy*. Homewood, Ill., Dow Jones–Irwin.

Ansoff, H. Igor (1965) *Corporate Strategy: An Analytic Approach to Business Policy for Growth and Expansion*. New York, McGraw-Hill.

Burgelman, Robert A. (1983) A process model of internal corporate venturing in the diversified major firm. *Administrative Science Quarterly*, June.

Hofer, Charles W. and Schendel, Dan E. (1978) *Strategy Formulation: Analytical Concepts*. St Paul, Minn., West Publishing.

Lorange, Peter and Vancil, Richard F. (1977) *Strategic Planning Systems*. Englewood Cliffs, NJ, Prentice-Hall.

Porter, Michael E. (1980) *Competitive Strategy*. New York, Free Press.

3

STRATEGIC VISION OR STRATEGIC CON? RHETORIC OR REALITY

Colin Coulson-Thomas

Chairman, Adaptation Ltd

Most executives assume the value of a compelling corporate vision that 'grabs the attention' of customers and 'turns on' employees. Externally, the vision differentiates. Internally, it motivates people to achieve. Chief executives consider themselves negligent if their companies are without a mission statement that is generally available to all employees. Much effort has been devoted to 'communicating the vision' throughout corporate organizations.

Surely all this activity must have been worthwhile? Three recent reports (Coulson-Thomas and Coe, 1991; Coulson-Thomas and Coulson-Thomas, 1991a, b), based on questionnaire and interview surveys completed in 1991, suggest that many attempts to formulate and implement visions and missions have been naïve, and in some cases destructive. A wide gulf has emerged between rhetoric and reality, and between aspirations and achievement. Instead of inspiration and motivation there is disillusionment and distrust (Coulson-Thomas, 1992a, 1992b).

This article examines what has gone wrong, and the longer term and sometimes hidden consequences of the short-term reactions of corporate boards to economic pressures. It highlights some arenas of conflict that are to be found in many companies, and emphasizes that changing attitudes and perspective generally takes longer than is first thought. Greater unity and commitment is needed in the boardroom, and new approaches to communication are required.

International Review of Strategic Management, volume 4.
Edited by D. E. Hussey. Published 1993 by John Wiley & Sons Ltd.

THE SURVEYS

But first, the sources of the evidence, the three 1991 surveys:

(1) The British Institute of Management (BIM) report *Managing the Flat Organisation* (Coulson-Thomas and Coe, 1991) is concerned with the management of the transition from a bureaucratic to a flexible organization. It is based upon a survey of 59 organizations employing 1.3 million people and with a combined turnover of £180bn.
(2) The survey *Quality: The Next Steps* (Coulson-Thomas and Coulson-Thomas, 1991a) is concerned with quality priorities and barriers. It was carried out by Adaptation Ltd, and involved over 100 organizations with a combined turnover of £85bn and employing 1.6 million people. The survey was sponsored by ODI International.
(3) The survey, *Communicating for Change* (Coulson-Thomas and Coulson-Thomas, 1991b) examines the role of communications in the management of change. It was undertaken by Adaptation Ltd, and involved 52 organizations with a combined turnover of £90bn and employing 1.2 million people. The survey was sponsored by Granada Business Services.

Table 3.1 gives the job titles of the individuals completing the returned questionnaires. A majority of the respondents in all three surveys are at director level. Those completing the questionnaires were asked to categorize the main activities of their organizations. In all three surveys the largest category of participating organization is represented by 'manufacturing/production'.

Table 3.2 provides a breakdown of the turnover of the participating organizations. The proportion of organizations with a turnover in excess of £1bn ranges from about a quarter in the case of *Quality: The Next Steps*, to some two-thirds in the *Managing the Flat Organisation* survey.

There is a preponderance of 'UK headquartered' or 'UK national' organizations in all three surveys. The participation of 'non-UK headquartered' or 'non-UK

Table 3.1 Job titles of survey participants

	Managing the Flat Organisation (%)	*Quality: The Next Steps* (%)	*Communicating for Change* (%)
Chairman and CEOs	61	26	33
Director	17	32	25
Manager	14	29	35
Other	8	13	7

Table 3.2 Turnover of respondents' organizations (£)

	Managing the Flat Organisation (%)	*Quality: The Next Steps (%)*	*Communicating for Change (%)*
1bn+	65	24	33
501m–1bn	22	14	14
101–500m	7	46	45
51–100m	2	5	8
11–50m	0	7	0
0–10m	4	4	0

national' companies is generally through the chief executive or a director of the UK subsidiary or operating company.

THE IMPORTANCE OF VISION

The *Managing the Flat Organisation* survey is the third of a series of annual BIM surveys. The 1989 and 1990 surveys revealed that directors and managers face a turbulent and demanding business environment (Coulson-Thomas and Brown, 1989, 1990; Coulson-Thomas, 1991a). In order to survive in the face of multiple challenges and opportunities, companies are having to: (i) differentiate themselves from competitors; and (ii) become more flexible, responsive and adaptable (Coulson-Thomas and Brown, 1989, 1990; Coulson-Thomas, 1991a).

The 1991 survey (Coulson-Thomas and Coe, 1991) reveals the extent to which changes are now occurring within organizations: 'Approaching nine out of ten of the participating organizations are becoming slimmer and flatter, while in some eight out of ten more is being undertaken in teams, and a more responsive network organization is being created' (Table 3.3).

Table 3.3 What respondents' organizations are doing to better respond to challenges and opportunities within the business environment

	(%)
Creating a slimmer and flatter organization	88
More work is being undertaken in teams	79
Creating a more responsive network organization	78
Functions are becoming more interdependent	71
Procedures and permanency are giving way to flexibility and temporary arrangements	67
Organizations are becoming more interdependent	55

In such circumstances, involving change and uncertainty, a clear vision and strategy is essential. Without it organizations can become fragmented as devolution and delegation occur during the transition from the bureaucratic to the emerging network organization (Coulson-Thomas and Coe, 1991; Coulson-Thomas and Brown, 1989, 1991; Coulson-Thomas, 1991a). One CEO confessed: 'We almost lost control. People went off in all directions. I have had to put the old restrictions back on. They will have to stay until we can communicate or share the vision of what we are trying to do.'

The 1991 survey evidence confirms the importance of vision:

- In the *Managing the Flat Organisation* survey: 'Every respondent assessing it believes clear vision and mission to be important, and about three-quarters of them consider it "very important"' (Table 3.4).
- The *Quality: The Next Steps* survey concludes that: 'A clear and shared quality vision and top management commitment are essential.'
- In the *Communicating for Change* survey, 'Clear vision and strategy' and 'top management commitment' are jointly ranked as the most important requirements for the successful management of change (Table 3.5).
- The *Communicating for Change* survey concludes that: 'Clear vision and strategy, and top management commitment are of crucial importance in the management of change. The vision must be shared, the purpose of change communicated, and employee involvement and commitment secured.'

Sir John Harvey-Jones believes a vision should present 'an attractive and clear view of the future which can be shared. It must motivate, be ambitious, and should stretch people to achieve more than they might ever have thought possible' (Coulson-Thomas and Coe, 1991).

Table 3.4 Factors for creating a new philosophy of management in order of 'very important' replies

	(%)
Clear vision and mission	74
Customer focus	66
Harnessing human potential	66
Attitudes, values and behaviour	52
Personal integrity and ethics	40
Individual learning and development	29
Processes for ongoing adaptation and change	29
Turbulence and uncertainty	19
Organizational learning	14
Management techniques	5
Others	3

Table 3.5 Change requirements in order of 'very important' replies

	(%)
Clear vision and strategy	86
Top management commitment	86
Sharing the vision	71
Employee involvement and commitment	65
Communicating the purpose of change	65
An effective communications network	54
Communicating the expected results of change	44
Understanding the contributions required to the achievement of change	42
Communicating the timing of change	38
Linking a company's systems strategy with its management of change	38
Project management of change	27
Ongoing management education and development programmes	23
One off management education and development programmes	8

THE FAILURE OF IMPLEMENTATION

Given this agreement on the importance of vision, why is there thought to be a problem? Our family of three surveys suggests the answer to this question lies in a failure of achievement and implementation. The *Managing the Flat Organisation* survey reveals that:

- *'There is an emerging consensus concerning what is sought. The uncertainty is about how it might be achieved.'*
- Managers are not being equipped to handle the new demands that are being placed upon them. One chairman confided 'I worry that every change, every extra demand, may turn out to be the last straw.'
- In many companies both vision and mission are regarded as just 'words on paper'. As one director put it 'A document is dead'. A vision needs to live in the hearts and minds of all employees.
- The short-term responses of many boards to economic recession are not always consistent with either a company's vision or the building of long-term relationships with its customers. The 'gap' between rhetoric and reality suggests 'a lack of top management commitment'.
- In some (particularly UK and US) companies 'short termism' appears to have exacted a severe toll of the managerial spirit: 'Many managers appear to have "had enough" of forever "doing more with less", when the reality of the vision they are offered is corporate survival for another few months.'

These findings are not 'out of step with other results'. They are supported by the second 1991 survey *Quality: The Next Steps* which reveals that:

- Many organizations lack both a common understanding of what quality is, and a shared 'quality vision' of what it ought to be. One quality manager complained *'quality is now all things to all people'*.
- The quality message is not being effectively communicated. Over seven out of ten respondents agree that 'quality too often consists of "motherhood" statements'.
- Quality in many organizations is largely a matter of rhetoric. One general manager described it as 'a communication device, an umbrella, an adjective, a label or a slogan'.
- Short termism, and the perceived constraints upon directors and boards to focus excessively upon financial ratios has become a significant issue. A CEO summed up the dilemma. 'I face a real conflict of interests, between the long-term demands of the vision and a short-term imperative to survive. I don't want the vision to become an epitaph.
- *The main quality barrier*, by a large margin, in terms of 'very significant' replies is *'top management commitment'*. Over nine out of ten respondents consider this to be a 'very significant' barrier to the successful implementation of a quality process.

The *Communicating for Change* survey provides further support for these conclusions:

- 'There is widespread awareness of the need to change. However, commitment to significant change is rarely matched by a confident understanding of how to bring it about.'
- 'Simple and superficial change, such as shifting priorities, or those involving the use of words, can and sometimes do occur overnight. Fundamental changes of attitudes, values, approach and perspective usually take a longer time to achieve. The timescale to achieve such changes may extend beyond the lifetime of the change requirement.'
- 'Most companies believe the communication and sharing of vision and strategy throughout their organization could be much improved.' Top management commitment emerges as a significant barrier to effective internal and external communication.
- *'In many companies there is a feeling that visions and missions are just words on paper. Directors and senior managers are not always thought to be committed to their implementation.'*
- 'The recession has increased the extent of cynicism and mistrust as boards have felt it necessary to take short-term actions that conflict with longer term objectives.' A managing director confided in despair 'I know I'm doing things that will weaken us in the long term. What's worse almost everyone else

> knows as well. I'm surviving, but one day when the recession is over what we have done will come back to haunt us.'

DIRECTION AND MANAGEMENT

Respondents in all three of our 1991 surveys emphasize the need for 'top management commitment'. It is thought essential in view of the complex nature of the change task, and the number of individuals and groups that must be involved.

Commitment begins in the boardroom. Among the key responsibilities of the board are (Coulson-Thomas and Wakelam, 1991; Coulson-Thomas, 1992b, 1993; Taylor, 1988):

- Determining a purpose for the company, a reason for its continued existence, and articulating a vision that can be communicated.
- Establishing achievable objectives derived from the vision and formulating a strategy for their achievement.

Both vision and strategy have to be communicated and shared (Coulson-Thomas and Coe, 1991; Coulson-Thomas and Coulson-Thomas, 1991a, b). The results of communication should be monitored to ensure that it leads to understanding. One managerial interviewee pulled a mission statement out of his wallet: 'Here it is. They put it on a piece of card. I couldn't tell you what it says. It's one of those things that doesn't stick, but we've all got one.'

A board and its directors need to be persistent. The *Quality: The Next Steps* survey concludes: 'commitment needs to be sustained if barriers to full implementation are to be identified and overcome'.

The qualities that distinguish directors from managers derive from: (i) their different legal duties and responsibilities; and (ii) the role of the board. Directors require strategic awareness, the ability to see a company as a whole and understand the context within which it operates (Coulson-Thomas, 1990a). Formulating a distinctive vision and a realistic strategy requires objectivity and the ability to look ahead (Coulson-Thomas and Wakelam, 1991; Coulson-Thomas, 1993; Taylor, 1988; Coulson-Thomas, 1990a). Not surprisingly, strategic awareness, objectivity, and communication skills rank high among the qualities sought in new appointees to the board (Coulson-Thomas, 1990a).

Managers, particularly those in larger and international companies, also need strategic awareness, communication and team skills etc. Increasingly, they need to understand the business environment (Coulson-Thomas 1990b). In the *Managing the Flat Organisation* survey the only 'management quality' assessed as of importance by every respondent is 'understanding the business environment'.

FOCUS AND HORIZON

A 'traditional' view has been that: 'directors ... (focus) ... on the external business environment ... and are concerned with long-term questions of strategy and policy', while 'in comparison the great mass of employees are thought to concentrate upon short-term questions of implementation'. 'In reality' both directors and managers 'concentrate upon both the outside world and the company, and also the inter-relationship between the two' (Coulson-Thomas and Wakelam, 1991).

The efforts of companies to articulate and communicate a longer term and customer focused vision have shifted the focus of many managers to the extent that distinctions of perspective between many directors and managers may have become a matter of emphasis or degree. As a result 'sharing a vision' has increased the potential for conflict where vision and conduct are perceived to be incompatible (Coulson-Thomas and Coe, 1991; Coulson-Thomas and Coulson-Thomas, 1991a, b).

Figure 3.1 illustrates the conflicting pressures at the heart of the relationship between both head office and business unit, and between holding company and subsidiary or operating company:

- Business unit managers and the directors of operating or subsidiary companies are striving: (i) to build longer term relationships with customers,

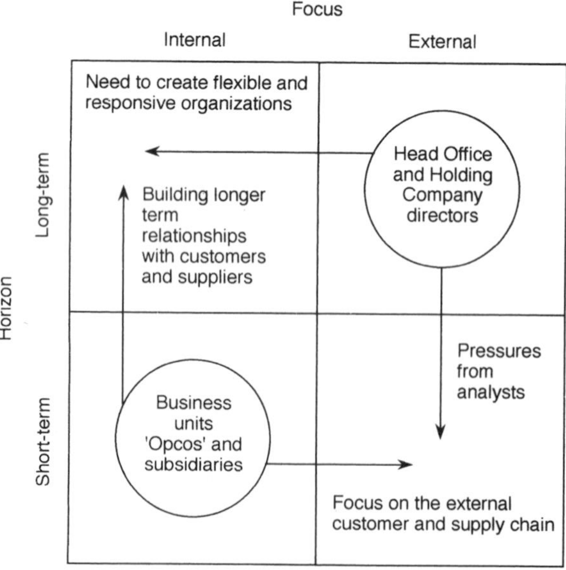

Figure 3.1 Focus and horizon

and in many cases also with suppliers; and (ii) to focus externally on the customer and relationships within supply chains. Corporate visions and strategy have encouraged them to 'think long term' and to develop more of an external focus.
- At the same time, those occupying head office and main board positions feel under pressure from analysts to maintain short-term performance. They are also putting more emphasis upon the transformation of the internal corporate bureaucracy, as they strive to create more flexible and responsive organizations.

ARENAS OF CONFRONTATION

The three 1991 surveys suggest that four arenas of conflict have been exacerbated by the drive of CEOs to communicate and share a longer term vision.

Directors vs Managers

Directors and managers do not agree on the question of where a lack of commitment is to be found within their companies:

- CEOs and directors tend to interpret the 'top management barrier' as the senior management team constituting the first couple of layers below the board (Coulson-Thomas and Coulson-Thomas, 1991a). While CEOs report receptive employees further down the organization, many managers, to quote one CEO, 'assess changes in terms of the impacts upon their own roles and standing in the corporate bureaucracy'.
- Interviews with CEOs suggest that 'vested interests', 'organizational politics' and 'cynicism' tend to be associated with senior rather than junior managers. Those thought by CEOs to be less committed to change are those with the greatest stake in, or having most to gain from, the 'status quo'.
- Managers have a different perspective on the source of the 'commitment barrier'. Many of those interviewed interpret 'top management' as those 'above' them, particularly the board (Coulson-Thomas and Coulson-Thomas, 1991a). It is felt that many boards remain sceptical and are not committed.

A CEO who 'changed companies' during the course of interviews now shares the 'managerial' view: 'Looking back I realise some of my colleagues in the boardroom were just playing with words. They would nod agreement, and then do nothing in their divisions. When people say things like "if you say so" or "you're the boss", you know you are in trouble. We should have kept at it until they were all committed.'

Head Office vs Business Unit

Head offices and business units can have conflicting views and perspectives on the steps needed to implement a vision. The *Quality: The Next Steps* survey identified the tension which 'short termism' can cause between a head office and operating units. One director of quality summed up the dilemma: 'Business units are confused. *We have really pushed customer satisfaction, and we have asked them to put everyone through quality training. Some of them are now quite committed. But at the moment we have frozen headcounts and new consultancy contracts so they can't do the training.'*

At the level of business units there is much dissatisfaction with the criteria used to measure performance. One divisional director complained: 'I bought into quality, and the vision, as did my team. Everyone talks about quality, but I'm measured by the same old ratios. Quality is great, and we all know it's important, but numbers are real. The ratios decide my next move, not how many quality improvement projects I've got.' In many companies the relative bottom line performance of operating companies reveals little more than the basis of the allocation of 'HQ' overheads.

The need to recover the cost of head offices is also a 'bone of contention'. One business unit general manager expressed frustration: 'I'm supposed to buy and hand out corporate videos on the vision, but our prices and margins are being squeezed, and I'm being squeezed. I get memos from head office to reduce headcount and cut costs, while my reallocated overheads have increased.'

Holding Company vs Subsidiary or Operating Company

Differences of perspective and emphasis are also endemic in the relationship between 'subsidiaries and parents'. Problems referred to in interviews during the *Quality: The Next Steps* survey include: (i) achieving 'consistency' across a group made up of diverse units; and (ii) the imposition upon a subsidiary of a group approach to quality which may not be appropriate. Some UK companies have resisted the use of a 'quality package' designed for a US parent on the grounds of incompatibility with UK culture.

According to one international personnel director of a MNC: 'Many of my colleagues never think about how much our strategic vision is bound up with our own culture. They don't relate to it in South America. My CEO expected a problem in Europe, but not in South America. Everywhere it's the same, it's not their vision—it's our vision. We're telling them about it, not sharing it with them.'

As corporations seek to 'slim down', many subsidiary companies believe they are bearing an unfair proportion of 'corporate savings'. One subsidiary managing director took the view: 'Who gets the misery depends upon power, and there's still a lot of it at the centre. We worry about long-term vision and the investments it requires, but we make the cuts. Yet the headcount at holding company level hasn't really changed. What on earth do they all do?'

A national operating company director answered this question in the case of one global company: '1992 has a lot to answer for. We had announced a run down of central overheads, and along comes 1992. The head office politicians jumped at the opportunity to create another layer of bureaucracy at the regional level. Just when I need to cut prices to survive in a more competitive market I'm having to fund the staffing up of a European headquarters.'

Generalist vs Specialist

Surveys of IT (Coulson-Thomas, 1990c; 1991b) personnel (Coulson-Thomas and Brown, 1989; Coulson-Thomas, 1991c), marketing (Coulson-Thomas and Brown, 1990; Coulson-Thomas, 1991a), and quality (Coulson-Thomas and Coulson-Thomas, 1991a) issues have all revealed a gap of perspective and understanding between CEOs and the heads of specialist functions. The differences of perspective appear to have widened as a result of differing interpretations of, and commitment to, corporate vision.

Many 'functional' directors and managers are critical of their CEOs. Economic recession, particularly that in the UK, has made many specialists more aware of the gap between the rhetoric of the long-term corporate vision of the CEO, as portrayed in the corporate video, and the reality of short-term cuts and tactical compromise (Coulson-Thomas and Coe, 1991; Coulson-Thomas and Coulson-Thomas, 1991a, b). The *Quality: The Next Steps* survey concludes: 'recession is clearly distinguishing the companies that are committed to quality from those that pay lip service to it'.

Functional specialists are at odds with the perceived 'short termism' of CEOs. Quality is regarded by its 'champions', as a continuing process and long-term commitment (Coulson-Thomas and Coulson-Thomas, 1991a). A director of quality claimed to be 'on a quest for the holy grail. I won't get there, but I'm obsessive. I feel, but I can't always prove, that I'm doing the right thing.' Almost all of those interviewed were experiencing some difficulty in quantifying 'benefits' and putting a satisfactory economic or 'cost justified' case for substantial quality 'investments'.

CEOs complain that their 'specialists' lack strategic awareness and business acumen (Coulson-Thomas and Brown, 1989; Coulson-Thomas, 1991c). Their perspectives are described by CEOs as 'functional' rather than 'strategic' (Coulson-Thomas and Coulson-Thomas, 1991a; Coulson-Thomas and Brown, 1989, 1990; Coulson-Thomas, 1990c, 1991a, 1991b, 1991c, 1992b, 1993).

IMPLEMENTING THE CEO VISION

The vision of many CEOs is of a network that embraces both customers and suppliers (Coulson-Thomas and Brown, 1990; Coulson-Thomas, 1991a). It is realized that in some sectors the individual company alone cannot deliver the whole of the value added sought by customers without working closely with other companies in the total supply chain (Coulson-Thomas and Coulson-Thomas, 1991a; Coulson-Thomas and Brown, 1990; Coulson-Thomas, 1991a, 1991b).

Customers are now regarded as a part of the organization, rather than 'outsiders'. However, many marketing directors are perceived as not sharing this vision of customers as colleagues or business partners (Coulson-Thomas and Brown, 1990; Coulson-Thomas, 1991a). According to one chairman: 'customers have been treated by our marketing people as cannon fodder for generalized ads and direct mail shots'.

The view of many 'generalist' CEOs, especially those trying to implement a vision, is that 'specialist' directors in the boardroom are often obstacles to, rather than facilitators of, change (Coulson-Thomas and Brown, 1989, 1990; Coulson-Thomas 1991a; Coulson-Thomas, 1990c, 1991b). According to one CEO: 'Trying to transform the culture brought it home to me. They are all great as heads of a function, but they are not a team. They look at everything from their own particular perspective. I have a corporate vision. They have a marketing, or personnel, or whatever vision. It came to me one day—we don't have the same view of where we are going, or of what is important.'

Companies now compete on the flexibility and speed of their processes for responding to evolving customer requirements. Some of the CEOs interviewed consider their priority roles to be those of catalysts and facilitators of the management of continuing change. This is thought to imply responsibilities in the boardroom that are 'broader' or 'beyond' many of the 'traditional' concerns of 'functional' directors (Coulson-Thomas and Coulson-Thomas, 1991a).

A theme of many interviews with CEOs across a succession of surveys (Coulson-Thomas and Coe, 1991; Coulson-Thomas and Coulson-Thomas, 1991a; Coulson-Thomas and Brown, 1989, 1990; Coulson-Thomas, 1991a) has been the extent to which many issues on the boardroom agenda transcend traditional functional divisions. There is need for everyone to be involved in 'the change process' (Coulson-Thomas and Coe, 1991), and there is a requirement in many boardrooms for facilitating roles such as directors of learning or thinking (Coulson-Thomas and Wakelam, 1991, 1992b). A growing range of responsibilities, including 'communicating the vision' will be shared within the boardroom team, rather than be regarded as the exclusive concern of one director.

BEGINNING IN THE BOARDROOM

So what needs to be done? First, let us consider the articulation of, and commitment to, a common vision in the boardroom. The survey *Quality: The Next*

Steps emphasizes the need for the board to: 'formulate a clear and shared quality vision, and communicate a commitment to quality'.

The board should be the source of the vision to be communicated. The Institute of Directors discussion document *The Effective Board* (Coulson-Thomas and Wakelam, 1991) reveals that there is little satisfaction with the performance of boards. Three-quarters of chairmen believe the effectiveness of the boards of their companies could be improved.

The key to sustained corporate success is an effective board, composed of competent directors who share and can communicate a common vision (Coulson-Thomas 1993; Taylor, 1988). Yet, only one in eight companies operates a periodic, formal appraisal of personal effectiveness in the boardroom (Coulson-Thomas and Wakelam, 1991). To improve the effectiveness of individual directors, and of the board as a whole, there are various checklists of questions which every company chairman should consider (Coulson-Thomas, 1992a, 1992b, 1993; Taylor, 1988). These include:

- Are your directors committed to a common vision and an agreed strategy?
- How effective are the members of your board at sharing the vision, and communicating with customers, employees and business partners?

Training and changing the composition of a board are the two most commonly cited means of improving the effectiveness of a board (Coulson-Thomas and Wakelam 1991; Wakelam, 1989; Coulson-Thomas, 1990d, 1993). Poor teamwork is frequently given as a factor that is limiting the effectiveness of boards. Improved communication, open discussion, regular meetings and a shared or common purpose are all given as ways of ensuring a board works effectively as a team (Coulson-Thomas and Wakelam, 1991; Coulson-Thomas, 1992b, 1993; Taylor, 1988).

WHO IS RESPONSIBLE?

Within the boardroom there are two distinct and key roles and responsibilities (even if both roles are occupied by one person) which will largely determine the extent to which a compelling vision is articulated, agreed, communicated and shared:

The Chairman

The chairman should be responsible for ensuring that a company has an effective board composed of directors who work well together as a team (Coulson-Thomas and Wakelam, 1991; Coulson-Thomas, 1992b, 1993; Taylor, 1988). The chairman is generally the individual who is best equipped to form an overview of the board and its operations. At minimum (Coulson-Thomas and Wakelam, 1991):

- A chairman should ensure that all directors are aware of their legal duties and responsibilities (Institute of Directors, 1991), and are properly prepared to make a contribution to the board (Coulson-Thomas, 1993; Taylor, 1988; Coulson-Thomas, 1990e).
- At least once a year a board ought to review its 'roles and responsibilities', size and composition, and its effectiveness.
- The personal effectiveness of all directors in the boardroom should be assessed at least once a year by the chairman.

The Chief Executive

The chief executive should take a lead in: (i) securing commitment; and (ii) communicating and sharing the vision. The CEO can also play a key role in preventing the occurrence of 'perspective gaps' and 'arenas of confrontation'.

Almost all those interviewed during the course of the three 1991 surveys, and who were not CEOs, referred to the importance of CEO commitment. CEOs themselves acknowledged the importance of their 'lead', as fellow directors and many senior managers tend to base their own level of commitment upon the priority being given to 'change' or 'quality' by the CEO.

One CEO summed up the dilemma of the 'fellow traveller' director: 'I lived for too long with directors who did not really believe in what we were trying to do. They didn't raise objections in the boardroom. What's worse, they sometimes said yes, and then went away and did nothing. They didn't implement the changes in their divisions, and everyone knew it.'

THE NEED FOR MORE EFFECTIVE COMMUNICATION

Once agreed by a competent and committed board, a vision has to be communicated and shared (Coulson-Thomas and Didacticus, 1991). Sir John Harvey-Jones believes that 'effective communication requires effort, commitment, time and courage. Full commitment is the result of integrity, openness and real two way communication' (Coulson-Thomas and Coe, 1991).

Visible commitment is crucial. Vern Zelmer, Managing Director of Rank Xerox (UK) believes that: 'the role of the manager must change from one of managing the status quo in a command and control environment to one of managing change through active teaching, coaching, and facilitating in a participative work group' (Coulson-Thomas and Coe, 1991).

Participants in the *Managing the Flat Organisation* survey were asked to rank in importance the management qualities which will enable their organizations to respond more effectively to challenges and opportunities within the business environment. When these are ranked in order of 'very important' replies, the 'ability to communicate' comes top. Two-thirds of the respondents consider it to be 'very important'.

The *Quality: The Next Steps* survey emphasizes the need for more effective communication:

- A broader view of quality needs to be communicated. Nine out of ten respondents consider 'too narrow an understanding of quality' to be either 'very significant' or 'significant' as a quality barrier.
- *Managers need to be better equipped to manage change. The 'quality of management', followed closely by 'quality behaviour, attitudes and values', are the top quality priorities. Over eight out of ten respondents expect to give them a 'higher priority' over the next 5 years.*

Further confirmation of the need for the more effective communication of a shared vision comes from the *Communicating for Change* survey:

- Communicating or 'sharing the vision' is considered 'very important' by over seven out of ten respondents, followed by 'communicating the purpose of change' and 'employee involvement and commitment'—both considered 'very important' by two-thirds of the respondents.
- 'Communication skills' are felt by respondents to be the top barrier to both internal and external communication. A third of the respondents consider 'communication skills' to be a 'very significant' barrier to internal communication.

Whatever their boards might think or hope is the case, in reality many companies are finding it difficult to articulate and communicate a compelling vision. Words and slogans are passed on without being fully understood.

THE EFFECTIVE COMMUNICATOR

The effective communicator needs to think through what is being communicated, to whom and why. According to David O'Brien, Chief Executive of The National and Provincial Building Society, 'Often people will pick up and use the words associated with change, but without really thinking through what they mean' (Coulson-Thomas and Coe, 1991).

Messages must be straightforward, and related to the needs and interests of the audience if they are to 'come alive' (Coulson-Thomas and Didacticus, 1991; Bartram and Coulson-Thomas, 1991). The communicator must be open and willing to learn. The communicator must share the vision, must feel the vision and must be visibly committed to it (Coulson-Thomas, 1992b, 1993).

The vision itself should 'paint a picture' of a desired future that is preferable to the present, and should motivate people to strive to bring it about (Coulson-Thomas and Didacticus, 1991). A vision should be succinct. It should inspire and liberate. In contrast to the compelling vision, many corporate mission statements are over long, too detailed, and bland (Coulson-Thomas, 1992b; Taylor, 1988; Coulson-Thomas and Didacticus, 1991).

Customers and employees are attracted to those organizations whose principles they share. The vision must empathize with people's values, and it must be believed. Sir John Harvey-Jones stresses the importance of both integrity and commitment. He believes 'the manager should not be afraid to show emotion' (Coulson-Thomas and Coe, 1991). Honesty is even more important in an era of recession and retrenchment, when there is bad news to communicate. The *Managing the Flat Organisation* report concludes: 'in a few companies urgent action is needed to re-establish an atmosphere of trust.'

SUMMARY AND CONCLUSIONS

The key lessons of the three 1991 surveys we have examined are that:

- Clear vision and strategy, top management commitment and communication skills are of crucial importance in the management of change.
- The vision must be compelling. It must be shared, the purpose of change communicated, and employee involvement and commitment secured. The chief executive should assume responsibility for communicating and sharing the vision.
- The distinct role of the director, and the difference between direction and management, needs to be better understood.
- The competence of directors, and the effectiveness of boards, should not be assumed. The chairman of the board should take responsibility for the effectiveness of the board as a team, and for the quality of the contributions of individual directors in the boardroom.
- The ability to communicate is an essential directorial and management quality. The focus needs to be upon attitudes and approaches to communication. Significant change will not occur in many organizations unless managers are equipped with the skills to bring it about.

REFERENCES

Bartram, Peter and Coulson-Thomas, Colin (1991) *The Complete Spokesperson*. London, Kogan Page.

Coulson-Thomas, Colin (1990a) *Professional Development of and for the Board*. A questionnaire and interview survey undertaken by Adaptation Ltd of company chairmen. A summary was published by the Institute of Directors, February 1990.
Coulson-Thomas, Colin (1990b) *Human Resource Development for International Operation*. A Survey sponsored by Surrey European Management School. London, Adaptation Ltd.
Coulson-Thomas, Colin (1990c) *Developing IT Directors*. An Adaptation Ltd report to the Department of Computing Science, Surrey University.
Coulson-Thomas, Colin (1990d) Developing directors. *European Management Journal*, 8 (4). 488–499.
Coulson-Thomas, Colin (1991a) Customers, marketing and the network organisation. *Journal of Marketing Management*, 7. 237–255.
Coulson-Thomas, Colin (1991b) Directors and IT, and IT directors. *European Journal of Information Systems*. 1 (1). 45–53.
Coulson-Thomas, Colin (1991c) *The Role and Development of the Personnel Director*. A survey undertaken by Adaptation Ltd in conjunction with the Research Group of the Institute of Personnel Management.
Coulson-Thomas, Colin (1992a) *Creating the Global Company*, London, McGraw-Hill.
Coulson-Thomas, Colin (1992b) *Transforming the Company*, London, Kogan Page.
Coulson-Thomas, Colin (1993) *Creating Excellence in the Boardroom and Developing Directors*. London, McGraw-Hill.
Coulson-Thomas, Colin and Brown, Richard (1989) *The Responsive Organisation, People Management: the Challenge of the 1990s*. London, BIM.
Coulson-Thomas, Colin and Brown, Richard (1990) *Beyond Quality, Managing the Relationship with the Customer*. London, BIM.
Coulson-Thomas, Colin and Coe, Trudy (1991) *Managing the Flat Organisation*. London, BIM.
Coulson-Thomas, Colin and Didacticus Video Productions Ltd (1991) *The Change Makers, Vision and Communication*. Booklet to accompany integrated audio and video tape training programme by Sir John Harvey-Jones. Available from Video Arts.
Coulson-Thomas, Colin and Susan (1991a) *Quality: The Next Steps*. An Adaptation Ltd survey for ODI International.
Coulson-Thomas, Colin and Susan (1991b) *Communicating for Change*. An Adaptation Ltd survey for Granada Business Services.
Coulson-Thomas, Colin and Wakelam, Alan (1990) *Developing Directors*. A survey, funded by the Training Agency, undertaken by Adaptation Ltd with the Centre for Management Studies, University of Exeter. The main findings are summarized in Coulson-Thomas and Wakelam (1991).
Coulson-Thomas, Colin and Wakelam, Alan (1991) *The Effective Board, Current Practice, Myths and Realities*. An IOD discussion document.
Institute of Directors (1991) *Guidelines for Directors*, fourth edition, May. London, Director Publications.
Taylor, Bernard (ed.) (1988) *Strategic Planning: The Chief Executive and the Board*. The best of *Long Range Planning*, No. 1. Oxford, Pergamon Press.
Wakelam, Alan (1989) *The Training & Development of Company Directors*. A report on a questionnaire survey undertaken by the Centre of Management Studies, University of Exeter, for the Training Agency, December.

4

CORPORATE VISIONING

Jagdish Parikh

Managing Director Lemuire Group of Companies (India) and Visiting Professor of various International Management Institutes

Fred Neubauer

Faculty Member in Multinational Corporate Strategy and Planning, IMD, Lausanne

THE PERSPECTIVE

A corporate vision is defined as an image of a desired future state of an organization. In very practical terms, it is an answer to the question: 'What do we want to create?' This means, unlike the traditional strategic planning approaches, a vision is: *a future to be created,* and *not* a forecast. The concept of a vision is based on a model of the management process shown in Figure 4.1 (Leavitt, 1986).

The lines between the three aspects of the management process have been made wavy on purpose; they indicate that the borderlines between them in real life are blurred. To unfold this further, each of the subprocesses shown in Figure 4.1 reflects the different roles that an effective leader in business is supposed to perform: Namely that of an entrepreneur, that of a professional and that of a manager. This is shown in Figure 4.2.

What are the 'energies' necessary to facilitate the performance of these roles? Primarily they are intuition, reason, and emotions. A more complete model is therefore shown in Figure 4.3.

This chapter is a condensed version of two chapters on visioning in the forthcoming book *Intuition: The New Frontier in Management,* (1993) Oxford, Basil Blackwell by Jagdish Parikh in collaboration with Fred Neubauer and Alden G. Lank.

International Review of Strategic Management, volume 4.
Edited by D. E. Hussey. Published 1993 by John Wiley & Sons Ltd

It must be emphasized, however, that the above classifications of the processes, roles, and energies should not be taken as either totally comprehensive or mutually exclusive. The purpose of such a somewhat simplistic model is to emphasize the major issues and elements that an effective leader should be concerned with. In fact, as it is not commonly possible for one single person to be equally strong in all the above facets, one has to make sure that the team at the top of an organizational unit is chosen in such a way that the members of the team complement each other. Moreover, the various aspects of the entire management process, roles, and energies do not occur sequentially; more often they happen simultaneously, that is, real life does not follow linear, orderly Cartesian thinking, rather it is organic and may even appear 'messy'.

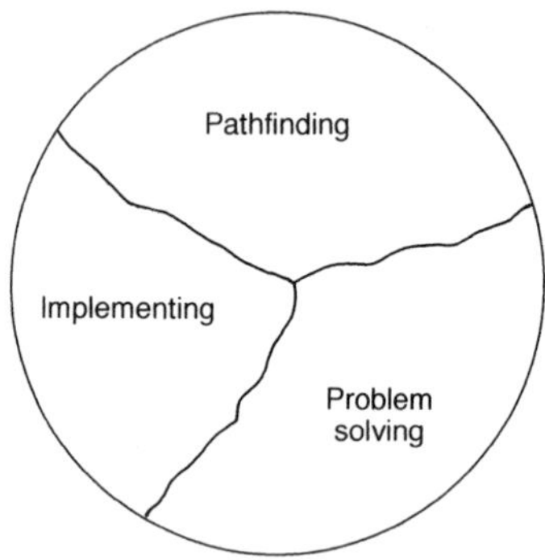

Figure 4.1

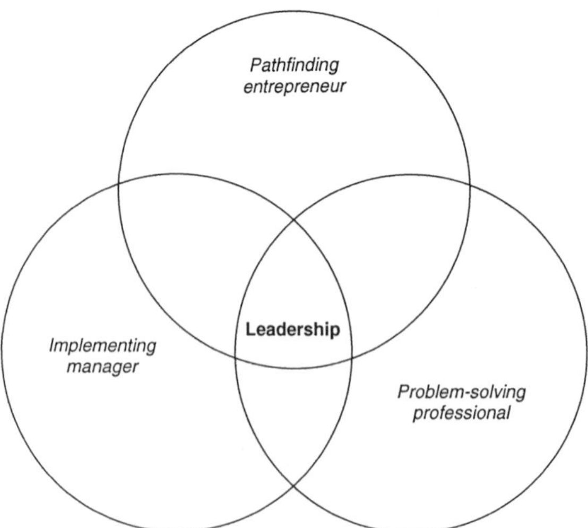

Figure 4.2

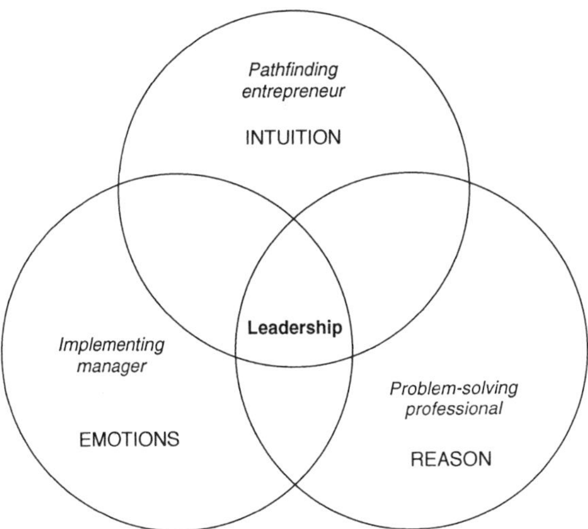

Figure 4.3

The Task of the Manager

Implementing in management—one of the main tasks of a manager—means primarily getting a job done. Generally, in the contemporary scenario, implementing requires changing the behavior of employees. We know from the behavioral sciences that people most often change behavior for emotional rather than for rational reasons. The key word in implementing therefore is *emotions*: It is by appealing to their pride, loyalty, ambition, and so on that we motivate people to improve, for instance, product or service quality. Managing emotions effectively is a key competence of a good manager.

The Task of the Professional

Management, however, is not only about doing, changing behavior; it is also about thinking: Taking complex problems and analytically breaking them into more manageable ones and tackling them rationally—is a major task of a professional in business. If the key word in implementing is emotions, the key word or key skill in this area is *analysis*: Managing as a rational, logical activity, helping to identify options and to select from among them systematically and judiciously has been the preferred focus of modern Business Administration. Unfortunately, there is evidence that relying exclusively on it may well drive out creativity, the essence of entrepreneurship.

The Task of the Entrepreneur

Behind these two aspects of managing is a third one which is more difficult to grasp but which is nevertheless critical for the health of organizations. This aspect has to do with entrepreneurship, with determining the direction of an organization or of a discrete unit within an organization, through the creation of a vision for it. The key word here is *intuition*: The power of knowing without recourse to inference or reasoning (Webster's). This term does not denote something contrary to reason, but something beyond the province of reason. The typical innovative entrepreneur will, of course, analyze every bit of data he has; but the sheer nature of his activity—breaking new ground—compels him to go beyond the data typically available for analysis. To a large degree, entrepreneurs therefore rely on their intuition.

In today's and tomorrow's context, cultivating and skillfully blending these three elements, namely reason, emotions and intuition, are essential requirements of leadership. The process that unfolds and enhances these elements, competencies and qualities in the executives is Vision Building. Before we turn to Vision Building, it is appropriate to examine the concept of vision.

VISION: FREQUENTLY MISUNDERSTOOD

The word vision is perhaps the most avant-garde concept in the management world today. Unfortunately, it also happens to be frequently misunderstood and sometimes even misused. Quite often one finds the word vision applied almost as a substitute for the terms target, goal or objective. This may sound better, but used in that way it does not create any difference.

In the context of accelerating change in the face of complexity, uncertainty, and conflict, it is imperative to generate much greater strength and coherence within organizations, to ensure not only sustainable success, but even survival. The most effective and empowering element that can facilitate this, is the creation and maintenance of a shared vision throughout the organization. The mission statement, the objectives, targets, strategies, flow from such a vision. The essential difference is that the organization does not push itself *towards* a vision—it operates *from* a vision: Unlike the traditional incremental approach, this concept asks the company to jump ahead, say, five years (by creating an image of a desired future state of the organization at that point in time) and, looking back, to raise the question what steps would have to be taken now to achieve the desired state.

It is in this perspective that three questions have to be asked:

Why to create a vision?
What is the structure of a vision?
How to develop a vision?

Our approach, the PN Model, addresses itself to the context, the content and the process of corporate visioning. It also explains the profile of the emerging new paradigm in business, contrasts the characteristics of an organization's structure and culture in the traditional with those in the emerging paradigm (including the shift in management styles), and describes different approaches to visioning: Reflective visioning, intuitive visioning and integrative visioning.

Why to Create a Vision?

Good visions can have several positive impacts on a company; here are the most important ones among them:

- Good visions are *inspiring*, they are actually *exhilarating*. To ask employees, even managers for 'ten percent plus' (in profits or sales, for instance) hardly motivates people any more; they have been through that exercise too many times. Visions, in contrast, create the spark of excitement that lifts the organization out of the mundane.
- Unlike the incremental approach to planning ('x per cent a year will get us there in year y'), visions *represent a discontinuity, a step function, a jump ahead*. To take an example from the business sphere: The authors of a business vision describe in it what they want the company to *be*, not to *become* in, say, five years time and then look back and ask what their organization would have to do today to arrive at the desired future state in due time.
- Good visions *align* people in an organization. By creating a common identity, a shared sense of purpose, a vision provides a first step in allowing people to work together who may not have trusted each other before. Such an alignment frees energies which up to then may have been eaten up by internal friction and infighting.
- Good visions are *competitive, original, unique*. 'Powerful visions are statements of intent that create an obsession with winning throughout the organization' (Hamel and Prahalad, 1989; Day, 1990). By focusing attention on a desired leadership position, continuously searching for new ways to gain competitive advantage, the actions and aspirations mean more than merely striving to catch up to competition and to match best practices.

  At the same time good visions *make sense in the market place*; that is, they are not utopian in the negative way. Unfortunately, this economic sense is often difficult to document with hard facts at the outset. This very point is frequently the source of friction between traditional, analytical managers and the entrepreneurial visionary: The analytical manager insists on data; for him, propositions which cannot be substantiated with hard facts are half-baked ideas. The visionary, however, as he typically enters uncharted territory, does not have facts and figures to prove that his idea is going to pay off. A good case in point here is Steve Jobs and the founding of Apple; when he tried to convince several of the large traditional computer companies of his vision—to put computing power into the hand of large portions of the population—the established firms citing their own market research (facts and figures!) told him that in their view there was no market to speak of for personal computers out there. This brings up a major characteristic of a vision and of visioning: The hallmark of the true visionary is that he or she reads the environment differently than 'the pack' and, as a result, comes up with unique business ideas.

This ability to combine dreams and reality seems to be a common quality of leaders throughout the ages. As a good example, Napoleon can be mentioned here; his biographer Louis Madelin writes: 'His vision ... was capable of both breadth and depth. Perhaps the most astonishing characteristic of his intellect was the combination of idealism and realism which enabled him to face the most exalted visions at the same time as the most insignificant realities. And indeed, he was in a sense a visionary, a dreamer of dreams' (quoted in Hutt, 1972).

- Being immersed in a vision also *fosters risk taking and experimentation*. The existence and the widespread understanding of a vision instills in an organization a sense of direction. Such an 'umbrella' provides members of even complex organizations with rules of inclusion and exclusion, and by doing so, allows them to take risks, develop initiatives and take decisions on their own. As an example, John Stamford Raffles, the founder of Singapore, comes to mind. Raffles was an officer of the British East-India Company stationed in the Far East, that is, he was so far away from headquarters in London (or from his immediate superior in India) that any communication with London would have taken months. At one time, Raffles in a surprise coup created a British settlement at the tip of the Malay Peninsula right at the edge of the Straits of Malacca and at the site of the ancient city of Singapura; this was in the middle of a territory which the Dutch claimed as their sphere of interest. The settlement, which later on became Singapore, prevented the Dutch from getting a stranglehold on the route to China. How did Raffles know how to function such a remote place? There was a vision of the British Empire in which he was fully immersed; it was clear to Raffles that in order to realize that vision, the British would need a stepping stone to the Far East; so, when the opportunity offered itself, Raffles acted relatively autonomously (and, as the records show, to the horror of headquarters who feared a war with the Dutch over Singapore; history vindicated Raffles however—at least from a business point of view) (Collins, 1988).

The parallel of this situation with today's broadly based companies—productwise as well as geographically—is obvious. If top management in such a vast company wants to promote entrepreneurial behaviour in its rank and file, it has to make sure that managers down the line are guided by a powerful vision, otherwise these eager beavers are all over the map with their activities.

So, to sum up: A good vision empowers and enables people.

- A good vision also *fosters long-term thinking*. Thoughtful observers of the business scene (among them Peter Senge, who stresses this point particularly), pose that it simply may not be possible to convince human beings *rationally* to take a long-term view. He argues that in every instance where one finds a long-term view actually operating in human affairs, there is a long-term vision at work appealing to the guts of people. 'The cathedral builders of the Middle Ages laboured a life time with the fruits of their labours still a hundred years into the future' (Senge, 1990).
- There is an additional, indispensable characteristic of a vision: Its *integrity*— in at least two respects. First, a vision has to be truly genuine 'which proves crucial to visionary leadership' (Westley and Mintzberg, 1989). Employees recognize very soon to what extent management really stands behind a vision, not only with their minds, but also with their hearts. The very moment the employees start doubting the seriousness of top management, cynicism is invariably the consequence.

  There is however, also a second aspect to be taken into consideration: A vision is a powerful tool and like any tool it can be used to the benefit of people as well as abused terribly. As in every aspect of human life, a good vision has to be governed by ethical principles. After all, one has to realize that for instance Martin Luther King's great rhetorical gifts, which enabled him for instance to paint a grandiose vision of America in his landmark speech 'I have a dream ...' given in 1966 in Washington, could also have been abused for demagogical purposes.

What is the Structure of a Vision?

In our work with companies we found it most practical if a vision statement addresses itself to the following content dimensions:

- *The basic idea the business is built on*. Why should a customer come to a company's doorstep? A good business idea has three major elements to it. The *first two* are closely related: A *strong, enduring customer problem* in the market the company has identified as its territory on the one hand and a *unique, attractive and accepted solution* to that problem offered by the company on the other. If one or both of these factors show any weakness, the attractiveness of the business idea is reduced. This idea is usually expressed with the help of the product and/or service offered by a business, as well as with the help of the market to be served (Neubauer, 1990).
- The third major element of a business idea is the 'business system': There is more to a business than a product, and a market; 'there is in fact an entire chain of activities from product design to product utilization by the final customer, that must be mobilized to meet certain market expectations. The

most commonly accepted term to designate this chain of activities is the *business system*' (Gilbert and Strebel, 1988). Part of this system is the organization structure, the resources, the organized knowledge, the leadership style (including major values), the links to subcontractors, the reward system and the like. The question to be answered here is, how does one want to shape the different elements of the business system to serve as a source of differentiation (or, for that matter, as a competitive barrier).

As important as the content of a vision is the way in which it is communicated. Westley and Mintzberg believe that every vision is surrounded 'by a kind of halo designed to gain its acceptance; it heightens the vision's motivational appeal and determines whether it will be sufficiently memorable to influence the day-to-day decision-making of an organization' (Conger, 1991). As Conger observes, some of the main tools in this context are metaphors, analogies and organizational stories. The power of metaphor and analogies comes from their ability to capture and illustrate an experience of reality by appealing simultaneously to the various senses of the listener. There is an appeal to the emotions, to the intellect, to imagination, and to values. Conger resonates here a word by Ortega y Gasset, the Spanish philosopher, who once said, 'The metaphor is probably the most fertile power possessed by man.'

VISION BUILDING: HOW TO DEVELOP A VISION?

The three approaches to visioning mentioned above are outlined in Figure 4.4. There are three parts to it:

- creating a *reflective* vision (Analytical—Intellectual);
- creating an *intuitive* vision (Instinctive—Intuitive);
- creating an *integrative* vision (Pragmatic blend of Reflective and Intuitive).

The Reflective Vision

The upper left-hand part of the flowchart in Figure 4.4 outlines the steps in the reflective visioning process. It represents a more conventional way to establish a vision. According to this approach, creating a vision depends on two aspects: On the one hand the ability of a manager to see the world differently 'than the pack', that is differently than most of the other managers, and the capability to create a mental image of a desired future state of his organization on the other hand.

New ways of looking at the world

The hallmark of the entrepreneur is that he or she reads the breaks in the environment differently than anybody else. Here is an example: When Jan Carlzon set about to create the 'new' SAS, he faced an environment which was characterized by a large growth of the passenger market, in particular the tourist market. While many other airlines banked on the tourist business, Carlzon decided to bank on the (essentially price-insensitive) business traveller, and by researching the service needs of that business traveller (as well as by satisfying them), he turned around SAS (at the same time he revolutionized a good portion of the European airline industry). Carlzon did not have a single more piece of information available than the rest of the industry, but he 'read' the information differently (and acted according to his 'reading').

Creation of a desired future image

Like an artist who always has an image of the work he wants to create in his mind, an entrepreneurial, visionary manager has to be able to create an image of the desired future state of his organization and to share it with his fellow managers. 'If there is a spark of genius in the leadership function at all, it must lie in this transcending ability ... to assemble—out of all the variety of images, signals, forecasts and alternatives—a clearly articulated vision of the future that is at once simple, easily understood, clearly desirable and energizing' (Bennis and Nanus, 1985). An effective way of creating a reflective vision is to keep the 'breaks' in the different domains of the environment of one's organization in mind and to compose an article about the theme: 'What would you like Fortune Magazine to write about your organization five years from now?' In our workshops, the participants are asked individually to write an exciting story about their organizations as they want it to be seen five years hence.

In order to serve its purpose, a vision has to be a shared vision. This sharing is achieved in our workshops in a plenary session of the group. During this session, the participants discuss the presentations of the individual visions, identify areas they have in common as well as discrepancies. In these intensive sessions 'in sweatshirts, with flipcharts, cans of beer and sandwiches' (as John Harvey-Jones, the former Chairman of ICI, once characterized such a process) and under the guidance of skilled process facilitators, a reflective shared vision is hammered out with all the specificity needed to make it meaningful.

Intuitive Vision

The reflective vision—as big a step ahead as it may be—frequently does not appear radical enough. Due to the habitual tracks of the learnt professional thinking, most managers' reflective vision represents an answer to the question: 'What can we get?' To facilitate a real quantum leap in their thinking in a parallel move, the process encourages the participants to understand, experience and enhance their own intuitive abilities and to use them to create an intuitive vision.

Basically, this type of vision is a response to the question: 'What do we really want?' This portion of the process, which is described in the lower left-hand part of Figure 4.4, enables the participants to get in touch with their deep-seated, gut-level desires and urges, breaking through and beyond the barriers of 'rational' thinking and 'realistic' attitudes. In this way, they can get access to significantly different and innovative ideas which represent the essence of entrepreneurship. In a step-by-step process the participants learn the 'inner language' of imaging, visualizing, projecting, symbolizing and finally creating a visual image and a verbal statement of their intuitive vision, free from the limitations imposed by the more 'realistic' approaches to visioning. As in the case of the reflective vision, each of the participants first creates an individual intuitive vision; then, in an intensive plenary session, the different individual visions are again converted into a shared visual image or symbol and an intuitive vision statement.

The purpose of embarking on two streams of Vision Building is to guide the participants from a more familiar approach to a meaningfully radical way to establish the vision. By doing so, one provides the participants on the one hand with the sense to be well-grounded in a more traditional way of creating a 'possible future' and at the same time—with the help of the second, intuitive prong—one gives them access to the exciting opportunity to experience the creation of a more daring 'desired future.'

Creating an Integrative Vision

The high point of the process is the generation of an integrative vision, a synthesis of the reflective and the intuitive vision. This portion is shown in the right-hand side of the flowchart in Figure 4.4. This step is again carried out in an intensive plenary session. The result of this step is creation of the vision finally to be shared and followed by the entire organization. For 'marrying' the two visions, a continuum of options is available which reaches from the two conceivable extremes—selecting either the reflective or the intuitive vision as the final vision to be pursued—to any pragmatic blend or synthesis of both. Experience shows that generally the latter way is followed by the participants. This synthesis is cast in a shared integrative symbol and statement.

The integrative vision addresses itself to aspects like: The product or service activity to be pursued, the ways to go about pursuing it, the management style of the unit, its structure, and its major values.

It is the aim of the process to make sure that the integrative vision meets two requirements:

- it should be unique and exciting,
- it should be shared and owned by the management team.

FROM VISION TO ACTION

The purpose of the visioning process is to transform the organization into a new, desired state. In order to do this, one not only has to describe such a future state in a cogent vision statement, it is also necessary to establish the departure point. This means the participants have to 'view' the reality of the current state of their organization through the optics of their integrative vision. This implies creating an image/symbol and a verbal statement of their current reality. Again this is first done individually; thereafter, in plenary, one condenses these individual statements in a common, shared view. In a subsequent step, this common view is contrasted with the integrative vision.

The differences observed between both—the shared integrative vision and the current reality—are usually significant; as a rule, these discrepancies lead to a substantial amount of creative tension which in turn requires resolution. To achieve this resolution is the aim of the next step.

The participants are guided to specify what has to be done, by whom, within what time frame, and with what resources. The dimensions discussed in this context are: strategy, organization structure, management style and skills, resources, and other relevant elements.

ON-GOING REVIEW

Ensuring that the organization arrives at the desired future state is a process which requires constant recalibration of the course of action chosen. As the Apollo spaceship was off course roughly 80% of the time on its way to the moon, in the same way the organization of the participants will be off course time and again on its way to the desired future state. This requires a continuing review and mid-course corrections. This activity is indicated by the feedback loop at the right hand side of Figure 4.4. As part of this process, the integrative vision has to be challenged and reviewed at regular intervals to ensure that it continues to resonate within the organization and with its changing reality.

The process is highly interactive, and thought- as well as emotion-provoking. It has been tested successfully several times not only in the classroom but, more importantly, in a company setting. It is a powerful response to a problem more and more companies are experiencing: The old, incremental mode to planning hardly motivates managers any more. They want to be involved in an exciting experience: A quantum leap of their organization, well in line with a word by the Greek historian Thukydides (460–400 BC), who once said: 'But the bravest are surely those who have the clearest vision of what is before them, glory and danger alike, and yet notwithstanding go out to meet it.'

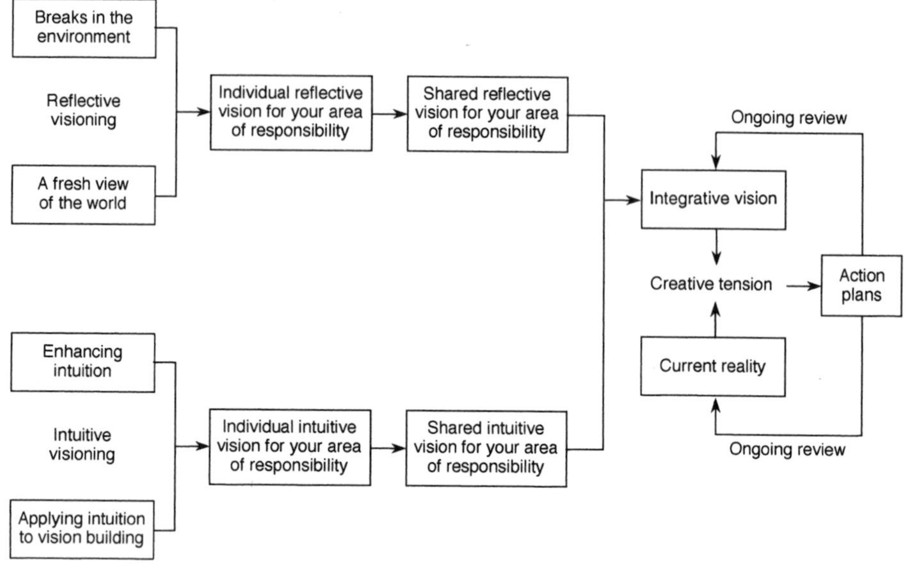

Figure 4.4 Vision Building process (PN Model)

REFERENCES

Bennis, Warren, and Nanus, Bert (1985) *Leaders*. New York, Harper & Row.

Collins, Maurice (1988) *Raffles*. London, Century.

Conner, Jay A. (1991) Inspiring others: The language of leadership, *Academy of Management*, 5, No. 1. 31–45.

Day, George S. (1990) *Market Driven Strategy*. New York, The Free Press.

Gilbert, Xavier and Strebel, Paul (1988) *Developing Competitive Advantage*. In James Brian Quinn, Henry Mintzberg and Robert M. James (eds), *The Strategy Process*, Englewood Cliffs, NJ, Prentice-Hall.

Hamel, Gary and Prahalad, C. K. (1989) Strategic intent, *Harvard Business Review*, May–June, 63–75.

Hutt, Maurice (ed.) (1972) *Napoleon*. Englewood Cliffs, NJ, Prentice-Hall.

Leavitt, Harold J. (1986) *Corporate Pathfinders*. Homewood, Ill. Dow-Jones Irwin.

Neubauer, Franz-Friedrich (1990) *Portfolio Management*. Deventer, Kluwer.

Senge, Peter (1990) *The Fifth Discipline*. New York, Doubleday-Currency.

Westley, Frances and Mintzberg, Henry, (1989) Visionary leadership and strategic management, *Strategic Management Journal*, 10. 17–32.

5

WILL HUMPTY DUMPTY WIN?

Foreword to a reprinting in 1993 of: 'Rescuing Leadership from Humpty Dumpty'

John Nicholls

Principal, John Nicholls Associates

In my 1990 article (see Chapter 6), I tried to develop a coherent view of leadership that would counter the natural Humpty Dumpty tendency for everyone to use the word differently. Leadership is such a rich concept that there is ample opportunity for people to seize on a particular aspect to the exclusion of others or, perhaps worse, to slip unconsciously from one to the other as the mood takes them.

Will Humpty Dumpty win in spite of our efforts to control him? That depends on whether the framework proposed:

(1) is strong enough to constitute a coherent view;
(2) becomes accepted and widely used.

On the first point, a further two years' work with the concepts has reinforced my belief in the framework. This reinforcement has come from both theoretical discussion with colleagues in the field and practical experience with consultancy clients. On the second point, this reprinting will contribute to a wider dissemination of the framework and, hopefully, its acceptance and use. It would be wise to become familiar with the framework by reading the original article before going on—or, at least, the three overheard conversations at the beginning. These describe different types of leadership as displayed by three different managers—Bob, Harry and Susan.

International Review of Strategic Management, volume 4.
Edited by D. E. Hussey. Published 1993 by John Wiley & Sons Ltd

I will discuss in a moment how the framework ties together much of the work of prominent US contributors in this field—most notably, Bass (1992), Bennis (1989) and Kotter (1990). First, I should like to take the original article and explore what changes I would make to refine the ideas or express them more clearly.

THE OVERALL FRAMEWORK

The overall framework—as illustrated by the meta, macro and micro leadership of Susan, Harry and Bob, respectively—stands firm.

I find, however, that these three aspects of leadership have much more appeal to managers when I refer to them, these days, as the *heart*, *head* and *hands* of leadership. This, in turn, encourages the addition of qualifying adjectives, that is inspirational, organisational and supervisory, respectively.

Thus, inspirational leadership by the *heart* is shown by the (meta) *inspiration* that Susan gave to her department, releasing people's energy so that everyone was whole-heartedly contributing their full talents.

On the other hand, organisational leadership by the *head* is shown by the (macro) path-finding and culture-building *role* that Harry plays in building an effective organisation.

Finally, supervisory leadership by the *hands* is shown by the way Bob adapts the level and balance of task and relationships behaviour in his leadership *style* to the given (micro) situation, to achieve efficient performance.

Incidentally, I now prefer to call micro leadership 'supervisory' rather than 'situational'—it is a more familiar term with a broader application. The heart, the head and the hands of leadership have a much more intuitive appeal than meta, macro and micro. It is also much easier for managers at all levels to see how they could lead in all three ways. As well as applying their hands to supervisory leadership of the situation, as expected of any manager, they also have to think in terms of path-finding and culture-building, using their heads as they perform their leadership roles. While leading in both of these ways, they can also use their hearts to give inspiration as transforming leaders.

THE PACE MODEL

The PACE model of leadership skills has a strong intuitive appeal and continues to gain acceptance. People can easily see that leaders need to have *perception, articulation, conviction* and *empathy*. These skills will, however, not produce a leader unless they are applied. Every study of leadership recognises that leaders have special characteristics of will and determination that drive them on. Although there is no agreement on a definitive list, they all include such things as energy, courage and a refusal to admit defeat.

So the PACE model has been extended, by adding *resolution*, to become the PACE(R) model. Adding resolution recognises that, while the PACE skills are necessary, they are insufficient in themselves if they are not put into effect by someone with the resolve to make a difference. We shall see later how this expression 'make a difference'—with the interesting initial letters MAD—is crucial to the definition of leadership. Resolution is put in brackets in the PACE(R) acronym. This recognises that it is something that drives the leader to apply the PACE skills. It also allows for the phenomenon of the 'reluctant' leader.

The reluctant leader is the one who has all the necessary PACE capability but, for one reason or another, does not have the drive to lead—they lack the resolution (R). A good example of this is Vaclav Havel, the democratically elected president of Czechoslovakia—now the Czech Republic. Although he led the Forum movement during the break-up of the communist regime, he was reluctant to stand for president in the elections once democracy was established. It was only at the insistence of his colleagues that he did so.

In business organisations, of course, the reluctant leader is rare. The drive to be in charge is usually all too obvious. Those who are more devious will, naturally, try to moderate a too-aggressive exhibition of their ambition—giving an impression of being the reluctant leader. Julius Caesar's attempts to reject the crown of kingship when it was offered to him did not convince people that his reluctance was genuine.

DEFINITIONS OF LEADERSHIP

Having applied the framework with clients for several years now and gained a growing confidence in it, I tend to go directly to the definition of leadership that underlies it as: 'That activity which intentionally influences outcomes by changing the way people look at the world around them and relate to each other.' From this definition we see that the first essential characteristic of leadership is that it influences outcomes. In other words, leaders make things happen that otherwise would not have happened—they make a difference. In this sense, as remarked above, they can be thought of as 'mad'.

Leaders are uncomfortable people to have around. Not only are they always stirring things up, they do it in ways that have a direct impact on people—changing the way they look at the world around them and how they relate to each other.

We can see how these characteristics of the central definition of leadership are reflected in the definitions of leadership by the heart, the head and the hands.

Inspirational (meta) leadership, by the Heart:

is that activity which—without the use of coercive power or authority—triggers purposeful action in others by creating the psychological ground for common action. It does this through an *inspirational vision* which reduces uncertainty about the environment and produces alignment around a common cause.

Organisational (macro) leadership by the Head:
is that activity which creates an effective organisation. It does this by performance of the leadership *role* which combines *path-finding*—to find the way through the business environment—and *culture-building*—to build people into a purposeful unity to follow the path.

Supervisory (micro) leadership, by the Hands:
is that activity which produces efficient performance in a given *situation*—i.e. a specific combination of people and job to be done. It does this by adopting the appropriate leadership *style*, i.e. level and balance of task and relationships behaviour.

These are operational definitions of the leadership illustrated by Susan, Harry and Bob, respectively.

LEADERSHIP AND MANAGEMENT

Influence on outcomes and change in the way people behave are the two essential elements of leadership. These aspects of leadership make it sound very close to 'getting things done through people'—a common definition of management. In spite of this, the two are different. Although different, however, they are not mutually exclusive. Nor is management a lesser activity. Quite the contrary. Leadership is, in fact, a vital component of management. To see why, we must have a proper understanding of the word management—a word that it is important not to devalue. To help avoid this, it is worth spending a moment to look at some other associated Humpty Dumpty words.

Apart from leader, potential Humpty Dumpty words are: *executive, manager, administrator* and *bureaucrat*. Although not strict synonyms, the words are clearly related and have a great deal of overlap. There is a tendency, especially in American work, to make a distinction between managers and leaders— although there is less likelihood of denying that executives are leaders. On the other hand, managers are usually distinguished from administrators—and certainly from bureaucrats—although, paradoxically, the principal management degree is the MBA, master of business administration.

The easiest way to resolve these inconsistencies is to restore management to its central position. Management is the uniquely special activity required for the successful running of an organisation. As such, it has two essential components: leadership (which is also an implicit attribute of an executive) and administration (which can too easily decay into bureaucracy).

The manager as administrator deals with the *complexity* of organisational life by the traditional activities of planning, organising, monitoring, controlling, and so on. The manager as executive deals with *change and uncertainty* by exercising leadership. Both activities of the manager are necessary to 'get things done through people'.

Thus, the manager must simultaneously act as executive *and* administrator. On the one hand, the manager provides leadership to cope with change and uncertainty. On the other hand, the manager administers the complexity of the operation—while avoiding the temptation to become a bureaucrat.

The words relate to each other in the sequence: leader–executive–manager–administrator–bureaucrat. This puts management in the central position as the word which encompasses both aspects of 'getting things done through people'—leadership and administration.

TRANSFORMING LEADERSHIP

In the above, it is clear that we have been thinking of leadership in the context of the organisation—in other words, leadership through the head (macro). In 'getting things done through people', the focus has been on people collectively as members of the organisation. This has established the left-hand half of Figure 5.1, showing the way in which leadership through the head (macro) and administration may be viewed as complementary aspects of management, with respect to the complexity and uncertainty in the environment.

When talking of 'getting things done through people' it is equally valid, however, to think of people individually—interacting personally. This gives us the other dimension of Figure 5.1, allowing us to show how the other two forms of leadership also complement the administrative aspect of management.

Thus, in the fixed environment of a particular job, managers lead individuals personally through the hands (micro), adjusting their style to be congruent with people's level of competence and commitment. When facing uncertainty in the environment, however, individuals require the meta inspiration of leadership through the heart.

Figure 5.1 shows how the sequence from bureaucracy to leadership, derived earlier, requires the two dimensions of people and environment to relate all three aspects of leadership as complements to administration—illustrating the full richness of management. It also provides us with a way to visualise the meaning that may be given to Burns's political concept of transforming leadership when put into an organisational context.

Starting at the origin, the administration of people collectively in an environment of fixed complexity can decay into bureaucracy. Moving in one dimension, focusing on people as individuals, the manager must complement the administration of fixed complexity with supervisory leadership by the hands

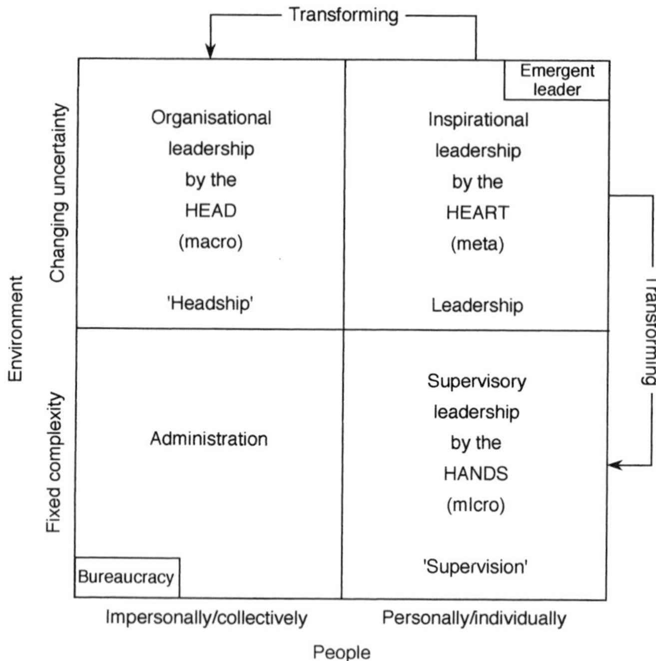

Figure 5.1 Management: administration complemented by leadership

(micro). Moving in the other dimension, as uncertainty increases, the manager must complement the administration of people collectively with organisational leadership by the head (macro).

These two aspects of leadership are associated with managers as executives in an organisation. Some, however, would reserve the word leadership for a combined move in both dimensions. The confines of the organisation begin to weaken and one approaches the domain of the emergent leader. Thus, when dealing with individuals in an uncertain environment, the manager must complement administration with the meta inspiration of leadership by the heart.

One might call this the 'strict' interpretation of transforming leadership in the organisational context. Management is a combination of administration in one corner of the figure with its inspirational leadership complement in the diagonally opposite corner. The two other quadrants of the figure do not qualify as leadership. They are part of management but are better described by terms such as 'headship' for the one and 'supervision' for the other.

In my experience, however, most managers are content to view as leadership their executive activities in dealing with individuals and with uncertainty. This allows another interpretation of transforming leadership—the addition of meta visioning to both aspects of executive leadership as shown by the arrows, thus bringing inspiration of the heart to both neighbouring quadrants. With this addition of meta inspiration, both quadrants—performing the macro role and adjusting the micro style—qualify as leadership. Together, the injection of meta inspiration of the heart into headship and supervision constitutes transforming leadership in the organisational context.

Figure 5.1 is a major step forward in understanding how leadership relates to management, how the three aspects of leadership relate to each other and to the operational meaning of transforming leadership in an organisational context. Summing up, one can say that all managers must keep their feet on the ground (administration), while they lead with their head (organisation) and their hands (supervision). At the same time, good managers make their managerial leadership transforming by infusing it with inspirational leadership of the heart.

RELATING THE 'HEART, HEAD AND HANDS' MODEL TO THE PRINCIPAL US RESEARCH

The work of Kotter (1990) and Bennis (1989), the leading US researchers in this field, lends a great deal of encouragement to the 'heart, head and hands' model of leadership.

The distinction made in the previous section between leadership and administration as the two complementary aspects of management is closely parallel to that made by Kotter (1990). In common with many American writers, however, he makes the distinction in a different way by viewing managers and leaders as fundamentally different. This confuses the distinction between two modes of behaviour by embodying it in personality. If this were true, it would seem that organisations would need parallel structures for career advancement to accommodate the two types—managers and leaders.

Alternatively, people making a career would have to metamorphose from managers to leaders as they progressed. This latter is, in fact, close to what actually happens. But it is not that people mysteriously convert from being one sort of person (managers) to another (leaders). It is, rather, that as they progress they spend less time on one aspect of their management behaviour (administration) and must develop their skill in another aspect (leadership).

Looking at leadership in organisations, Kotter (1990) sees both the path-finding and the culture-building activities that make up leadership of the 'head'—the macro role. Path-finding is called 'setting a direction' and is described as '... developing a vision of the future (often the distant future) along with strategies for producing the changes needed to achieve that vision.' Culture-building is called 'aligning people' and is described as '... communicating the new direction to those who can create coalitions that understand the vision and are committed to its achievement.'

A third aspect of leadership which Kotter calls 'motivating and inspiring' is closer to the inspiring leadership by the heart (meta): 'keeping people moving in the right direction, despite major obstacles to change, by appealing to basic but often untapped human needs, values, and emotions.'

This moves into the broader field of leadership, where Bennis has been active, going beyond the confines of the business organisation. Here we find encouraging support for the PACE(R) model. From his study of leaders in a wide variety of fields—business, sport, medicine, education, religion, the arts—Bennis (1989) concludes that leaders are those who '... know what they want [Perception], why they want it [Conviction], and how to communicate what they want to others [Articulation], in order to gain their cooperation and support. Finally, they know how to achieve their goals [Empathy]' (p. 3).

As pinpointed by the words I have added in brackets, this passage neatly encapsulates the PACE capabilities. A page or two later Bennis (1989) adds Resolution when making the point that leaders have '... an abiding interest in expressing themselves'. Expanding on this as 'desire', he quotes one of his sample of leaders as saying, 'I was the one with the energy and enthusiasm and drive and determination, so I became the leader.'

In spite of the differences in emphasis and terminology, it is interesting to find such a close correspondence between the American work of Kotter and Bennis and the 'heart, head and hands' model that we gave to Humpty Dumpty. Adding further support, Bernard Bass—author of *Leadership and Performance Beyond Expectations* and director of the Center for Leadership Studies— comments on the article that 'I endorse your conception of meta, macro and micro leadership'.

TRANSFORMING LEADERSHIP, VALUE TO THE CUSTOMER AND TQM

In recent years, the leadership ideas have developed into a methodology for the in-depth implementation of TQM (Total Quality Management). As I have noted elsewhere (Nicholls, 1990), TQM is becoming an 'umbrella' word that encompasses almost any activity that contributes to 'excellence'—another umbrella word! In its broadest sense, TQM is a continually evolving vehicle to give expression to two fundamental paradigm shifts in management thinking—towards *people* and towards *customers*:

(1) it is no longer possible to regard people at work as mere 'hands'. The complexity and speed of change in today's business environment demands people who are committed to their work, empowered to contribute their full energies and talents;
(2) going beyond marketing, everyone in the entire organisation must be focused on delivering value to their customers—be they internal or external.

Competitive success depends on creating an organisation in which everyone is excited about serving their customers—where they are constantly giving of their best to *delight* them with value beyond their expectations. This can only happen when managers have learned to lead their organisations differently—in a way that supports and helps implement the paradigm shifts in their way of thinking about people and customers. In effect, they must turn the organisation *upside-down*—to flatten the controlling hierarchy—and *inside-out*—to focus everyone on the customer.

From this viewpoint, it is easy to see why the successful implementation of TQM requires an understanding and adoption of transforming leadership. The 'vision' of the visionary/enabler directs attention outwards to the customer, via the mission statement, while the 'enabling' allows people to devote their full energies and talents to delivering value to the customer.

'Value' is a term that embraces both effectiveness and efficiency—a product or service must both perform and be affordable. It avoids the counter-intuitive drawbacks of defining quality as 'conformance to specifications'—as does Crosby (1979), for example. As I have pointed out elsewhere (Nicholls, 1992b), this has the disadvantage of implying that a Skoda, for instance, is a quality car because it meets its specs. Or that on-spec instant coffee is top quality for honoured guests.

But, whereas nobody would include Skoda in their list of quality cars, a Skoda can perfectly well be seen to be good value—not much of a car but dead cheap! Similarly, instant coffee is good value at its price.

The way in which transforming leadership is applied to the implementation of TQM, via value to the customer, is described in more detail in my recently published *Leadership of Customer-Driven TQM: A Handbook for Managers* (Nicholls, 1992a).

CONCLUSION

Looking back, this review inclines me to the feeling that the 'heart, head and hands' model is sufficiently robust to keep Humpty Dumpty on the run. Not only is it coherent and well-accepted by managers, it has intellectual support from its correspondence to leading American research.

In this review, I have provided operational definitions of the three types of leadership exhibited by Susan, Harry and Bob. Fresh light has been thrown on the relationship of leadership to management and a clarification of the meaning of transforming leadership provided.

Finally, I have outlined how transforming leadership is being used to provide the vital under-pinning to the implementation of TQM, via value to the customer.

REFERENCES

Bass, Bernard (1992) Private communication.

Bennis, Warren (1989) On Becoming a leader. London, Hutchinson Business Books.

Kotter, John (1990) What leaders really do. *Harvard Business Review,* May/June.

Nicholls, John (1990) Value to the Customer. *TQM Magazine,* April.

Nicholls, John (1992a) *Leadership of Customer-Driven TQM: A Handbook for Managers.* London, Technical Communications Publishing Ltd.

Further Reading

Crosby, Phillip (1979) *Quality is Free*. New York, McGraw-Hill.

Nicholls, John (1992b) Is Quality Free? *TQM Magazine,* June.

6

RESCUING LEADERSHIP FROM HUMPTY DUMPTY

John Nicholls

Principal, John Nicholls Associates

> It is in the very nature of modern, large-scale organisations that the only hope of vitality is the willingness of a great many people, scattered throughout the organisation or the society, to take the initiative and perform leadership acts, identifying problems at their level and solving them.
>
> (John Gardner, author *Self Renewal* and Director, The Leadership Studies Programme)

> 'When *I* use a word,' Humpty Dumpty said, in rather a scornful tone, 'it means just what I choose it to mean—neither more nor less.' 'The question is,' said Alice, 'whether you *can* make words mean so many different things.' 'The question is,' said Humpty Dumpty, 'which is to be master—that's all.'
>
> (Lewis Carroll, *Through the Looking-Glass: And What Alice Found There*)

RESCUING LEADERSHIP FROM HUMPTY DUMPTY

This article is dedicated to Humpty Dumpty who, apart from falling off his wall, uses words in any way he likes: to Alice's great confusion.

Leadership these days is the 'in' topic! After years in which we were content to talk about how to manage a business, the talk has now turned to leadership. John Gardner is one voice among many in emphasising the need for leadership throughout the organisation (see quote at head). But leadership is a seductive word that has a multitude of meanings. No one is short of a definition but, like

International Review of Strategic Management, volume 4.
Edited by D. E. Hussey. Published 1993 by John Wiley & Sons Ltd

Humpty Dumpty in *Through the Looking-Glass: And What Alice Found There,* everyone uses the word in his or her own way.

This lack of cohesion in our ideas about leadership makes it hard to know exactly what John Gardner might be getting at when he stresses the need for leadership at all levels. Is everyone going to be trying to run the organisation? Don't 'leadership acts' require leadership talents that only few possess? Is problem-solving all that leaders do? What about inspiration, guidance and standard-setting? Humpty Dumpty would have a field day with leadership! No wonder he falls off walls if they are built of such a jumble of concepts.

In this article we see how the many strands of current leadership thinking can be cast as solid bricks that will build a 'leadership wall' strong enough to hold Humpty Dumpty securely.

Let's first get an idea of what different people mean by leadership by eavesdropping on three very ordinary workplace conversations:

- Two machinists are chatting over their coffee in the canteen during a break from work:

  1st voice: 'It's a funny thing but Bob seems much better as section head than I thought he would be.'
  2nd voice: 'How do you mean?'
  1st voice: 'Well, I had my doubts when they promoted him last year, but he has turned out really well. He seems to adjust to suit everyone. If you know how to do something, he lets you get on with it—providing you show willing, of course.'
  2nd voice: 'He certainly doesn't let you get away with things! If something's wrong, he gets in there to sort out why.'
  1st voice: 'Too true! But at the same time he's very flexible. Some things I'm good at so he never watches me closely or interferes. But he's helping me a lot with the new milling machine. I'm really getting the hang of it.'
  2nd voice: 'Same with me. Mostly, I'm left alone, but he knows I'm hopeless with jig-setting and helps me through it.'
  1st voice: 'Yes, its funny how the job seems to have brought out his leadership talents—I wouldn't have thought it possible.'

- Two executives of the same medium-sized company are talking at the water-cooler on the 7th floor of their smart headquarters:

  1st voice: 'I hear Harry Coleman's finally decided to retire next year. The place won't be the same without him.'
  2nd voice: 'You're right! I can't think of many others who could have pulled us through the things we've just faced in the last couple of years.'
  1st voice: 'It's amazing how he sorted out the mess old Fred had left us in.

He seemed to have an instinct for what had to go and what to hang on to.'

2nd voice: 'Mind you, he trod on a few toes in the process! He'd never have got all those new projects going if he hadn't. But, by George! the medicine worked!'

1st voice: 'That's the whole point. He didn't mind whose nose he put out of joint. If he felt it was right he would go for it. After he'd cleared out the dead wood at head office, the others soon got the message.'

2nd voice: 'Too right! We'd have gone right under without his leadership. He really turned us around.'

- The company's manufacturing director is talking to the personnel director before a board meeting:

Mnftg director: 'Susan's done a magnificent job with the management services division since she took over last year.'

Personnel director: 'They've really found their feet. It seems to me they have a much clearer idea of their role.'

Mnftg director: 'Yes, she's shifted the emphasis to helping the operating divisions perform better and make better decisions—not imposing systems on them like they used to.'

Personnel director: 'Not only that, everyone seems to be pulling together. She's managed to overcome that traditional rivalry between design and operations. They actually talk to each other now!'

Mnftg director: 'That's it. There's a real enthusiasm that was never there before. I bumped into Joe Thompson, their chief systems analyst, the other day. He tells me everyone feels now that they are really able to give their best. Sometimes they get so stuck into things he actually has to throw them out at night!'

Personnel director: Sue really knows how to get people turned on. We could do with a bit more leadership like hers around here!'

In these examples, Bob, Harry and Sue are performing at widely different levels in their organisations, and the speakers have focused on markedly different aspects of their behaviour as managers. Hearing them one after the other like this, our impression is of three very different activities—yet each is referred to as leadership. No wonder Humpty Dumpty finds it a confusing word!

While Bob is creating a productive working environment for the machinists in his section, Harry is acting as a 'mover-and-shaker' to transform the fortunes of his organisation. Sue, on the other hand, has been transforming in another way—by revitalising her division, filling her people with enthusiasm. And yet we can readily appreciate why the speakers feel that leadership is involved in all three examples—even though it is hard to pin down precisely.

But, in responding to John Gardner's call, are we expecting people to behave more like Bob, like Harry or like Sue? Our Humpty Dumpty tendencies to use the word in these widely different ways makes it difficult to tell. If we really want to change the way we run our companies, getting people to act differently, we are going to have to be more precise about what we are asking them to do. We need to help Alice seat Humpty Dumpty more securely by developing bricks for his wall that embrace the wide variety of leadership behaviour evident in the three conversations. In doing so we will have a surer guide to action and, hopefully, a clearer idea how we might respond to John Gardner's call for leadership in depth.

A CLOSER LOOK AT LEADERSHIP

Examining the first two conversations, it is clear that Harry's leadership is on a scale quite different from Bob's. Whereas Bob has been successful in getting willing cooperation from his people in doing their job, Harry is being praised for pulling his company back from the brink of disaster. One could say that Bob was skilful in adapting his leadership *style* to the people working for him, whereas Harry performed well in the leadership *role* of creating a successful organisation.

As a starting point, this distinction between style and role seems to be a matter of scale. On a small scale, leadership style is adapted to particular people doing a particular job. On a larger scale, the leadership role is concerned with the organisation as a whole. Reflecting the difference in scale, these are called micro and macro leadership, respectively.

To some extent, this question of scale is connected with the focus of attention. Bob, as a section head, has an inward focus on the job to be done; whereas Harry, as the man at the top, has an external focus on the organisation's performance in the business environment.

There are other differences between Bob's micro leadership and Harry's macro leadership. Bob is more concerned with adapting to people as they are in their present job, while Harry's focus was on the things people should be doing and how they must adapt. Bob is trying to get the best out of people's present capabilities, whereas Harry made the most of their growth potential: one is focused on now and the other on the future.

It is not a question of one being right and the other wrong: one being better than the other or superior. They are simply concerned with different aspects of 'getting things done through people'. Bob's micro leadership concentrates on efficiency here and now, *adapting his leadership style* to 'doing things right'. Harry's macro leadership was looking to effectiveness in the future, *performing his leadership role* by 'doing the right things'.

Distinguishing between micro and macro leadership in organisations helps us to come to grips with its wide spectrum of meanings. It helps us to see why Bob and Harry's colleagues would say that what both of them are doing is leadership, although so vastly different in many respects of scale, time and intent.

The major differences between micro and macro leadership can be summed up as:

Micro	Macro
particular	general
job/task	team/organisation
short-term performance	long-term: career/climate
as things are	as things could be
present/reactive	future/proactive
inward-looking	outward looking
internal environment	external environment
doing things right	doing the right things
efficiency	effectiveness
Adapting one's leadership STYLE to a given situation	Performing the leadership ROLE in an organisation

The need for Bob's sort of micro leadership in organisations has long been recognised and widely studied. Most of the familiar models for leadership training are at the micro level. Hersey and Blanchard's (1969) Situational Leadership, for example, directs attention to the task and relationships aspects of leadership behaviour. It indicates how the balance of attention to these two dimensions should vary in response to the capabilities of the particular people doing the particular job in the given situation. In a related model that I have developed with my clients, the leader's style is adjusted to match or be 'congruent' with the subordinates' level of competence and commitment (Nicholls, 1986).

Bob's leadership skill is undoubtedly important but the need for it is already widely recognised. Although micro leadership is the first brick in our wall, it is not what John Gardner means when he calls for leadership in depth. But can he have meant that everyone should start behaving like the chief executive? It sounds unlikely, but a clearer idea of our second brick—the macro leadership role—would be useful before going further.

THE MACRO LEADERSHIP ROLE

In its broadest terms, the responsibility of the chief executive is to create a successful organisation. For a profit-making corporation, a successful organisation can be created in one (or both) of two ways:

(1) successfully finding the way through a changing environment, correctly identifying the opportunities and avoiding the threats;
(2) creating the capability to follow your own particular path or to perform better than others on the commonly-acknowledged beaten track.

These two components of success appear widely in the management literature. As long ago as 1957, Selznick (1957) recognised them as 'policy formation' and 'organisation building'. He saw the function of the chief executive as being '... to define the ends of group existence, to design an enterprise distinctively adapted to these ends, and to see that the design becomes a living reality'.

Adapting terms from recent works by Leavitt (1986) and Schein (1985), we can call them 'path-finding' and 'culture-building'. Path-finding can be summed up as finding the way to a successful future, while culture-building can be viewed as drawing people into a purposeful organisation.

In Figure 6.1, we see these two activities in diagrammatic form, showing how the leader performs the macro leadership role by:

(1) relating the organisation to its environment, through path-finding;
(2) relating people to the organisation, through culture-building.

This model of the macro leadership role helps us see why some management thinkers regard leadership as a red herring. Path-finding and culture-building, in one way or another, are managerial activities that chief executives have always concentrated on. Traditionally, they have been viewed as top management functions.

For many people, however, they are seen as sufficiently different and special as to warrant the use of the word leadership. Indeed, Selznick chose to refer to them as functions of the leader/statesman. In this view, path-finding and culture-

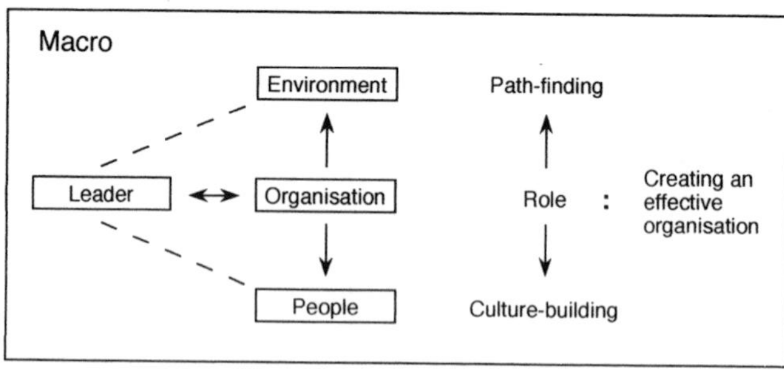

Figure 6.1 The macro leadership role

building are two components of the macro leadership role in creating an effective organisation. Look on them, if you wish, as 'managerial' components of the macro leadership role.

With this clearer view of the macro leadership role we have a firm second brick in our wall. Macro leadership corresponds much more closely to the activities that John Gardner suggests are needed at depth in organisations. The need is not for micro leadership to accomplish the pre-determined job/task but for people at all levels to take path-finding initiatives, to identify problems, and build a culture that is capable of solving them.

Bob and Harry have given us two bricks for the leadership wall but what about Sue—how does her leadership fit in? If anything, her success is like Harry's in revitalising her department at the macro level. The transformation, however, seems to have more to do with how her people are behaving—all pulling together in the right direction, at last—than to a great recovery in the fortunes of her group; although their chances of success are, indeed, much brighter now.

Our thinking about Bob and Harry's leadership has been firmly in the context of an organisation. Since Sue's leadership success seems to be somewhat different, it is useful to step outside the organisation for a moment and consider leadership in a broader perspective.

LEADERSHIP OUTSIDE ORGANISATIONS

How do some people emerge and become accepted by their followers as leaders, even though they have no power or authority and there is no mechanism for them to be elected or appointed? How did Martin Luther King, for example, become the leader of the Civil Rights movement? Or, getting down to the grass-roots, how does a ringleader emerge in an unofficial industrial dispute? Personality clearly comes into it, but what can be said about the process itself and the abilities that are important?

From everyday experience, it is easy to accept that leaders emerge and become accepted because they help their potential followers to make sense of an environment that is confusing and hard to understand. Leaders are instrumental in creating 'the psychological ground for cooperative common action' (see Vaill, 1987). The complex process by which they do this is referred to as 'visioning'. Visioning has two main components that are at the heart of emergent leadership—the sort that arises because it is accepted rather than being imposed:

(1) it reduces uncertainty and helps in making choices;
(2) it aligns people and gives them a sense of common purpose.

As visioning occurs, energy is released and people become enthusiastic about the leader and the vision that is emerging.

There are clear parallels between these two components of emergent leadership and those that were identified for the macro leadership role within organisations. This is not surprising. They are simply models of different aspects of that elusive concept—leadership. Whereas emergent leaders energise people as individuals, regardless of the power and authority structure, performance of the macro leadership role takes place within organisations.

Emerging leaders seem to have four main abilities that interact in a complex way in visioning. Firstly, their *perception* of the confusing environment is more accurate than that of the people around them. This perception may not be perfect, but emerging leaders see things significantly more clearly than those around them. Secondly, they are very *articulate* in expressing their perception. Depending on the circumstances, this may or may not involve great oratory; clarity of exposition can be equally as potent. The emerging leader's sharper perception, clearly articulated, starts to reduce the uncertainty that people feel and helps them in making choices.

Thirdly, the emerging leader has basic values and beliefs, tempered by experience: these support strong *convictions* about what should be done and provide a drive to do it. Finally, conviction is very often accompanied by a strong *empathy* with the potential followers, an understanding of their aspirations, hopes and fears. The emerging leader's strong convictions and empathy with others encourages people to align themselves in the same direction and feel a sense of common purpose.

The initial letters of the four abilities—perception, articulation, conviction and empathy—form the acronym PACE which summarises the abilities that the emerging leader combines. These interact in the process called visioning, to create the psychological ground for common action.

In addition to the four PACE abilities, however, emergent leaders seem to have a number of personal characteristics that give them the will or resolution to be a leader. Although these are commonly recognised by most researchers and authors, there is no complete consensus about them. Typically, lists include such things as determination, refusal to quit, inner strength, enthusiasm and courage. These characteristics are recognised under the heading *resolution* to complete the PACE(R) model of emergent leadership.

The word 'charisma' is frequently heard as an explanation for the emergent leader. Charisma is an ill-defined word which implies certain personal characteristics. It could be fitted into the PACE(R) model under resolution (R)—the general heading for personal characteristics. It is arguable, however, that charisma is a catch-all word which is applied to those lucky few who have a high natural level of the PACE abilities. This high endowment, in itself, allows them effortlessly to create a compelling vision and emerge as a leader. In this interpretation, they do not necessarily have a special will to lead or high resolution.

Through the complex interaction of the four PACE abilities—depending on the emergent leader's particular talent and driven by their resolution (R)—uncertainty is reduced and people become aligned, sharing a common purpose. As a result, energy is released through enthusiastic followers.

Visioning through PACE is called *meta* leadership since it goes beyond the exercise of power or authority in organisations. Meta leadership is, as the word implies, distinct from the macro and micro leadership that occurs within organisations. Figure 6.2 illustrates how the leader's PACE(R) abilities interact in meta visioning to release the energies of enthusiastic followers.

We can use the PACE(R) model of meta visioning to explain how Martin Luther King, driven by a determination (R) to achieve change, became accepted as the leader of the Civil Rights movement. He perceived the true nature of what was happening at that time in the Southern United States and was able to articulate it in terms of his own convictions—'I have a dream ...'—with empathy that struck a chord with the hopes and fears, needs and aspirations of his listeners.

At the grass-roots too, ringleaders emerge on the factory floor through their personal resolution (R) and the interaction of their abilities in the PACE model. They perceive more clearly than their fellows what is going on in the workplace and articulate this in a clear call to action. Strong convictions drive them to act and, being part of the workforce, they have a strong empathy with their fellow workers.

In both of these typical cases, it is visioning—through personal resolution (R), coupled with talent in the interaction of the four PACE abilities—that achieves the key functions of meta leadership: reducing uncertainty (which helps in making choices) while aligning people (which gives them a sense of purpose). This

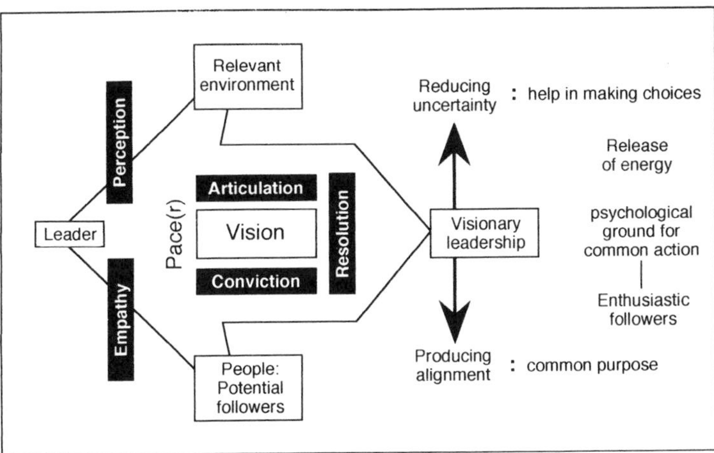

Figure 6.2 Meta leadership through visioning

generates the psychological ground for common action—releasing the energy of enthusiastic followers.

Sue's meta visioning has given us a third brick in our wall by demonstrating an aspect of leadership which goes beyond the macro role. Although it is not explicit in John Gardner's call for initiatives to be taken at every level, it is, nonetheless, a vital ingredient. One cannot imagine initiatives being taken on the scale required, or creative solutions being found, without the sort of leadership that generates enthusiastic followers and permits them to act.

So far, Bob and Harry have shown us that John Gardner's call for leadership in depth means raising people's attention from their micro leadership style by making them conscious of their macro role of path-finding and culture-building. Beyond that, Sue's leadership has reminded us of the need to release the energies of enthusiastic followers by meta visioning while performing that macro role.

Although these three bricks—meta, macro and micro—have given us a firm foundation for Humpty Dumpty's wall, the concept of transforming leadership is still balancing precariously. For example, Harry's leadership was quite different from Sue's and yet, earlier, we saw how both could be described as transforming. First coined a decade ago—and boosted by a mention in the best-selling *In Search of Excellence*—this word has been widely applied to leadership in organisations. In spite of its popularity, however, its meaning has remained imprecise. Clearly, it is another word we need to pin down for Humpty Dumpty!

TRANSFORMING LEADERSHIP

The political scientist James MacGregor Burns first made the distinction between *transforming* and *transactional* leadership. As first proposed by Burns (1978), transforming leaders *engage* people in a way that uplifts them and transforms both leader and led: '... the transforming leader looks for potential motives in followers, seeks to satisfy higher needs, and engages the full person of the follower. The result of transforming leadership is a relation of mutual stimulation and elevation that converts followers into leaders and leaders into moral agents.' Although imprecise and difficult to transpose to an organisational setting, this concept has great intuitive appeal, as witnessed by its ready acceptance by a wider management audience.

Transactional leadership, on the other hand, is equally difficult but has been subject to neglect rather than confusion. In contrast to transforming leadership, it excludes engagement and is restricted to 'exchange' relationships between leader and followers: 'you scratch my back, I'll scratch yours.'

In a nutshell, Burns' distinction between transactional and transforming leadership, when applied to an organisation, lies in how the macro role is performed. Transactional leadership is limited to the 'managerial' aspects of the macro role. Much has been written about what one might call these 'managerial' aspects of leadership: how to formulate a strategy, how to create a supportive climate to implement the strategy. Notable examples are Kanter (1983) and Tichy and Devanna (1986). They include the actions that management can take to encourage commitment in the workforce by creating a sense of belonging and excitement in the job (Nicholls and Martin, 1987).

Transforming leadership goes beyond this and engages people through meta visioning. When it comes to performing the macro leadership role within organisations, however, meta visioning is only part of achieving engagement. The transforming leader in an organisation must be both a *visionary* and an *enabler*—making sure that the energy released is allowed to flow productively. The power and authority structure of an organisation is so seductive that the visionary, to be a real transforming leader, must also strive to engage people as an enabler.

To make the concept of a transforming *visionary/enabler* more concrete, it is useful to contrast it with the polar opposite that springs from the extreme of autocratic, transactional leadership.

Authoritarians view leadership as the prerogative of a few. Only those with special insight are able to perform the macro role, especially the path-finding. They, alone, know where the organisation ought to be going and will exercise *control* to get it there. While exercising control, very often, the visioning of meta leadership is disdained. There is no need to inspire people and release their energies: the power and authority mechanisms can be *manipulated* by those at the top to get people to comply in following the path which has been 'heroically' defined by the autocrat.

Leadership of this *controller/manipulator* sort is widespread. Rather than exhibiting 'TLC' for people, it is characterised by 'TDC'. These less familiar initials, coming from Tom Peters' *Passion for Excellence,* express the implicit view of their subordinates held by many managers: that of 'thinly disguised contempt'—somehow there is not much talent around and people don't have a great deal to offer. If the boss is not there, knocking heads together or generally stirring things up, nothing much gets done: as for creativity, enthusiasm or initiative—they stand no chance!

If the circumstances are right, as we saw with Harry, controller/manipulators can be highly successful in transforming the fortunes of an organisation. These successful autocrats transform things by being transactional 'movers-and-shakers'. They are not, however, transforming leaders in Burns' sense—at best they could be called 'transforming autocrats'. As pointed out elsewhere (Nicholls, 1988), transforming autocrats create a vision but behave autocratically in its pursuit. Although often successful—witness Lee Iaccocca's rescue of Chrysler—they lack the engagement/enabling characteristics of the true transforming leadership of the visionary/enabler.

From what we overheard at the beginning, Harry transformed the organisation's fortunes by behaving as a controller/manipulator. He was a successful autocrat—or, at best, a transforming autocrat. Sue, on the other hand, would better qualify as a transforming leader. By acting as a visionary/enabler she transformed the behaviour of the people in her division, filling them with enthusiasm. The energy she released may indeed make success more likely. It is, however, through her effect on people, as a visionary/enabler that her leadership merits the adjective transforming.

THE LESSONS FOR LEADERSHIP BEHAVIOUR

Our discussion of the range of meanings given to the word leadership shows why Humpty Dumpty had such scope for misunderstanding. Having built a more secure wall for him to sit on, what lessons can we draw for leadership behaviour?

First of all, we can now see that, in organisations, leadership can be exerted in both the micro and macro senses. Micro leadership is familiar to all managers. It involves getting the best out of a particular group of people (or person) doing a particular job. From this focus on a given situation, it is often called 'situational' leadership.

Like Bob, good leaders adjust their style—in terms of task and relationships behaviour—to match, or be congruent with, the situation. They achieve congruence by ensuring that the level and balance of task and relationships behaviour in their leadership style matches the ability and willingness of those they are leading in a given job.

Macro leadership, on the other hand, is concerned with the creation of an effective organisation. This leadership role consists of path-finding and culture building. Although macro leadership is what is required in depth, many managers are unaware that they have a leadership role to play—it is not just for people at the top, like Harry. Anyone on whom others look as their boss or manager has the potential to play a leadership role. Their path-finding and culture-building will, of course, be constrained by that of those above them—but the opportunity exists.

In today's fast-changing and uncertain business environment, it is becoming more and more essential that managers at all levels—right down to the shop floor—recognise their potential leadership role and perform it. It helps in doing this to think in more familiar terms than path-finding and culture-building. These can be put more colloquially as 'finding a better way' and 'getting it done'. The more people there are who take responsibility for doing this the better.

We can now see more clearly how to respond to the call for leadership in depth. It does not require more skill in adjusting one's style to the micro situation. Although, of course, more skill in adjusting style would be desirable, managers have always been aware of the need to lead people in the efficient performance of the job. What is needed now is for more managers, right down through the organisation, to become aware of their responsibility to fill a macro leadership role. This goes beyond efficiency in doing today's job. It involves the broader responsibility of leading their team to find a better way and get it done.

Before thinking how managers might go about performing their leadership role, we should remind ourselves of what is meant by transforming leadership. From Burns' original work we saw that transforming leadership engages with people and lifts them above themselves, eschewing the use of coercive power—as contrasted with transactional leadership which operates at an exchange level of 'you scratch my back, I'll scratch yours'.

We also saw that transforming leadership in organisations implied the use of meta visioning in performing the macro leadership role—while enabling people to contribute their talents to the full. This visionary/enabler leadership was contrasted with that of the controller/manipulator. Whereas it is possible for an autocratic leader to transform the fortunes of an organisation as a controller/manipulator, the true transforming leader is the visionary/enabler.

It is evident that if managers are to be urged to fulfil leadership roles they should be encouraged to do it as a transforming visionary/enabler. The benefits of leadership initiatives in depth—finding a better way and getting it done—will only be realised if the leader is able to engage with people and liberate their potential rather than attempting to coerce innovative behaviour as an autocratic controller/manipulator.

Thus we see that leadership in depth implies greatly increased initiative as managers at all levels become more active in finding a better way and getting it done. This does not mean that they will all be trying to run the organisation as mini-chief executives. They will simply be performing the leadership role as it is appropriate to their level.

Anything that managers can do to enhance their PACE(R) skills will be of benefit in their attempts to fulfil their leadership role. The more they understand how their team fits into the organisation and the vital contribution it makes the better will be their perception. Their conviction will be enhanced by the experience they gain and any appropriate training they undergo. Using a mission statement as a vehicle to help articulate a vision, while showing empathy, through TLC rather than TDC, will help them in being transforming visionary/enablers.

Their resolution to lead can be enhanced by an understanding of their potential leadership role, a realisation of the benefits which many firms are experiencing from the practice of transforming leadership and using prominent visionary/enablers as role models—Sir John Harvey-Jones, former chairman of ICI, for example.

These lessons have derived from our attempts to clarify the concept of leadership and rescue it from the arbitrary abuses of Humpty Dumpty. At the same time, we have been able to derive much valuable guidance for practical managers. With the insights provided from the examples of Bob, Harry and Sue, Alice should now be well equipped to hold her own.

REFERENCES

Hersey, P. and Blanchard, K. L. (1969) *Management of Organisational Behaviour*. Englewood Cliffs, NJ, Prentice-Hall.

Kanter, R. M. (1983) *The Change Masters*. London, Allen & Unwin.

Leavitt, H. L. (1986) *Corporate Pathfinders*. Washington, DC, Dow-Jones Irwin.

Macgregor Burns, J. (1978) *Leadership*. New York, Harper & Row.

Nicholls, J. R., (1986) Beyond situational leadership—Congruent and transforming models for leadership training. *European Management Journal*, 4, No.1. Spring.

Nicholls, J. R., (1988) The transforming autocrat. *Management Today*, March.

Nicholls, J. R. and Martin, P. (1987) *Creating a Committed Workforce*. London, IPM and McGraw-Hill.

Schein, E. (ed.) (1985) *Organisational Culture and Leadership*. San Francisco, Ca., Jossey-Bass.

Selznick, P. (1957) *Leadership in Administration*. New York, Harper & Row.

Tichy, N and Devanna, M. A. (1986) *The Transformational Leader*. New York, Wiley.

Vaill, P. (1987) The purpose of high performing organisations. *Organizational Dynamics*, Autumn. Phrase attributed to Norton Long.

7

LEADERSHIP-FOCUSED MANAGEMENT DEVELOPMENT: ARE TODAY'S PRACTICES MEETING TOMORROW'S NEEDS?

Karen E. Soderberg

Associate Director, Harbridge Consulting Group Ltd, London, UK

Today, as we study the needs of middle managers and the initiatives being taken to train and develop them to assume leadership roles, we find ourselves challenging the traditional beliefs about and approaches to management development as well as past prescriptions:

- Are the behaviors and characteristics traditionally associated with successful managers distinct from those of successful leaders?
- Can middle managers in today's new, delayered organizations be effective leaders as they are called upon to demonstrate skills not previously expected of them?
- Are new approaches to management development needed to bridge critical behavioral and skills development gaps in order to prepare middle managers for organizational leadership?

This article presents Harbridge House's point of view about manager effectiveness and management development. Our observations and hypotheses are based on client work as well as our own data gathering and proprietary

International Review of Strategic Management, volume 4.
Edited by D. E. Hussey. Published 1993 by John Wiley & Sons Ltd

research performed in support of this work. All of these efforts point to the need for middle managers to exercise new leadership behaviors and skills that go beyond conventional business management practices, behaviors that require substantive knowledge and understanding of the business traditionally expected only from senior managers. They also point to the critical need for new approaches to management development that better prepare middle managers for their new role. For these reasons, we believe that companies need to reassess their thinking about the skills and capabilities their managers need in order to be successful in the new organization.

THE MANAGER'S NEW REALITY

Why now? Why revisit tried and tested theories about managers and approaches to management development? The reality is that the role of all managers, and particularly middle managers, is changing. Yet organizational support to develop middle managers and ensure their success—and the success of their organizations—has been lagging.

In recent years intense competition has forced most companies to change, to engage in major restructuring efforts that eliminate jobs and positions and significantly reduce management ranks. The organizational ideal that has emerged has been simultaneously positive and painful, generating benefits in the form of greater customer responsiveness, improved quality, and enhanced cost effectiveness, but eliminating tens of thousands of jobs and requiring millions of individuals to let go of 'business as usual' practices and embrace new ways of doing business.

The movement toward corporate delayering has revised the definition and flow of organizational responsibility and changed the nature of the tools that managers need to employ in order to succeed. In the past, organizations achieved goals and results through elaborate planning and control mechanisms. In the 1970s and 1980s, strategic planning was heralded as the key to success. Senior executives held sole responsibility for formulating and articulating the corporate vision, setting strategic direction, and executing long-term plans. Today, however, the senior executive role has shifted dramatically to creating a vision that will take an organization to a future desired state and getting the organization committed to and lined up behind an agenda for bringing about that change.

The role of the middle manager has also changed as middle managers, such as work unit managers, have become increasingly responsible for translating the corporate vision into concrete operational terms—that is, specific direction, goals, and priorities—for their units. However, with many of the old but comfortable 'command and control' processes being set aside, middle managers face a great deal of uncertainty. The abandonment of these traditional management tools and the sudden widening of their scope of responsibilities in the new slenderized, self-managed organization have created an enormous behavioral and skills gap to be filled. Properly retooling these managers so they can step up to their new role poses a bold challenge to management developers.

MANAGEMENT AND LEADERSHIP: HOW ARE THEY DIFFERENT?

A major shift in thinking about the roles of management and leadership has taken place over the last 30 years, making many of the traditional conceptual distinctions between management and leadership no longer valid.

Abraham Zaleznik, a prominent writer and pioneer in exploring management/leadership issues, argued in the late 1960s and throughout the 1970s that fundamental differences exist between the two. 'Where managers act to limit choices, leaders develop fresh approaches to long-standing problems and open issues to new options' (Zaleznik, 1977, p. 129). Zaleznik believed that leaders had very different attitudes and motivations that influenced how they worked and related to others. He saw the role of the leader as forward looking, focusing on 'what' events mean to the organization rather than 'how' events get done (p. 131).

The more recent work of John P. Kotter has codified the thinking of many writers since then. Kotter distinguished management from leadership in terms of capacity for coping. He defined management as 'coping with [the] complexity' of large organizations by bringing order and consistency to key business processes, and leadership as 'coping with change' by recognizing and understanding its driving forces (Kotter, 1990a, p. 104). Working within these definitions, Kotter assigned to management responsibility for 'planning and budgeting,' 'organizing and staffing,' and 'controlling and problem solving'—the traditional management activities; 'setting a direction,' 'aligning people,' and 'motivating and inspiring' (Kotter, 1990b, pp. 4–5), were the equivalent leadership activities. In Kotter's interpretation, management falls short of anticipating and leading, activities considered to be the responsibility of senior management.

David A. Nadler and Michael L. Tushman (1990), extended the discussion of leadership by introducing the concept of the 'charismatic' leader, someone who is capable of articulating a credible, compelling future state ('envisioning'); generating personal support and empathy ('enabling'); and expressing personal excitement and confidence ('energizing') to lead an organization during times of strategic organizational change (Nadler and Tushman, 1980, p. 82). They believed that what is needed is an 'instrumental leader,' someone simultaneously capable of managing (structuring, controlling, and rewarding) and introducing change. They cautioned, however, that charismatic leadership has some limitations and may result in the 'disenfranchisement' of middle and lower levels of management and the inability of the leader to deal with all of the issues involved in a transformational change (Nadler and Tushman, 1990, p. 84).

Charles C. Manz and Henry P. Sims, Jr, writing in 1991, questioned the appropriateness of the image of the charismatic or heroic leader. 'In many modern situations,' they observed, 'the most appropriate leader is one who can lead others to lead themselves. We call this powerful new kind of leadership "SuperLeadership" ... a leader's strength [is in the] ability to maximize the contributions of others through recognition of their right to guide their own destiny, rather than the leader's ability to bend the will of others to his or her own' (Manz and Sims, 1991, pp. 18–19). With this view, Manz and Sims shifted the leadership focus to others, 'followers' as they called them, to become self-leaders, causing the distinctions between managers and leaders to fade further.

Leadership, as described by these prominent thinkers/writers, is not dependent on hierarchical relationships but instead demands special people with distinct skills and qualities. How does an organization develop such individuals?

Although writing at a time when both the hierarchy and the bureaucracy of the corporate world tended to be rigid, Zaleznik (1977) demonstrated considerable insights about leadership-focused management development. Insisting that there is an inherent conflict in the parallel development of managers and leaders, Zaleznik asserted: 'What it takes to ensure a supply of people who will assume practical responsibility may inhibit the development of great leaders. On the other hand, the presence of great leaders may undermine the development of managers who typically become very anxious in the relative disorder that leaders seem to generate. It is easy enough to dismiss the dilemma of training managers, though we may need new leaders or leaders at the expense of managers, by saying that the need is for people who can be both (Zaleznik, 1977, p. 127).

Although Kotter viewed management and leadership as complementary, he suggested that the development of management skills compromises the development of leadership capabilities. The real need, he explained, is to enhance the management development process so that a strong cadre of organizational leaders can be built. To do this, the organization must offer its neophyte managers opportunities for risk-taking and broaden their experience and knowledge base.

Nadler and Tushman (1990), offered a different approach for developing and institutionalizing leadership throughout an organization, one that begins with defining critical managerial competencies. Institutionalizing leadership would leverage the skills of the organization's senior management teams and empower the individuals in those teams to empower themselves; develop each of their members; alter their respective compositions; and, as teams, become 'learning systems' (Nadler and Tushman, 1990, p. 90). This top-down rollout approach for systematically extending leadership capability down through an organization is highly dependent on the ability of senior managers to learn quickly and to pass their learnings on to others.

Under the concepts set forth by Manz and Sims (1991), everyone is a self-leader and all individuals are responsible for building the necessary work skills that will allow them to contribute to the success of the organization. As self-leadership becomes the task of all managers, the behaviors of middle managers can be expected to mirror those of their superiors, at least with respect to role and responsibility for setting direction.

In the final analysis, it does not matter whether middle managers are called managers, leaders, leader-managers, or whatever. What is important is that they recognize that in order to carry out their new and expanded responsibilities, they must master new skills that will make them effective leaders. Transitioning them from managers to leaders will require defining their current skills and capabilities, their future needs and those of the organization, and any gaps that exist between these two states. It will also require adapting both the content of most current management development programs and the process and approach for helping managers build and exercise new competencies.

A MODEL OF EFFECTIVE LEADERSHIP

Several frameworks have been put forth for thinking about the critical elements of management and approaches to management development. Harbridge House used the most practical litmus test to develop our own model, applying it directly to client situations and asking, 'What works?'

As management development practitioners, our interest in creating a model was spurred by changes we were beginning to see in the business environment as well as by work we were doing with managers of several Fortune 1000 clients to improve managers' leadership of change. It also came from our desire for a tool that would help us assist managers in getting their jobs done—that is, leading and managing change.

In developing a model, we conducted research to identify and validate behavioral patterns or practices that we believed determined manager effectiveness. As part of this effort, we interviewed managers in order to understand what they had actually done to become successful innovators or leaders of change—in other words, to find out what worked and what didn't work. We then created a list of practices that reflected the behaviors of these managers and surveyed over 1000 of their peers and/or reports to get their perspectives on the extent to which the managers engaged in the critical behaviors. When we grouped these practices into what we defined as the three major components of effective leadership—Vision, Commitment, and Management—and performed a statistical analysis of the data collected (806 responses), we found that 44 of the practices had a significant relationship to leadership.

In our model, which we call the Effective Organizational Leadership (EOL) model,[1] we have defined the three components of leadership as follows:

- Vision—A clear view of a desirable future state that is realistic, motivating, and meaningful, so that people clearly understand where an organization is going and what they must do to move it there.
- Commitment—The 'buy-in,' support, and agreement of people whose efforts or investments are essential to making the vision a reality.
- Management—The ability of an individual to influence, guide, and discipline others' performance; to develop challenging new ways of doing business; and to accept personal responsibility for bringing about change.

The EOL model makes no explicit distinctions between leaders and managers. Rather, it is predicated upon an equation where effective leadership requires a relative balance among these three components and the behaviors they represent. Balance among the components ensures that efforts to change direction remain grounded in reality, that key players are on board, and that results are achieved in a disciplined and focused manner. Thus, Management prevents Vision from becoming mystical and obscure and Commitment from becoming a sort of organizational 'love-in;' Vision and Commitment keep Management moving in the right direction and ensure that the shared commitment to the larger cause is not lost or compromised when the pressures of executing day-to-day work decisions encroach upon the individuals involved.[2]

Although our first use of the EOL model was tied into our work in the area of innovation, we have since found it to be a useful tool for bringing about any number of organizational changes. We use the model in our management training and development activities as a vehicle for communicating and reinforcing some general leadership themes, and for assessing an individual's leadership strengths and weaknesses. When applied within the context of a particular organization, the model can show what skills or behaviors a manager must demonstrate in order to be successful in bringing about change or, in innovation terms, 'the process of developing better things to do or better ways to do existing things.'

Over time, effective managers need to exhibit all of the behaviors represented by the model; and, at different points in an individual's career, the emphasis or balance needs to shift to bring about particular changes. But bringing about a fundamental shift in the way managers need to think and act in their new role is not easy.

For example, in a recent client experience, Harbridge House worked with a group of newly promoted managers in a company that was undergoing a significant leadership change. Our objective was to help these managers understand their new role as part of the larger organizational context, broaden their focus to include process issues as well as outcomes, and change their behaviors accordingly. However, after working with them for several months, we observed that:

- They were not fully embracing new business initiatives such as total quality management, process improvement, and change management; rather, they were adopting these as themes—'flavor of the week'—for efforts they were already leading.
- Many of the managers saw their job as one of managing a 'steady state' business and their role as that of a block, buffer, protector, and decision enforcer rather than a decision-making strategist.

These managers had failed to understand the implications of current business realities and were applying almost programmatic thinking to new situations, which was perpetuating their current management behaviors and limiting their effectiveness. This kind of thinking was causing them to fall back on traditional roles, even when these roles were inappropriate for meeting new challenges. As this example attests, middle managers in today's organizations are having great difficulty in transitioning to the leadership role expected of them.

IDENTIFYING GAPS IN LEADERSHIP BEHAVIORS

In 1990, as part of our continuing efforts to validate our EOL model and practices and develop the design for a program on leadership, Harbridge House conducted a series of focus groups with eight US and European Fortune 100 companies.[3] While each company noted issues or challenges specific to its line of business, numerous similarities appeared in the responses. For example:

- Every group identified change as an issue having a tremendous impact on an individual's ability to perform effectively and agreed that the amount and rate of change were increasing at levels never before experienced. Managers concluded that change was becoming a way of organizational life, but admitted finding it difficult to get others to accept this.
- Several groups pointed to their organization's focus on short-term performance and the speed at which some decisions were now being made. Many managers felt that they didn't always have the information they needed to make decisions and that demands for short-term results were conflicting with broader, longer term strategic goals.
- Most of the managers were in organizations that had experienced a recent downsizing or streamlining that was requiring fewer people to do more work. They claimed that they were finding it harder to motivate and reward individuals, some of whom were now performing twice as much work and carrying out a variety of tasks that they were not necessarily qualified to do.

- Managers noted that their organizations were looking to differentiate themselves through a more focused approach to identifying customer needs and providing better customer service. As a result, they said they were needing to identify opportunities to improve customer relationships and share knowledge and perspectives.
- Cross-functional collaboration was identified as a crucial measure of organizational and individual effectiveness. Managers stated that they were now working more across functional lines with individuals with whom they traditionally had very little contact and whose goals, priorities, and operations were usually quite different from their own.

These managers were clearly finding it difficult to break out of their current patterns of behavior; further, many of them felt they did not have the skills they needed to do their job well. Having been groomed for a specific role with a limited scope of responsibility and a fairly narrow span of control, they were not prepared to assume leadership responsibility for bringing about change in the workplace.

More recently, Harbridge House has done extensive data gathering on the practices that support our leadership model. In our analysis of a subset of the database we have built, we have found that two of the Vision practices broadly associated with the leadership role of setting direction—providing others with a clear picture of where the organization is going and generating a sense of purpose or mission to guide others' activities—have been ranked lowest among middle managers (see Figure 7.1).

There has seldom been an equal balance in the use of all of the practices among the managers we have surveyed and profiled. Typically, we have found that most managers are relatively weak in the Vision practices and disproportionately strong in some of the Management practices. Our one-on-one coaching sessions with middle managers generally reveal that most middle managers do not have a clearly defined vision for the organization in which they work, a situation that presents problems for their peers and reports. When asked to comment on their manager's leadership practices, peers and reports often note that managers spend a lot of time down in the trenches, fighting fires, and helping them deal with their problems. Reports also comment that managers spend too much time trying to control what is going on, often with little success and therefore giving too little time to their own job responsibilities; lack specific job knowledge; and rarely communicate anything substantial about what is going on in the many meetings they attend. Peers see managers as being detached from the business world and the community at large, though they almost always manage to make the numbers. Thus, the prototypical and still dominant type of manager is the traditional 'command and control' manager.

This stagnant, narrow manager profile would not be so unsettling if there were great stability in the business environment and if organizations themselves

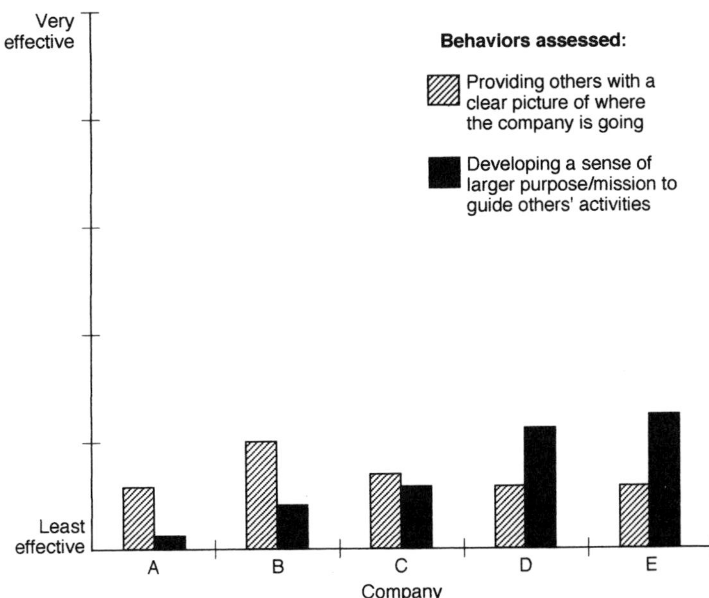

Figure 7.1 Effectiveness of management behaviors. The data examined were drawn from a subset of five companies representing a cross-section of industries (manufacturing, high technology, pharmaceuticals, insurance, and financial services) and ranging in size from 3000 to 45 000 employees. The data for each company were collected through a management survey, as part of a management development training program or an extensive needs assessment

represented constant forces. However, the reality of being leadership focused requires managers to be able to identify and interpret current business realities, articulate a direction for where their work unit needs to be, and step up to the trade-offs that must be made. Managers need to acquire a clear understanding of substantive issues such as economic leverage, sources of competitive advantage, and strategic thinking that will allow them to make informed decisions, address problems, and lead others.

Our belief that a content-rich business understanding is critical to the process of leadership is not new. Zaleznik recognized that if a manager is to succeed as a leader, 'he must be able to contribute to the substantive thinking necessary to move a business beyond problems into opportunities (Zaleznik, 1989, p. 214), defusing once and for all the 'managerial mystique' that managers, in their limited roles, do not have or necessarily require these kind of ambitions in order to fulfil their responsibilities.

If all we needed to do was focus on developing the vision skills perceived to be missing in a manager's profile, the solution would be simple. Yet there is another way to interpret the results. Our survey questionnaires tap normative perceptions—what ought to be—and in effect ask people to speculate about unreal states. Manager behaviors, however, reflect real choices made each day about what individuals see as important for getting the job done. In fact, when comparing survey participants' self-assessments against those of their reports and peers, we find that managers often identify for themselves similar patterns of strengths and weaknesses, suggesting that they are aware of their deficiencies.

In a survey conducted for a diversified transportation and natural resources organization to determine what managers perceived as the gap between the organization's current and desired leadership profile, we collected data from a representative sample of 500 managers from six operating companies. Managers in all six companies indicated that they wanted to see greater Commitment and less Management in the organization. To respond to these managers and close the leadership gap, the organization needed to support the development of new Commitment-building skills and the change to a less Management-dominant behavior. Both developmental approaches needed to be implemented in order to achieve a more desirable balance.

In summary, our studies show that most middle managers do not exhibit a strong and balanced set of leadership-focused behaviors. Management development efforts that build skills or behaviors in isolation of the greater business context—a sort of Skinnerian box-like approach—perpetuate patterns of imbalance. As a result, managers continue to operate in their traditional roles rather than lead—and may even be discouraged from leading—while responsibility for making decisions and effecting change rests with their superiors. Organizations need to develop their managers' understanding of the business and beliefs about their roles. They also need to provide them with opportunities to rehearse new behaviors. Models of leadership that accomplish this take external and organizational realities into consideration.

DEVELOPING MANAGEMENT FOR NEW ROLES

In the throes of rapid change and absent well-tested ways for accomplishing a wholesale upgrading of their managers' capabilities, many companies are experimenting with a variety of development approaches. Some are using traditional training methods, even though they consider them to be too time-consuming and not always effective for today's needs. Others are adapting standard training and development methods to satisfy a different set of organizational requirements. Still others are forging new territory, applying new approaches to help their managers acquire the requisite knowledge and skills.

Based on our own efforts to help middle managers change their behaviors and become more leadership focused, we believe that organizations must provide better forums for integrating their various development initiatives in a meaningful way. With greater integration, middle managers will develop the requisite focus, one that reflects a substantive grasp of the business.

One highly successful approach for jump-starting the change process is to work with 'live' pilot teams, helping these groups work through real-time projects and issues while reinforcing a growing understanding, appreciation, and practical application of their new role and responsibilities.

This approach echoes concepts presented by Peter Senge in his 1990 articulation of the 'learning organization' (Senge, 1990, p. 8). Senge argued that the capacity for corporate learning through the conscious development and application of its leadership talent must be pursued throughout the organization. He ascribed to the leader three roles: 'teacher, designer, and steward' (p. 10). He explained that the teacher guides the organization's perception of and reaction to the external realities; the designer constructs systems and processes that foster organizational learning; and the steward reinforces and promotes the values of the organization and its employees. The ideal organization would create management-team 'practice fields' (p. 21), or real-life settings, in which managers would practice constructing, shaping, and expanding their shared capabilities as a way of effectively adopting all three roles.

The practice field notion is an interesting one for management development practitioners because, while it reflects approaches that have been used for years (pilot testing of training programs, individual skill building, in-class role modeling, and on-the-job action planning), it also poses new possibilities for designing almost holistic approaches to management development that ensure that managers:

- Recognize and accept that the definition of leadership includes implementing change and accepting responsibility for doing so.
- Have a clear understanding of both the positive and the negative consequences of their new role.
- Have a solid understanding of current business realities and areas where the organization needs to improve.

In some of our recent work, we have helped clients develop critical masses of managers through programs designed to build new skills, and by conducting one-on-one coaching/counseling sessions to help them individually identify ways to improve their leadership behaviors and develop plans for increasing their effectiveness back on the job.

In one engagement, a large consumer packaged goods company believed that a radical restructuring of its entire field sales and marketing organization was needed in order to achieve some major productivity improvements. We used a training program approach to help field sales people develop a solid grasp of the business and prepare themselves to lead the way and bring out the best in others in order to achieve the goals inherent in the company's new business direction. Using a 'practice field' approach and simulating the managers' true work environment, we provided individuals with a means for developing the critical skills needed. This effort created tremendous pressures for the organization's managers to become part of the change process and to learn the new techniques and skills being developed by field personnel in order to lead their own teams to achieve the desired results.

This bottom-up approach has had an upward impact. The organization has mapped out a strategy to become more customer driven by working in partnership with its customers and by drawing on the knowledge, skills, and resources of all team members. To help implement these changes, a core skills training program was designed to integrate team development concepts with company-specific case studies and business dynamics exercises.

Another approach to individual development took into account state-of-the art technologies and processes to develop managers' coaching effectiveness. A large financial services firm had radically restructured, downsized, and moved its major 'backroom' function to a new location. It staffed this function with a largely new workforce that was technically savvy but not sufficiently knowledgeable about the business itself.

The new structure was designed around self-directed work teams and a group of middle managers, selected for their functional expertise, was chosen to coach the teams. Although the physical relocation process was an unequivocal success, the coaches had difficulties establishing a culture that would facilitate rapid, decentralized decision making and empowerment. We worked with these middle managers to put in place a coaching model framework that helped them achieve the transition to the new organizational vision. Coaches received one-on-one counseling and personal feedback to reinforce the positive behaviors they would need to develop in others. Their individual and team practice fields provided opportunities for them to rehearse their new role. With continued practice, expectations are that the behaviors remnant of the old hierarchy will gradually be replaced with leadership-focused management.

SUMMARY

The challenge of adapting to the new realities of lean, delayered, customer-responsive organizations will be with us for many years. The success or failure of every organization will ride on the creativity and insights with which managers at all levels jointly address this opportunity. Here we have made an attempt to add one more chapter to the continuing discussion of leadership.

ACKNOWLEDGMENTS

The concepts and findings we report here are the product of work of the Organizational Change Practice of Harbridge House, Inc. In addition to the lead author of the chapter, the following individuals, in particular, have been largely responsible for the development of these ideas, for conducting and summarizing the studies described here, and for numerous other client engagements that contributed to this effort: Janet Bailey, Ken Boughrum, Deborah Cornwall, Paul Croke, Jack Cronin, John Dinkelspiel, Marshall Goldstein, Paul McKinnon, Matt Nash, Sara Mannle, Maura Shannon, and Beth Webster. Deanna Brown drafted a first review of the literature on leadership; Marcia Gallichio conducted a further search of the literature used for the completion of this chapter. David Morton and Lorraine Goldstein provided writing and editing assistance. The statistical analysis was performed by Robert E. Taylor and Alec S. Fernandez of Robert Taylor Associates, Chapel Hill, North Carolina.

NOTES

1 The Harbridge House Effective Organizational Leadership (EOL) model was first described to this readership by Janet Bailey and John Dinkelspiel in *International Review of Strategic Management*, 2, No. 1 (1991). The foundation and framework of this model were developed by Paul McKinnon, PhD. The practices that embody the three components of the model were derived from a set of behavioral descriptions (i.e. development skills) researched and defined by Harbridge House.

2 Given the applicability of the EOL model to all layers of management, we have changed the name of the Management component to Execution in order to avoid confusing the set of management behaviors or practices with individuals who hold management positions.

3 The participating companies represented a range of industries (agriculture and specialty chemicals, banking and financial services, insurance, pharmaceutical, food and tobacco, media and entertainment). The primary data collection methodology was face-to-face interviews in which a standardized interview guide was used.

REFERENCES

Kotter, J. P. (1990a) What leaders really do. *Harvard Business Review*, May–June.

Kotter, J. P. (1990b) *A Force for Change*. New York, The Free Press.

Manz, C. C. and Sims, H. P. Jnr (1991) SuperLeadership: Beyond the myth of heroic leadership. *Organizational Dynamics*, Spring.

Nadler, D. and Tushman, M. (1990) Beyond the charismatic leader: Leadership and organizational change. *California Management Review*, Winter.

Senge, P. M. (1990) The leader's new work: Building learning organizations. *Sloan Management Review*, Fall.

Zaleznik, A. (1977) Managers and leaders: Are they different? *Harvard Business Review*, May–June. (Reprinted March–April, 1992).

Zaleznik, A. (1989) *The Managerial Mystique*. New York, Harper & Row.

8

LEADERSHIP AS A FORM OF CULTURE: ITS PRESENT AND FUTURE STATES IN JAPAN*

Akira Ichikawa

Professor, Fuji Junior College
Chief, Fuji Junior College Management Research Institute
Senior Managing Director, Japan Strategic Management Society

THE NATURE AND FUNCTION OF LEADERSHIP

Leadership Driving People

Leadership can be understood either as the power to drive people, or as influence over people. Not only is leadership necessary for those who have subordinates and are in formal positions to guide them, but it also has a critical meaning for individuals to enable them to cope within their groups.

For example, a president of a firm, a head of a department, or a coach of an athletic club demonstrates his or her leadership to the people in his or her organization. It is a matter of course for the leader to drive people. Needless to say, leaders in these kinds of organizations are given formal authority with which they are expected to demonstrate leadership within their organizations.

However, in some cases it is possible or desirable to have situations in which a person who does not possess a formal authority drives people through influence.

* Translated from Japanese by Professor Gen-Ichi Nakamura and Dr Dae-Ryong Choi. See Editor's Note at end of chapter.

International Review of Strategic Management, volume 4.
Edited by D. E. Hussey.

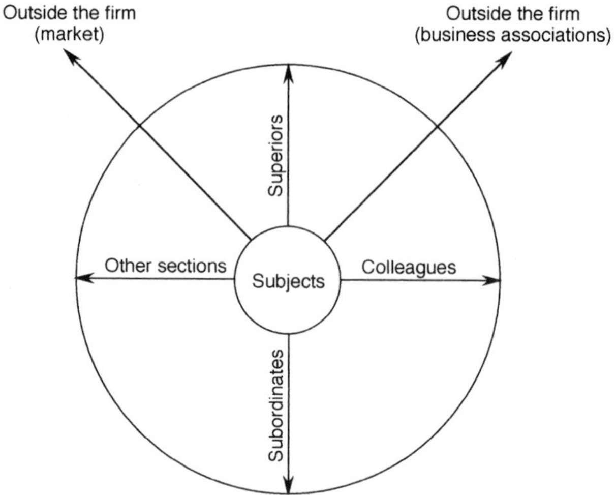

Figure 8.1 Omnidirectional leadership (middle managers of firms)

A President or a Prime Minister of a country has formal power in his or her own country, but is supposed to have mutually equal power with Presidents or Prime Ministers of other countries. The same can be said of a CEO of a business firm. However, a degree of difference in the power to drive through influencing people clearly exists among those who do not possess formal power. As a simple example, varying degrees in the power to influence people exist among colleagues or friends.

These differences are brought about by factors other than formal authority. Thus it is possible for subordinates to lead superiors if the subordinates learn and demonstrate the means to lead other people. It can also be possible for a business person to lead customers, or other people with whom he or she has business associations (Figure 8.1).

Although the word 'leader' may not be appropriate in the above cases, the author believes that it is genuine leadership. It is critical for formal superiors to master and demonstrate this genuine leadership if they want to fulfill their own roles and improve the performance of their organizations.

Importance of Respect to People's Willingness

We should now like to give some consideration to the power of driving and compelling people. In general, the most definite and strongest power is a formally approved authority. Here, the relationship between a position where the power is held and a scope where the power extends is made explicitly. Furthermore, some punishment (e.g. demotion in the case of business firms) may

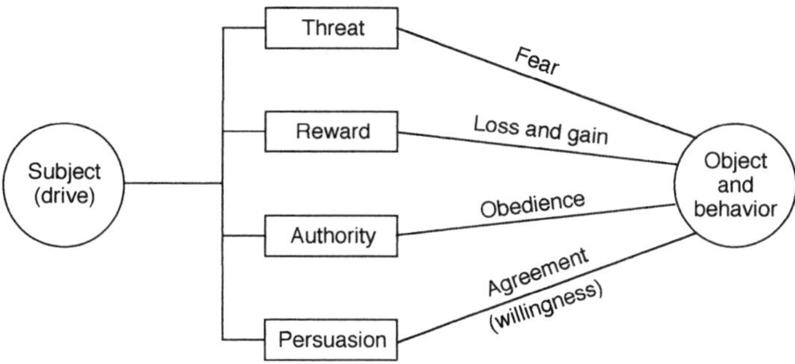

Figure 8.2 Means to drive people

be imposed on a person who does not obey the order of his or her formal superior.

Even though authority bestows the power to drive subordinates, it is doubtful whether such authority comprises genuine leadership. Leadership should be considered as a process for driving people through influencing them in a specific but broad sense, not as a driving power which aims at a small part of a group. Also, when leadership is applied for the improvement of the organization's performance and on the leader's own assessment, relying on formal power or position to drive subordinates through compulsion does not necessarily produce desirable consequences in the long run.

In other words, it is necessary to consider leadership as an instrument, means, or process for persuading people to comply willingly (Figure 8.2). How should we persuade people to comply willingly without threatening or materially rewarding them? One of the objectives in studying leadership is to answer this question.

There are various factors in genuine leadership that drive people, besides formal power, threats, or material rewards. First, consider examples of acknowledged great leaders' behavior or that of people who do not possess any authority to drive others through compulsion. We can find a rational proof of the reasons why they drive people, and at the same time, a certain relationship between the condition of groups and the style of leaders.

This leads us to believe that leadership is a product of an epoch and a form of culture. When leadership is matched with its environment, it will prove significantly effective. In other words, it can be said that leadership is a form of a culture.

Rational and Cultural Aspects of Leadership

It can generally be said that a culture is a common value shared by a group of people, or a type of thought and behavior based on common values even though the existence of a culture can also be applied to an individual. There is a culture in a tribe or country. Furthermore, there may be one culture in a political world, and another culture in an economic world. Also, a particular culture can be seen in every industry or corporation.

Of course, because there are common characteristics in people or organizations over generations, or tribes, there are common conditions or factors with which certain aspects of leadership hold good in any country or field. However, in reality, different types of leadership or leaders can be seen in different countries, fields, or generations. This is the reason why we should understand that leadership is significantly related to a culture.

Therefore, in order to take people in a desired direction, and influence them so that they willingly go in that direction, it will be necessary to consider carefully the following two aspects.

The first is a rational aspect of leadership which corresponds to the elements that people or organizations hold in common, and appeals to the nature of people or the fundamental characteristics of organizations. Of course, there is no universal standard rational aspect because the people, organizations, or situations involved are extremely complicated.

The second is a cultural aspect which corresponds to particular characteristics of individuals, tribes, or groups. At first glance, a cultural aspect seems irrational. However, if it is matched with the values, styles, or rules of a group, persuading the people in the group will be easy. Also, It can be said that the cultural aspect is often appropriate to the objective of the group.

Before discussing the main issue of this article, which is the examination of this cultural aspect of leadership, we shall in the next section briefly discuss a rational aspect of leadership.

EFFECTIVE LEADERSHIP

Essential Attributes in Demonstrating Rational Leadership

What are the essential attributes needed to drive individuals or groups? The nature of the attributes is the same for individuals or groups even though we shall here focus on the attributes needed to drive groups. The essential attributes are the following:

(1) Objectives or specific goals of a group.
(2) External environments of a group.
(3) Characteristics of a group.

An organization (or individuals or groups in an organization) can be naturally driven by an understanding of the above three attributes, and through proposals and guidance of the organization (that is, transmitting information) which match them. This will be discussed more specifically below.

If information which matches the objective of an organization, such as a business firm, is transmitted throughout the organization, it will be easier to persuade individuals or groups to follow it. There are various objectives for business firms. Some aims are based on corporate philosophy; there are also fundamentally common objectives such as improvement of profit, survival and expansion, response to customers' requests, or contribution to society. In any case, individuals or groups in an organization will be persuaded and driven if a leader proposes, guides, or requests a certain response from them after he or she has made it clear that this response is needed to achieve their objectives, or is related to the achievement of specific goals.

It is also important to understand and assess the external environments of an organization. Some say that external environments generate the behavior of organizations. In order to drive the people within an organization, it is necessary to explain their external environments to them, to make them realize what behavior is necessary, and sometimes even to build internal environments for guiding the organization. If necessary, leaders should suggest, or sometimes guide, the way to apply a certain behavior.

For example, when a firm faces a certain difficulty, a leader should make subordinates understand the meaning and characteristics of the problem and make them come up with appropriate behavior to deal with it. In some cases it will be enough to provide suggestions, in others it will be desirable to impose strong guidance or command. This depends on the degrees of importance and urgency of the difficulty or problem and the situations of the individuals or groups that the leader intends to drive.

It is also important to understand the characteristics of a group in a broad sense. That is both to understand and to match the level of experience, knowledge or characters of individuals or groups, and to understand and relate to the external environment.

If people are inexperienced, it may be necessary to provide some guidance, but if they are experienced it may be inadvisable to give fully detailed guidance. This also depends on the personal character or nature of each individual. Some people perform best when they have autonomy, but on the other hand, others do better when they are carefully guided. This involves the issue of a culture.

We also have to take into consideration the fact that many characteristics of a group depend on personal relationships. Is it a relationship between a person and his or her subordinate in an organization? Is it a relationship between a person and his or her colleague in an organization? Is it a relationship between a person and his or her customer? Is it a relationship between a person and his or her business partner? Every characteristic of a group will change depending on a specific human relationship or power relationship. Therefore, it will be necessary to drive people in ways which an understanding of those relationships shows to be appropriate.

Leadership Created by Personality

A rational leader is someone who can transmit essential information throughout a group by relating it clearly to the group's objectives, environments and characteristics.

In this context, it is important to know how subordinates perceive their leader. If the above mentioned essential information is perceived as unimportant by the subordinates, it will be impossible to drive them and make them behave willingly.

In order to make subordinates understand and to convince them to follow their leader's intention, it is necessary that the leader should be trusted by subordinates and receive their goodwill either as an individual, or as an authority. Even though the information itself and the method of transmitting it are the same in every case, the information will be perceived differently by individual subordinates, depending on the person who transmits it. It is a fact of life that human beings cannot avoid having such differences of perception to some degree.

After all, this perception is created by an individual's personality or background. Here, it is important to note that we have to realize and distinguish between the power we possess naturally and the power of authority we are given.

Some leaders may confuse their formal power to drive subordinates with the natural power they personally possess. If one can motivate people and make them compliant without exerting any authority, it should be considered as genuine leadership. (Of course, this does not mean that a person in a position of authority should not take advantage of it. However, a senior person should not rely too heavily on the authority he or she possesses.

This kind of leadership, generated by personality, contains more facets than a purely rational aspect of leadership, such as, for example, suitability, trust, and attractiveness. It may come primarily from inherent personal characteristics. However, it is possible in some degree to acquire it by learning techniques of rational persuasion, behaving with honesty and sincerity, and building up a track record of one's own achievements. Here the importance lies in a natural human desire to trust and respect others.

For instance, although it may not be an entirely appropriate example, if a man does not trust and love his dog, the dog does not love the man at all. The same is true of relationships between people.

LEADERSHIP AND CULTURE IN JAPAN

Characteristics of Japanese Culture and Requisites of Japanese Leaders

Some of the characteristics of leaders discussed in the previous section cannot be rationalized, because they might be related to individual characters and styles. However, as a whole, most of them are the common principles of leadership which hold good to some extent in all societies and groups.

On the other hand, there are particular leaders or styles of effective leadership which are suitable only to a specific community, society, or organization. In other words, different situations for leaders can be found by country or by activity, such as politics, economics, education, and sports. Different leaders can be found in different groups, with very varying requirements.

This, in a sense, can be considered as an aspect of the external environment discussed previously. However, it will be much easier to understand if the difference of leadership is related to culture. After all, the leader of any organization is bred, selected, and functions only when he or she possesses both the common characteristics of a leader and the conditions desired by that organization's culture.

We will now discuss the relationship between cultures and leaders mainly by taking cases in Japan and making comparisons between Japan and the Western world.

Essential Characteristics of Japanese Leaders Based on Japanese Culture

Who are the leaders of Japan? There are various views on this. First, we will take the political world. Formally, a political leader is a Prime Minister. In addition, those who have held the position before and those who are aspiring to the position are considered to be the leaders, or the top people, in the political world.

Consider the following case. In Japan, it is customary for journalists to interview acknowledged politicians by surrounding them and walking along with them before and after conferences at the Diet or a Cabinet council. We can see from this that most of the politicians are hidden by the group of journalists. That is because the height of politicians tends to be shorter than that of journalists. This is not only because of the generation gap (although young people have become taller recently); there is another reason for this gap in the height between leaders and journalists, which is that the height of political leaders tends to be short as a whole. For example, look at the Prime Ministers who have been supreme leaders in the political world: the present Prime Minister Miyazawa and ex-Prime Ministers Kaifu, Uno, or Takeshita are all of them short. Furthermore, the leaders of the Takeshita faction (the leading political faction in Japan), including Mr Kanamaru, are all shorter than the average height for their generation. The only recent exception might be Mr Nakasone. We can see the gap in height between the political leaders of Japan and the leaders of the Western countries, such as ex-President Bush of the USA and Chancellor Khol of Germany, at every summit conference.

Looking at this gap, many Japanese may wish they had a taller Prime Minister, but things are not as easy as that, because this has roots deep into their culture.

It is not by chance but an inevitability because of Japanese culture, especially culture in the political world, that many Japanese Prime Ministers or other leaders are short.

The same applies even in the Japanese business world. It is not too much to say that there is a key to understanding the relationship between Japanese culture and the conditions of Japanese leaders or styles of Japanese leadership.

Physical Appearance of Japanese Leaders

The height of many leaders in the Japanese political and business world is short. This means that the physical appearance of not being tall is a major weighting factor in the nomination of leaders, or in Japanese selection criteria. Of course, this condition is not explicitly stated but, laying aside whether or not the Japanese are conscious of it, it is an undeniable fact.

More strictly speaking, a successor as a leader in Japan should not exceed a predecessor in terms of physical appearance. In other words, a Japanese leader does not select as his or her successor a subordinate who physically looks down at the leader. Although 'stout and short' is one of the images of leaders which the Japanese have, most leaders only become fat after achieving leadership. People who want to be leaders must not be fat before they become leaders. It is very rare for Japanese leaders (even though they themselves are physically stout) to select as their successors people who look bigger than them. This is not just a joke. It is a symbolic appearance of the Japanese culture.

Comparisons between Predecessors and Successors of Japanese Leaders

Based on the actual situations mentioned above, the conditions for becoming leaders and the styles of leadership in Japan can be considered as the following.

First, the essential condition is that people becoming leaders should not outdo their predecessors in either appearance or achievement. Successors should follow their predecessors' direction even after becoming leaders, and they should 'save the predecessors' faces,' and not despise them.

Current leaders should never have reason to suspect that their successors will ignore them and just do as they want after taking their place. Otherwise, the prospective successors will lose the opportunity of becoming the next leaders. A candidate who wishes to become a future leader should, for example, share the same interests as, and pledge loyalty to, the present leader as well as the leader's family. In addition, even if the candidate considers himself or herself to have greater ability than the current leader, such ability must be concealed.

The most comfortable choice of a successor, for a leader, is to select a member of his or her own family. That is heredity. Here, physical appearance is the second criterion. If you see a tall leader, it will be safe to assume that he or she comes from his or her predecessor's family.

We can find the main criterion for the selection of leaders in Japan by asking the following questions. What finally happened to the person who was listed as a candidate to be the new president in a company (other than a person from the same family as the current president)? Who was eventually elected as the president from among many candidates? What was the reason for the discord between a very important CEO and a president?

Selection Processes of Leaders in Japan

The reason why a successor should not surpass a predecessor in many ways may be a result of the processes of leader selection in Japan. As an example, a Prime Minister in Japan is not selected through direct election. A future president of a firm is selected from inside the firm. A proper person as a president is not sought from outside, neither does he or she fight to become a president (even a general meeting of stockholders does not substantially have much power to select a president).

Above all, a top manager is not selected openly. The selection is made in a closed society or group. Therefore it is natural that the present incumbent's intention should be emphasized.

There is another interesting fact. The physical appearance of many top managers of business ventures, where they seem to have established their positions through their own efforts, is short. They did not have any predecessors, so why are they short? Many of them have achieved their successes by having support, favors, and patrons from people outside their firms. Their supporters may be the top managers of clients, or corporate executives who help entrepreneurs. Here, the previously mentioned principle about physical appearance again applies. Very few people favor or patronize a taller man or woman who looks down at them even though he or she is younger than their supporters.

Critical Decision Factors for the Selection of Leaders among Various Choices in Japan

The above-mentioned conditions for the selection of leaders are certainly irrational. Many people may ask the question, 'Will the leaders who are selected by such criteria and processes ever function well?' However, in reality these physically small politicians and managers have established Japan as one of the leading countries, at least in the economic world. That is, they have brought leadership into play. In other words, we can say that this style of leadership has matched the culture of Japan's society and the cultures of its political or business world.

That is not to say that those leaders do not have any abilities or have succeeded only through apple-polishing. As one CEO says: 'There are many people who have the abilities to be a president of my company. But the critical factor to become a president is personality. Getting beloved by many people and getting along with them are requirements for the next president.'

In this sense, the political or business world in Japan may be a highly competitive society. Excellent top managers have controlled their subordinates well by making the subordinates compete at the last moment and keep a close eye on each other. It can be one of the leadership styles in Japan.

What are these leadership styles? Why do they work well? Before answering these questions, it is necessary to understand the characteristics of Japanese culture.

CHARACTERISTICS OF JAPANESE CULTURE AND TRADITIONAL JAPANESE-STYLE LEADERSHIP

Japanese Collectivism

The main characteristic of Japanese culture can be summed up in a word: collectivism. Although this collectivism has actually been changing gradually, the differences between collectivism in Japan and individualism in the Western countries are clearly seen.

We shall now discuss the three aspects of its typical characteristic as follows.

Relationships between a group and its members

In other words, this is the unification and identification of individuals to their group. This is quite different from the individuals' autonomous contribution to the group. Autonomy itself is left with the group.

Specifically, the interests of the group become those of each member. For the sake of the group, the members do not mind sacrificing themselves. Furthermore, they are proud of devoting all of what they have to the group and have no sense of being sacrificed.

Relationships among members in the group

An important key word to explain this is homogeneity. A member is expected to think and behave in the same way as others do. If there is a person who thinks and behaves differently from the others, that person will be pressured to conform. Failure to comply with the pressure means that he or she will be eliminated from the group. A heretic is ostracized by the villagers.

Strictly speaking, that is not to say that everyone has the same way of thinking or the same style of behavior. One person behaving differently or showing his or her excellent ability may destroy the order of the group, that is, cause the group to be in trouble. Above all, various negative reactions and emotions of jealousy will be aroused in the group. Rather than destroying the order of the group, the members may consider that it is easier to restrain themselves and keep pace with others. In this sense, they are homogeneous.

Relationships between the group and outsiders

A group protects its benefits and avoids any damage from outsiders. This is the natural tendency for a group. However, in the case of the group under collectivism, this appears in an extreme form. That is, a group justifies any means used to protect its interests, and does not care about outsiders at all. The group possesses egoistic thoughts and behavior and may even try to increase internal centralization by creating imaginary enemies outside.

A group in Japanese society is collective, comprised of the same sort of members who have strong loyalty to the group. When a group faces outside enemies or critical situations, the members of the group strongly unite to protect the group's interest. This is truly like a village or Japanese mafia (*Yakuza*) protecting its own territory. Of course, a business firm also has the same characteristic.

Then what are the leader's characteristics in these kinds of societies? To understand them, it is necessary to go back to the society which became the basis of collectivism formation, a so-called agricultural society.

An Agricultural Society as the Origin of Japanese Culture

Characteristics of an agricultural society, compared with those of a hunting society, can be the following:

(1) People settle down in one place. Naturally, the regional and blood relationships become closer, and the opportunities for human interaction and information exchange with outsiders will decrease.
(2) As their work is based on the seasons, their life styles come to have periodicity. As people can anticipate the next opportunity coming round, they will possess a passive attitude rather than seeking active changes.
(3) Everyone does the same work, such as rice-planting, weeding a rice field, and harvesting in rice-cropping. The difference between individual abilities is buried there and becomes an unimportant matter.

These characteristics of an agricultural society become much clearer by comparison with those of a hunting society. In a hunting society, people move around to chase animals, and their work does not have the same periodicity. So they make much of each moment. And that is the society in which an individual role is clear, and a leader who heads up the followers is needed.

Leaders in an Agricultural Society

The previously mentioned collectivism seems to be developed from a society with an agricultural-style culture. Further, this culture may characterize the culture of present Japanese society. Therefore, what types of leaders are suitable in this agricultural society? The answers are as follows:

(1) Leaders should have the style of settlers. It is more important for leaders to listen to others, find a point of agreement, and settle down rather than to put themselves in the forefront and lead people. It is important to maintain the harmony of a group. This, for example, leads to the sentence, 'Harmony is precious' which was written in the Seventeen Article Constitution by Shotoku-Taishi. Apart from this, the constitution also says that plenty of discussion is important. This is to maintain and manage a group by bottom-up decision-making and consensus.

(2) Leaders should possess the ability of extrapolating actual conditions from the past as specific knowledge. Even if leaders face some problems or obstacles, they are able to deal with them by drawing from a pile of past experiences as in most of the cases in an agricultural society. And it is also important to persuade people that good times will always come through bearing up under the present conditions.

(3) Leaders should strengthen the feeling of unity and increase collectivity inside a group. At the same time, leaders should keep the group's feeling of tension and consciousness of competition against outside groups, such as neighboring villages. Specifically, many events such as village festivals were used to arouse a hostile feeling against the other groups.

Leader–Follower Relations Commonly Used Through the Modern Age in Japan

The above-mentioned portraits and functions of leaders, that is leadership, exactly overlap the portraits of current leaders in Japan. It is the traditional Japanese style of leadership. Although this may be to repeat what has been mentioned previously, a leader is selected from the group, based on his or her length of service and personality. A leader is the one who listens to others well and is trusted as a settling influence. A leader is the one who guides followers and increases collectivity by emphasizing the harmony of the group, arousing a competitive spirit against outsiders, and increasing a crisis atmosphere within the group.

In other words, a leader is not the person who establishes a position with their own high ability or activity, or with clear objectives based on a philosophy or vision, nor the one who is accepted as having strong characteristics to motivate people by using creativity and innovation.

This Japanese-style or agricultural-style leadership can function well with particular types of followers. These are people possessing high loyalty to their groups, being collective, respecting harmony, and willing to work for a long time without distinguishing between private and official time.

These followers do not possess any autonomy. They understand the relationship between individuals and groups as loyalty and sympathy not as an agreement of rights and obligations.

Essential Environmental Conditions for the Success of Traditional Japanese-Style Leadership

There is another important condition necessary for the achievement of successful results by these leaders and followers. That condition is related to the objectives, the characteristics, and the external environments of the society or group.

Stating the conclusion in advance, postwar Japan achieved surprising success in economic development because those factors matched well with each other. These matches are specified as the following:

(1) The Japanese government set its priority of policies on economic rehabilitation to recover from the ruin of the war, and put the emphasis on industrial policy.
(2) Many of the Japanese saw the difference between the spiritual and materiality as the reason for their defeat in the war, and aspired to the materialism of the Western countries, especially the materialistic culture of the USA.
(3) After their defeat, many of the former political and business leaders in Japan lost power either by being ostracized or for some other reason. Therefore strong leadership allied to a philosophy did not come into existence. Also the leadership controlling operating activities became dominated.
(4) By following the advanced countries, the Japanese objectives became very specific and persuasive. Having people who made efforts as a group to achieve their objectives of adapting to and catching up with the advanced countries was extremely effective.
(5) The role of top managers was in stirring up and drawing on their followers' willingness, and creating conditions to realize that willingness.
(6) The Japanese applied decision-making processes of bottom-up and consensus such as the Ringi system, lifetime employment, a seniority system, and negativistic personnel evaluation which phases out a person with problems. These Japanese-style management systems were also very effective in the activities of achieving economic growth and efficiency with

suitable models for the moderately changing environment in terms of both impact and speed.

In other words, leadership emphasizing the maintenance of passive, consensus-centered, and harmonious groups was the ideal style for the Japanese society that pursued economic development in the postwar era.

This has been the case up to now. What is going to happen in the future? Will this Japanese-style leadership continue to be effective? If not, what type of leadership will be required? This issue will be discussed next.

FUTURE OF TRADITIONAL JAPANESE-STYLE LEADERSHIP

Future Environment and Culture of Japan

To discuss the future of leadership in Japan, it will be necessary to consider the two aspects stated previously. One is the issue of the future of the culture in Japanese society. If the culture changes, that is changes occur in people's values and the behavioral styles of the Japanese, traditional Japanese-style leadership will lose its effectiveness.

Another aspect is the issue of the external environment and the objectives of societies or groups, specifically Japan as a nation, or Japanese business entities. If those too change, then traditional leadership will not function.

In fact, both of these aspects have already begun changing greatly. Even individuals' loyalty to their groups and their consciousness of respecting harmony have begun to collapse in the Japanese younger generation. Also the Japanese management system, for example the seniority system, has faced difficulties caused by the end of high economic growth. Furthermore, behavior which gives priority to a company or to profit is a focus of censure, not only from outside but also inside Japan.

In addition, the world has been changing rapidly, and the West has been losing its significance as a model to Japan. And Japan itself is now expected to act as a nation which has a philosophy and autonomy with a global perspective.

This is not a subject only at the national level. The situation is exactly the same in an industrial sector or a company. In other words, Japan has been greatly changing, or is expected to change, its direction and culture. Therefore, Japanese leadership inevitably needs to change qualitatively.

Future Direction of Japanese Society

Therefore, what should leaders do? This is a very delicate issue. First, we shall consider Japanese culture. The characteristics of collectivism and egoism still remain deeply embedded in Japanese cultures even though they are on the way to collapse. Consciousness of autonomy or co-existence still barely exists. Values or styles which give priority to the economy or to seeking materialistic sufficiency have grown stronger. What should leaders do in these situations?

Leaders have to aim at the following societies as well as business firms:

(1) The society which puts importance on fairness and co-existence with the world by having a clear philosophy.
(2) The society, as a nation, business firm or individual, which establishes its own autonomy and respects others' autonomies.
(3) The society which creates conditions for individuals to demonstrate their individual abilities and to live fruitful lives.

Needless to say, each culture or social structure has been established by various factors and processes over a long period. Therefore, it cannot be changed in a day, although undoubtedly, drastic remedy may be needed at some time. The collapse of Eastern Europe and the Soviet Union and the worsening of the world environment should be considered as good reasons for a change. In addition, the collapse of the economic bubble in Japan gives us many opportunities to reconsider our society.

However, we must not only break down the present situation, but also build up a new society. In order to do this, appropriate leadership for a new society is necessary.

From Traditional Japanese-style Leadership to New Leadership for the Twenty-first Century in Japan

The new leadership for the twenty-first century should:

(1) Have a clear philosophy, and be able to visualize it, to make it appeal adequately to people, and to get empathy for it. This philosophy must be based on a consciousness of co-existence and fairness.
(2) Make clear what should be done to realize that philosophy and vision. In other words, leaders should provide specific schemes to make them materialize.
(3) Respect and trust individuals, to find, improve, and utilize individuals' abilities and characters. In short, leaders should develop the conditions for positive participation by individuals.
(4) Apply properly the means to induce individuals' autonomous behavior, such as taking the initiative, scolding and encouraging, or transmitting information according to the external environment or target individuals.
(5) Have an unselfish and strong problem-finding consciousness or mission.

In every generation, the fact that leadership is exceedingly cultural will not change. Therefore the culture of a society or group itself needs to match with the leadership in order for the leadership outlined here to be accepted and become effective.

The priority of the whole world has been gradually changing from military strength or economic wealth to an emphasis on human beings. Within its change, Japanese culture has been shifting importance from collectivism to co-existence and individuality. However, we are still far from the desired situation.

The essential goal for the future of Japan will be to respect an individual and his or her characteristics and establish a society which has consciousness of being part of the world. This in itself needs proper leadership. After all, leadership changes a society, and the changed society breeds the leadership suitable to it.

EDITOR'S NOTE

The word translated as 'drive' is used in two senses:

(1) To force people by compulsion to take a certain course of action.
(2) To influence people through leadership.

After discussion with Professor Ichikawa through the translators, we believe that we have changed the word, or added qualifications, so that the appropriate difference in meaning is clear. However, it may be helpful to the reader to be aware of the two senses, in case I have done the translators and the author a disservice by making alterations at the wrong time.

Part Three

OTHER TOPICS

9

EMPIRICAL SUPPORT FOR A PARADIGMIC THEORY OF STRATEGIC SUCCESS BEHAVIORS OF ENVIRONMENT SERVING ORGANIZATIONS

H. Igor Ansoff and Patrick A. Sullivan
with Peter Antoniou, Hassane Chabane, Setiadi Djohar, Reuben Jaja, Alfred Lewis, Abainesh Mitiku, Tamer Salameh, and Pien Wang

United States International University School of Business and Management, San Diego, California

HISTORICAL BACKGROUND

The empirical research reported in this paper was preceded by ten years of theoretical research by Ansoff (Ansoff, 1979). This research was triggered by unsatisfactory experience encountered in the 1960s by business firms which used a management technique called Strategic Planning.

Strategic Planning, which was independently invented by a number of American business firms, and was codified and expanded by Ansoff and other writers (Ansoff, 1965), originally received an enthusiastic reception from the business community. But experience with Strategic Planning led to mixed results.

International Review of Strategic Management, volume 4.
Edited by D. E. Hussey. Published 1993 by John Wiley & Sons Ltd

In a minority of firms it became an established part of the management process. In a majority three phenomena were observed.

One, named 'paralysis by analysis', was failure by firms to convert strategic plans into new profits in the market place. The second phenomenon, named 'death in the drawer', was observed when, after several years of frustration, firms abandoned Strategic Planning. The third phenomenon occurred in some firms which, having retreated from Strategic Planning, returned to it later and made it work, sometimes as a result of several abortive starts, as was the case in the American General Electric Company.

This mixed record led to a disillusionment with Strategic Planning. A popularly accepted explanation was that it was a bad invention which should be written off to experience. Another explanation was that since planning dealt with only a part of the firm's strategic behavior process, it was an incomplete invention, like a car with a body but without an engine and without wheels. This second explanation was subscribed to by Ansoff who committed himself to a protracted search for the 'missing wheels'. This search eventually led to formulation of a number of hypotheses about success behaviors of ESOs built around a central Strategic Success Hypothesis.

EVOLUTION OF THE STRATEGIC SUCCESS HYPOTHESIS (SSH)

The first step in identification of the 'missing parts' was to broaden the scope of interest from business firms to a larger class of Environment Serving Organizations (ESOs) and to broaden the perspective from Strategic Planning, which terminated with a written plan, to Strategic Management, which terminates with an ESO's entry into new markets and/or introduction of new products or services.

The second stage was recognition that the driving 'engine' which determines the success of an ESO's Strategic Behavior is the turbulence in the external environment. This insight came from a seminal paper by Emery and Trist entitled *Causal Texture of the Environment* (Emery and Trist, 1963) which described the external environment as composed of several distinctive segments at different levels of turbulence.

The third step was inspired by two findings reported in another seminal work, *Strategy and Structure* by Alfred P. Chandler (1962). The first finding showed that, when the environment undergoes a discontinuous change, firms which remain successful do so through discontinuous transformation of their strategies. Ansoff generalized this finding by hypothesizing that in successful ESOs strategy matches the turbulence of the ESO's environment (Ansoff, 1979).

Chandler also found that, while alignment of strategy with turbulence was necessary for success, it was not sufficient, and that the structure and dynamics of the ESO's behavior must also undergo a discontinuous transformation. Ansoff labelled the structure and dynamics *ESO's Capability*, and generalized this second finding by hypothesizing that in successful ESOs capability must be aligned with the environmental turbulence.

The integrating concept of the SSH was suggested by the Requisite Variety Theorem in Cybernetics advanced by Ross Ashby (Ashby, 1956) which, liberally translated, states that to succeed in a complex environment an ESO must match the 'variety' of the response to the variety of the environment.

Using this integrating concept, the Strategic Success Hypothesis combined the concepts of turbulence, strategy and capability:

> For optimum performance both strategy and capability of an ESO must be aligned with the turbulence of the ESO's environment. (Ansoff, 1979)

OPERATIONALIZING THE STRATEGIC SUCCESS HYPOTHESIS

The Strategic Success Hypothesis subsumes two key hypotheses which have important implications to both research and the practice of Strategic Management. These are:

SSH-1. There is no single strategic behavior which assures success;
SSH-2. Environmental Turbulence is the driving variable which determines the type of strategic behavior which will succeed in an environment.

The next stage in the development was to operationalize the Strategic Success Hypotheses. The key insight for operationalizing turbulence (and consequently Strategy and Capability) came, curiously enough, from an early model of the atom proposed by the great Danish physicist Niels Bohr. Bohr hypothesized the atom to consist of a nucleus surrounded by electrons which rotate around it in discrete stable orbits and which change orbits when external forces add (or delete) to their discrete quanta of energy.

(1) Following this model in SSH, *Environmental Turbulence* was operationalized by a *five-point scale of discontinuous levels of turbulence* measured by four variables:

(i) *Complexity* of events in the environment;
(ii) *Familiarity* of successive events;
(iii) *Rapidity* with which these events evolve;
(iv) *Visibility* of future events.

Figure 9.1 presents the hypothesized turbulence scale in descriptive theoretical language.

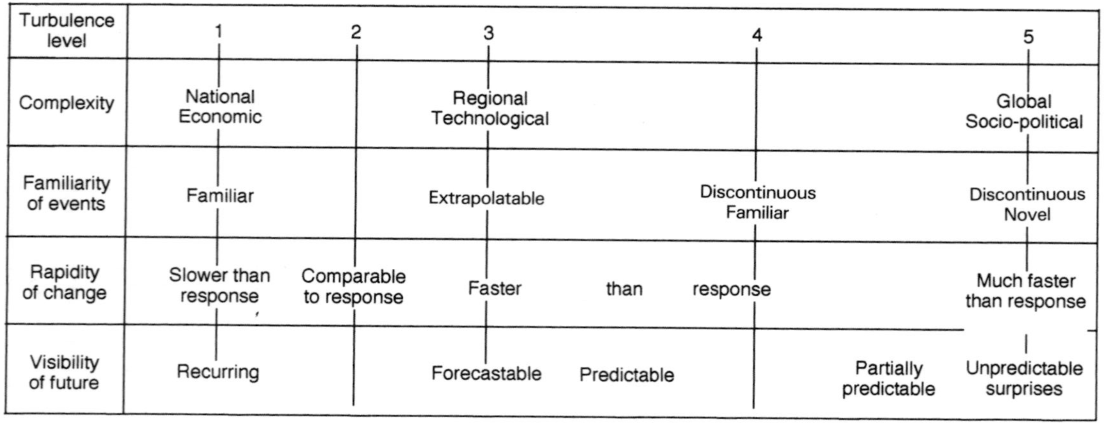

Turbulence level	1	2	3		4		5
Complexity	National Economic		Regional Technological				Global Socio-political
Familiarity of events	Familiar		Extrapolatable		Discontinuous Familiar		Discontinuous Novel
Rapidity of change	Slower than response	Comparable to response	Faster	than	response		Much faster than response
Visibility of future	Recurring		Forecastable	Predictable		Partially predictable	Unpredictable surprises

Figure 9.1 Environmental turbulence scale

Turbulence level	1	2	3	4	5
Environmental turbulence	<u>Repetitive</u> No change	<u>Expanding</u> Slow incremental change	<u>Changing</u> Fast incremental change	<u>Discontinuous</u> Discontinuous predictable change	<u>Surpriseful</u> Discontinuous unpredictable change
Strategic aggressiveness	<u>Stable</u> Stable based on precedents	<u>Reactive</u> Incremental change based on experience	<u>Anticipatory</u> Incremental change based on extrapolation	<u>Entrepreneurial</u> Discontinuous new strategies based on observable opportunities	<u>Creative</u> Discontinuous novel strategies based on creativity

Figure 9.2 Matching aggressiveness to turbulence

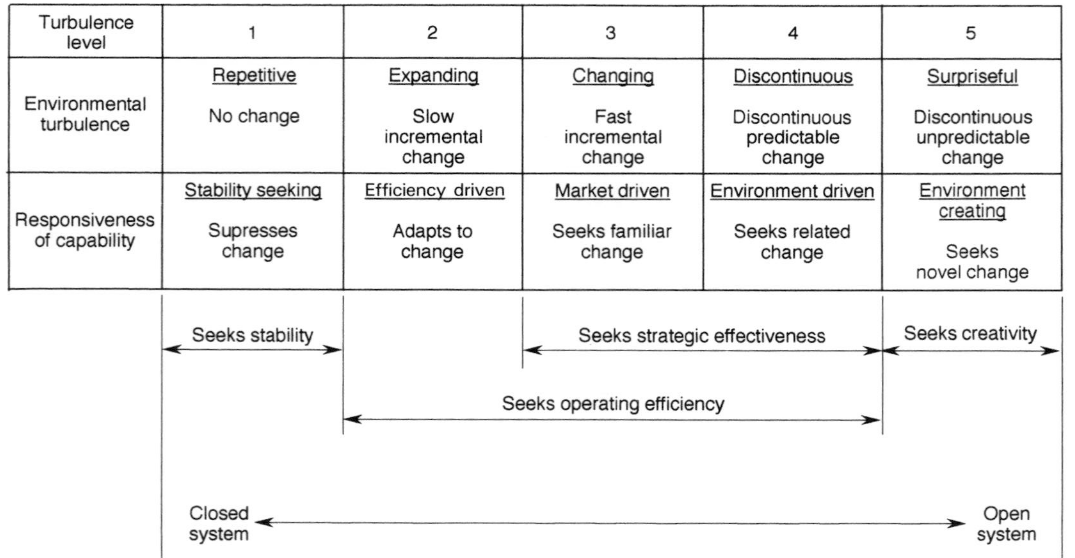

Turbulence level	1	2	3	4	5
Environmental turbulence	Repetitive No change	Expanding Slow incremental change	Changing Fast incremental change	Discontinuous Discontinuous predictable change	Surpriseful Discontinuous unpredictable change
Responsiveness of capability	Stability seeking Supresses change	Efficiency driven Adapts to change	Market driven Seeks familiar change	Environment driven Seeks related change	Environment creating Seeks novel change

Figure 9.3 Matching responsiveness to turbulence

Turbulence level	1	2	3	4	5
Environmental turbulence	Repetitive No change	Expanding Slow incremental change	Changing Fast incremental change	Discontinuous Discontinuous predictable change	Surpriseful Discontinuous unpredictable change
Strategic aggressiveness	Stable Stable based on precedents	Reactive Incremental change based on experience	Anticipatory Incremental change based on extrapolation	Entrepreneurial Discontinuous new strategies based on observable opportunities	Creative Discontinuous novel strategies based on creativity
Responsiveness of general management capability	Stability seeking Rejects change	Efficiency driven Adapts to change	Market driven Seeks familiar change	Environment driven Seeks related change	Environment creating Seeks novel change

Figure 9.4 Matching turbulence/aggressiveness/responsiveness triplets

(2) *Strategy* was operationalized as a five-point scale of *Strategic Aggressiveness* measured by two variables:

(i) *Discontinuity* of successive strategic moves by an ESO;
(ii) *Time perspective of the database* used for selection of the strategic moves.

Figure 9.2 presents a hypothesized scale of strategic aggressiveness expressed in descriptive theoretical language.

(3) *Capability* was operationalized by a five-point scale of *responsiveness of capability* measured by three variables:

(i) *Type of change management behavior by the ESO;*
(ii) *Goal of ESO's behavior;*
(iii) *Openness of ESO to the environmental influences.*

Figure 9.3 presents a hypothesized scale of responsiveness of capability.

Figures 9.1, 9.2 and 9.3 are consolidated in Figure 9.4 which presents 'matching triplets' which are required for success at the respective levels of turbulence. In terms of Figure 9.4, the SSH can be restated as follows:

> *For optimum performance strategic aggressiveness and organizational responsiveness of an ESO must be aligned with the turbulence level of its environment.*

LIMITATIONS ON THE SCOPE OF RESEARCH

Research Presented in this Paper Was Focussed on Strategic Responsiveness

Success of an ESO depends on two basic variables (Ansoff, Declerck and Hayes, 1976), *Strategic Responsiveness,* which generates future profitability potential, and *Competitive Effectiveness,* which transforms the profitability potential into actual profits.

Strategic Responsiveness is a measure of how well an organization positions itself in attractive markets, anticipates the needs of its customers, and develops responsive products/services, which use the most effective technologies. Competitive Effectiveness is a measure of how efficiently the organization produces goods and/or services and how effectively it markets them.

The two variables are a formal description of a well known dictum by Peter Drucker (1974) which says that, to succeed, a firm must first 'do the right thing' and second, 'do the thing right.' The relationship between the two variables can be represented by the symbolic equation:

Performance = f (Strategic Responsiveness × Competitive Effectiveness)

Eight of the nine research projects presented in this paper were focussed on the relationship between Strategic Responsiveness and organizational success. The Competitive Effectiveness variable was not controlled. This was done on the assumption that Strategic Responsiveness was the dominant variable in determining an organization's success.

As will be shown, the results of the first eight projects validated this assumption by showing significant and strong correlations between performance and Strategic Responsiveness.

In addition to validating this assumption, the eighth research project (Djohar, 1991) was designed to make explicit the role of Competitive Effectiveness in organizational success. The project found that, at high turbulence levels (Levels 4 and 5), Strategic Responsiveness is the dominant correlate of success.

The ninth project (Mitiku, 1991) tested the Strategic Success Hypothesis on Ethiopian state-owned industries at low turbulence levels. The results show that, while Strategic Responsiveness dominates Competitive Effectiveness at high turbulence levels, it becomes less important at Levels 1–3.

Focus on General Management Capabilities

Another important and highly consequential limitation of the research studies was in the treatment of organizational capability. Organizational capability has two major components: *General Management Capability* which plans, guides and controls ESOs' behavior and *Logistic (or Functional) Capability* which invents, develops, produces, distributes, and markets the goods and/or services produced by the ESO.

The research reported in this paper assessed only the General Management Capability of ESOs. The underlying assumption was that responsiveness of General Management Capability to Environmental Turbulence is strongly correlated to the success of an ESO. As will be seen from the results, this assumption was validated.

RESEARCH HYPOTHESIS

To facilitate empirical research, the Strategic Success Hypothesis was reformulated in terms of the *gaps* between actual behavior of an ESO and the behavior which is optimal for the turbulence level in the organization's environment.

Using this concept SSH can be described by the following equation:

$$\text{PERF} \propto \text{PERFOPT} \times [\text{STRATEGIC GAP}]$$

$$\text{STRATEGIC GAP} = 1 - \frac{|\text{AGROPT} - \text{AGRACT}| + |\text{RESOPT} - \text{RESACT}|}{2}$$

$$\text{PERF} \propto \text{PERFOPT} \times \left[1 - \frac{|\text{AGROPT} - \text{AGRACT}| + |\text{RESOPT} - \text{RESACT}|}{2}\right]$$

Where: PERF = Actual Performance
PERFOPT = Optimal Performance
AGROPT = Optimal Strategic Aggressiveness
AGRACT = Actual Strategic Aggressiveness of the Organization
RESOPT = Optimal Organizational Responsiveness
RESACT = Actual Responsiveness of the Organization

The Strategic Success Hypothesis can now be rewritten in two parts as follows:

(1) *Performance of an Environment Serving Organization is optimized when the Strategic Gap is zero.*
(2) *The absolute size of the gap is negatively correlated with the organization's performance.*

RESEARCH POPULATION

Research was confined to the set of *Environment Serving Organizations (ESOs)*, which are sometimes referred to as purposive organizations. These are organizations which derive a significant part of their income in return for goods and services which they provide to their environment.

The following *Domain of Applicability Hypothesis* guided selection of the research populations for the eight research projects:

> *The Strategic Success Hypothesis is applicable to the set of Environmental Serving Organizations (both profit-seeking and not-for-profit) in different social, political and economic settings.*

Table 9.1 lists the nine projects which have been completed to date and identifies the type of ESO which was studied in each project.

Table 9.1 Research population samples by project

Project	Research population	Researcher/Year
1	43 Manufacturing and 16 wholesale and retail firms in the United States	Hatziantoniou (1986)
2	25 Commercial banks in Abu Dhabi, United Arab Emirates	Salameh (1987)
3	45 State-owned manufacturing firms in Algeria	Chabane (1987)
4	69 United States Navy public works organizations	Sullivan (1987)
5	15 Banks in San Diego, California, United States	Lewis (1989)
6	28 Major commercial banks in the United States	Jaja (1989)
7	39 Savings and loan associations in the United States	Wang (1991)
8	97 Manufacturing firms in Indonesia	Djohar (1991)
9	54 State-owned enterprises in Ethopia	Mitiku (1991)

RESEARCH QUESTIONNAIRE AND DATA COLLECTION

All of the research projects used the same basic questionnaire, which was designed to assess three aggregate variables:

(1) The average Turbulence Level of the ESO's environment.
(2) The Strategic Aggressiveness of its behavior.
(3) The Responsiveness of its General Management Capability.

In each project the questionnaire was enlarged to test additional hypotheses assigned to the respective projects.

For application in the field, Figures 9.1, 9.2 and 9.3, which use descriptive theoretical language, were expanded into a field questionnaire expressed in managerial language. An example of the field questionnaire is shown in Appendix A.

Table 9.2 (p. 184) shows the research population, data collection method, and percentage response to the questionnaire for each of the nine projects.

The last column of Table 9.2 shows that in five of the projects Environmental Turbulence was diagnosed both by the responding senior managers in the subject population and by outside industry experts. This independent evaluation was important to control for the strategic myopia which was observed among ESO top managers (Salameh, 1987).

The time perspective for which data were collected was for a recent three-to-five-year period. The data gathered were averaged over this period.

Table 9.2 Data collection methods

Project/Researcher	Data collection method	Response	Turbulence level diagnosed by
US manufacturing, wholesal, retail firms Hatziantoniou (1986)	Secondary sources analysis of 59 case studies	100%	Researcher analysis of cases
United Arab Emirates commercial banks Salameh (1987)	Structured questionnaire administered during interview	71% 25 banks	Bank managers + expert observers
Algerian state-owned manufacturing firms Chabane (1987)	Self-administered questionnaire w/prior researcher instructions	75% 34 firms	Researcher analysis
US Navy public works organizations Sullivan (1987)	Mailed questionnaire	70.4% 69 organizations	Researcher analysis
San Diego, California US banks Lewis (1989)	Structured questionnaire administered during interview	100%	Bank managers + expert observers
US major banks Jaja (1989)	Mailed questionnaire + selected interviews	80% 28 banks	Bank managers + expert observers
US savings and loan associations (S&Ls) Wang (1991)	Mailed questionnaire	64% 99 S&Ls	S&L managers + expert observers
Indonesian manufacturing firms Djohar (1991)	Mailed questionnaire	22% 97 firms	Manufacturing firm managers + expert observers
Ethiopian state-owned enterprises (SOEs) Mitiku (1991)	Self-administered questionnaire preceded by researcher instructions	75% 54 SOEs	State-owned enterprise managers

FINDINGS

The findings of the nine research projects discussed in this paper are in two categories. The first category is the proof of the Strategic Success Hypothesis which was replicated by all nine projects.

The second category of findings is based on additional hypotheses about success behavior which were tested in each of the research projects.

FINDINGS BASED ON THE STRATEGIC SUCCESS HYPOTHESIS

The SSH Domain of Applicability Hypothesis Presented Earlier in this Paper Was Validated

Reference to Table 9.3 (p. 186) shows that the relationships specified by SSH are highly significant across a range of different ESOs including: manufacturing,

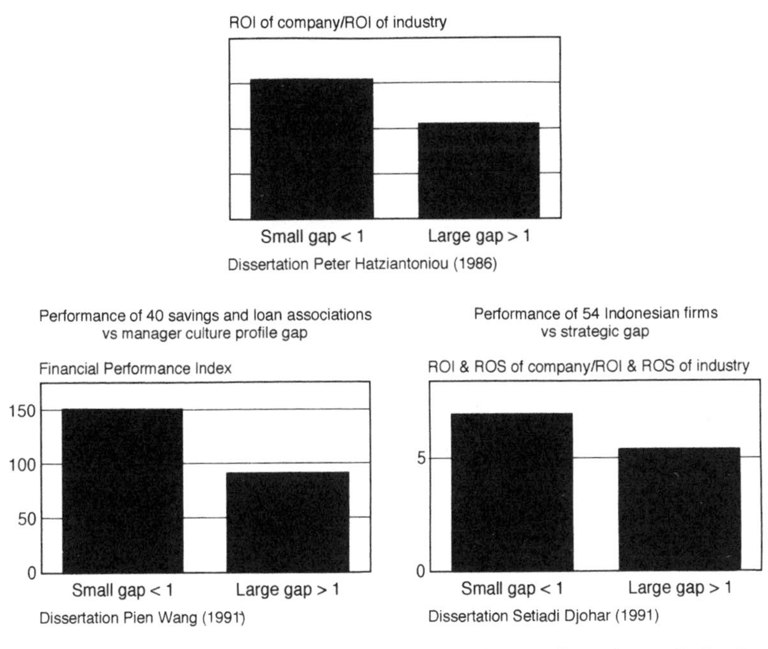

Figure 9.5 Strategic effectiveness vs performance: US manufacturing, wholesale, retail firms, savings and loan associations, Indonesian firms

Table 9.3 Findings

Researcher	Independent variable	Dependent variable	Test	Results
Hatziantoniou (1986)	Total Gap = Mean [Strategy Gap + Capability Gap]	Net profit to net worth	Mann–Whitney U Test	$U = 555$ $z = 1.82$ $p = 0.034$
Salameh (1987)	Observer's Total Gap = mean [Strategy Gap + Capability Gap]	Return on equity (ROE)	Pearsonian Correlation	$r = -0.716$ $p < 0.001$
Chabane (1987)	Gap = Optimum Profile – Current Profile	Plan achievement (% of plan target)	t Test	$t = 2.14$ $p = 0.043$
Sullivan (1987)	Strategic Gap = Optimum Profile – Current Profile	Number of commercial activities studies won	Pearsonian Correlation	$r = -0.336$ $p = 0.008$
Jaja (1989)	Strategic Gap = Mean [Perception Gap + Key Gap + Technology Aggressiveness Gap + Capability Gap]	Return on equity (ROE)	Pearsonian Correlation	$r = -0.579$ $p < 0.001$
Lewis (1989)	Total Gap = Mean [Perception Gap + Strategy Gap + Capability Gap]	Return on equity (ROE)	Pearsonian Correlation	$r = -0.914$ $p < 0.001$
Wang (1991)	Manager Culture Profile Gap = Optimum Profile – Current Profile	Financial performance bank index	Pearsonian Correlation	$r = -0.351$ $p = 0.026$
Djohar (1991)	Strategic Gap = Mean [Strategy Gap + Capability Gap]	Performance	Pearsonian Correlation	$r = -0.352$ $p = 0.009$
Mitiku (1991)	Strategic Gap – Strategy Gap × Capability Gap	Return on assets (ROA)	Pearsonian Correlation	$r = -0.162$ $p = 0.033$

retailing and service firms, regional banks, major banks, and not-for-profit ESOs. The findings are also applicable to countries in different stages of political and economic development.

The Strategic Success Hypothesis Was Validated

Table 9.3 shows the variables used in the respective projects, the tests performed, and the statistical significance of the findings. As the table shows, the significance of the results ranged from $p = 0.043$ to $p < 0.001$, thus significance of all projects was better than the $p = 0.05$ which is normally required in social science as the minimum acceptable level of significance.

The importance of the Strategic Success Hypothesis to ESOs' success is shown in Figures 9.5, 9.6 and 9.7, which present ESO performance as a function of the Strategic Gap. As the figures show, in capitalist economies, the difference in performance between ESOs with a gap less than one and ESOs with larger gaps ranged from 50% to 300%.

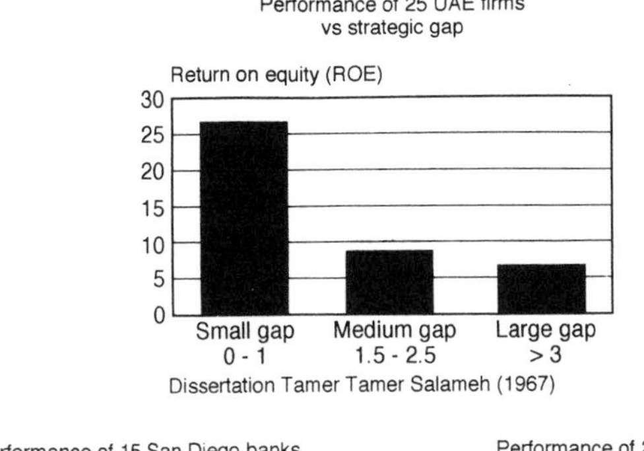

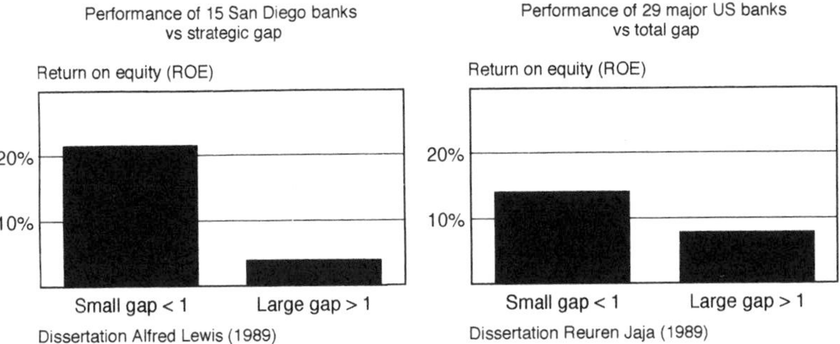

Figure 9.6 Strategic effectiveness vs performance: San Diego banks, major US banks, United Arab Emirates banks

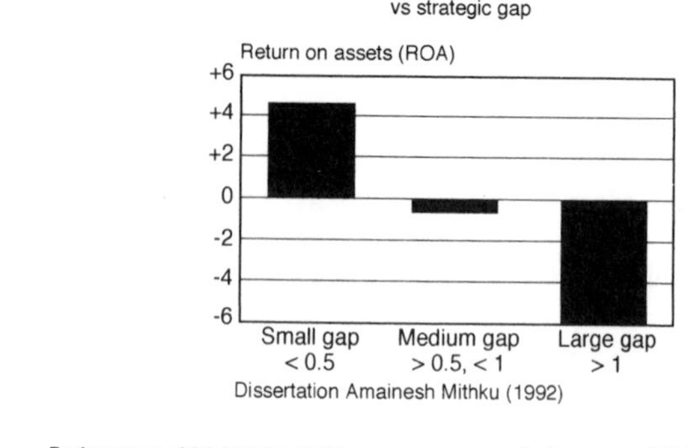

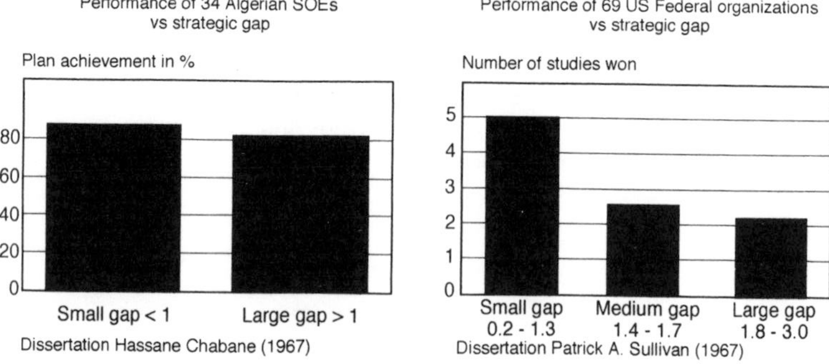

Figure 9.7 Strategic effectiveness vs performance: Ethiopian state-owned enterprises, Algerian state-owned enterprises, US Federal public works organizations

OTHER FINDINGS

Characteristics of Suboptimal Behaviors

(1) *ESOS' performance declines as the Strategic Gap Increases.* (See Figures 9.5, 9.6 and 9.7).

(2) *The break-even (zero) level of performance is in the vicinity of 1.5 to 2.0.* (See Figure 9.8).

Impact of Competitive Intensity on Decline of Performance as a Function of Gap

In 1984 Ansoff advanced a hypothesis which stated that:

> *As the strategic gap increases, performance of ESOs in highly intense competitive environments declines more rapidly than performance of ESOs in less intense competitive environments.* (Ansoff, 1984)

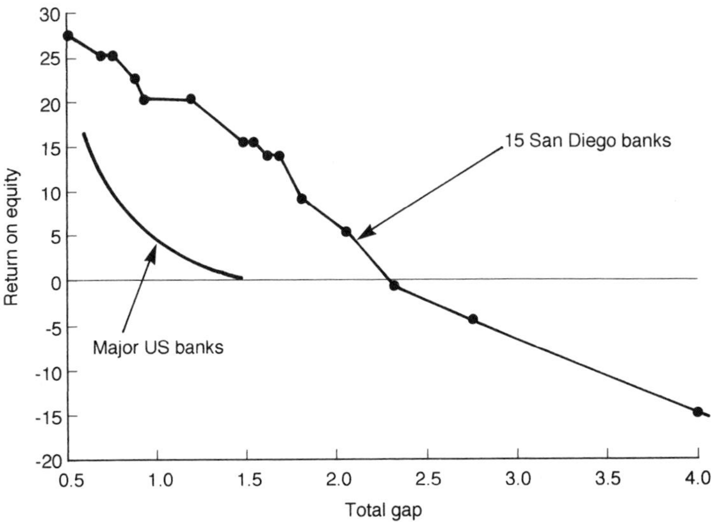

Figure 9.8 Zero performance gaps

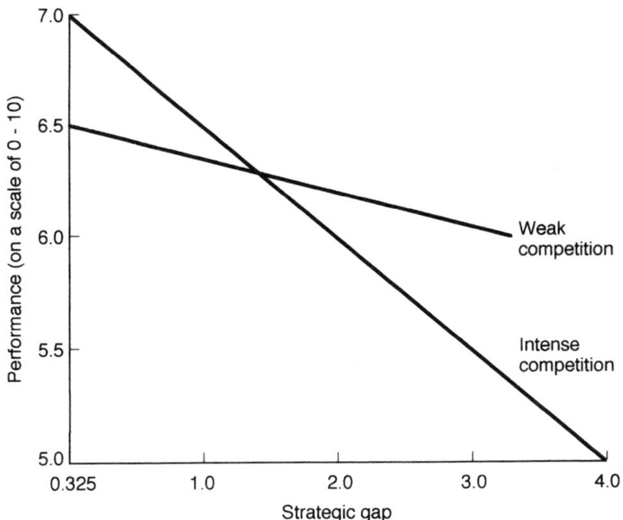

Figure 9.9 Effect of competitive intensity on performance

This hypothesis was empirically validated by Djohar (1991), as shown in Figure 9.9.

Impact of Environment Dependence on Behavior

In 1979 Ansoff advanced an Environmental Dependence Hypothesis which states:

> *The optimality of an ESO's behavior in its market environment is positively related to the percentage of its total income which it derives from the market environment. (The other source of income being the ESO's subsidy environment.)* (Ansoff, 1979)

This hypothesis was validated by Chabane (1987) and Sullivan (1987). The hypothesis was also validated by a study of parastatals in Kenya (Gutu, 1989—not reported in this study).

Chabane (1987) found that Algerian state-owned enterprises moved closer to the optimum response as subsidy income of enterprises decreased, and the percentage of total income derived from the market environment increased. The change between the subsidy and reduced subsidy behaviors was tested using a t test. The results were significant at $p < 0.001$.

Sullivan (1987), obtained the same result in Federal Agency Public Works Organizations. The relationship was tested with Pearsonian Correlation, and the results were significant at $p < 0.0005$.

Importance of Strategic Responsiveness to ESO Success as a Function of the Environmental Turbulence Level

In 1976 Ansoff, Declerck and Hayes proposed a hypothesis which states:

> *The importance of Strategic Responsiveness to an ESO's success (as compared to Competitive Effectiveness) is positively related to the Environmental Turbulence Level.* (Ansoff, Declerck, Hayes, 1976)

This hypothesis was validated by Djohar and Mitiku. Djohar (1991) studied the pharmaceutical and electronics industries, both of which were at Environmental Turbulence Level 4, and the textile industry which was at Turbulence Level 2.3. The relationship between Strategic Responsiveness and success was highly significant for the Level 4 industries, but the relationship was not significant for the low turbulence textile industry.

Similar results were obtained by Mitiku (1991) who studied four industries at turbulence level 2.4. Even though her results supported the Strategic Success Hypothesis, the relationship was weak ($p = 0.033$ and $r = 0.1618$).

Relative Importance of Technological Aggressiveness to ESOs' Success

In his study Jaja hypothesized that:

> *In technologically turbulent environments the technological component of a bank's strategic aggressiveness makes a significant contribution to the bank's financial performance.* (Jaja 1989)

Jaja validated this hypothesis by performing a stepwise multiple regression analysis on the relative importance to success of the following variables:

(1) Technological Aggressiveness Component of the Business Strategy Gap.
(2) Technological Turbulence Perception Gap by Key Managers and Technologists.
(3) Key Managers' Strategic Mentality Gap.
(4) Technological Capability Responsiveness Gap.

The results of the regression analysis showed that Technological Aggressiveness Component of the Business Strategy Gap was the only significant variable ($p = 0.002$), and that it explained 31% of the Return on Equity.

Impact of Strategic Myopia on Performance

Managers who perceive the level of environmental turbulence to be less (or greater) than it actually is are said to suffer from strategic myopia. Strategic myopia is frequently observed after environmental turbulence rapidly shifts to a new level.

As a part of his study Salameh hypothesized that:

> *Banks whose top managers are not myopic perform better than banks whose managers are myopic.* (Salameh, 1987)

He tested this hypothesis using one way analysis of variance. The result was significant at $p < 0.001$ level.

During the period covered by Lewis' (1989) study of San Diego banks, 30% of the banks in the original sample declared bankruptcy. Lewis took advantage of this unfortunate phenomenon to demonstrate the impact of strategic myopia by advancing a three-part hypothesis which states that:

> *Gaps in perception of turbulence are significantly smaller in the surviving banks than those in the failed banks.* (Lewis, 1989)

The hypothesis was sustained at the level of $p < 0.001$.

Irrationality of Managers' Response During Changes of Turbulence Levels

Wang found that, while S&L managers clearly perceived their environmental turbulence levels, their choices of strategic aggressiveness level were guided by their personal success models (mindset) and not by the aggressiveness necessary for success according to the Strategic Success Hypothesis.

In the light of the fact that a shift in turbulence level was relatively recent in S&Ls, this finding suggested a hypothesis which states that:

> *When the environmental turbulence shifts rapidly to a new level, the choice of strategic response is likely to be guided by manager's personal models of success and not by the response necessary to optimize performance at the new level of turbulence.*

This hypothesis has been subsequently proved by Al-Hadramy (1992) in a dissertation which is not reported in this paper.

As discussed earlier, the research results presented in the first eight projects were based on a total gap measured as the sum of Strategic Aggressiveness and Management Capability Gaps.

Impact of a Multiplicative Measure of The Total Gap

In her project Mitiku found that, using a multiplicative total gap formula, she obtained a significant confirmation of the Strategic Success Hypothesis which could not be obtained when she used the additive measure.

This result suggests a hypothesis which states:

> *The multiplicative measure is a better predictor of strategic success than the additive one.* (Mitiku, 1991)

This hypothesis suggests that support for the Strategic Success Hypothesis would have been further strengthened by using the multiplicative measure in the other projects.

SUMMARY OF FINDINGS: A PARADIGMIC THEORY OF STRATEGIC SUCCESS BEHAVIORS

Considered together, the empirical findings of the nine projects reported in this paper offer a predictive explanation of Strategic Behavior which is sufficiently comprehensive and coherent to deserve, in our opinion, the title of an Empirically Validated Paradigmic Theory of Strategic Success Behaviors.

Presented below is a summary of the validated theorems which comprise the theory.

Paradigmic Scope

Theorem 1.1 Institutional scope

The theory applies to the class of Environment Serving Organizations (ESOs) which depend (to a smaller or larger degree) on the market environment for their survival.

Theorem 1.2 Societal scope

The theory applies to the class of ESOs in both capitalist and socialist economies.

Theorem 1.3 Scope of behaviors

The theory comprises the full range of Strategic Behaviors observed in practice and found in business and management literature.

Optimal Behavior

Theorem 2.1 Multiplicity of success behaviors

There is no universal strategic success behavior.

Theorem 2.2 Behavior driving variable

The variable which determines the strategic behavior necessary for success is the Turbulence Level in the ESO's environment.

Theorem 2.3 Strategic success formula

An ESO's performance is optimized whenever its Strategic Responsiveness (Strategic Aggressiveness plus Organizational Responsiveness) is aligned with the Turbulence Level of the ESO's environment.

Theorem 2.4 Importance of technology

In a technologically turbulent environment the technological aggressiveness of an ESO is a major contributor to its success.

Theorem 2.5 Importance of strategic behavior to success is a function of turbulence

The importance of Strategic Responsiveness to success of an ESO increases with the Turbulence Level in the ESO's environment.

Suboptimal Behavior

Theorem 3.1 Performance decline

An ESO's performance declines as the Strategic Gap between Strategic Responsiveness and the Turbulence Level increases.

Theorem 3.2 Impact of competitive intensity

As the Strategic Gap increases, ESO performance declines more rapidly in high-intensity competitive environments than in low-intensity environments.

Theorem 3.3 Zero performance gap

At a Strategic Gap in the vicinity of 1.5 to 2.0 an ESO's performance declines to zero.

Theorem 3.4 Impact of environmental dependence

ESOs which receive their total income from their market environment perform better than ESOs which derive a part of their income from government (or other) subsidies.

Theorem 3.5 Impact of strategic myopia

Performance of ESOs whose top managers are strategically myopic (i.e. have a distorted perception of the Environmental Turbulence) is inferior to ESOs whose managers are not strategically myopic.

Theorem 3.6 Strategic irrationality

Managers' choice of strategic behavior is determined by a combination of their mindset and their perception of Environmental Turbulence.

Theorem 3.7 Strategic irrationality as a function of turbulence

The influence of managers' perception of the environment on their choice of Strategic Response is positively related to the level of turbulence. In addition to Wang's findings, this theorem was strongly supported by subsequent research by Al-Hadramy which is not reported in this paper (Al-Hadramy, 1992).

Figure 9.10 presents a one-page summary of the Paradigmic Theory of Strategic Behaviors.

Paradigmic scope	1. Theory applies to all Environment Serving Organizations 2. Applies in both Capitalist and Socialist economies 3. Comprises all observable Strategic Behaviors
Optimal behavior	1. There is no universal success behavior 2. Success behavior is determined by the Turbulence Level 3. ESO's performance is optimal at zero Strategic Gap 4. Technological Aggressiveness is a key success variable in High Technology Environments 5. Strategic Responsiveness is the key success variable in High Turbulence Environments
Suboptimal behavior	1. Performance declines monotonically as Strategic Gap increases 2. Performance decline is more rapid in highly competitive environments than in less competitive environments 3. Performance drops to zero around Strategic Gap 1.5 to 2.0 4. Performance decreases as Environmental Dependence of an ESO increases 5. General Managers' Strategic Myopia depresses ESO's performance 6. Choice of Strategic Behavior is determined by a combination of managers' mind sets and their perceptions of the environment 7. Influence of the perception on choice increases with the Turbulence Level

Figure 9.10 Overview of Paradigmic Theory of Success Behaviors

IMPLICATIONS FOR STUDY OF STRATEGIC BEHAVIOR

The Paradigmic Theory of Success Behaviors provides a comprehensive empirically validated *conceptual umbrella* for the study of organizational behavior.

The theory:

(1) Proves that none of the competing prescriptions for success found in both management and academic literature can claim universal validity, or superiority over other prescriptions.

(2) That different success behaviors are needed at different levels of Environmental Turbulence.

(3) Identifies turbulence levels at which a majority of the apparently conflicting prescriptions are valid. Figure 9.11 demonstrates this finding for a number of the best known prescriptions.

(4) Provides a strong argument for shifting the historical context-free search for universal descriptions of organizations to a search for context-dependent (contingent) description and prescriptions.

(5) On the other hand, the Paradigmic Theory provides a strong argument in favor of broadening the research domain of study of organizational behavior to include both for-profit and not-for-profit members as a class of Environment Serving Organizations.

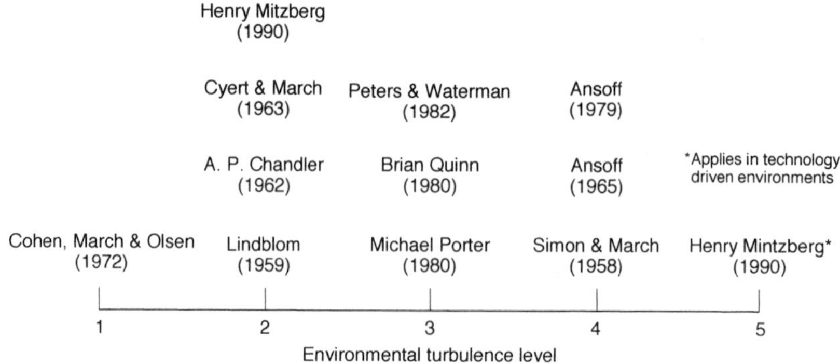

Figure 9.11 Paradigmic nature of the Strategic Success Theory

IMPLICATIONS FOR PRACTICE OF MANAGEMENT

Survival Threat to Firms Misaligned from the Environment

The findings of our research have threatening implications for many firms in the United States which face the problem of declining competitiveness in the global marketplace. It is commonly believed in the US business sector that the problem of competitiveness can be solved through increasing worker productivity on the shop floor. But the research findings reported in this paper show that exclusive focus on productivity will not solve the competitiveness problem and will endanger the survival of many American firms during the 1990s.

The research results which point to this conclusion are the following.

(1) Figure 9.4 in this paper shows that productivity is the key success variable at Turbulence Level 2, but at Levels 3, 4 and 5 market effectiveness, entrepreneurship, and creativity respectively, become the keys to success.
(2) A ten-year-long survey of senior managers' expectations of future turbulence conducted by Ansoff around the world (Ansoff and McDonnell, 1990) shows that roughly 80% of managers in developed countries expect turbulence Levels 4 and 5 in their environments during the 1990s.
(3) Thus, firms which persist in focusing on shop floor productivity can expect to experience a Strategic Gap of 1 to 3.
(4) Figure 9.8 in this paper shows that when the Strategic Gap reaches 2, the profitability of a firm drops to zero. *Thus in the 1990s American firms (and firms in other countries) which focus on productivity as the single key to success will increasingly face the prospect of bankruptcy.*

Optimizing Performance during the 1990s

The findings of our research also point the way toward assuring survival and success in the 1990s. This way is through continual use of the Strategic Diagnosis which logically follows from our findings. The relevant steps in the Strategic Diagnosis are the following:

(1) Our research shows that there is no universal success formula and that the success behavior is determined by the Turbulence Level in an ESO's environment. *Therefore. ESOs must continually diagnose the future turbulence of their environment*. The Environmental Turbulence assessment instrument, which was used in the research, has been translated into a practical management tool which can be used to diagnose future Environmental Turbulence (Ansoff and McDonnell, 1990; Ansoff, 1991).

(2) Our research proved that in turbulent environments General Management Capability (and not the shop floor productivity!) becomes the key factor in an ESO's success. Therefore *ESOs must follow the future turbulence diagnosis with a diagnosis of the readiness of their PRESENT CAPABILITY to respond to the future turbulence*.

The General Management Capability instrument used in the research has been translated into a General Management Capability diagnosis tool usable by practicing managers (Ansoff and McDonnell, 1990; Ansoff, 1991). Figure 9.12 presents a summary of the General Management Capability profiles which are necessary for success at the respective Turbulence Levels.

Turbulence level	1	2	3	4	5
Key manager(s)	Custodian	Controller	Growth leader	Entrepreneur	Creator
Culture	Stability seeking	Efficiency seeking	Growth seeking	Opportunity seeking	Opportunity creating
Rewards for	Longevity	Cost minimization	Profitability	Future profit potential	Creativity
Problem solving	Change control	Diagnostic	Optimizing	Opportunity finding	Opportunity creating
Key management system	• Policies • Procedures	• Financial control • Budgeting	• Extrapolative strategic planning • Issue management	• Entrepreneurial strategic planning	• Surprise management
Key data base	Precedents	Past performance	Extrapolation of past performance	Vision of the future	Weak signals

Figure 9.12 Optimum general management profiles

CHARACTERISTIC	STRATEGIC PLANNING	STRATEGIC MANAGEMENT
1. Turbulence level	1 - 3	4 - 5
2. Assumption about future environment	Extrapolation of the past	Discontinuous from the past
3. Planning of	Strategy	Strategic posture (strategy + capability + strategic investment)
4. Planning method	Historical success which matches ESO's strengths	Creatively visualized success which will optimize ESO's performance
5. Type of risk	Familiar	Unfamiliar
6. Organizational renewal	Incremental	Discontinuous
7. Anticipation of surprises	None	Active participation
8. End product	Strategy	New products and services transformed capability

Figure 9.13 Comparison of Strategic Planning to Strategic Management

(3) If there is a gap between an ESO's present General Management Capability and the future Turbulence Level, an *organizational transformation program must be designed and executed*.

(4) It is important to point out that, thanks to the Strategic Success Hypothesis, the *capability transformation program can be launched as soon as the Capability Gap is diagnosed without waiting for identification of the ESO's future strategy*.

(5) The research instrument used for diagnosis of an ESO's Strategic Aggressiveness has also been translated into a practical tool for Strategic Diagnosis (Ansoff and McDonnell, 1990; Ansoff, 1991). *In turbulent environments, this instrument must be used to diagnose the Strategy Gap between an ESO's present Strategic Aggressiveness and the future Environmental Turbulence. If the diagnosis shows a Strategy Gap, a new strategy must be formulated for the future.*

(6) The research results show that, depending on the level of the diagnosed future turbulence, different approaches to strategy formulation must be used. If the future environment is expected to be *extrapolative*, the well developed and practiced technology of Strategic Planning must be used. However, if the future environment is expected to be *discontinuous* (Turbulence Level 4 and 5) a newer planning technique called Strategic Management becomes necessary (Ansoff and McDonnell, 1990). Differences between Strategic Planning and Strategic Management are illustrated in Figure 9.13.

SUMMARY

This paper has described the evolution of the concept of the Strategic Success

Hypothesis and presented the results of an extensive empirical research program which validated the hypothesis.

The program also included a number of auxiliary hypotheses which illuminated various aspects of Strategic Behavior by Environment Serving Organizations. This auxiliary research made it possible to broaden the scope of the inquiry, which led to formulation of The Paradigmic Theory of Success Behaviors by Environment Serving Organizations.

Implications for research on Environment Serving Organizations and for the practice of management were presented.

REFERENCES

Al-Hadramy, Ahmed (1992) General Managers' personality characteristics and perception of environmental turbulence as determinants of rationality of choice in small firms. Unpublished doctoral dissertation, School of Business and Management, United States International University.

Ansoff, H. Igor (1965) *Corporate Strategy*, New York, McGraw-Hill.

Ansoff, H. Igor (1979) *Strategic Management*, London and Basingstoke, Macmillan.

Ansoff, H. Igor (1991) Strategic Diagnosis. Unpublished diagnostic procedure, Ansoff Associates.

Ansoff, H. Igor, Declerck, Roger P. and Hayes Robert L. (1976) From strategic planning to strategic management. In H. I. Ansoff, R. P. Declerck, R. L. Hayes (eds), *From Strategic Planning to Strategic Management*, New York, John Wiley.

Ansoff, H. Igor and McDonnell, Edward J. (1990) *Implementing Strategic Management*, 2nd edn. New York, Prentice-Hall.

Ashby, W. R. (1956) *Introduction to Cybernetics*, New York, John Wiley.

Chabane, Hassane (1987) Restructuring and performance in Algerian state-owned enterprises: A strategic management study. Unpublished doctoral dissertation, School of Business and Management, United States International University.

Chandler, Alfred D. Jr (1962) *Strategy and Structure: Chapters in the History of the American Industrial Enterprise*, Cambridge, MIT Press.

Cohen, Michael D., March, James G. and Olson, Johan P. (1972) A garbage can model of organizational choice. *Administrative Science Quarterly*, 17, No. 1. 1–25.

Cyert, Richard M. and March, James G. (1963) *A Behavioral Theory of the Firm*, Englewood Cliffs, NJ, Prentice-Hall.

Djohar, Setiadi (1991) The relationships between strategic effectiveness, competitive efficiency and performance in Indonesian firms. Unpublished doctoral dissertation, School of Business and Management, United States International University.

Drucker, Peter F. (1974) *Management: Tasks, Responsibilities, Practices*. New York, Harper & Row.

Emery, F. E. and Trist, E. L. (1963) The causal texture of organizational environments. *Human Relations*, 18. August, 20–26.

Gutu, Jackan M. (1991) Strategic management of state owned corporations (parastatals): An investigation of environmental dependence for resources by parastatals in Kenya.

Unpublished doctoral dissertation, School of Business and Management, United States International University.

Hatziantoniou, Peter (1986) The relationship of environmental turbulence, corporate strategic profile, and company performance. Unpublished doctoral dissertation, School of Business and Management, United States International University.

Jaja, Reuben Mietamuno (1989) Technology and banking: The implications of technological change on the financial performance of commercial banks. Unpublished doctoral dissertation, School of Business and Management, United States International University.

Lewis, Alfred Olanrewaju (1989) Strategic posture and financial performance of the banking industry in California: A strategic management study. Unpublished doctoral dissertation, School of Business and Management, United States International University.

Lindblom, C. E. (1959) The science of 'Muddling Through'. *Public Administration Review*, Spring, No. 19, 79–88.

Mintzberg, Henry (1990) The design school: Reconsidering the basic premises of strategic management. *Strategic Management Journal*, 11, No. 3. 171–195.

Mitiku, Abainesh (1991) The relationship of general management capability with performance in state-owned industrial enterprises in Ethiopia: A strategic approach. Unpublished doctoral dissertation, School of Business and Management, United States International University.

Peters, Thomas J. and Waterman, Robert H. Jr (1982) *In Search of Excellence*. New York, Harper & Row.

Porter, Michael E. (1980) *Competitive Strategy: Techniques for Analyzing Industries and Competitors*. New York, The Free Press.

Quinn, James Brian (1980) *Strategies for Change: Logical Incrementalism*. Homewood, Ill., Richard D. Irwin.

Salameh, Tamer Tamer (1987) Analysis and financial performance of the banking industry in United Arab Emirates: A strategic management study. Unpublished doctoral dissertation, School of Business and Management, United States International University.

Simon, Herbert A. and March, James G. (1958) *Organizations*. New York, The Free Press.

Sullivan, Patrick A. (1987) The relationship between proportion of income derived from subsidy and strategic performance of a Federal Agency under the commercial activities program. Unpublished doctoral dissertation, School of Business and Management, United States International University.

Wang, Pien (1991) Determinants of perceptions of environmental turbulence and strategic reponses of savings and loan top managers. Unpublished doctoral dissertation, School of Business and Management, United States International University.

APPENDIX A: SAMPLE RESEARCH INSTRUMENT

(A) The following questions relate to changes which occurred in the external environment of your firm during the period from 1981 to 1984.

(1) For the past three years (1981–1984), which of the following statements best describes your firm's familiarity with events in the environment of your industry?
   (a) Nothing really changes much in the environment.
   (b) Changes in the environment were repetitions of the firm's past experience.
   (c) Changes in the environment were understood when we thought of historical development.
   (d) Changes in the environment were different, but we explained them when we thought of past experience.
   (e) Changes in the environment were new, and not experienced before.

(2) For the past three years (1981–1984), which of the following statements best describes the speed of change in the environment of your industry?
   (a) Speed of change in the environment was much slower than the speed of my firm's response to it.
   (b) Speed of change in the environment was slower than the speed of my firm's response to it.
   (c) Speed of change in the environment was comparable to the speed of my firm's response to it.
   (d) Speed of change in the environment was faster than the speed of my firm's response to it.
   (e) Speed of change in the environment was much faster than the speed of my firm's response to it.

(3) For the past three years (1981–1984), which of the following statements best describes the visibility of the future in the environment of your industry?
   (a) My firm's environment remained substantially unchanged.
   (b) My firm's environment evolved in a historically logical manner.
   (c) My firm's environment was predictable through analysis of threats and opportunities.
   (d) My firm's environment was difficult to predict.
   (e) My firm's environment was characterized by unpredictable surprises.

(4) For the past three years (1981–1984), which of the following statements describes the scope of your firm's business operations?
   (a) The scope of business operations was local.
   (b) The scope of business operations was national.
   (c) The scope of business operations was national plus adjacent countries.
   (d) The scope of business operations was regional.
   (e) The scope of business operations was global.

(B) The following questions relate to your firm's strategies in response to the changes in the external environment during the period from 1981 to 1984.
- (1) For the past three years (1981–1984), which of the following statements best describes your firm's response to customers?
  - (a) We neglected response to customers.
  - (b) Our service is what the customer wanted.
  - (c) We anticipated the customer's needs.
  - (d) We identified unfilled customer needs.
  - (e) We identified needs which were expected to occur in the future.
- (2) For the past three years (1981–1984), which of the following statements represents your firm's focus on new service development?
  - (a) We did not develop new services.
  - (b) Our focus on service development was the imitation of existing services in the industry.
  - (c) Our focus on service development was the improvement of existing services.
  - (d) Our focus on service development was the adoption of new developing services in the industry.
  - (e) Our focus on service development was on pioneering new services in the industry.
- (3) For the past three years (1981–1984), which of the following statements represents your firm's approach to market development?
  - (a) We stuck to our existing customers.
  - (b) We followed competitors in their market development.
  - (c) We expanded to familiar markets.
  - (d) We expanded to foreign markets.
  - (e) We created new markets.

(C) The following questions relate to top management's capabilities to support your firm's response to the changes in the external environment during the period from 1981 to 1984.
- (1) For the past three years (1981–1984), which of the following statements best describes top management's willingness to accept risk?
  - (a) They rejected risks.
  - (b) They accepted familiar risks.
  - (c) They sought familiar risks.
  - (d) They sought unfamiliar risks.
  - (e) They sought novel risks.
- (2) For the past three years (1981–1984), which of the following statements describes top management's way of solving problems in your firm?
  - (a) They solved problems through trial and error.
  - (b) They solved problems through diagnosis.
  - (c) They solved problems through choosing among existing alternatives.

   (d) They solved problems through searching for alternatives.
   (e) They solved problems through creating alternate solutions.

(3) For the past three years (1981–1984), which of the following statements best describes the personal knowledge required by top management in the firm for conducting the business?
   (a) Knowledge of internal politics was all that was needed.
   (b) Knowledge of internal operations.
   (c) Knowledge of traditional markets, competitor's behavior, and new technologies.
   (d) The knowledge of global opportunities.
   (e) The knowledge of changes in the environment.

(4) For the past three years (1981–1984), which of the following statements describes top management's model of success for your firm?
   (a) Top management's model of success was stability and repetition.
   (b) Top management's model of success was service and efficiency.
   (c) Top management's model of success was the balance of internal efficiency and marketing responsiveness.
   (d) Top management's model of success was investment in the most profitable opportunities.
   (e) Top management's model of success was creativity.

(5) For the past three years (1981–1984), which of the following statements describes your firm's information system?
   (a) Our firm's information system was based on past precedents.
   (b) Our firm's information system was based on information about past performance.
   (c) Our firm's information system was based on statistical projection of past performance.
   (d) Our firm's information system was based on data relative to developing changes collected by environmental surveillance.
   (e) Our firm's information system was based on data relative to possible changes collected by environmental surveillance.

(6) For the past three years (1981–1984), which of the following statements describes the rewards and incentives system of your firm?
   (a) Rewards and incentives were based on length of service.
   (b) Rewards and incentives were based on past performance.
   (c) Rewards and incentives were based on contribution to growth.
   (d) Rewards and incentives were based on contribution to growth and innovation.
   (e) Rewards and incentives were based on creativity.

10

MANAGING STRATEGIC CHANGE IN A HIGH-TECHNOLOGY ENVIRONMENT: THE CASE OF RANK XEROX (UK)

David Asch

School of Management, The Open University, UK

INTRODUCTION

This chapter reports on a longitudinal study of strategic change in Rank Xerox (UK) Ltd (RX(UK)). RX(UK), 'The Document Company', supplies a full range of document management hardware and software to UK customers from its headquarters in West London. The company was of particular interest for a number of reasons. First it has experienced periods of profitable growth and downturns in performance in recent years. Secondly it was possible to get a reasonable grasp of the strategic influences on the company as it was not too large or complex in structure. Thirdly, it allowed the researcher complete freedom of access.

The nature of strategic management will be established first, followed by the arguments for the use of one case study. The way in which the research was conducted is then discussed. The nature of strategic change is analysed and some background material on RX(UK) presented. Findings of the research will be discussed and some conclusions drawn. Finally, the implications for managing strategic change will be discussed.

International Review of Strategic Management, volume 4.
Edited by D. E. Hussey.

Defining Strategic Management

Chaffee (1985) proposed three models of strategy—linear, adaptive and interpretive. The linear model of strategy making assumes a progressive series of steps (setting objectives, analysis, evaluation, selection and implementation) to achieve long-term goals. The adaptive model is characterized by concern for the development of a viable match between the external environment and the organization's resources and capabilities. The organization continually assesses external and internal conditions leading to adjustments to align capabilities and resources to environmental opportunities and risks. The interpretive model is based on a social contract which portrays the organization as a collection of cooperative agreements. It assumes that reality is socially constructed, that is not something objective or real to the perceiver.

Johnson (1988) argued that these three models of strategy encompass two broad thrusts. First, that strategy can be seen as a logical, rational process—either through planning or through logical incrementalism. Secondly, strategy may be seen as the product of political, cognitive, or symbolic action.

Strategic decisions are related to the environment, they are also non-routine, substantial and important enough to affect the overall welfare of the company, and organizationwide in their consequences (Hambrick, 1980; Hickson, Butler, Cray, Mallory, Wilson, 1986). Strategic decision-making has been found to be a complex, multi-organizational level phenomenon (Fahey, 1981). Strategy is concerned with: the scope of an organization's activities; the matching of an organization's activities to its environment and to its resource capability; the allocation and reallocation of major organizational resources; the values, expectations and goals of those influencing strategy; the long-term direction of the organization; implications for change throughout the organization (Johnson & Scholes, 1988). Strategic management may then be defined as 'the process of making and implementing strategic decisions, ... [it] is about the process of strategic change' (Bowman & Asch, 1987, p.4).

The use of a single case

Given the nature of strategic management briefly outlined above, it is necessary to explain why the focus of the research is on one organization. There is no attempt here to claim that RX(UK), or its managers, are representative of all organizations or all managers. The research is designed to illustrate and examine a complex issue. The aim of the research is to provide a rich contextualist (Pettigrew, 1985a) study so that strategic change can be examined '...theoretically sound and practically useful research on change should explore the contexts, content and process of change together with their interconnections through time' (Pettigrew, 1990). In undertaking the research, the researcher endeavoured to become 'intimately familiar' (Mangham, 1986, p. 8) with RX(UK). The aim was to utilize a case study to (a) describe events in some detail, (b) explore and analyse the relevance of differing models of strategic management, and (c) attempt to provide an explanation of such complexity (Yin, 1984).

Some other issues are linked to this. RX(UK) allowed the researcher complete freedom of access to documents and, more importantly, to managers and meetings. To emphasize this point the current CEO stated 'You can talk to who you like, wherever you want to. You can visit any of our locations, look in any office.' Buchanan, Boddy and McCalman (1988) argue that an opportunistic approach to fieldwork in organizations is permissible due to the necessity to exploit the opportunities available. They qualify their position by stating that 'The ultimate goal of the research enterprise is to gather empirical evidence on which theories concerning aspects of behaviour in organizations can be based.' Greiner and Bhambri (1989) note that the risk in using a single case is defensible given the continuing problem of access to senior executive teams. Furthermore, as Calori and Atamer (1990) observed recently, there is still a lot to learn on the management of strategic change—'In depth case studies bring new insights to the understanding of the 'alchemy' between conservation and the transformation of companies.'

Research methodology

The focus in the study is the period from the early 1980s to the present time. The basis of the research took the form of extended, discursive interviews with directors and senior managers. Secondary data were also collected both from the company and from external sources. This type of triangulated methodology is useful as different types of data can be used to cross-check events. Pettigrew (1990) noted that the triangulated approach draws on the particular strengths of a variety of data collection methods. So, while interviews can provide depth and subtlety factual detail may be low. Documents can provide facts but are subject to selective deposit and survival. Direct observation enables access to group processes and allows the researcher to distinguish between what people say they do and what they actually do.

The timing of the interviews was as follows:

- A first round of interviews was conducted with all nine directors and eighteen senior managers in November and December 1990. Table 10.1 sets out some data on the interviewees.
- A second round of interviews with the same people who were interviewed in late 1990 was carried out in September and October 1991.

A number of meetings were attended where company results or future directions were discussed. In addition, in November 1990, all directors and senior managers (65 people in total), were asked to complete a 'Perceptions of Strategy'

Table 10.1 Profile of sample of interviewees

	No.	Age		Length of service		No. with degree or equivalent
		Ave	*Range*	*Ave*	*Range*	
Directors	9	44	37–47	20	17–23	8
Managers	18	41	36–48	15	1–20	13

(a) Of the 18 managers interviewed, 5 were from sales, 3 from marketing, 3 from distribution and service, 3 from finance and administration, 2 were general managers, with one each from quality and personnel. Two were women.
(b) Length of service denotes time spent in the industry, not just with RX(UK).

questionnaire (Bowman, 1990). In September 1991 the same people were asked to complete the 'Perceptions of Strategy' questionnaire again. This questionnaire contained 21 statements designed to explore three dimensions of RX(UK)'s strategy—priorities about cost efficiency, priorities about being differentiated, and the extent of change in the organization.

The secondary data collected included market research reports, annual reports, company newspapers, employee surveys, industry and customer surveys, plus a host of internal management reports. The use of triangulation and the interaction of different data (Jick, 1979), whereby disparate data sources (collected at different times and from different people) are used to examine the same phenomena, enabled an understanding of the nature of the organization and of the changes which had taken place to develop.

STRATEGIC CHANGE REVISITED

Tichy (1983) sees strategic change mainly in terms of a major intervention by top management to overcome organizational inertia and accomplish radical change. Consultants and behavioural science techniques are often used. Pettigrew (1985b) takes a longer term view and uses both political and cultural perspectives to describe decision processes in which managers bargain and compromise their way to unpredictable outcomes. Mintzberg and Waters (1985) draw a useful distinction between deliberate and emergent approaches and utilize the idea of intentionality to distinguish between planned and emergent events imposed perhaps by external environmental forces.

Lindblom (1959) developed the idea that strategic change is incremental. He noted that 'Policy is not made once and for all; it is made and remade endlessly.

Policy making is a process of successive approximation. . . . It is at best a very rough process.' Incrementalism was then almost elevated to a prescription for strategic management by Quinn (1980). He developed Lindblom's thesis and suggested that senior managers proceed 'flexibly and experimentally from broad concepts to specific commitments, making the latter concrete as late as possible' (Quinn 1980, p. 56). Strategic change is seen as a cautious step-by-step process, that is, logical incrementalism. Quinn's view that strategies emerge in a continuous incremental, and hence additive, fashion is contradicted by others. A number of writers (e.g. Greiner, 1972; Miller & Friesen, 1980) have developed some form of punctuated equilibrium model involving periods of relative stability or convergence which for one reason or another leads to a frame-breaking or revolutionary change.

Miller and Friesen's (1980) model of organizational change is based on the notion that momentum is the dominant factor; because reversals in the direction of evolution are resisted, and because an elaborate set of programmes, goals and expectancies grows up around the organization's modus operandi. Momentum then is pervasive. Organizational change is also likely to be characterized by periods of dramatic revolution when there are reversals in the direction of change across a large number of variables of strategy and structure. The focus of Miller and Friesen's research was on major changes, and they identified eight critical decisions or events:

(1) The replacement of a top executive (president or CEO).
(2) The introduction of a new product–market strategy that might involve entering a new market, geographical expansion, new product introduction, etc.
(3) The decision to build a major new facility or to adopt a significantly different production technology.
(4) A major change in distribution, promotion, or pricing strategies and techniques.
(5) Modification of organizational structure and the distribution of authority.
(6) A change in the external environment caused by competitor strategies, technical obsolescence, economic booms and recessions.
(7) Acquisitions, mergers, or the addition of new departments.
(8) A change in administrative practices pertaining to control and information systems and planning methods.

Miller and Friesen found that momentum was the dominant tendency for all variables given the preponderance of continuous links. Simultaneous continuity was found to be a powerful form of organizational momentum. Significant pressure was needed for momentum to end in a revolution. Miller and Friesen concluded that the pervasiveness of momentum may lie in a reluctance to tamper with tried and tested formulas, the effects of cognitive limitations, gestalts, or integral relationships among environmental, organizational, and strategy-making orientations, and the nature of forces of power and ideology.

The work of Miller and Friesen is broadly confirmed by research conducted by Tushman, Newman and Romanelli (1986). This illustrated periods of incremental change or convergence, punctuated by discontinuous changes throughout the organization. Executive leadership in initiating and implementing major change was also illustrated. In considering incremental change these researchers distinguished between fine tuning and incremental adjustments to environmental shifts. Fine tuning involves filling out and elaborating consistencies in strategy, structure, people and processes. As such the organization's social system becomes even more interconnected and stable. Incremental adjustments to environmental shifts involve some adaptation, but not transformation, in the overall system. Changes are compatible with existing structures, systems and processes.

Tushman, Newman and Romanelli identified a number of reasons for frame-breaking change, which they argue arises from one or a combination of industry discontinuity, shifts in product life cycles and internal company dynamics. The scope of frame breaking change usually involved:

- refining the company mission and core values;
- changing the distribution of power;
- modifications in structure, systems and procedures;
- revised interaction patterns, such as new work flows, communication networks and decision-making patterns; and
- new executives, often brought in from outside the organization.

These shifts reshape the entire nature of the organization. Interestingly, Tushman, Newman and Romanelli note that the more effective examples of major change were implemented rapidly. It is possible to characterize major organizational change as involving one or more of the following:

- a change in CEO;
- a new product–market strategy;
- a significant change in organizational interactions (e.g. due to revised working methods, new/different facilities);
- a change in the organizational structure;
- a change in information/control systems;
- significant change in the external environment.

Many of these features may well be related. For example it is difficult to conceive of the introduction of a new product–market strategy without also changing associated information systems. The development of a new product–market strategy, or changes in working methods, may, for example, have been triggered by events external to the organization.

It seems clear that organizations tend to incremental change with periodic major upheavals. Mintzberg and Waters (1982) found that there were only major shifts once every ten years on average. The consequences of incremental change have been identified as increasing momentum and reinforcing complacency, coupled with decreased flexibility and an unwillingness to learn (Tushman, Newman & Romanelli, 1986). Lorange and Nelson (1987) noted that problems were not recognized, and that refusal or inability to see problems early on can lead to escalating negative effects leading to organizational decline.

Johnson (1987, pp. 245–247) argues that even though managers may see themselves as managing logically incrementally, such a conscious approach will not necessarily succeed in keeping pace with environmental change. Johnson identified a number of reasons why this might be the case:

(1) Some environmental signals will not be perceived as being relevant in terms of the organization's paradigm and will, therefore, be ignored.
(2) Other signals might be seen as 'consonant' with the paradigm in that they can be interpreted and acted on within bounds of the paradigm.
(3) Some signals are seen as 'dissonant' with the paradigm, in which case responses seem to follow this pattern:
    (a) dissonance is coped with symbolically through the mechanisms within which the paradigm is embedded;
    (b) since the threat may challenge those most associated with the core constructs of the paradigm such threats may well take on a political complexion and be strongly resisted;
    (c) the dissonance will be resolved by adapting the organization within the bounds of the paradigm.

Thus, strategic drift occurs imperceptibly and managers are unlikely to be aware of strategic drift until it is so marked that a state of crisis is perceived either within or outside the organization.

BACKGROUND INFORMATION ON RX(UK)

The plain paper copier segment of the industry in which RX(UK) competes was estimated to have European revenues of US$ 14 000m in 1986 (up from less than US$ 6000 in 1981) so the industry is not insignificant. In considering the impact of technological change on industry structure Ghazanfar, McGee and Thomas (1987) identified four recurring themes:

- step changes in technology led to changes in market structure and competitive conditions which had serious implications for the survival of incumbent firms;

- technological change enabled firms from outside the industry to capture a series of submarkets;
- market structure was the result of strategic decisions by firms as well as technological change;
- step changes in technology enlarged the market, boundaries were redefined and new dimensions of competition created.

Ghazanfar, McGee and Thomas argue that technology can change market structure and the nature of competition. They also infer that successful firms are able to redefine their industry boundaries and engage in a continuous series of innovations.

RX(UK) was one of a number of operating companies of the Xerox Corporation. It had responsibility for exploiting all Xerox products in the UK. RX(UK) has a wide range of products, from those which are highly differentiated on the one hand to those which are virtually commodities on the other. In the industry in which it competes it is the only competitor with such a wide range. Most of its major rivals seem to compete either on the basis of differentiated offerings (e.g. Kodak) or on a cost leadership basis (e.g. Canon) (Porter, 1980). In effect RX(UK) was a marketing, sales, distribution and service company which relied on Xerox for both product development and product supplies.

Within this general role each operating company selected from the Xerox portfolio of products those which suited its own territory best. Thus there would be a different product–market emphasis in each country depending on the requirements of the customers, the strength and effectiveness of competitors, and the relative strength of the Xerox operating company. In selling and servicing office equipment RX(UK) competes in quite different markets. Some products are highly differentiated (e.g. Docutec, 5090 photocopier) while others are, to all intents and purposes, commodity type products (e.g. fax, 5014 photocopier).

Until the mid 1970s Xerox Corp. and RX(UK) were very successful, growth was rapid and profits large. However, from the mid 1970s competition intensified both in the UK and worldwide. Market share slumped, growth and profits declined sharply. As part of its response in 1983 Xerox Corp. launched a massive quality programme designed to re-establish it as the leading office equipment vendor.

Leadership Through Quality (LTQ) was introduced to all operating companies, including RX(UK), throughout Xerox. LTQ is intended to change the way people think about their jobs by focusing on the customer. The LTQ process prescribes a six-step problem-solving process and a nine-step quality improvement process. Company documents stress that quality is not something added to the daily activities of an employee's job, it is the way the job gets done.

By the mid 1980s Xerox Corp. had developed a new office systems product range at its Palo Alto Research Centre (PARC). These products were revolutionary for Xerox, moving it arguably into a quite different product–market environment. Office Systems were launched in the UK by RX(UK) in 1985.

The basic organizational structure of RX(UK) was functional. Key operational functions were sales, indirect sales, marketing, distribution and service, supported by personnel, finance, and legal. Each function was headed by a director, and the directors with the CEO formed the top executive team. RX(UK) operated a nationwide system of branches which included sales, marketing and service personnel. A few large customers were handled on a 'major account' basis. Table 10.2 provides a brief summary of RX(UK)'s annual reports from 1983 to 1990.

In 1985 a new CEO (Smith) was appointed to RX(UK) and he took up his post in January 1986. New CEOs were appointed to other operating companies within Xerox at about the same time. They were all appointed from outside the group with a brief to develop the new product. Initial expectations were that the office systems product range would account for nearly 50% of revenues by 1990. At that time RX(UK)'s systems and processes were geared to selling the existing product range. The sort of skills needed to sell Office Systems would need to be developed.

Smith kept the current executive board in place and appointed two new directors as 'facilitators'. The two new directors were both former colleagues of Smith's. They were responsible for: Strategic Business Development, which

Table 10.2 Summary financial reports

	1983	1984	1985	1986	1987	1988	1989	1990
Sales	248	271	287	302	361	406	445	410
Net profit after tax[a]	25	37	23	4	15	18	0	4
Fixed assets	44	45	43	42	38	38	28	29
Rental equipment	81	68	54	37	26	24	26	19
Working capital	92	107	102	85	95	107	117	203
Average number of employees								
Selling	1417	1469	1491	1522	1632	1687	1690	1700
Distribution and service	2391	2311	2247	2214	2187	2258	2277	2300
Administration	648	639	576	552	525	510	470	500
TOTAL	4456	4419	4314	4288	4344	4455	4437	4500*

* Denotes estimate

Source: Company annual reports.

Note:

[a] Because the company is a wholly owned subsidiary of Xerox Corp. it would be unwise to rely on published profit figures as a measure of performance. This is due to the fact that prices paid for products by RX(UK) (i.e. the transfer price) are determined by Xerox and may not be market prices.

included new business development, management training, LTQ, and organization development; and Business Management Systems, which included information systems, business and management processes.

In order to effectively develop the Office Systems market, account management techniques were introduced and a focus on cross-functional teamwork developed. New processes were used to supplement/replace the LTQ approach, and to reinforce the integrated approach to customers (Chapman, 1988, provides a more complete description of these events).

Initially the results, in a buoyant economy, were good. In 1987 revenues increased by 20% and profitability improved, RX(UK) was 'Opco of the year'. In 1988 revenues grew by 12.5% and in 1989 by just under 10%, but profits were very poor. By 1990, with the UK economy heading towards a recession, revenue growth was negative and profits were effectively non-existent. Even during the good years of 1987 and 1988 it appeared that profit was generated by the existing core business rather than the office systems product range.

In May 1990 Smith left RX(UK) and a new CEO (Jones), from one of Xerox's US operations, took up the reins in July 1990. A detailed assessment of the state of the company was undertaken and a number of changes to the board of directors took place. Between Smith's departure in May 1990 and the start of the company's new financial year on 1 November three executive directors left, and Strategic Business Development was disbanded. Business Management Systems took over the LTQ role (which was considerably reinforced).

The branch network was redefined by making sales and service regions common, and more importantly by creating regional partnerships (with effect from February 1991). The regional partnership consisted of the respective region managers for sales, for service, and administration effectively running their own business. In November 1990, at the start of the new financial year, these changes were announced along with what was known as the 'Blue Book' which set out the way in which RX(UK) related to Xerox, and the things that needed to happen to return the company to an acceptable level of performance (in financial and competitive terms).

Underpinning these events were a range of other changes including changes to the management philosophy which focused on cross-functional processes, self-managed work groups, and a team orientation. Xerox shifted its corporatewide priorities to Customer satisfaction, Employee satisfaction, Return on assets, and Market share (in that order). This, coupled with the LTQ emphasis, sought to establish a re-engineering of management processes. 'Management by Fact' and the use of statistical information was reinforced, and new ways of presenting management information introduced. Business processes (e.g. customer billing cycles) were critically reviewed and simplified (Walker, 1992, provides a more complete description of these changes).

1991 also saw a number of new and updated products launched by Xerox. The most significant of these was probably the Docutec product—a sophisticated piece of document management technology. Xerox also sought to redefine its business by focusing its efforts on 'Document Management'. RX(UK), in line with the new product strategy, also started to position itself as 'The Document Company'. While not an entirely new concept to the organization (it had been using the words for some years) it did mark a shift in emphasis away from the office systems approach.

FINDINGS

In this section the output of the first (November 1990) 'Perceptions of Strategy' questionnaire will be considered first, followed by the findings of the first round of interviews (conducted in November and December 1990). In this way strategic changes up to that date can be identified and discussed prior to considering the changes up to late 1991.

The Situation up to 1990

Figure 10.1 is a plot of the questionnaire output. The vertical axis indicates the extent to which respondents believe the company is pursuing a differentiation strategy (unique products, premium prices, distinctive image/products etc.). The horizontal axis measures the extent to which respondents believe the company is pursuing a strategy of efficiency (price-sensitive customers, similar products to competitors, focus on cost control, etc.).

As Figure 10.1 reveals, there seems to be little consensus concerning the major strategic thrust of the company (the directors are those marked A to J on the plot). Most seem to believe that the company is pursuing a differentiation strategy, while only 6 see it as pursuing a cost efficiency strategy. Of some concern is the group of 23—35% of the total—in the lower left quadrant who seem unable to perceive any clear strategic direction. Perhaps of more interest is the lack of consensus between the 9 directors.

There are a number of potential explanations for this outcome. In the RX(UK) employee satisfaction survey conducted at the same time, over 75% thought the company had a well-defined business strategy. It should be noted that this was a response to one question and did not attempt to unravel in any way the dimensions that the strategy may involve. It has already been noted that RX(UK) has a wide range of products, from those which are highly differentiated on the one hand to those which are virtually commodities on the other. The fact that RX(UK) competes across the whole spectrum may then have led respondents to complete the questionnaire on the basis of the products/product groupings with which they were most familiar. Given that three of the directors had only been in the post for a short time (from two weeks to three months) their knowledge of

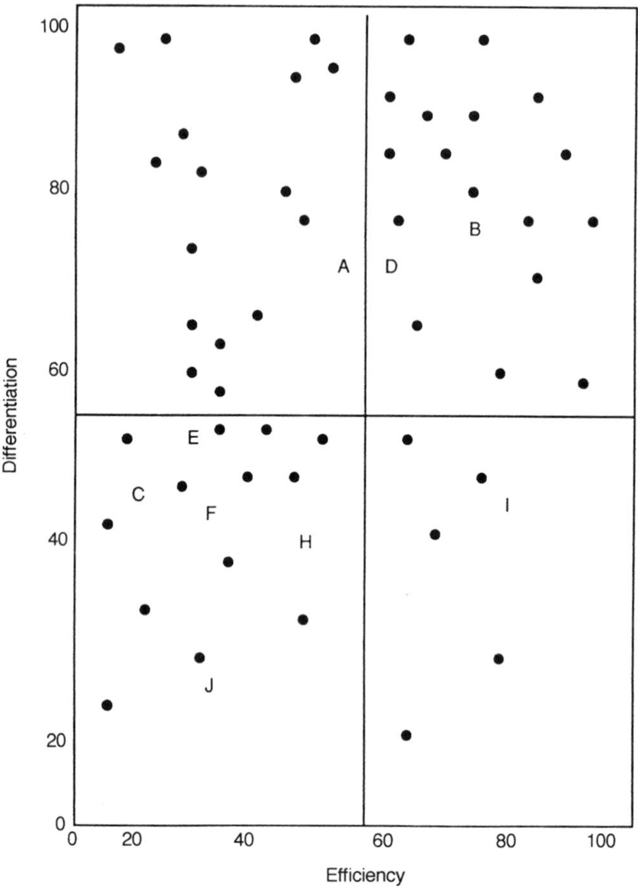

Figure 10.1 Perceptions of strategy 1990

how RX(UK) competes in the UK arena may have been incomplete. Nevertheless, the lack of consensus at the top management level was of some concern.

The questionnaire also revealed that respondents believed there had been quite a lot of change in the company in terms of the strategic direction being pursued, product changes, and the way the company was structured.

Given the questionnaire results outlined above, the responses of the directors to a question concerning sources of competitive advantage were illuminating. They were illuminating in the sense that their responses collectively produced a list with over a dozen sources. The wide range of responses would tend to support the lack of consensus revealed by the questionnaire and discussed earlier.

As a result of the variety of responses by the Board an alphabetical list of all sources of competitive advantage mentioned by the directors was circulated to them. They were asked to rank them in order of importance. This produced four clear 'favourites'—the quality approach with its focus on customer satisfaction, the distribution and service function, the commitment of people in the organization, and the products (range, reliability, innovations etc.).

Senior managers' responses to the same question seemed much clearer. Nearly all of them mentioned the product as a key source of competitive advantage. The quality approach and distribution and service function were ranked next, followed by the sales force. The fact that these rankings differ from those of the directors probably reflects respondents' different positions in the company (Stevenson, 1976). The commonality in the responses may also be interpreted to mean that the lack of consensus revealed by the questionnaire may be overstated.

There was virtual unanimity concerning major changes which managers and directors saw as having happened during the past. Three major changes were identified—changing the CEO (in 1986 and 1990), changing the products (to more sophisticated offerings like the office systems product range), and the introduction of LTQ (in 1983 when it was originally introduced, and the reinforcement in 1990). One interviewee who was unsure of whether changing the CEO was an important event noted 'I've worked here 13 years and I am on my fifth [CEO]. I'm not sure that is a real change, just look at the numbers employed.'

What became clear was that the change to Smith (the outsider) in early 1986 was directly related to product changes—the introduction of Office Systems. At that time performance was poor 'the company was in poor shape, performance had trended down, it was pretty chaotic, low morale etc. The intention was to put together a team that would turn it round.' It also seemed to signal other perhaps more subtle changes. One interviewee put it thus:

> it [hiring Smith] set the seal on how we developed over that four year period because that was the great experiment. Smith was given, effectively, a free hand and a brief to try and see if an operating unit could demonstrate to the rest of the corporation whether we could actually break into being what people then called a Systems type company. ... Yes, there was massive delegation and total divergence from corporate policy, philosophy and strategy on a whole series of things.

The appointment of Jones (a Xerox man) in 1990 seemed to represent a return to the corporate fold; the same interviewee said 'Now we have absolutely become the satellite of the corporate thinking in all respects. Everything is done to the corporate book.' Jones's arrival was also to do with the very poor performance of RX(UK) during 1989 and 1990.

The change in products also led to changes in working practices for large parts of the company. The advent of Office Systems, and Smith's arrival, led to a restructuring of the sales force and a focus on key accounts. The development of a key account approach meant that RX(UK) started to focus on customer needs by setting up cross-functional teams to interface with major customers. Another interviewee summed the situation up: 'we had the marketing triangle absolutely loaded at the top end, driven to key accounts. ... we had the sales force heavily focused on Office Systems, which were the least profitable and hardest to sell piece of our business. ... our focus on the reprographics business went, our focus on Electronic Printing (EP) went, we didn't advertise EP and we got a fall that was pretty rational.'

However, the failure of the office systems product range and what went with it was not seen as all bad news. As another of the interviewees put it: 'I think the penetration into the Office systems market place and the understanding that we have grown in there [was most important]. We are now able to operate at the higher levels. ... I think that has been one of the major achievements.'

The introduction of LTQ influenced the way in which people in RX(UK) approached problems, as has already been noted. The sorts of processes that are involved in managing an organization in an LTQ way would facilitate the sorts of changes (e.g. to account management) undertaken. One interviewee put it this way: 'I think if you go back to the decision to become a quality based company I would say that is the most significant decision that we have ever made. ... I don't see how you can be a company that is keen on customer satisfaction without attempting to be a quality organization... .' As one would expect it was not without some problems. The same individual ruefully noted in referring to the Smith era: 'the whole b..... thing was so complex—a lot of people talked about it all with little understanding. So inevitably the implementation was, as soon as you turned your back, it was gone. But you had to say the words or else you were in deep s.:. .'

The arrival of Jones as CEO in 1990 has already been touched upon. A lot of changes were then introduced in a short period of time—region partnerships, the 'Blue Book', restructuring the sales force, restructuring marketing, reinforcing LTQ, board level changes, and so on. 'Jones has come in and in 3 to 4 months has changed a lot of things without very much resistance ... if he had tried to do the things he is doing today 4 to 5 years ago I think he would have come up against a lot more resistance. ... the organization is a lot more adaptable than it once was... .'

In late 1990 a number of managers expressed uncertainty around the changes being introduced by Jones. Indeed there was some cynicism, perhaps best expressed as 'well empowerment, breaking the business down into smaller units, just makes it easier to sell off bits... .' At this stage, while most respondents appeared to view the changes favourably they did express concern around the long-term commitment to them

> One of my concerns about RX(UK) always is that we don't give things long enough, we change very quickly and don't allow people time to settle. Perhaps that is why we

are not good at understanding the facts because we have never stayed in one place long enough to really study what they are. I hope that they allow this philosophy to develop and to give us a better understanding rather than in two years time saying well, that was a good idea but how about trying this now.

Thus in late 1990, although there was clear agreement concerning major organizational changes, RX(UK) seemed to be in a state of transition. This appeared to involve some uncertainty, some ambiguity, novelty, and a lack of clarity regarding the future direction of the company. Although there were quite clear implications for RX(UK) around issues like long-term commitment to espoused policies (e.g. empowerment, LTQ, partnerships, etc.), the employee survey indicated that 70% of managers believed, in looking ahead, that the company will have changed for the better.

The situation in 1991

Figure 10.2 plots the results of the 'Perceptions of Strategy' questionnaire administered in September 1991. Because 6 managers had left the company the results show responses to 59 of the original 65 respondents in 1990. Figure 10.2 reveals much more consensus concerning the strategic thrust of the company: 46 (78%) now believe the company is pursuing a differentiation strategy, as opposed to 36 (55%) in 1990. Only 9 (down from 23) are unable to discern any clear strategic direction. Perhaps more significantly, the 9 directors now appear to have a clearer more consensual view of the direction being pursued by RX(UK).

The interviews tended to confirm the questionnaire results. Most seemed to welcome the move to position RX(UK) as 'The Document Company'; more importantly, it seemed to be understood. Most interviewees observed that the policies and processes announced in late 1990 had been consistently applied. This in turn seemed to have developed a sense of more openness and enthusiasm in the company than was evident in the transitional period in late 1990. Certainly there was less evident cynicism around what was being proposed and implemented.

The focus on LTQ meant that it was now seen as a much more rigorous process than hitherto. As one interviewee put it, 'in the past we used to count the QITs (Quality Improvement Teams), and the more the better. Now it is the quality of the output that is important, not the numbers.' The use of 'Management by Fact' and the new reporting formats appeared to be better understood and more widely used. However, the view was expressed that there was still a long way to go: 'We need to improve our analysis of root causals, some of those presented to us are not root causals at all, they are merely symptoms.'

If late 1990 was characterized by uncertainty and lack of clarity over the direction of the company then the management processes introduced and reinforced during the year seem to have addressed most of those issues. 1991

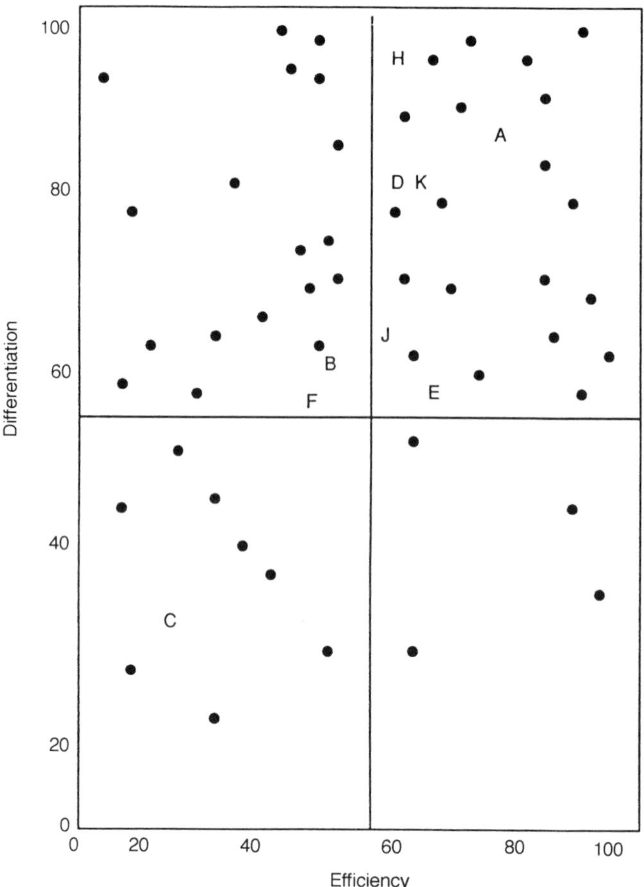

Figure 10.2 Perceptions of strategy 1991

was, however, a very difficult trading year. For example, market research estimates indicated that the size of the market had declined by some 25%. Nevertheless, the year also saw improvements in some external performance measures like customer satisfaction and market share.

CONCLUSIONS

The findings outlined above appear to confirm that incremental change is a dominant tendency with periodic revolutions. So the punctuated equilibrium model of organizational adaptation would appear appropriate. However, this research has demonstrated that the gap between revolutions may be quite short. Indeed in this case the gaps were only 3 and 4 years—that is considerably less than the 10-year average noted above by Mintzberg and Waters (1982) and largely confirmed in Johnson's (1987) study of Foster Bros.

There are two possible reasons for this, firstly the extent of the change being measured may be different, and secondly the competitive arena for all three studies was quite different. The extent of the revolutionary change in this research has been quite marked and has incorporated at least four of the six dimensions noted earlier. The change in 1985/86 involved CEO, product–market strategy, organizational interactions, and the structure of RX(UK). The change in 1990 involved all six dimensions. Even given different interpretations of the data, and the problems inherent in measuring strategic change 'objectively' (Asch, 1989) it seems clear that RX(UK) underwent major changes as identified. RX(UK)'s deep structure, that is the design of the playing field and the rules of the game, was altered (Gersick, 1991). The frequency of the major change may then have more to do with the organization's competitive arena, and how the company seeks to compete within it. As was noted earlier, the influence of the pace of technological change and its effect on industry structure may be profound.

The evidence in this case would also lend support to the notion of the organizational paradigm (Johnson, 1987), as it is arguable that 'evidence' of decline was available but for one reason or another was not accepted. This is not unusual, for as Kuhn stated in discussing scientific revolutions, '[phenomena] that will not fit the box are often not seen at all' (1970, p. 24). It is of interest to note that, in this industry, strategic drift appears to happen quite quickly. This is probably caused by the degree of product innovation, both real and perceived.

The ability or otherwise of RX(UK) to adapt to changes in the environment may also reflect its inability, in part, to adopt a new 'recipe' (Grinyer & Spender, 1979). This seems to be the case even though a tried, tested and presumably currently successful recipe was brought in by Smith in 1986. The importance of the CEO should not be understated. Stopford and Baden-Fuller (1990) found that the chief executive was crucial in terms of setting the direction to be followed, asking questions that systems geared to the needs of old 'recipes' could not answer, challenging past beliefs, and breaking the old 'rules of the game'. Certainly, in the research discussed in this chapter it became clear that the CEOs played a pivotal role in managing the content, process and pace of strategic change.

As noted at the outset RX(UK) is but one case. It appears to have confirmed some accepted ideas about the way in which organizations adapt, but at the same time to have raised a query concerning the time frames for that process. Other studies of organizations in different industries would add to the growing, but still small, number of cases on which researchers can draw and from which our understanding of the complex of organizational change can develop.

MANAGING STRATEGIC CHANGE

Having explored the way in which RX(UK) has changed over the last few years a key issue remains—is there a usable prescription for the management of strategic change? The answer to this question has to be mixed. One point does emerge with a reasonable degree of clarity—for an organization to achieve a real transformation in the way that it competes involves changing the whole because the inertial forces tend to be pervasive.

Inertia is pervasive because of the reluctance to tamper with tried and tested formulas, and managers' inability to perceive the danger, which leads to strategic drift. Both this research and the work of others already discussed has referred to the importance of the CEO and the top executive team (Tushman, Newman & Romanelli, 1986; Stopford & Baden-Fuller, 1990). These individuals are crucial because, as Tushman and Romanelli (1990) point out, 'executive leadership is the primary agent capable of mediating between these contrasting forces for stability and change'.

In the case of RX(UK) it would appear that, although the period 1986 to 1990 was mixed in terms of competitive performance, the scene was set to enable the organizational transformation put in place in late 1990 early 1991 to happen. Without that earlier period it seems unlikely that the changes introduced by Jones would have happened quite so quickly. Undoubtedly the company's poor performance in 1989 and 1990 helped to focus the effort. Nevertheless, the scope of the changes introduced in late 1990 was all pervasive, and indeed impressive to observe. They involved developing a new product–market strategy, a significant change in working methods—due to the reinforcement of LTQ, regional partnerships etc., changing the company's structure by using cross-functional teams and work groups, changes in information systems involving the development of 'management by fact', as well as facing a declining market.

Another lesson from the RX(UK) experience is that it demonstrates that strategic change can take place quickly. In this case most of the changes were in place within six months, and the company started to benefit from learning both how to utilize the new methods and how to develop them further within the first year. The evidence here, then, is that major change can, and needs to, be implemented speedily, if the inertial properties are to be overcome and a new paradigm established.

The key was not only to drive the change, but also to demonstrate to an uncertain and cynical (at that time) management cadre that effective leadership was in place. In this way the new top team, in particular the CEO, demonstrated that they had the qualities needed to succeed,—industry and organizational knowledge, a good reputation and track record, the right sort of abilities and skills (good judgement, strong interpersonal skills etc.), integrity, and motivation (Kotter, 1988, p. 30). Although it is too early to say whether or not RX(UK) has been transformed completely, its performance in a depressed very competitive arena has been impressive. The work done to address and redefine the management philosophy, business and management processes is starting to establish a company that is more responsive and adaptable. The real test of the new RX(UK) may well come when the economy picks up, but for now the judgement would be that it is well positioned to take advantage of any upturn.

For organizations and their management the challenge is to maintain both flexibility and direction (Isenberg, 1987). It is also to recognize that there is no magic formula for balancing the here and now against the long-term strategy. Kanter (1984, p. 350) sums up the position: 'Piecemeal—segmentalist—change is not enough to help companies develop the innovations they need to survive and prosper. Innovation derives from the whole structure, culture, and approach to problems characterizing an organization.'

ACKNOWLEDGEMENTS

The research reported here was made possible by the cooperation of the Directors, Managers, and Staff of Rank Xerox (UK) Ltd. In order to respect the confidentiality of the interviews, questionnaires, meetings, and so on, individuals' names are not revealed.

REFERENCES

Asch, D. (1989) Strategic control: An overview of the issues. In D. Asch, and C. Bowman (eds), *Readings in Strategic Management*, Basingstoke, Hants, Macmillan.

Bowman, C. (1990) Shared understanding of strategic priorities. Paper presented to the Strategic Management Society Conference, Stockholm, Sweden,

Bowman, C. and Asch, D. (1987) *Strategic Management*, Basingstoke, Hants, Macmillan.

Buchanan, D., Boddy, D. and McCalman, J. (1988) Getting in, Getting on, Getting out, and Getting back. In A. Bryman (ed.), *Doing Research in Organizations*, London, Routledge, pp. 53–67.

Calori, R. and Atamer, T. (1990) How French managers deal with radical change. *Long Range Planning*, 23, No. 6. 44–55.

Chaffee, E. E. (1985) Three models of strategy. *Academy of Management Review*, 10. 89–98.

Chapman, P. (1988) Changing the corporate culture of Rank Xerox. *Long Range Planning*, 21, No. 2. 23–28.

Fahey, L. (1981) 'On strategic management decision processes. *Strategic Management Journal*, 2. 43–60.

Gersick, C. J. G. (1991) Revolutionary change theories: A multilevel exploration of the punctuated equilibrium paradigm. *Academy of Management Review*, 16, No. 1. 10–36.

Ghazanfar, A., McGee J. and Thomas, H. (1987) The impact of technological change on industry structure and corporate strategy: The case of the reprographics industry in the United Kingdom. In A. Pettigrew (ed.), *The Management of Strategic Change*. Oxford, Basil Blackwell.

Greiner, L. E. (1972) Evolution and revolution as organizations grow. *Harvard Business Review*, July–August, 37–46.

Greiner, L. E. and Bhambri, A. (1989) New CEO intervention and dynamics of deliberate strategic change. *Strategic Management Journal*, 10. 67–86.

Grinyer, P. H. and Spender, J.-C. (1979) Recipes, crises, and adaptation in mature businesses. *International Studies of Management & Organization*, IX, No. 3. 113–133.

Hambrick, D. C. (1980) Operationalising the concept of business level strategy in research. *Academy of Management Review*, 5. 567–575.

Hickson, D. J., Butler, R. J., Cray, D., Mallory, G. R. and Wilson, D. C. (1986), *Top Decisions: Strategic Decision-Making in Organizations*. Oxford, Basil Blackwell.

lsenberg, D. J. (1987) The tactics of strategic opportunism. *Harvard Business Review*, March–April, 92–97.

Jick, T. D. (1979) Mixing qualitative and quantitative methods: Triangulation in action. *Administrative Science Quarterly*, 24. 601–611.

Johnson, G. (1987) *Strategic Change and the Management Process*. Oxford, Basil Blackwell.

Johnson G. (1988) Rethinking incrementalism. *Strategic Management Journal*, 9. 75–91.

Johnson G. and Scholes, K. (1988) *Exploring Corporate Strategy*. Hemel Hempstead, Herts, Prentice-Hall International.

Kanter, R. M. (1984) *The Change Masters*, London, Unwin.

Kotter, J. P. (1988) *The Leadership Factor*. New York, The Free Press.

Kuhn, T. S. (1970) *The Structure of Scientific Revolution*. Chicago, University of Chicago Press.

Lindblom, C. E. (1959) The science of muddling through. In D. S. Pugh (ed.), *Organization Theory*, Paperback edn, 1984, Harmondsworth, Penguin, pp. 238–255.

Lorange, P. and Nelson, R. T. (1987) How to recognize—and avoid—organizational decline. *Sloan Management Review*, Spring, 41–48.

Mangham, I. L. (1986) *Power and Performance in Organizations*. Oxford, Basil Blackwell.

Miller, D. and Friesen, P. H. (1980) Momentum and revolution in organizational adaptation. *Academy of Management Journal*, 23, No. 4. 591–614.

Mintzberg, H. and Waters, J. A. (1982) Tracking strategy in an entrepreneurial firm. *Academy of Management Journal*, 25, No. 3. 465–499.

Mintzberg, H. and Waters, J. A. (1985) Of strategies deliberate and emergent. *Strategic Management Journal*, 6. 257–272.

Pettigrew, A. M. (1985a) Examining change in the long term context of culture and politics. In J. M. Pennings (ed.), *Organizational Strategy and Change*. San Francisco, CA, Jossey-Bass, pp. 269–318.

Pettigrew, A. M. (1985b) *The Awakening Giant*. Oxford: Basil Blackwell.

Pettigrew, A. M. (1990), Longitudinal field research on change: Theory and practice. *Organization Science*, 1, No. 3. 267–292.

Porter, M. E. (1980) *Competitive Strategy*. New York, The Free Press.

Quinn, J. B. (1980) *Strategies for Change*, Homewood, Ill, Irwin.

Stevenson, H. H. (1976) Defining corporate strengths and weaknesses. *Sloan Management Review*, Spring, 51–68.

Stopford, J. M. and Baden-Fuller, C, (1990) Corporate rejuvenation. *Journal of Management Studies*, 27: 4. 399–415.

Tichy, N. M. (1983) *Managing Strategic Change*. New York, John Wiley.

Tushman, M. L., Newman, W. H and Romanelli, E. (1986) Convergence and upheaval: Managing the unsteady pace of organizational evolution. *California Management Review,* XXIX, No. 1. 29–44.

Tushman, M. L. and Romanelli, E. (1990) Organizational evolution: A metamorphosis model of convergence and reorientation. In B. M. Staw and L. L. Cummings (eds), *The Evolution and Adaptation of Organizations*. Greenwich, Conn, JAI Press, pp. 139–190.

Walker, R. (1992) Rank Xerox—management revolution. *Long Range Planning,* 25, No. 1. 9–21.

Yin, R. K. (1984) *Case Study Research: Design and Methods,* Newbury Park, CA, Sage.

11

ACQUISITION REGIMES: MANAGING CULTURAL RISK AND RELATIVE DEPRIVATION IN CORPORATE ACQUISITIONS

Kenneth David

Associate Professor, Michigan State University
Visiting Research Fellow, Universiteit van Utrecht

Harbir Singh

Associate Professor, University of Pennsylvania

INTRODUCTION

Acquisition cultural risk refers to complementary processes (cultural and relative power issues) that profoundly affect pre-acquisition evaluation and negotiations as well as post-acquisition integration. In previous work far more attention has been paid to strategic fit than to organizational and cultural fit of acquiring and target firms. More recently, Haspeslagh and Jemison (1991) discussed how cultural differences have to be seen in the context of the integration mode chosen by the acquiring firm; Bastien (personal communication) has been working on impacts of relative power following acquisitions. We intend, in this paper, to pursue both of these directions of inquiry. In a nutshell, *managing cultural and*

International Review of Strategic Management, volume 4.
Edited by D. E. Hussey. Published 1993 by John Wiley & Sons Ltd

power issues is an essential task if the acquiring firm expects to implement a coherent post-acquisition strategy.

Cultural compatibility is critical to post-acquisition performance. Hans Werthen, Chairman of the Board of the Swedish corporation, Electrolux, suggests: 'We have in the past very carefully examined whether prospective acquisition candidates will be able to adapt to the Electrolux style of doing business. This factor is as important to us as acquirers as the financial aspects of the acquisition.' (Field research, H. Singh). Compatibility is not a state of being, but an objective that is achieved through processes of inter-organizational learning and then constructing a common cultural discourse (an adequately shared set of understandings). Establishing a common cultural discourse between organizations is crucial.

Cultural compatibility is only part of the cultural story of integration. Managing power dynamics between the acquiring and target firms is essential to enlist commitment to a common cultural discourse. In discussions of corporate acquisitions, much attention has focused on winning over the target firm's top management: they are offered strong financial incentives to stay or to leave. In addition, winning over the middle and lower ranks' commitment is important to avoid staff defection or non-compliance with the strategic objectives and to promote cultural understandings within the new merged organization. Neutralizing relative deprivation (perceived inequity and power imbalances) by financial or other incentives to the lower ranks as well as to top management is also crucial.

OBJECTIVES

Our objectives in this paper are a segment of a larger research program aimed at combining strategic and cultural analyses for the study of inter-organizational relationships—mergers and acquisitions, joint ventures, strategic alliances, and long-term, large-scale projects. These inter-organizational relationships have supplemented the multinational corporation as means of business expansion. Our objectives in this work are as follows: The first part of the paper reviews prior research on corporate acquisitions; the second part explores a framework for analysing acquisition culture risk. This framework covers problems of cultural misunderstanding (cultural risk) and power issues (relative deprivation) in the acquisition transaction. Concepts transposed from cultural anthropology as well as the organization and culture literature are brought to the service of merger and acquisition studies.

The third part links these cultural and power issues with strategic issues. Cultural and power issues become problematic depending on the acquirer's strategic choices. We introduce the notion that acquiring firms employ a variety of *acquisition regimes*, planned or unplanned programs to approach and integrate target firms; these regimes have trade-offs just like any other organizational program.

Exposition and illustration of the framework appears in the fourth part. To study acquisition cultural risk, we present detailed case studies—the takeover actions between a French and a British advertising firm (BDDP and BMP) General Motors' acquisition of Electronic Data Systems, General Electric's integration strategy, Deloitte Haskins & Sells' merger with Touche Ross—and shorter contrast cases. These cases meet the following criteria: (i) the companies involved in the transaction have a good strategic fit, (ii) the companies' assets are complementary, and (iii) the acquisition is an appropriate response to industry conditions. Space prohibits full documentation of these points in all cases presented.

A concluding statement summarizes our findings and places points of our argument in their theoretical context.

PRIOR RESEARCH

We now review prior work on corporate acquisitions. Because this paper focuses on cultural and power issues in acquisitions, our coverage of strategic fit in acquisitions is relatively brief.

Strategic Fit

Strategic fit is defined as 'the degree to which the target firm augments or complements the parent's strategy' (Jemison and Sitkin, 1986) in terms of industry, market, or technology. Research on strategic fit focuses on corporate and business (market and product) relatedness between acquiring and target firms (Singh and Montgomery, 1987; Shelton, 1988; Lubatkin, 1987; Chatterjee, 1986). These works relate strategic fit to stock market based financial performance indicators: the principal insight is that the competitive bidding process yields small appropriable gains to the bidding firm but high gains to the target firm. Close fit in products and markets does not result in higher returns to the acquiring firm's stockholders.

Organizational Fit

Organizational fit between an acquirer and a target firm relates in part to strategic fit, but includes issues of implementation of the acquisition strategy. Strategic fit can result in potential synergies; organizational fit is a necessary condition for effective realization of the potential synergies.

Research on organizational fit has therefore concerned itself with organizational structures, incentives, cultural factors and human resource issues relating to implementation of acquisition strategy. Organizational fit is defined as 'the match between administrative practices, cultural practices, and personnel characteristics of the target and the parent firms and may directly affect how the firms can be integrated with respect to day-to-day operations once an acquisition has been made' (Jemison and Sitkin, 1986).

Previous studies have related post-acquisition outcomes to particular organizational features such as structure, matches in corporate management styles, matches in control systems and differences in the willingness of employees in the two firms to adapt to the other's culture and systems. Mismatches can result in negative consequences to motivation and productivity of individuals within the firms (Mace and Montgomery, 1962; Marks, 1982). Further, there is resistance to changes in structure on both sides of the transaction (Pitts, 1976). These results suggest that difficulties in implementing planned changes in the acquired and acquiring firms after the transaction are underestimated by acquirers. Matching control and compensation systems after acquisition also appears to be a more complex task than typically envisioned by managers prior to the transaction (Kitching, 1967; Mace and Montgomery, 1962; Shrivastava, 1986). That is, managers underestimate the degree to which these systems are idiosyncratic to particular organizations, given their histories and their cultures.

We note that while the set of organizational fit studies addresses a range of organizational dimensions, each study typically addresses only one or several dimensions. By contrast, Walter (1985) attempts a holistic approach regarding impacts on a target firm's organization and culture when an acquiring firm's organization and culture is superimposed on it. He discusses six dichotomies stemming from core conflict of human versus property values[1] and finds that acquirers tilt priority towards property values in the period after an acquisition.

A recent study (Chatterjee, Lubatkin, Schweiger, and Weber, 1989) considers both cultural fit and strategic fit in corporate acquisitions. This study controls for strategic fit by studying only related mergers, studies cultural fit by questioning top managers involved in mergers about their perceptions of cultural differences and the buying firm's tolerance of multiculturalism, and relates these findings to post-merger stock market performance. They find that a perception of higher cultural similarity by the top executives is positively related to higher post-acquisition stock market returns. The findings are very interesting in that the stock market does recognize externally visible cultural compatibilities between the two firms. A possible limitation of this work, acknowledged by the authors, is that their characterization of cultural compatibility is somewhat narrowly focused on top management.

Modes of Acculturation and Cultural Diversity in Acquiring Firms

Only a few studies focus on modes of acculturation of the target firm after the acquisition transaction. Walter (1985) relates merger motives and degree of relatedness to post-acquisition acculturation. He discusses the varying post-acquisition consequences to target firms depending on the type of acquisition (vertical, horizontal, concentric, or conglomerate): in general, target firms experience far greater interference with their operating policies when the acquiring firm is pursuing one of the first three types than with the last type. When the motive of a merger is operating synergy, the target firm is likely to be more closely strategically related to the acquired firm and more closely integrated with it following acquisition. In this case, the acquirer is likely to impose its culture on the target firm in order to integrate operations and to reduce duplication; such cultural imposition, however, may place acculturative stress on members of the target firm. When the motive is financial synergy, the two firms are less likely to be related and there is little need for integration beyond financial systems. In unrelated acquisitions, therefore, target firm members have less stress of acculturation to the dominant culture of the acquiring firm. Nahavandi and Malekzadeh (1988) further suggest that post-merger integration stress is reduced when the acquiring firm is multicultural, that is, when the firm tolerates cultural diversity within its organization and is better able to tolerate cultural differences of the target firm.

Types of Capability Transfer and Cultural Issues

Haspeslagh and Jemison discuss three types of capabilities that create value if successfully transferred in an acquisition: resource sharing, transfer of functional skills, and transfer of general management capability (1991, pp. 140, 141). These types have implications for autonomy and culture of the target: 'autonomy should be provided the acquired unit if the survival of the strategic capabilities on which the acquisition is based depends on preservation of the organizational culture from which they came' (1991, p. 143).

Summary

Strategic analyses dominate the literature. Extensive research on strategic issues in acquisitions concludes that relatedness in products and markets is not a guarantee for acquisition success. Strategic analysis is appropriate, but needs to be complemented with studies of the organizational consequences of acquisitions.

Studies relating organizational fit to acquisition performance underscore the need for more research identifying patterns of successful and unsuccessful acquisition strategy implementation. Previous writings are top management centered, focusing primarily on impacts to the top management with less emphasis on other ranks. Further, since most previous studies mainly address the effects on post-acquisition integration of organizational fit in particular dimensions, such as structure, compensation systems, etc., while only several address cultural impact issues, it is appropriate to call for two types of research. First, extensive case studies can highlight the sequence and choice of post-acquisition management techniques used in particularly successful or unsuccessful acquisitions. Second, survey research or other large-sample research can relate the incidence of particular attributes of the two firms (such as compatibility of incentive systems and organizational structure) to post-acquisition outcomes. In this paper, we view acquisition success as an outcome of effective strategic analysis combined with management of cultural and power issues and use case studies to illustrate our points.

A FRAMEWORK FOR UNDERSTANDING ACQUISITION CULTURE RISK

We now propose an analytic framework for assessing cultural and power risks in both pre- and post-acquisition phases. This scheme rests on conceptions of organizational culture, cultural distance, cultural impact, and relative deprivation derived from the organizational culture and cultural anthropology literatures.[2]

Culture and Organizational Culture

All human societies require a system of reasonably shared understandings in order to incite predictable, coordinated activity among societal members. Cultural understandings can be described as four operations that individuals learn while growing up in a society. Culture *classifies* phenomena into discontinuous units. Culture sets forth appropriate *codes for conduct* for the phenomena so classified. Culture specifies *priorities* for the use of different codes for conduct in different social contexts. Culture *legitimizes* and incites commitment to all of these understandings about reality. For elaboration, see Terpstra and David (1991, ch. 1).

All human organizations have *culture*: an imperfectly shared system of understandings with which organization members orient themselves to internal and external relationships and processes. We define *organizational culture* along three axes (cultural operations, media of communication, and cultural access).

The *operations* of classifying, coding, prioritizing, and legitimizing reality construct a system of understandings. The culture of an organization is interwoven within its business activities. *Media of communication* refers to the spectrum of media—from the formal organizational chart to informal communications—through which understandings are quite frequently *imperfectly* transmitted. The notion of *cultural access* focuses on an ordinary structure within organizations: that units within organizations benignly or consciously conceal their backstage effective codes for conduct, yielding a structure of diverse understandings that are not completely accessible to one another.

These concepts have two immediate applications for understanding acquisitions. First, they highlight the difference between what an acquiring firm can easily learn about a target firm's organizational culture (its frontstage culture: formally communicated, relatively standardized understandings that guide conduct for members of the firm) and what an acquiring firm can learn only with greater difficulty (its effective backstage culture: less formally communicated, and more ambiguous or divergent understandings that are effective guides to conduct). Not all acquiring firms choose to learn and respond to a target firm's culture. If the acquirer wishes to enlist the target firm's culture as part of its integration program, it faces a task of delving into the target's backstage as well as frontstage culture.

Second, these concepts highlight a source of anxiety on the part of a target firm regarding an acquiring firm's communications. After a merger, upper management usually delivers a frontstage-mode, encouraging and reassuring version of the new reality. A Rhône-Poulenc Agrochemical executive's statements on his company's acquisition regime may be interpreted in this light. According to Desmarescaux (1989), Rhône-Poulenc's negotiating team includes not just financial and legal officers, but also future operational officers (one in financial/legal; one in human resource management; one for business coordination). The idea is to reduce discontinuity between acquisition planning and implementation. The key features of implementation are participative design and meritocracy staffing. Rhône-Poulenc installs a matrix of steering committees including personnel from both sides. Staffing decisions are based on competence and potential for the future rather than on fairness to past employment or balance between the two parties. Rhône-Poulenc's post-acquisition staff policy emphasizes equal jeopardy: the best person is chosen for each job. This criterion is prioritized over other criteria such as previous history or maintaining a sense of balance between personnel from acquiring or target firms. Thus a major message is communicated to target firm personnel: they are not categorical second-class citizens.

Depending on the acquirer, the frontstage presentation may or may not closely resemble the effective backstage reality that follows. Jack Welch of General Electric is quite straightforward in his message that counterparts from an old GE division and a newly acquired company are in open competition: 'after an acquisition, one plus one equals one!' For GE, backstage practice closely resembles this frontstage statement. Such a statement is culturally unacceptable in the Netherlands, where it is expected that a company does not casually discard its personnel. In Holland, acquiring firms make frontstage statements that target firm managers will be retained; in the ABN–AMRO case reported later, the Welch formula is fully operative backstage in practice.

Potentials for Acquisition Cultural Risk

This section introduces two inescapable facts of life, cultural distance and power asymmetry, that pose *potential* problems for all coordinated social activity. An organization can learn about them, manage them, even manipulate them. Or an organization can ignore them and experience their impact.

Cultural distance

Our notion of *cultural distance* refers to the fact that before they enter organizations, individuals have already been socialized in their national culture and frequently socialized in a professional culture—such as business, legal, engineering, or medical culture: see Figure 11.1. This is a simplified statement: in various apprenticeship situations, a person enters a company and acquires a professional culture while on the job (Terpstra and David, 1991).

No matter how rigorous the regime of corporate selection and training, individuals retain earlier socializations that affect their perceptions and understanding. A massive study on work-related values in 60 country offices of IBM is evidence of the continuing impact of national culture. Despite IBM's well-known selection and training regime, IBM employees were surveyed as differing strongly along four major dimensions of work-related values (Hofstede, 1980).

Power asymmetry

All human societies—even the structurally least complex band societies—are

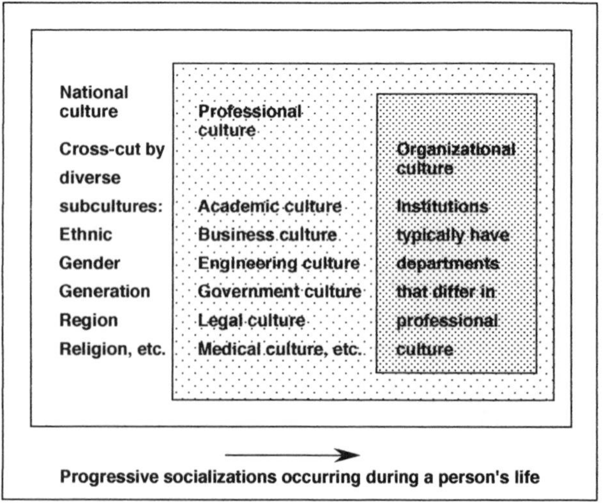

Figure 11.1 Triple socialization and cultural distance

structured with an unequal distribution of power. Individuals, groups, and organizations have unequal control over resources and resource allocation decisions, over strategic information, over followers, etc. Whatever the source of control, relative control is power. Power differentials or asymmetries always pose the potential for non-compliance, opposition, conflict, and change. As we shall see, power asymmetry is present in all acquisition transactions—even in 'mergers of equals'.

Acquisition Cultural Risk

We introduce the concept *acquisition cultural risk* as a cover term for related processes (cultural impact and relative deprivation) that are important determinants both of the advisability of engaging in a corporate acquisition and of the post-acquisition strategy a firm may adopt.

Cultural impact

Whereas *cultural distance* only represents a potential for misunderstanding, *cultural impact* refers to threats to effective integration of post-acquisition activities due to imperfectly shared understandings. Later, we develop the theme that—depending on integration choices—cultural distance between an acquiring and a target firm may or may not become operative as cultural impact. Said again, cultural impact is a problem that occurs when people who differ in backstage culture must work together. As was indicated above with the notion of cultural access, risk of cultural misunderstanding is present even within organizations; such risk is a greater, generic problem in all inter-organizational relationships (acquisitions, joint ventures, strategic alliance, and long-term service contracts). The common element is that two or more organizations make a connection for sound business reasons without, typically, previous knowledge of one another's backstage cultures. Managers with excellent interpersonal communications skills may still have little skill in reading and responding to another organization's culture.

Relative deprivation

Whereas *power asymmetry* only represents a potential for non-compliance, *relative deprivation* refers to threats to effective integration of post-acquisition activities due to a social mobilization of non-compliant behavior. Because acquisitions entail coordinating behavior in the context of directed change, a concept from anthropological social movements theory is appropriate here. Aberle (1962) defines *relative deprivation* as a

> negative discrepancy between legitimate expectation and actuality. Where an

> individual or a group has a particular expectation and furthermore where this expectation is considered to be a proper state of affairs, and where something less than the expectation is fulfilled, we may speak of relative deprivation.... The deprivation is not a particular objective state of affairs, but a difference between an anticipated state of affairs and a less agreeable actuality.

People make three key judgments when comparing expectations and actuality: Are our present circumstances as favorable as someone else's circumstances? Are our present circumstances as favorable as our past? Are our future prospects as favorable as our present circumstances? These judgments may refer to practical interests (possessions, power, rank) or ideological ones (adherence to a cultural order felt to be fair and legitimate). These three judgments may be experienced as personal or as a member of a group. The concept of relative deprivation is familiar to cultural anthropologists who study the mobilization of collectivities of persons into social movements.

In social movements, perceived relative deprivation results in poor adherence to the understandings that have been established by a dominant class in society and poor compliance with behavioral codes (David, 1977). A similar relationship occurs with acquiring and target firms. Until it is proven otherwise, members of an organization perceive a merger or acquisition as a situation of profound change. If, in addition, they perceive relative deprivation in their changing situation, the most well-orchestrated program for developing shared understandings between the acquiring and target firms may fall on deaf ears.

Summary: acquisition cultural risk

Acquisition cultural risk includes two related processes. Cultural impacts due to imperfectly shared understandings occur between persons who differ in, at least, backstage organizational culture. These cultural impacts can be managed by organizational routines that specifically aim to construct an adequately shared set of understandings among people who will have to work together. Power asymmetry between the parties may be collectively perceived as relative deprivation; relative deprivation usually results in poor adherence to a common cultural order that acquirers try to establish. Organizational routines can neutralize relative deprivation.

Figure 11.2 shows the combined impact of cultural sharing and adherence to understanding on post-acquisition activity. Neither dimension alone results in the integrated, well coordinated activity necessary to achieve the expected benefits of combination. Managing cultural risk and relative deprivation issues are processes critical both to approaching target firms and to coordinating activities in the post-acquisition period. Coordinated behavior among people requires not only shared understandings about what is expected of them; it also requires *adherence or commitment* to this social construction of their reality. Along

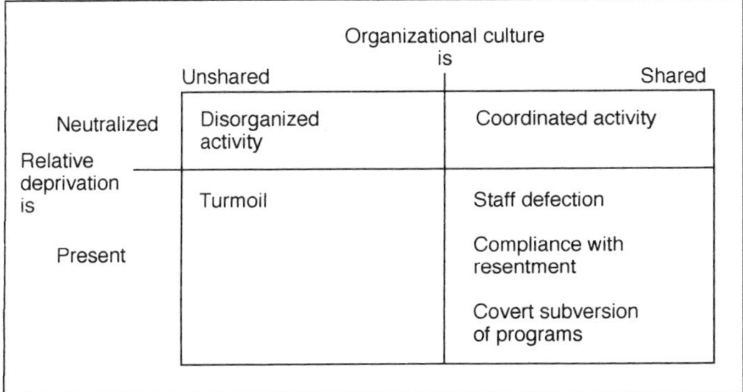

Figure 11.2 Cultural sharing, relative deprivation, and activity

with strategic factors, such coordinated activity is a determinant of post-acquisition performance and value creation. See Figure 11.2 which foreshadows observations from the following set of acquisition cases. It is equally applicable to the analysis of attempted takeovers (see below, Case V). Such discussion of related cultural and power issues is barren until it is linked with strategic issues, a topic to which we now turn.

LINKING STRATEGIC, CULTURAL AND POWER ISSUES

The acquisition cultural risk framework intends to avoid two pitfalls: an overly simplistic version of organizational culture and a narrow conception of cultural determinism. These pitfalls are avoided by linking organizational strategies and processes on one hand and cultural and power issues on the other.[3] See Figure 11.3.

Acquisition Regimes

A linking concept is necessary. The concept of *acquisition regime* is here defined as an acquiring firm's set of pre- and post-acquisition organizational processes and policies for approaching and subsequently integrating target firms. We shall present cases to illustrate the following points.

First, these regimes have a common overt purpose: to implement strategic choices of how to acquire a firm, how much of the acquired firm's operations are to be integrated, and how strongly are target units linked with their counterparts.

Second, we suggest that prior approaches to acquisition management can

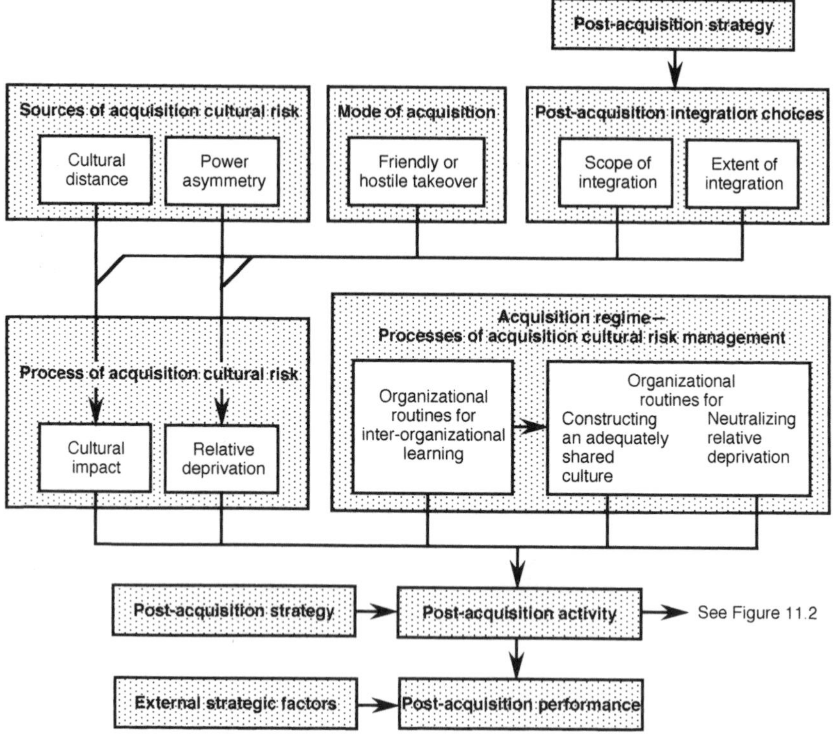

Figure 11.3 Power and cultural issues in relation to strategic factors

be substantially enriched by identifying quite distinct varieties of acquisition regimes.

- All acquisition regimes distribute benefits and opportunities to the acquiring and target firms: some regimes incite relative deprivation, others neutralize it, and still others eliminate it.
- All regimes bear on the cultural gap between the acquiring and target firms: some regimes include pre-acquisition learning routines while others forge ahead without pre-learning; some regimes have no specified cultural policy, others include cultural policy routines that bridge the cultural gap, still others forcibly impose their culture on the target.

Third, analysis of cases brings our work within sight of relatively standard business analyses. For acquisition regimes have trade-offs just like any other business factor (raising market share for the long term may require reducing profit per unit on the short term). Whether or not planned by the acquirer, the routines that comprise acquisition regimes have trade-offs—there are various impacts on cultural and power issues.

Summing up, the notion of acquisition regime is a linking concept in the acquisition cultural risk framework, that is, linking strategic, cultural, and power issues that are always present in completing and implementing acquisition transactions.

Strategic Factors and Cultural Distance

In this section, we link the factor of cultural distance with certain strategic factors:

(1) Scope of integration: how much of the acquired firm is to be integrated?
(2) Motivation of takeover: operating or strategic synergy
(3) Extent of post-acquisition integration: how tightly are the target firm's units linked? fully integrated into a merged organization? loosely federated with units from the acquiring firm? remain autonomous? sold off?
(4) Mode of takeover: friendly or hostile?

One strategic factor, the scope of integration, is unambiguous. When more units must be integrated to attain benefits of combination, there is more work and difficulties are more likely to occur. The remaining factors require more discussion.

A standard classification for takeovers is horizontal, vertical, concentric, and unrelated categories. Walter's propositions relate the motivation of takeover to post-acquisition acculturation stress. Units in firms acquired for operating synergy may face much acculturation stress because they are pressured to be tightly linked with counterparts in the acquiring firm; whereas units in firms acquired for financial synergy may face little post-acquisition stress because they are left to run autonomously. (A variant of financial acquisition, of course, is acquiring a firm and then selling off undervalued units. In this case, stress faced by sold-off units is indirectly a problem for the acquiring firm; units that are retained may react with heightened uncertainty).

Theoretically, acquisitions motivated by solely operating or financial synergy are possible. In real transactions, mixed cases also occur. Acquiring firms confront multiunit, heterogeneous target firms. The acquiring firm may face a variety of integration decisions: the extent of post-acquisition integration differs for various units; some units are linked more tightly than others. *It is more precise to consider impacts of both motivation for takeover and extent of post-acquisition integration (including cultural risk to integration) at the level of business units within the target company rather than at the level of the entire target company.*

ACQUISITION REGIMES AND THEIR TRADE-OFFS

Cases: Strategic Factors and Cultural Risk

We now propose to show that the four strategic factors listed above must be considered in the context of culture distance. The following set of cases[4]—the ABN–AMRO merger, the NMB–Postbank merger, and the Japanese acquisition of a Dutch firm—differ in cultural distance; these cases will show that cultural distance is not an implacable force but becomes mobilized as cultural risk under specifiable strategic conditions.

Alternatively, cultural distance can be neutralized by cultural bridging techniques such as Sony's strategy of acquiring CBS only after joint venturing with the latter for some years. See Figure 11.4.

Case I: Merger of ABN and AMRO banks: firms differing only in organizational culture

When full integration of business units is required for a post-acquisition strategy, then even minor cultural distance can be a problem—even in the case of a friendly merger between strategically-related companies.

ABN and AMRO are two Dutch wholesale and retail commercial banks with contrasting organizational cultures. AMRO is rather more informal in interpersonal relationships, more aggressive and domestically oriented. ABN culture is rather conservative and formal in interpersonal relationships and relatively

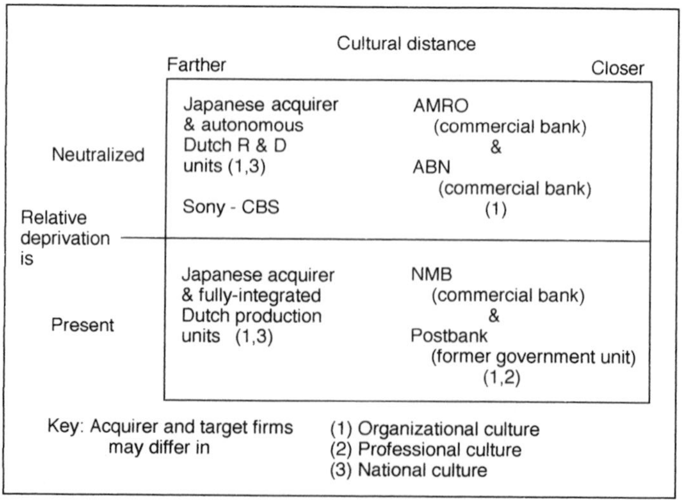

Relative deprivation is	Cultural distance: Farther	Cultural distance: Closer
Neutralized	Japanese acquirer & autonomous Dutch R & D units (1,3) Sony - CBS	AMRO (commercial bank) & ABN (commercial bank) (1)
Present	Japanese acquirer & fully-integrated Dutch production units (1,3)	NMB (commercial bank) & Postbank (former government unit) (1,2)

Key: Acquirer and target firms may differ in (1) Organizational culture (2) Professional culture (3) National culture

Figure 11.4 Cases of cultural distance and strategic factors

more internationally oriented. With an orchestrated effort, the two banks elicited from personnel ways the banks might work together and communicated their intended changes in a weekly publication called *Fusie Nieuws* (Merger News). In our terms, such a media of communication usually communicates *frontstage* messages that attempt to encourage personnel engaged in the integration.

The regime and its trade-offs

As the combination is billed as a merger of equals, we might speak of a merger regime rather than an acquisition regime. Certainly, a major feature of the integration regime was to include all the previous boardmembers into a rather large new board. Such a move is one variant of an *equity* solution to avoid relative deprivation in the top management. This action has had two trade-offs. First, various executives just below the board level perceived their route to the board blocked and defected to other major Dutch banks such as NMB and Rabobank. Second, doubling up of the top leaves boardmembers with spare time to supervise the activities of previously more powerful executives one level down.

Even though these banks have relatively less cultural distance than the cases that follow, the integration is intricate because of wide-scale integration. Billed as a merger of equals, closer inspection reveals a series of takeovers. ABN's very powerful international division has taken over the moderate sized AMRO counterpart division with little fuss. On the other hand, various home country divisions such as back office transactions and the system of bank regions in the Netherlands now clearly follow the AMRO mold. Projects are undertaken to acquire benefits of combination. For example, a project to harmonize the information system is underway. Managers report that ABN's information system is outdated and that AMRO's information system is becoming the template for the integrated system. The combined work group charged with this project has had to rectify modes of communication and decision-making in order to complete the project. Some dilemmas of relative deprivation remain to be solved concerning regional and branch organization. Because the old AMRO organization had thirty regions while the former ABN organization had just sixteen, any ABN regional manager who stays at that level has lost power. Because AMRO and ABN branches are present in every moderate sized town and city, the merged organization must choose one branch manager out of two currently present at each location. Middle managers are faced with their specific takeover situation rather than an overall integration.

Case II: NMB and Postbank: firms differing in organizational and professional culture

This case of combining two organizations that differ only in organizational culture contrasts with another recent friendly merger between two Dutch banks with apparent market and financial complementarity. This merger is facing integration difficulties because one bank, NMB, has a conventional private sector culture while the other, Postbank, was formerly a government agency.

The regime and its trade-offs

This is, strictly speaking, a clash between two professional cultures. For example, a project to harmonize a part of the information system is currently in progress. A manager reports that differences in management style are definitely affecting progress. NMB personnel are used to a fair degree of autonomy when working and bridle when working under a Postbank supervisor who expects fairly frequent and detailed reports. Conversely, Postbank personnel are accustomed to strong supervision and feel they are receiving insufficient guidance when working under an NMB supervisor.

This situation became tense when the direction of integration moved unilaterally in the direction of NMB. Protests by the workers' council were widely reported in the popular press. The situation was mitigated by several factors over time. First, only about one-third of the banking operations were integrated. NMB's funds transfer system is part of the national commercial bank network. Postbank's funds transfer system is a separate system that reflects the former government agency status of the bank. This *Giro* system is the channel for citizens' tax payments as well as for many companies' payroll systems. These systems are not to be integrated. Second, the NMB–Postbank Group merged with a large insurance company, Nationale Nederlanden, late in 1990. In mid-1991, Nationale Nederlanden stated that its prime motivation was to use the widespread Postbank branch system—every locale has one—to distribute a second tier of insurance products. Postbank's sense of relative deprivation has decreased following this announcement.

Case III: Japanese acquisition of a Dutch company: firms differing in organizational and national culture

A Japanese company acquired a moderate sized Dutch company five years ago. Several units within the target company were left severely alone because they fitted the parent company's normal strategy of buying a foreign company to acquire innovative product technology rather than leasing the technology; with full, unrestricted access to the proprietary technology, they would then expend research and development effort to modify the technology in relation to their production technology. These units experienced little intervention ('Nothing has changed here except the name on the door') and thus no culture shock of accommodating to Japanese management.

On the other hand, production units within the target company were expected to accommodate. Japanese management is often noted for consensual decision-making. Consensus is not always practiced in managing a foreign acquisition.

The Japanese company initially installed their personnel down to the shopfloor supervisory level. Because the Dutch workers—who are in general far less adversarial than American counterparts—were covertly rebelling against what they experienced as arrogant, autocratic communications and decision-making with the supervisors, communications and decision-making were compromised in the Dutch production sites.[5] After two years of poorly coordinated activity, the Japanese installed Dutch managers nearly to the top. Local communication improved but the Japanese top management were often caught in a cross-fire when communicating with the parent company. The Japanese wife of a Dutch executive (from another company) was hired as a cultural mediator.

By contrast, the following case of a Japanese acquirer and a US target illustrates conduct in which strong cultural distance is neutralized. The acquirer engages in routines to know enough about the target firm's culture to facilitate post-acquisition management.

Case IV: SONY–CBS: pre-acquisition learning by joint venturing

The highly visible acquisition of CBS by Sony, Inc. in 1987 was made nineteen years after establishing a joint venture with CBS records in 1968. The venture's aim was to further sales of American music in the Japanese market. In the course of the joint venture Sony became very familiar with CBS's internal operations and top management.

Armed with this knowledge of CBS, Sony was able to pursue a post-acquisition cultural policy of minimal intervention. They had determined that minimal intervention would be generally consistent with three premises generally true of Japanese acquirers in the late 1980s (Peterson, 1990). First, a strategic orientation to long-term partnership: Japanese firms are more concerned with obtaining market share than with immediate profitability. The Japanese parent is looking for long-term operating success rather than short-term rewards gained from divesting assets of the acquired firm. Second, local acceptance: acquirers are concerned with public opinion. For example, when Mitsubishi Real Estate bought 51% of Rockefeller Center, public opinion was against them, even though Rockefeller Center initiated the deal. Peterson notes that other Japanese firms became reluctant to acquire other US cultural symbols, despite economic benefits. Third, management–labor relationships: the tradition of loyalty to the firm is carried across borders in that it is rare for a new Japanese parent to lay-off substantial numbers of managers at the time of the acquisition. Sony has been true to this philosophy in retaining CBS's governing group.

This acquisition strategy sequence has implications for Sony's image as an acquirer at a time of controversy over the Japanese direct investment in the United States. Sony's non-intervention in CBS's daily operations has allayed fears of massive post-acquisition disruption (see below, the TWA and General Electric cases). Yoshihido Kondo, a senior analyst at Daiwa Securities, summed up the expectations of the cultural matches and mismatches between US and Japanese firms best when he remarked, 'Sony may be the only company with a corporate culture that is Americanized enough to pull it [the acquisition of a Hollywood studio] off. Matsushita, JVC—they are all too conservative for this' (Kondo, 1990).

Implications of Cases I–IV for acquisition cultural risk management

The theoretical point is to avoid a simplistic formula such as greater cultural distance results in greater problems of post-acquisition integration. The two bank cases are friendly mergers between firms in the same industry subsector, retail and wholesale banking: in each pair, the companies are strategically related. The pairs differ in the degree of cultural distance. First, both cases involve companies with the same national culture. NMB and Postbank differ in professional and organizational culture while ABN and AMRO differ only in organizational culture.

This is not the end of the story. Relative deprivation and extent of integration patterns differ. NMB has dominated Postbank but the extent of integration is only moderate—about one-third of the total operations have been combined. Recent changes stemming from a third merger partner, Nationale Nederlanden insurance company, have alleviated the deprivation problems to some extent. On the other hand, particular units within ABN and AMRO have taken over counterpart units and the linkage of units is very tight. Deprivation problems occur. We can *not* conclude that the merger case where companies differ only in organizational culture is having easier sailing than the case where the companies differ both in organizational and professional culture.

The first international acquisition case—where a Japanese company took over a Dutch company—holds the degree of cultural distance constant and records varying cultural outcomes depending on the mode of integration of specific business units in the acquired firm. Culture shock due to cultural distance is not relevant in the case of the autonomous R&D units but is fully operative in the case of the fully integrated production units. This problem has not been solved but only transferred to the middle management. The second international case—Sony's acquisition of CBS—demonstrates how an acquisition regime that combines pre-acquisition learning and post-acquisition multicultural tolerance succeeds in neutralizing cultural distance.

All these cases illustrate the need to consider cultural and strategic factors together: cultural distance is not an implacable force but becomes mobilized as cultural risk under certain conditions.

Case V: BDDP's attempt to acquire BMP: interplay between cultural issues and relative deprivation[6]

This next case, the failed attempt of BDDP (a French advertising firm) to acquire BMP (a British advertising firm) also avoids a simplistic cultural distance explanation in favor of showing the interplay between cultural differences and relative deprivation. See Figure 11.5.

BMP: background, culture and acquisition regime

Boase Massimi Pollitt (BMP) was the fifth-ranked UK-based communications group. Founded in 1968 as an advertising agency, they diversified into marketing services and developed an international presence, especially in the United States. Martin Boase, the current chairman and CEO, was the only remaining key founder. BMP once attempted to expand by a merger of equals. During the 1970s, they briefly associated with Univas, a French company to whom they sold 50% of their equity; they repurchased this stake in 1979. BMP has more typically expanded by acquiring relatively smaller entities—large advertising agencies and marketing services companies.

BMP's management was driven by its priority on the quality of its creative reputation. Highly rated by industry peers, the agency had won both effectiveness and creativity industry awards every year since 1983. BMP and Martin Boase were viewed as the pioneers of British advertising. The culture was said to be highly intellectual and democratic with very accessible managers.

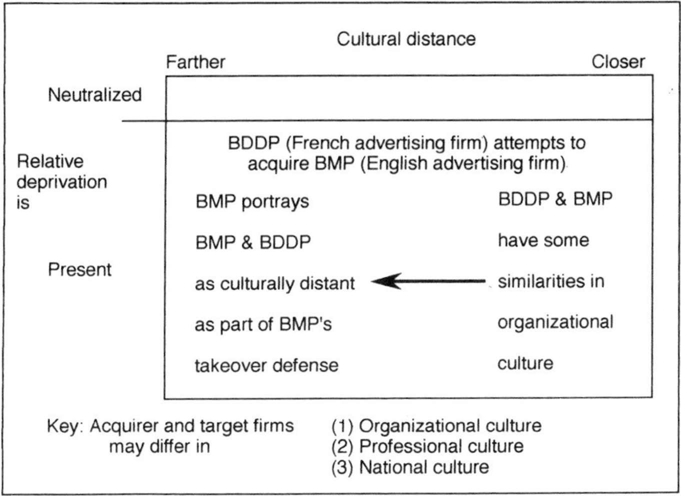

Figure 11.5 Exaggeration of cultural distance during takeover defense

BMP was known for strong strategic planning skills; each subsidiary was controlled by centralized planning although each entity was encouraged to operate independently. Founders of each acquired company could remain shareholders of their own firm.

BDDP: background, culture, and acquisition regime

BDDP (Boulet–Dru–Dupuy–Petit) was a privately held French advertising and communications group, founded in 1984. Their creative reputation and their dynamism were uncontested in France, where industry peers viewed them as an effectively managed and highly entrepreneurial company.

From its inception, BDDP's ambitious strategy was to become a major international communications group built around a network of creative advertising agencies with a strong position in their national or regional markets. They expanded rapidly during their first three years by both internal growth and acquisitions. Their billings ranking in France improved from tenth in 1986 to seventh in 1987 and to fifth in 1988. By 1987, they had begun developing an international network through start-ups and small acquisitions. By December 1988, agencies in London, Milan, Barcelona, Madrid, Brussels, and Dusseldorf were added to the group: BDDP had a European network.

Expansion by acquisition had been successful due to key features of BDDP culture. They recognized that creativity is a driving force for success in a people's business; imposing an external culture on an acquired company would drive creative people away. Because BDDP granted autonomy to each subsidiary at the operating level, the subsidiaries could be quite responsive to their country markets. John Allen, managing director of WAHT subsidiary in the UK said that he 'could not ask for more' in terms of autonomy and that 'the French are much more aware [than the Americans] of the yawning culture gap in Europe, so that they are more prepared to allow you to do what you think will work'. (We earlier saw Sony's use of multicultural tolerance as a post-integration strategy.) Internal communications allowed coherence within the group. Planning was centralized through business plans designed at the subsidiaries level. Centralized budget and financial control management complemented planning and allowed close monitoring of each business unit's strategic directions.

Summing up so far, there are important similarities between BMP and BDDP. Despite different national origins, the two firms share not only professional culture (they are in the same sectors of their industry) but also various key features of organizational culture: priority on creativity and decentralization. Further, each firm had grown successfully through prior acquisitions, no mean feat in a creative business where human resources can easily be lost after an acquisition. Advertising requires culturally-responsive operations. Both firms had developed successful integration regimes: imposing centralized planning and financial monitoring while allowing the autonomy necessary to preserve each acquired firm's capability to operate effectively in its home country.

Strategic considerations

A strong case could be made for this transaction. Both were very creative and highly regarded groups. Both Boase and Boulet were ambitious for their respective groups. The industry was consolidating internationally. Benefits are available from pooling client portfolios, increased bargaining power in media purchasing, capability to effectively service the wide scope and varied needs of multinational client firms, and building critical mass in each country market. Assets of BMP and BDDP were complementary: the firms had complementary geographical coverage and few client conflicts (they served few competitors). An association, they concluded, would benefit their clients, their staffs, and their business.

Merger talks initiated by BMP

Consequent to BMP's plans for European expansion, Boase approached Jean Claude Boulet in 1976 and offered him the managing directorship of BMP's Paris agency. Although Boulet refused, BMP approached him again in 1987 and discussed the possibility of purchasing the BDDP group during most of 1988.

Relative deprivation difficulties arose. The two managements began competing via the idiom of valuing the French group. Since BDDP was privately owned, its valuation depended on the criterion chosen: BDDP could be valued as low as 40% smaller than BMP or comparable in size to BMP. Neither party wanted to be the junior partner. A solution with Boulet as CEO and Boase as Chairman (see the Deloitte–Touche *equity* solution to relative deprivation recounted below) was discussed. Finally, according to Boase, the 'competitive ambitions between the management of the two companies' stopped the negotiations.

Initiation of a hostile BDDP takeover

Following the collapse of these talks in late 1988, BDDP initiated a hostile takeover by hiring investment bankers and arranging financing. Leaks about cross-shareholding talks between BMP and Omnicom, a US communications group, forced BDDP to start building an initial stake quickly. After hostile private discussions, BDDP officially disclosed its 6.48% holding and the existence of previous merger discussions on 8th March. On 29th March, at which point BDDP owned 10.5% of BMP, BDDP formally launched its bid at £103 million (a multiple of eleven times expected 1988 earnings), a relatively high figure for an advertising agency on the London stock exchange.

The British financial press, whose influence is significant in takeover battles, gave a mixed reaction to BDDP's offer. Analysts held that because BMP was a healthy and profitable agency an acquirer would have little room for improvement. They questioned the international benefits: they agreed that an agency's clients require extra-national coverage but noted that BDDP's network was slim outside France. They mostly agreed that the business fit between the companies was good.

The public relations battle: cultural distance exaggerated as part of takeover defense
In what follows, we easily see stylish moves and countermoves by two talented advertising agencies using all their communications skills. Both BMP's attacks and BDDP's responses aimed at the same public relations targets: the UK and French press; both firms' employees, shareholders and clients; and BDDP's bankers (a hostile bid is problematic for bankers because it triggers high interest rates).

Even before the formal bid, BMP's public reaction was frankly hostile and xenophobic. At a press conference, Boase qualified the deal as 'ridiculous and inappropriate' and the offer 'frivolous and totally unwelcome'. He claimed that previous discussions about BMP purchasing BDDP were broken off due to Boulet's 'conquering, autocratic, and dominant' attitude. He viewed Boulet and the concealed stockbuilding as 'Napoleonic' and suggested that the latter 'Frog off!'

BMP's agenda was to discredit BDDP and create the impression that the acquisition would be an economic disaster for BMP, its clients, and its staff. Boase proclaimed that the transaction would remain hostile[7] and, in several articles, developed an 'empty shell' theme: the vast majority of his clients and employees would defect if the takeover were accomplished. He managed to get written support from twenty of his key clients for this assertion. Boase also wrote to BDDP's bankers and advised them to withdraw their support, arguing that the highly leveraged BDDP could not support further debt if merged with BMP.

Before the bid, BDDP contacted both its own and BMP's clients and key employees, explaining the philosophy and new opportunities of the transaction. The BDDP offer document was presented as an advertising brochure, featuring BDDP and BMP as pieces of a jigsaw puzzle representing worldwide advertising presence and emphasizing the commercial, cultural, and geographic fit of the business combination and benefits to clients and employees of the merger.

BMP immediately rejected the offer. BMP's creative staff wrote and published the 'Boulet Rap', a song using all anti-French clichés. An extract from the 'Boulet Rap' follows:

> It's been compared to Waterloo which might not mean that much to you
> 1815 the battle fall score England one France nought
> If Boulet is Napoleon then Boase he is Wellington
> So Boulet come up with the loot then Wellington gives you the boot
> If it's farce you want it's farce you'll get
> The boot and the farce without the F!

The price issue was featured in the public relations battle. Boase claimed that the price to earnings ratio of 11 grossly undervalued BMP's franchise.

On 12th April, Boase presented his defense document in a press conference in Paris. He emphasized the lack of fit between the cultures of both groups, the holes in BDDP's international network, the financial inadequacy of the bid and the hostility both of clients and staff. The document was also presented as an advertising brochure, spoofing precisely the images featured in BDDP's offer document: an image of the BDDP jigsaw where the pieces do not fit together, another image where BDDP is represented as much smaller than BMP, and another depicting BDDP's network as 'the Gruyère of European Networks'. These comments were effective. They worried BMP clients and staff.

The same day, Boulet held a press conference with his bankers and international branch managers to counter Boase's accusations. The managers praised the operating autonomy given them and described it as a key feature of BDDP culture. The bankers issued press releases to restate their support and confidence about the financial soundness of the operation. In order to test for BMP staff defections, BDDP's top managers personally contacted key BMP employees during April. Only some of BMP's staff were clearly hostile to the transaction; most understood its benefits. Similarly, BMP's clients were contacted; the feedback was generally positive, even for those who initially supported Boase.

A white knight

A series of events incited BMP to seek a white knight. A Swiss firm appeared as a second bidder. Publication of BMP's performance figures (5% higher than expected) allowed Boase again to denigrate BDDP's price. Boase changed his defense strategy from the 'empty shell' theme (that failed to repel BDDP) to arguments based purely on price. Finally, on 11th May, BDDP raised the offer to £118.5 million and increased its participation to 15% to repel white knights. Most analysts reckoned this bid was high enough for BDDP to gain control.

Realizing that fact, on 16th May Boase contacted Omnicom with whom he previously had held joint venture and minority share holding talks. Omnicom, the fourth largest advertising group in the world and well represented in the US and Europe, operated 260 advertising and marketing services companies. On 19th May, Omnicom unveiled its white knight counter-offer of £125 million. BMP's board of directors recommended the offer because the price was higher and the cultural and strategic fit better than those offered by BDDP. The stated objective was to create one of the largest advertising groups in Europe. Omnicom's presence in the UK was small and would be enhanced by combination with BMP. Client conflicts were limited to 5% of billings. Last but not least, BMP would merge with one of Omnicom's UK agencies; Boase would chair the combined group. BMP directors immediately sold their stakes to Omnicom.

On 9th June, BDDP announced it would tender its shares to Omnicom. The hostility of the transaction faded away in the declarations of BDDP, BMP, and Omnicom. 'Good luck BMP. Good luck Omnicom', said Boulet in a last press conference on the transaction.

Implications of Case V for acquisition cultural risk management

This rich case highlights the interplay between cultural and power issues in acquisition conduct. A strong strategic case can be made for the transaction. The advertising industry was reacting to increased globalization by means of cross-border expansion. Acquisition was a good expansion strategy if the target unit was talented and had a good client list and also if pooling talent and accounts yielded more effective operations. Our analysis suggests that although the firms differ in national culture, they have striking points of similarity in organizational culture: their reputation for quality, their core cultural features, and their regime of integrating previous acquisitions. Before BDDP's takeover attempt, they specifically knew one another fairly well because Boase had approached Boulet personally in 1976 to head his French agency. BMP and BDDP had engaged in discussions over joint ventures, and BMP and BDDP had discussed a merger a few months earlier. These talks foundered over relative deprivation issues (neither party wanted to be the junior partner) but were expressed in the idiom of cultural distance. In the takeover battle, relative deprivation resurfaced. One antagonist chose to use cultural distance as a weapon. BMP skillfully portrayed BDDP in hostile, xenophobic terms that aimed to enlist the historical enmities between the British and the French. BMP consistently used this weapon each time they had relative deprivation conflicts with BDDP.

A quick reading of the case would have overemphasized cultural distance as a determining factor in the failed takeover attempt. Culture distance is not an implacable fixed force but can be manipulated in line with one's practical interests: overcommunicated in order to wreck alliances or undercommunicated in order to forge them.

Cases of Relative Deprivation

The first pair of cases are selected from the well-publicized category of hostile takeovers where post-acquisition policy clearly puts members of the target firm at a disadvantage relative to members of the acquiring firm. Then, even in cases where the target firm understands what is expected of them, post-acquisition activity may be marked by staff defection or covert subversion of programs installed by the acquiring firm. See Figure 11.6.

Icahn's takeover of TWA airlines and Northwest Airlines' acquisition of Republic Airlines illustrate post-acquisition problems that occur when the acquirer rather transparently puts target firm stakeholders at a disadvantage relative to those in the acquiring firm. The third case is the reverse of the first two: due to integration policies, some personnel in the acquiring firm perceive deprivation.

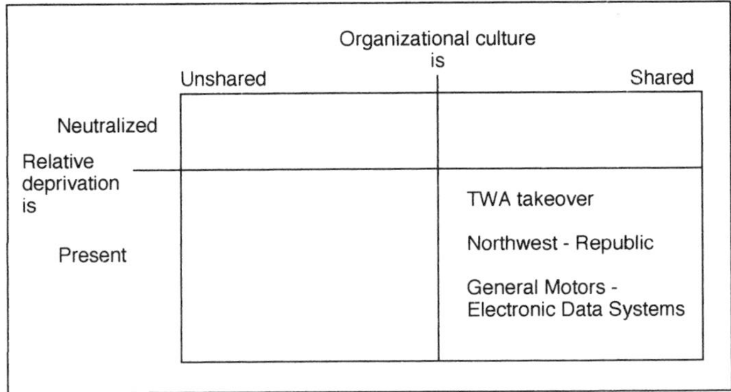

Figure 11.6 Cases: relative deprivation is present

Case VI: Airline cases: relative deprivation of target firm in a hostile takeover[8]

Carl Icahn's takeover of TWA in 1985 was hostile. It was actively resisted by managers who wanted to retain their jobs. Before he began investing in TWA, its 33 million shares traded at $8. He eventually bought 40% of the airline through open market purchases and the rest through a hotly contested tender offer. This takeover has attracted enough attention and commentary to provide us with sufficient data to assess stakeholder losses: in particular, after gaining control, Icahn lowered the wages and benefits of the three major TWA unions.

Before Icahn took control, TWA paid its 3000 pilots an average salary of $90 000 per year, including benefits. Icahn's agreement cut this figure around 30%, for an annual saving of approximately $100 million (Fortune, 'Takeover'). The company employed about 9000 machinists at an average cost of $38 000. They agreed to a 15% cut, saving TWA around $50 million a year. The story with flight attendants is more complicated, since no agreement was reached. On average, a TWA flight attendant made $35 000 a year. Some attendants (around 2500 out of 6000) were replaced within three months by rookies paid an average of $18 000 per year. This essentially transferred wealth from the existing flight attendants, who could presumably take entry-level jobs, to Icahn. In fact, some of them accepted wage cuts, and, over time, most who did not were replaced. Assuming an average saving of $10 000 per flight attendant, the total annual saving adds up to $60 million (Shleifer and Summers, 1989, pp. 48, 49).

When Republic Airlines was acquired by Northwest Airlines, the lower ranks understood well enough what was expected of them. One could hardly point to cultural distance as a factor because both airlines have headquarters in the midwestern United States. But when Republic flight crews and ground crews were placed at the short end of a two-tier pay scale, they protested with unofficial slow-downs that clearly impaired scheduled flight performance. Similar covert subversive behavior has been observed elsewhere in low-profile, non-confrontational forms of peasant resistance (Scott, 1985).

Implications of Case VI for acquisition cultural risk management

The two airline cases are not exceptional but rather typical cases of hostile takeovers. For our purposes, they are variations on the theme that shared understanding in the presence of relative deprivation is still dysfunctional. When members of a target firm think that they will be relatively deprived in or omitted from the new organization, they may react negatively. Types of reaction depend on position in the firm: top management may try to block the merger or quit if the merger succeeds; lower ranks cannot easily block a merger but may tend to subvert post-merger integration or quit if the merger succeeds.

Case VII: General Motors' acquisition of Electronic Data Systems: relative deprivation of acquirer in a friendly takeover

General Motors' acquisition of Electronic Data Systems (EDS) reverses the airline cases: certain personnel from the acquiring firm were disadvantaged relative to those in the target firm. EDS, a Dallas-based computer service company that specializes in system integration, focused its effort in government services (41% of revenue), insurance services (21%), and financial and commercial services (22%).

Strategic considerations

This acquisition was attractive. GM would benefit from EDS's high growth. As GM's business is acutely sensitive to the swings of the economy, EDS would be a major diversification and a hedge against volatility in the auto industry. The acquisition would markedly raise the technology level of an old line manufacturing firm. GM's chairman, Roger Smith, was concerned that GM was too rigid to anticipate and respond to the rapid environmental changes such as shifting fuel prices, increasing regulation and growing international competition. To close the competitive gap in costs and quality, Smith wanted to develop highly efficient methods of manufacturing and management. Improved technology (rather than lowering labor costs) was the answer; in particular, computer products and processors would become indispensable to the auto industry. EDS would give GM resources hard to develop internally.

EDS's proven ability to handle enormous systems was especially attractive to GM. Although GM was a leader in using computers to design car parts and robots to assemble them, a massive system integration would improve communications among GM suppliers, manufacturers and employees. EDS's experience in network design and system integration would resolve GM's internal communication and data processing problems: integrating the automaker's numerous and different computer systems into a worldwide data, voice, and video network, as well as streamlining electronic support for order processing, manufacturing material purchases. GM makes about 8 million long-distance telephone calls a month; EDS would build the nation's largest private telephone network, a $350 million network connecting telephones and computers. EDS estimated that it could install the system three times faster than GM had planned.

The acquisition was also attractive for EDS. While EDS's revenue in 1984 was $654 million, GM's data processing budget was about $6 billion per year: more than nine times EDS's operating sales. Meeting GM's data processing needs would increase EDS's size four to five fold.

The regime

This huge volume increase set up the challenge to post-acquisition integration: GM could not afford defection by EDS personnel and would have to add staff. GM invented an innovative financial tool to acquire EDS cheaply and retain EDS staff. Buying EDS for $2.5 billion, GM issued about 13.6 million shares of a new class of stock, designated class E or GME. GM aimed to give GME holders—mainly EDS employees—a vested interest by basing GME dividends on EDS performance.[9]

This golden leash for EDS employees was tethered to a condition: the promissory notes that guaranteed a higher rate of return were issued only to the EDS holders at the time of the acquisition. The package was attractive to EDS managers and employees who together took more than half the initial distribution. Another 15.4 million shares were issued to holders of GM regular stock on 10 December 1984 and another 3.1 million shares at a public offering of 15 February 1985. Share value rose dramatically.[10]

Trade-offs of the regime

Post-acquisition problems arose not from retaining EDS staff and management, but in integrating GM data processing staff into the vastly expanded EDS operation. Both companies underestimated integration difficulties. The first step towards consolidating technical expertise and economies of scale was to combine all of GM's data centers into regional operation under EDS control. About 10 000 GM data processing and telecommunications personnel worldwide were transferred to EDS. Many employees experienced organizational culture shock. They were alarmed by EDS's conservative codes of conduct (no beards, no suede shoes, no drinking during business hours), the demand that they give up overtime pay and accept less generous benefits, and the less secure tenure within EDS. Previously, they had enjoyed automatic index-linked salary increases as well as generous pension, dental, and medical benefits. At EDS, lower base salaries were augmented by bonuses based on profits and individual performance. Furthermore, unlike EDS employees, the 10 000 GM transferees did not participate in the lucrative GME stock plan.

These changes precisely fit two types of relative deprivation (see above, p. 236): the transferred GM employees perceived that their present situation was not as rosy as their past and that their situation was not as advantageous as that of their peers, that is, all the GM employees who had not been transferred to the EDS operation. Nearly 350 dissatisfied GM data processing employees jammed the union hall in Warren, Michigan, to join the United Auto Workers (UAW). They filed a class action suit against GM in the federal court alleging that GM had violated the employee retirement income security Act amendments of 1980. They asked for benefits they would have received had they stayed with GM: overtime pay and cost of living increases to salary (about 95% of GM's white-collar employees were receiving about $6000 a year for cost of living increases, payments made quarterly). Further, non-transferred as well as transferred GM employees perceived a disadvantage relative to EDS employees: the golden leash incentive—intended to inhibit EDS staff defection—was not available to them.

EDS faced union challenges at 14 of the 200 GM data processing sites it took over. GM and UAW reached a three-year settlement on 21 September 1984 for 350 000 UAW represented workers after about 16 hours of continuous bargaining and six days of selective strikes at 17 GM plants. Wage increases were modest; instead, the union's profit sharing at GM would reflect EDS earnings: about $1000 per worker during 1984 and $1100 during 1985 and 1986. The UAW got job security for its workers: a six-year, billion dollar program wherein laid-off workers would earn their normal wage and benefits while being trained for other jobs at GM or outside the company.

Implications of Case VII for acquisition cultural risk management

Post-acquisition programs can incite a perception of relative deprivation: problems were perceived by the target firms in the airline cases and by the acquiring firm in the GM–EDS case. One usually thinks of reduced conditions imposed on members of a target firm in a hostile takeover. The reverse can also happen, as when GM sought to avoid defection by the target firm's professional staff with an advantageous financial offer. Unfortunately, this offer was perceived as unfair by the acquiring firm's employees. In addition, reduced benefits received by GM employees who were transferred into EDS's operations were perceived as relative disadvantage. Post-acquisition integration difficulties fell squarely on the acquiring firm's employees. Relative deprivation can impede the progress of post-acquisition programs in both hostile and friendly takeovers and can affect personnel from either firm.

Cases of Relative Deprivation Neutralized

The following cases are variations on the theme of neutralizing relative deprivation. The major contrast here is between a meritocracy and an equity solution.

- A meritocracy solution to post-acquisition staffing is more typical of a recognized takeover; the acquiring firm gives equal opportunity (and equal jeopardy) to counterparts from the acquiring and target firms. This is General Electric's regime.
- By contrast, when firms try to stress a union of near-equals, they use varieties of an equity solution: either installing a system of equal power, participation, and financial return (the Deloitte–Touche merger) or creating a categorical inequity with a scheduled duration (the Ernst–Young merger). A contrast case from the same industry, Klynveld Peat Marwick Goerdeler, shows the dire consequences that occur when no such steps are taken. See Figure 11.7.

Case VIII: integration strategy of General Electric: imposing meritocracy to neutralize relative deprivation[11]

Companies that expand by recognized takeovers can employ a meritocracy solution to neutralize categorical relative deprivation between members of the acquiring and target firms. Choosing the best person for the job without reference to the person's predecessor firm creates equal opportunity but also equal jeopardy. This policy is very clear at General Electric. There is post-acquisition stress at General Electric—but not specifically for the target firm (as in the TWA case) or for the acquiring firm (as in the General Motors case). Jack Welch spreads the fear of post-acquisition lay-offs between the acquired business unit and its GE

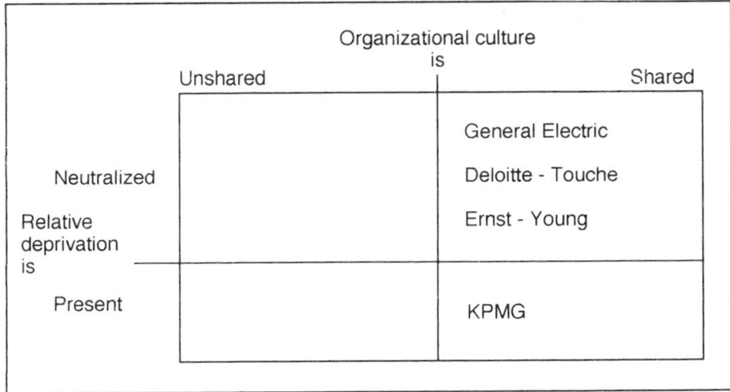

Figure 11.7 Cases: relative deprivation neutralized

counterpart with his dictum that after an acquisition 'one plus one equals one'. This management style of equal opportunity and equal jeopardy is consistently applied both to existing staff and to newly acquired companies.

Welch's strategic, organizational and cultural shifts

To understand this situation, we must back up and consider changes in GE strategy, organization, and cultural focus installed by Welch after he became chief executive in 1981. All these changes are applied to pre-Welch GE units as well as to newly acquired ones.

Any GE business must meet two criteria. First, GE invests in businesses with a chance of becoming number 1 or 2 in market share. Any other businesses are divested. Second, a business must fit within one of three circles: high-technology (Industrial Electronics, Medical Systems, Materials, Aerospace, and Aircraft Engine), services (Information services, Construction & Engineering, and Nuclear Services), and core businesses (Lighting, Major appliance, Motor, Transportation, Turbine, and Construction equipment). Businesses within the *high-technology* circle are to attain market leadership through acquisition and investment in research and development; those in the *services* circle, through acquisitions and the addition of 'outstanding people who can often create new ventures all by themselves' (1984 GE Annual Report). Strategy in the slower growth *core* businesses was to increase profitability through expenditure in automation to enhance productivity and quality. In addition,

> Outside the circles are businesses that provide support to the businesses within the circles. Outside as well, are other businesses: some have performed marginally, some are in low-growth markets; others are simply a poor strategic fit with the company. For these other businesses we have a fix, sell, or close strategy. (1984 GE Annual Report)

Concerning organizational and cultural shifts, key Welch phrases for approved GE management style are 'delayering' and 'developing a vision'. This translates as flattening organizational levels, removing bureaucratic barriers, and giving individual employees more responsibility. The idea is to create an environment in which employees' efforts determine whether their careers will flourish or perish. There are more opportunities for fast promotion and more opportunities to fail.

Meritocracy, then, is a way of life at GE—whether or not an acquisition has occurred. In response to criticism (see below) that the flourish or perish regime overextends and burns out employees, Welch responds that the regime intends to get employees to work smarter, concentrating on what's important. 'If we end up with key people browbeaten, working 16 hours a day trying to get the same amount of data as before, then we haven't done it right.' He believes that reducing the workforce while flattening organizational layers will help. 'I have a theory that an overextended leader—overextended by the number of direct people reporting to him—ends up being clearly the best leader because they don't have time to meddle and because they create under them people who by necessity have to take on more responsibility.'

The regime: applying changes to older and newly acquired GE units

Profound changes in administrative structure and staffing policy have affected units already present when Welch became the top executive in 1981. Reporting layers in the organization have been reduced from ten to five or six. After deleting two levels of administration standing between the CEO and business heads ('groups' and 'sectors'), corporate staff at the Fairfax, Connecticut, headquarters was reduced from 1700 in 1981 to 1000 in 1987. Similar trends occurred within the major business divisions. Roger W. Schipke, head of GE's major appliance business, deleted the separate staffs of marketers, salespeople, and controllers that existed for each appliance GE makes and rolled them into one unit that does the job for refrigerators, dishwashers, and other appliances. Job slashing is even more severe at lower levels in the company. Since 1981, over 100 000 employees, one employee in four have been dismissed.

Through the 1980s, GE divested over 350 business and product lines and acquired some 250 more. The divestitures generated over $9 billion used to fund acquisitions or strengthen other GE businesses. Application of the policies of three-circle fit, market leadership, delayering, and developing a vision results in clear expectations for companies newly acquired by GE. First, business units within the acquired firm will be retained for fit and leadership. After acquiring RCA in 1986, GE retained various units (RCA Aerospace & Defense fits inside the GE *technology* circle; NBC fits the *services* circle; RCA's Semiconductor Trading and Consumer Electronics fit the *support* sector) and sold off or closed six major businesses with 41 000 employees. Second, if the business unit is retained, it will be trimmed. NBC, the leanest television network at the time it was acquired, still lost 700 positions. Third, the former chief executive will be retained only if s/he has a management style compatible with headquarters and can run a business without interference from headquarters: Michael G. Fitt still runs the Employers Reinsurance Corp., acquired by GE in 1984. Otherwise, there will be a new chief executive: GE passed over several senior NBC executives and chose Robert C. Wright, the former head of GE's financial operations, as chief executive of NBC. Whomsoever is on top, the chief executive will 'develop a vision' as described above.

Another organizational feature, the 'Workout', was installed to replace the inter-unit coordination formerly provided by the multilayered GE bureaucracy. Horizontal boundaries still remained after Welch had destroyed various vertical layers. The workout is a companywide program designed to attack and eliminate functional boundaries *within* each business unit. Employees from all levels convene in a three-day session to examine current practices and present recommendations to senior management. The latter must either approve or disapprove (with explanation) the recommendation on the spot, or, with complex issues, request further analysis with a deadline given for a response. Because this process is available to personnel from newly acquired as well as older units, it serves as an integrating device for target firms.

Trade-offs of the regime

Formerly, adherence to GE culture was strong—an intense loyalty that few companies enjoyed and many envied. Traditionally, the company gave its employees a job-for-life promise. There was a cultural premise of stability.

Corporate performance under Welch has improved only with a cultural change towards instability. Sales have increased from $26.8 billion in 1980 to $58.4 billion in 1990, an annual growth rate of over 8% and a third better than inflation. During the same period, profits have grown at a rate of 11% per year, from $1.5 to $4.3 billion. Return on equity has averaged 19% per year. This performance was accomplished with an exacting criterion for a business unit to remain in the conglomerate: be number one or two in the industry or be 'fixed, closed, or sold'. Application of this criterion means instability. During this period when GE bought $25 billion worth of companies and sold $10 billion worth of companies, the workforce eroded from 410 000 to below 300 000. Not surprisingly, annual growth in labor productivity rose from 1.9% during Welch's first five years to 4.4% during his second five years.

Currently, some personnel appear to thrive in Welch's flourish or perish regime. A business head such as Jet Engine division chief Rowe enjoys relative autonomy because he meets financial targets. GE managers' opportunity to get big jobs when they are young gives them a strong mid-career résumé that is attractive to other companies: at least fourteen former GE executives are now chief executive officers at other companies. Proponents hold that the regime is not for everybody and that employees who cannot adjust do not belong at the new GE.

Currently, despite GE's efforts to blunt deprivation to fired persons by offering job-placement help and retraining as well as generous severance benefits, some personnel are disenchanted, dissatisfied, paralyzed and burnt-out because they are trying to do more work with fewer people and are uncertain whether they will have a job tomorrow. There were 'lots of 11-hour days, lots of sharing of secretarial help, having managers do it all on their own. I fear they're cutting into the very heart of our organization' (a former mid-level executive in the lighting business). 'Many GE people have called looking for jobs. A lot of people say they are just unhappy' (Alma Rothschild, who runs a consulting business with her husband, a former GE strategic planning executive).

Implications of Case VIII for acquisition cultural risk management

The General Electric regime cannot be described as a delimited acquisition regime because it applies companywide. The regime manages change and is clearly imposed upon both existing and newly acquired units. It can be interpreted in terms of the types of relative deprivation listed earlier (p. 236) There is no marked relative deprivation of the type 'our current situation is worse than their situation'. Due to equal opportunity and equal jeopardy management style, there is no categorical deprivation of newly acquired personnel relative to pre-1981 personnel. To this extent, we conclude, General Electric has neutralized deprivation for newly acquired units relative to older units. Some personnel (whether or not they belong to newly acquired units) perceive relative deprivation in the second and third types: our past situation was better than the current situation and the future looks bleaker than the present.

Top-down imposition of strategic criteria for retention, organizational delayering, horizontal integration via the 'work-out', and an organizational culture of meritocracy, taken together, result in high commitment to a relatively shared culture for those who stay and flourish. The trade-offs of such a regime are outplacement for many people and high stress for those who have been allowed to stay but do not quite flourish. Those in the last category share, but are not committed to, GE culture.

'Mergers' among major accounting firms[12]

This section focuses on so-called mergers among major accounting firms. We suggest that calling a transaction a merger is a social construction of an ambiguous situation to avoid the implication that one party will be dominated by the other. Deloitte Haskins & Sells and Touche Ross took elaborate measures to avoid that implication when they combined forces. By contrast, Ernst & Whinney and Arthur Young admitted inequity and proposed a short-term rectification. KPMG failed to address the problem.

Case IX: Deloitte–Touche: equity solution to neutralizing relative deprivation

In contrast with General Electric's meritocracy regime, an *equity* regime for post-acquisition staffing—filling positions with near equivalent representation from acquired and target firms—was found appropriate by two accounting firms: Deloitte, Haskins & Sells joined with Touche Ross to form Deloitte Ross Tohmatsu International (known as Deloitte & Touche in the United States).

Merger talks between Deloitte, Haskins & Sells and Touche Ross were reported on 6 July 1989; the merger became effective on 4 December 1989. Previously ranked seventh and eighth of the first tier accounting firms (then known as the Big 8[13]), the combined firm is number three in revenues in the accounting profession.[14]

Press releases presented the Deloitte–Touche merger to the world as a 'merger of near equals' and stated primary reasons for the merger: complementarities in geographic market, practice area, and industry strength and the need to deliver worldwide service. Pre-merger (1989) figures confirm the near-equivalence of the firms in the aggregate:

	Worldwide Income	Pre-tax Income	Billable Hours
DH&S	$890 million	$204 million	1523
TR	$917 million	$205 million	1500

Close examination of fits in geographic markets and client practice areas served and relative sizes of organizations at country and office levels shows that, depending on where you analyze the combined organization, some divisions are more equal than others.

As to geographic fit, the combined firm has a better balanced international network. In the Asia/Pacific region, DH&S's strengths in Hong Kong, Malaysia, and Singapore complement TR's strong position in Indonesia, the Philippines, Taiwan and Thailand. In addition, TR's long-standing connection with Tohmatsu Awoki & Sanwa became a formal link. Tohmatsu has the largest practice in Japan, extensive contacts with Japanese government and business and a strong list of Japanese clients. The Australian unit of TR, however, defected from the merger. There is strong complementarity in Europe and in North America.[15]

Concerning client service fit, there is some discrepancy among the practice areas—see Table 11.1. In two of the practice areas, Accounting & Audit and Consulting,[16] TR partners had significantly more revenue per partner than DH&S partners: 90 000 in Accounting & Audit and 110 000 in Consulting. If it is also true that Touche earned more profits (which is not disclosed), potential for friction between partners from the predecessor firms exists since—if no corrective action is taken—TR partners would suffer a decline in compensation.

This is a sensitive issue. The high figure for partners implies a low ratio of professsional staff to partners, a low 'leverage' or earnings potential per partner. D&T also has the lowest figure among the Big Six in the high-profit consulting practice area. In contrast, Arthur Andersen & Co. has the highest leverage of staff to partner ratio and the highest figure in the consulting practice area.

Concerning integration of personnel, this is a merger of equals according to the percentage of partners (DH&S: 48%/TR: 52%) or total staff (DH&S: 49%/TR: 51%) in the combined organization in the United States. The aggregate picture is less even in Europe where DH&S has 39% and TR has 61% of total personnel. These figures are misleading: there are discrepancies between the predecessor firms in the sizes of country units and individual offices that must work together if the intended synergies between the two firms' geographic, service, and industry strengths are to be realized as actual benefits of combination.

Table 11.1 Deloitte–Touche practice areas

	US Accounting and Auditing Practice		
	DH&S	TR	Combined
Revenue ($m)	$547	$486	$1033
Total revenue %	61%	53%	57%
Three-year growth	39%	42%	40%
Partners	528	429	957
Senior managers and managers	810	900	1710
Total professionals	4700	4300	9000
Revenue per partner ($m)	$1.04	$1.13	
	US Consulting Practice		
	DH&S	TR	Combined
Revenue ($m)	$121	$215	$336
Total revenue %	14%	23%	19%
Three-year growth	66%	57%	64%
Partners	105	174	279
Senior managers and managers	370	490	860
Total professionals	1010	1230	2240
Revenue per partner ($m)	$1.15	$1.26	
	US Tax Practice		
	DH&S	TR	Combined
Revenue ($m)	$222	$216	$438
Total revenue %	25%	24%	24%
Three-year growth	71%	57%	64%
Partners	207	201	408
Senior managers and managers	470	520	990
Total professionals	1840	1810	3650
Revenue per partner ($m)	$1.07	$1.07	

DH&S for the year ended 3 June 1989. TR estimated for the year ended 31 August 1989

The post-merger regime

In a merger of firms whose upper management is composed of partners, post-merger integration issues center on (i) power in the new organization and post-merger profit sharing among partners and (ii) power and cultural integration issues among the lower ranks in the organization. Deloitte Touche upper management have taken very firm steps to neutralize problems among themselves but are less specific in managing issues concerning the lower ranks.

Deloitte Touche upper management issued a statement of their 'goals for the design of management structure'. This list of goals deserves attention because it shows a tension between partner equity and matching skills to positions: (1) take advantage of synergies between the organizations, (2) select the most talented person for the position; while (3) maintaining a sense of a 'merger of equals'; (4) minimize the layers of management; (5) remain a 'field-driven' organization; and (6) build dedication of each member of top management. Items 3 and 6 clearly advocate the priority of equity, or, in our terms, neutralizing relative deprivation among the combined partnership; on the other hand, item 2 sets priority on matching skills with positions. Items 3 and 6 advocate the interests of top management while items 2, 4, and 5 prioritize the needs of the lower ranks in the organization.

Implementing these directives clearly prioritized the equity direction—with equity more explicitly guaranteed for the top management. The combined top management installed a highly ordered regime to avoid giving undue power to either predecessor firm:

(1) The initial Board of Directors is composed of equal numbers of persons from both predecessor firms; this equal representation is to last for five years.
(2) The initial appointment of a Managing Partner from one firm (TR) was matched by appointing a Chairman from the other firm (DH&S).
(3) After five years, the committee nominating the next Managing Partner and the Chairman will be composed of an equal number of partners from each predecessor firm.
(4) A Transition Advisory Group composed of three members from each firm is responsible for reviewing actions and appointments in order to ensure fairness to partners from both firms.
(5) While other management positions (administering the specific geographic and functional structure) are to be filled according to a merit criterion ('best person for the job'), such appointments are to be reviewed by the Transition Advisory Group.

By this set of structures and policies, the equity direction clearly dominates the meritocracy direction in decisions affecting the upper reaches of the firm; processes for decisions affecting the non-partner staff are not clearly stated.

Trade-offs of the regime

Deloitte Touche found this careful procedure to be appropriate on the premise that their merger is actually a matter of hundreds of specific mergers, that is, mergers of specific offices (before the merger, 176 cities had both DH&S and TR offices) of country units, and of practice divisions (Accounting, Audit, Information Consulting, and Tax divisions). Financial equity issues are easily seen for practice divisions. Profit sharing (earnings per partner) is a function both of total revenue and of leverage (the ratio of partners to other consulting staff.

Although revenues produced by the two predecessor firms were not appreciably different, Touche Ross had higher leverage than Deloitte Haskins & Sells in three divisions (Accounting, Audit and Consulting). Leverage was nearly the same in the Tax division. Then TR partners in three divisions faced a potential earnings dilution from the merger. Deloitte Touche has delayed facing this problem by decreeing that two separate earning systems will remain in effect for two years. To date these policies have reduced individual departures. Country member offices from DH&S did in fact defect in the UK, the Netherlands,[17] and Australia while the TR office in Italy also went its own way.

In practice, prioritizing equity among partners has led to some inefficiencies already recognized by Deloitte Touche. Although DH&S used to have only twelve members on its management committee, DT now has thirty members. DT executives also recognize that the current number of Group level Managing Partners, fourteen, should probably be reduced.

Ernst & Young and KPMG

The efficacy of the Deloitte–Touche policy to neutralize relative deprivation can be seen by briefly considering two other cases of mergers among major accounting firms. When Ernst & Whinney merged with Arthur Young, a large discrepancy existed in earnings per partner. The merged organization decided that Ernst & Whinney partners should receive 65% more than Arthur Young partners for the first two years after the merger. Far greater defections occurred after the 1987 merger between Peat Marwick (PM) and Klynveld Main Goerdeler (KMG) into Klynveld Peat Marwick Goerdeler. In that merger, according to a manager in the KPMG office in New York, PM partners defected in Europe, where KMG was dominant, and vice versa in the United States, where KMG partners earned 35% less on average than PM partners. Because no post-merger equity corrective actions were taken as in the Deloitte–Touche firm or in the Ernst & Young firm, Peat Marwick partners had an incentive to force out KMG partners located in the United States: of 525 KMG partners located in the United States, only 175 now remain. Country offices in Australia, Colombia, Canada, Mexico, New Zealand, Norway, Northern Ireland, and Spain defected after the KPMG merger. Uncorrected, relative deprivation has consequences in the post-acquisition period.

Implications of Case IX for acquisition cultural risk management

The three cases of mergers among major accounting firms can be arranged in an order of degree of elaboration of post-combination policies intended to reduce relative deprivation.

KPMG is reported as taking no action to offset the differential earning power of partners in the merged organization. The results were dire: many highly-priced consultants (partners) defected from both firms.

Ernst & Young, recognizing inequality of earning power per partner, adopted a categorical, short-term formula for rectification: former Ernst & Whinny partners are to take home 65% more than former Arthur Young partners. No massive partner defections have occurred. This transaction attained stability more quickly than KPMG where earning power issues were not dealt with decisively.

Deloitte Touche has opted for an elaborate set of measures to avoid categorical inequities in power, assignments, and earning power *at the partner level*. Even among the partners, there is potential for friction within the Accounting, Audit, and Consulting practice areas where, in each area, TR partners earned more than DH&S partners before the merger. Less strain is potential in the Tax practice where partners earned about the same amount. Next, demographics differ markedly for countries and for individual consulting offices.[18] The equity policies will not automatically reduce frictions at these levels. A merger is indeed composed of many integrations.

CONCLUSION

The Acquisition Cultural Risk Framework

Acquisition cultural risk

We have explored a framework for understanding acquisition cultural risk, that is, complementary processes of cultural risk of misunderstanding and perceived relative deprivation that—when linked with strategic factors—affect the outcome of an acquisition transaction.

Cases studied

All the transactions we examined had a strong strategic rationale for their consummation. In each case, industry conditions and firm-level specialized resources indicated that the acquisition decision was appropriate. Organizations that effectively respond to cultural and relative deprivation issues in post-acquisition management have access to the potent economic benefits available from such transactions. Variations in post-acquisition outcomes just from cultural and relative deprivation problems can be substantial, as the cases discussed here illustrate.

Sources of acquisition cultural risk: cultural distance and power asymmetries

Cultural distance always exists between target and acquiring firms because they differ in organizational culture (and may also differ in professional and national culture); some degree of power asymmetry is also present in most business relationships. While they are inescapable facts of life, neither cultural distance nor power asymmetry are automatic, implacable forces. The interplay between cultural distance and relative deprivation (in the BMP–BDDP affaire) shows that cultural distance can be a constructed event, not just a cause of events. Our analysis suggests that BMP (the British advertising agency) and BDDP (the French advertising agency) had similar organizational cultures. In this case, cultural discord was constructed and exaggerated by BMP as a ploy to fight off BDDP's takeover attempt. The eventual acquirer did not have higher economic synergies with BMP than did BDDP; the real driving force was the perceived future deprivation of BMP executives relative to BDDP counterparts. Cultural discord was amplified to avoid an economically justifiable transaction.

Processes of acquisition cultural risk: cultural risk and relative deprivation

Rather, cultural distance and power asymmetry can become problematic when mobilized (in post-acquisition work situations) as cultural risk of misunderstanding and as perceived relative deprivation. These processes are complementary: their combined impact affects post-acquisition activity. Perception of deprivation impedes joint, coordinated activity between parties even if they share sufficient understanding about expected activity. Conversely, cultural sharing and adherence to understandings together result in integrated, well-coordinated activity necessary to achieve the benefits of combination.

Acquisition cultural risk

The concept of *acquisition cultural risk* is used as a cover term for related processes (cultural risk and relative deprivation) that, in their combined impact, are an important determinant both of the advisability of engaging in a corporate acquisition and of the post-acquisition strategy a firm may adopt.

Linkage with Strategic Issues

Incidence of acquisition cultural risk

When do cultural and power issues become problematic? Our study suggests a counter-intuitive point: the mode of acquisition (friendly/hostile) does not have automatic impacts on integration but is strongly conditioned by the scope and extent of integration as well as the specific acquisition regime employed. For example, one usually thinks of reduced conditions imposed on members of a target firm in a hostile takeover: transparent pay differentials were perceived as unfair by the target firms in the airline cases. The reverse can also happen: GM sought to avoid defection by the target firm's professional staff with an advantageous financial offer. Unfortunately, this offer was perceived as unfair by the acquiring firm's employees. In addition, reduced benefits received by GM employees who were transferred into EDS's operations were perceived as relative disadvantage. Post-acquisition integration difficulties fell squarely on the acquiring firm's employees. Relative deprivation can impede the progress of post-acquisition programs in both hostile and friendly takeovers and can affect personnel from either firm.

Two strategic factors are closely related to the incidence of cultural and power issues: the scope of integration (how much of the firms is combined) and the extent of post-acquisition integration (are acquired units left to run autonomously, federated with acquiring firm units, fully integrated? or sold off?). For example, the extent of discord from unshared understandings depends partly on cultural distance and partly on the degree of interdependence necessary to achieve post-acquisition effectiveness. Cross-border acquisitions made *separately* by BMP and by BDDP (before the failed takeover attempt) illustrate this point. In the advertising industry, local responsiveness is essential. Both firms successfully maintained sufficient cultural and operating autonomy of their acquired firms to allow the latter to continue to perform well.

These cases support the argument of Haspeslagh and Jemison (1991) who discuss modes of integration necessary to transfer different types of competitive capabilities. For them, initial cultural distance is not the point; rather, whether maintaining the target firm's cultural autonomy is necessary to preserve the capability and create value.

Locus of acquisition cultural risk

What is the locus of these issues? While most writing deals with integration issues at the level of the firm, we suggest that these issues are more accurately dealt with at the level of more specific units.

Walter (1985) connects motivation for acquisition to post-acquisition stress at the level of the firm: firms acquired for financial synergy experience less acculturation stress than do firms acquired for operating synergy; he holds that the latter case is subject to more interference with operating policies. The Japanese acquisition of a Dutch company (Case III) tests this connection. The acquired firm's R&D unit experienced little stress after acquisition because it fitted the Japanese parent's strategy for buying innovative product technology; operational coordination with the parent was not required. Production units from the same firm were operationally integrated and experienced significant cultural discord. Our point is that one must look more closely at the differential impacts on units within a firm acquired for operating synergy.

This point also bears on studies classifying transactions as mergers or acquisitions. Various quantitative and qualitative measures have been proposed for deciding whether a merger or an acquisition has taken place: quantitative aggregate figures such as total assets, share capital, net profit, annual turnover, and number of employees and qualitative measures such as name and domicile of the new company after the merger as compared with names and domiciles of the predecessor companies; composition of the new company's board of directors; and composition of its advisory board (Nooter and Peterse, 1989).

In practice, the choice of the terms *merger* or *acquisition* is a rhetorical choice: executives use the term merger when they want to stress the equality, or, at least, the near equivalence of the two parties, while acquisition is used in an audience to whom it is safe to imply that our side has got the better of the deal and that we have dominant power after the deal has been completed. Our point, especially after examining the cases on mergers among banks and among major accounting firms, is that neither the aggregate quantitative measures nor the qualitative measures adequately deal with the fact that post-acquisition integration occurs at a variety of levels and units within the new organization and that various power asymmetries can occur lower in the new organization. Both the Deloitte–Touche and ABN–AMRO cases test the qualitative measure of board room composition: despite equity at the top, various asymmetries are being fought out in the middle management. In short, a merger/acquisition may entail hundreds of integrating processes between units. The potential for power asymmetries and thus relative deprivation is more usefully explored at the level of units.

Acquisition Regimes and their Trade-offs

Acquisition regimes

Companies implement a variety of practices that bear on cultural risk and cultural risk and relative deprivation management. As with all normally recognized business tasks, some companies manage them well and some undermanage them. *Acquisition regime* is defined as an acquiring firm's set of pre- and post-acquisition organizational processes and policies for approaching and later integrating target firms.

The notion of acquisition regime is a linking concept in the acquisition cultural risk framework, that is, linking strategic, cultural, and power issues that are always present in completing and implementing acquisition transactions. We have presented cases to illustrate the following points.

Overt purpose of acquisition regimes

These regimes have a common overt purpose: to implement strategic choices of how to acquire a firm, how much of the acquired firm's operations are to be integrated, and how strongly target units are linked with their counterparts.

Acquisition regime features

I. Cultural policy of acquiring firm: *Unspecified* — *Multicultural tolerance* — *Cultural dominance of acquiring firm*

II. Cultural process of acquiring firm: *Unspecified* — *Inter-organizational learning* — *Cultural imposition*

Outcomes in combined organization

III. Acquiring firm's policies regarding distribution of opportunities and benefits	o Cultural diversity is: *Present*	*Enlisted*	*Eliminated*	o Relative deprivation is
● Symmetrical treatment—Meritocracy Equal opportunity and equal jeopardy for acquirer and target firms			General Electric	*Neutralized*
● Selective o Symmetrical treatment—Equity: Balance of opportunity and benefits for acquirer and target and	ABN - AMRO (1) Deloitte - Touche (1) Japanese firm - Dutch R & D unit	Sony - CBS BMP (3) BDDP (3)		*Neutralized*
o Asymmetrical treatment— Unequal opportunity: * Some merger units dominate their counterparts * Acquirer units dominate their counterparts	NMB - Postbank ABN - AMRO (2) Deloitte - Touche (2) Ernst - Young (1) Japanese firm - Dutch production unit			*Present*
● Asymmetrical treatment: Acquirer units dominate target units or Some target units dominate acquirer units	TWA Northwest - Republic General Motors - EDS			*Present*

Key:
(1) Upper management
(2) Middle management
(3) In each firm's earlier acquisitions

Figure 11.8 Acquisition regimes and their outcomes

Varieties of acquisition regimes

Prior approaches to acquisition management can be substantially enriched by identifying quite distinct varieties of acquisition regimes. All acquisition regimes distribute benefits and opportunities to the acquiring and target firms: some regimes incite relative deprivation, others neutralize it, and still others eliminate it. All regimes bear on the cultural gap between acquiring and target firms: some regimes include pre-acquisition learning routines while others forge ahead without pre-learning; some regimes have no specified cultural policy, others include cultural policy routines that bridge the cultural gap, still others forcibly impose their culture on the target. See Figure 11.8.

Trade-offs of acquisition regimes

What are the trade-offs of these regimes? Analysis of cases brings our work within sight of relatively standard business analyses. For acquisition regimes have trade-offs just like any other business factor (raising market share for the long term may require reducing profit per unit on the short term). Whether or not planned by the acquirer, the routines that comprise acquisition regimes have trade-offs—there are various impacts on cultural and power issues.

Firms that overlook the relative deprivation issue in corporate acquisitions do so at considerable risk. The continued presence of relative deprivation impeded the post-acquisition process in the cases of TWA, Northwest-Republic, and KMPG. General Motors tried to avoid losing EDS staff and wound up depriving some of its own personnel. The BMP–BDDP affair was never consummated due to a power battle at the top; but Omnicom smoothly acquired BMP by installing BMP's CEO as head of their UK operations.

By contrast, other firms try to manage relative deprivation. There are trade-offs in the different regimes chosen. Both Deloitte–Touche and ABN–AMRO chose an equity solution for neutralizing relative deprivation; top management has parity. But this solution does not produce a lean upper management structure. Further, talented executives just below the top, perceiving blocked upward mobility, defected. General Electric imposes a meritocracy (flourish or perish) regime that gives equal opportunity and jeopardy to members of both the acquiring and target firms but can result in a more efficient management structure.

Bridging of cultural distance occurs in various processes of inter-organizational learning or multicultural tolerance. Sony learned about CBS by joint-venturing with them for years before acquiring them. Management on both sides developed routines for coordinating activity during the joint-venture period that facilitated smooth cross-cultural integration after the acquisition. As discussed elsewhere (David and Singh, 1992), national regulatory differences in acquisition conduct vary in the extent to which acquirers have direct access to target firm executives. In general, rules about public acquisitions in the United States severely curtail such access. European firms generally have this opportunity. National regulatory differences are then one source of acquisition cultural risk stemming from the wider environment. Sony's strategy of learning by joint-venturing before acquiring a company is one way to bypass this problem.

For Electrolux (a case reported in David and Singh, 1992) knowledge of target firms also occurs before acquisition. A distinctive feature of their integration process is tolerance for cultural differences, even to the point where core Electrolux values are contradicted. Although tolerance for cultural differences was not the strong point of BMP's takeover defense, integration routines in the earlier cross-border acquisitions of both BMP and BDDP included multicultural tolerance and operating autonomy for target firms. These cases, then, support Nahavandi and Malekzadeh's (1988) point that post-acquisition stress is reduced when the acquiring firm is multicultural and better able to tolerate cultural differences of the target firm.

Elimination of cultural distance is an alternate regime practiced by General Electric and The Limited (a case discussed in David and Singh, 1992). Although cultural issues in acquisitions have been largely ignored in the economics literature, the recent work of Shliefer and Summers (1989) states in economic language why cultural issues may be important. They suggest that acquirers may perceive potential value in a target firm by replacing the target firm's 'implicit contracts' with its stakeholders with new, more economical implicit contracts. We agree that an important challenge of pre-acquisition screening is the lack of access to the target firm's inner circle backstage culture and consequently to its implicit contracts. Next, although the Sony–CBS case just cited is a counter-example, we agree with them that acquisitions more typically result in new implicit contracts between the new management team and the firm's stakeholders. The General Electric case illustrates this point. General Electric acquires diverse firms and consistently supplants the old contracts with a very explicit new one which was described as 'developing a vision'. Although the new contract sets goals for the target firm that are very difficult to attain, it is not dysfunctional because the post-acquisition understandings are clearly communicated. The Limited is an even more extreme case of eliminating cultural distance; here, the acquirer's very uniform culture is directly imposed on each target firm; no deviation from the acquirer's management style is tolerated. We note that both cases illustrate how this regime can incite post-acquisition stress and yet, by eliminating cultural differences, arrive at a situation of closely shared understandings.

Impact of acquisition regimes on post-acquisition activity

What are the impacts of acquisition regimes? Managing cultural risk and relative deprivation issues are processes critical both to approaching target firms and to coordinating activities in the post-acquisition period. As depicted earlier in Figure 11.2, the regimes affect the degree to which planned post-acquisition activities between units of the acquiring and target firms will be coordinated, disorganized, subversive, or chaotic. Such activity, in turn, bears on the capability of the combined organization to implement strategic plans aimed to achieve benefits of combination (synergies). Said otherwise, as indicated in Figure 11.3, neutralizing relative deprivation and inciting sharing of cultural understandings does not guarantee success in acquisitions. What these processes do facilitate is implementing a coherent post-acquisition strategy. And, as Haspeslagh and Jemison (1991) point out, while potential synergies are the basis of pre-acquisition justifications for paying a premium price to acquire a firm, it is not until capabilities have been transferred and a strategy implemented that value is created from the transaction.

Research Agenda

As a research agenda note, cultural risk and relative deprivation issues are predictably present in all inter-organizational, project-mode relationships: not just acquisitions but also joint ventures, strategic alliances, and extended service contracts. Probing into these issues is a necessary step in understanding the management of these inter-organizational relationships. Noting that international expansion over the last twenty or so years has shifted from the intra-organizational mode (the multinational corporation and its system of subsidiaries) to the inter-organizational mode, this topic probably deserves some attention.

NOTES

1. Security versus flexibility; privacy versus scrutiny; identity versus substitutability; inclusion versus segregation; comparable competence versus superior competence; and self-determination versus organizational direction.
2. See Barley, Meyer, and Gash (1988); Beck and Moore (1985); Davis (1986); Deal and Kennedy (1982); Denison (1984); Gregory (1983); Hirsch and Andrews (1983); Louis (1985, 1986); Martin and Meyerson (1988); Martin and Siehl (1983); Morgan and Smircich (1980); Sathe (1985, 1986); Schall (1983); Schein (1984, 1985, 1986); Siehl (1984); Smircich (1983); Trice and Beyer (1984); Van Maanen and Schein (1979); Weick (1985); Wilkins and Dyer (1988).
3. Two related topics (i) legal issues concerning barriers to timely knowledge about the target firm and its culture and (ii) cultural risk due to target firm's pre-acquisition business operations are discussed in David and Singh (1992).
4. K. David, Field Research in the Netherlands, 1990–1991.
5. The Dutch cultural penchant for egalitarian relationships has also affected Dutch acquisitions of German firms. A Dutch investment banker who was stationed in Germany to arrange financing for acquisitions noted a rather

consistent pattern: Dutch acquirers that attempted to set up power-sharing relationships between counterpart units in the acquiring and target firms have fared less well than acquirers who set up a regime of rule-governed but clearly hierarchical relationships between counterpart units in the two firms (K. David, field research).

6. Case materials based (i) on field research by Hughes Lepic, (ii) on field research by Kenneth David, and (iii) from Boulet (1989).
7. The only significant hostile takeover in the advertising industry was Martin Sorrell's WPP acquisition of J. Walter Thompson in 1987. JWT's performance had declined for five years. Clients were defecting; senior management was internally and externally contested. Improvement of account management justified the takeover and resulted in improved profitability.
8. Case material based on Andrei Shleifer and Lawrence H. Summers (1989), pp. 33–67.
9. GME shareholders could choose a cash payment of $44 or a combination cash-stock-note package. Under the second option, EDS shareholders would receive $35.20 per share in cash plus one share of GME for each five EDS common shares. In addition, they would receive a non-transferable contingent promissory note which guaranteed for each GME share a pre-payment of $69 after three years and $125 after seven years. In other words, GM pledged to buy the shares back if they did not appreciate very much. Contingent note holders had the right, at the anniversary of the acquisition, to obtain pre-payment of their notes at substantially discounted principal prices ranging from $93 to $116 over the current GME market price. GM agreed to pay a further amount, if necessary, to offset any long-term capital gains tax. Holders of GME stock would have one half voting right and half the liquidation right of GM common, but the dividends would reflect the subsidiary's more rapid growth prospects. GME stock dividends were set at a percentage of EDS earnings, divided by the fully diluted share base. In fact, as the dividends would be declared at the sole discretion of GM's board of directors, healthy dividends were not in doubt.
10. Four months after the first GME was issued, the stock shot up 75%; by 25 February 1985, it was trading at 72, a multiple of 24 times its expected 1985 estimate of $3 per share. Less than one year after issue, GM declared a 2 for 1 stock split of GME.
11. Material for this case adapted from (i) field research by Bergelson and Larkin (1991) and (ii) Bernstein and Schiller (1987).
12. Case materials based on field research by Shigeru Nishiyama and Jeffry Zalla.
13. The Big Six accounting firms are Arthur Andersen & Co., Coopers & Lybrand, Deloitte Ross Tohmatsu, Ernst & Young (formerly Ernst & Whinney and Arthur Young), Klynveld Peat Marwick Goerdeler (formerly Klynveld, Main, & Goerdeler and Peat Marwick), and Price Waterhouse.
14. Figures are available in K. David and H. Singh (1991).

15. Figures are available in K. David and H. Singh (1991).
16. The scope of services in the consulting practice area ranges from strategic planning through the implementation of management information systems.
    The case of Arthur Andersen & Co. highlights the importance of practice area divisions within these firms, even when no merger has taken place. Arthur Andersen & Co. has the highest leverage of staff to partner ratio and the highest figure of partners in the consulting practice area. The Arthur consulting practice has been growing much faster than the original practice areas: Audit and Tax. This situation of relative deprivation lead to an internal power struggle because power was vested in the original divisions; recently, Andersen Consulting Co. has emerged as a partially autonomous unit within the firm.
17. Duiker, Van Doorn, and Dien—the pre-merger country member of DH&S—was Touche Ross's prime competitor in the Netherlands. Not surprisingly, this group split away when the DH&S/TR merger was announced. The Van Doorn group then allied with Coopers & Lybrand, another major accounting firm.
18. Figures are available in David and Singh (1991).

REFERENCES

Aberle, David (1962) A note on Relative Deprivation Theory as applied to Millenarian and other cult movements. In Sylvia Thrupp (ed.), *Comparative Studies in Society and History*, The Hague, Mouton, pp. 209–214.

Barley, Stephen R., Meyer, Gordon W. and Gash, Debra C. (1988) Culture of culture: Academics, practitioners, and the pragmatics of normative control. *Administrative Science Quarterly*, 33. 24–60.

Beck, Brenda E. F. and Moore, Larry F. (1985) Linking the host culture to organizational variables. In Peter J. Frost *et al.*, *Organizational Culture*, Beverly Hills, CA, Sage.

Bergelson, Bob, and Larkin, Larry (1991) The Transformation of General Electric, case prepared under the supervision of Harbir Singh.

Bernstein, Aaron and Schiller, Zachary (1987) *Business Week*, 14 December 1987, pp. 92–103.

Boulet, Jean-Claude (1989) President and CEO, BDDP. *BDDP's attempted acquisition of BMP*: Keynote speech at Strategic Management Society meeting, *The Wave of Mergers, Acquisitions, and Alliances: Towards a European or Global Firm*, Paris, 22 June.

Buono, A. F., Bowditch, J. L. and Lewis, J. W. (1985) When cultures collide: The anatomy of a merger. *Human Relations*, 38. 477–500.

Chatterjee, S. (1986) Types of synergy and economic value: The impact of acquisitions on merging and rival firms. *Strategic Management Journal*, 7. 119–140.

Chatterjee, Sayan, Lubatkin, Michael H., Schweiger, David M and Weber, Yaakov (1989) Cultural differences and shareholder value: Explaining the variability in the performance of related mergers. Paper delivered at Strategic Management Society, San Francisco, 12 October.

David, Kenneth (1977) Epilogue: what shall we mean by changing identities? In Kenneth David (ed.), *The New Wind: Changing Identities in South Asia*. In the series, *World Anthropology: Proceedings of the the Ninth International Congress of Anthropological and Ethnological Sciences*, The Hague, Mouton.

David, Kenneth and Singh, Harbir (1991) Cultural bridges and golden leashes: Managing cultural risk and relative deprivation in corporate acquisitions, Working Paper.

David, Kenneth and Singh, Harbir (1992) Sources of acquisition cultural risk. In Allessandro Sinatra, Harbir Singh, and Georg Voukrogh (eds), *Managing Corporate Acquisitions*, New York, Macmillan.

Davis, Tim R. V. (1986) Managing cultures at the bottom. In Ralph H. Kilman *et al.*, (eds), *Gaining Control of the Corporate Culture*, London, Jossey-Bass.

Deal, Terrence E. and Kennedy, Allan A. (1982) *Corporate Culture: The Rites and Rituals of Corporate Life*. Reading, MA, Addison-Wesley.

Denison, D. (1984) Bringing corporate culture to the bottom line. *Organizational Dynamics*, 13, 2. 5–22.

Desmarescaux, Philippe (1989) Success factors of a merger or acquisition operation. Speech by Executive Vice President and Chairman of Rhone-Poulenc Agrochemicals, at Strategic Management Society meeting, *The Wave of Mergers, Acquisitions, and Alliances: Towards a European or Global Firm*, 23 June, Paris.

Directors & Boards (1984) The success factor in acquisitions. *Directors & Boards*, Spring, 10–15.

The Economist (1991) Jack Welch reinvents General Electric—again. 30 March, p. 59.

Gregory, Kathleen L. (1983) Native-view paradigms: Multiple cultures and culture conflicts in organizations. *Administrative Science Quarterly*, 28. 359–376.

Haspeslagh, P. C. and Jemison, D.B. (1987) Acquisitions—myth and reality. *Sloan Management Review*, Winter, 53–58.

Haspeslagh, P. C. and Jemison, D. B. (1991) *Managing Acquisitions: Creating Value through Corporate Renewal*. New York, Free Press.

Hirsch, Paul and Andrews, J. (1983) Ambushes, shootouts, and Knights of the Round Table: The language of corporate takeovers. In L. Pondy, P. Frost, G. Morgan, and T. Dandridge, (eds), *Organizational Symbolism*. Greenwich, CT, JAI Press.

Hofstede, Geert (1980) *Culture's Consequences: International Differences in Work-Related Values*. London, Sage.

Hofstede, Geert (1980) Motivation, leadership, and organization: Do American theories apply abroad? *Organizational Dynamics*, Summer, 42–63.

Jemison, D. B. and Sitkin, S. B. (1986) Corporate acquisitions: a process perspective. *Academy of Management Review*, 17. 255–280.

Kets de Vries, M. (1980) *Organizational Paradoxes*. New York, Tavistock.

Kitching, J. (1967) Why do mergers miscarry? *Harvard Business Review*, March–April, 124–136.

Kondo, Yoshihide (1990) Sony wants to be called a U.S. company with Hollywood's support. *Nihon Keizai Sangyo Shinbun* (newspaper), Tokyo, Japan, 18 January.

Levinson, H. (1973) The psychological roots of merger failure. In H. Levinson (ed.), *The Great Jackass Fallacy*. Boston, Harvard Graduate School, Division of Research.

Louis, Meryl R. (1985) An investigator's guide to workplace culture. In Peter J. Frost *et al.* (eds), *Organizational Culture*, Beverly Hills, CA, Sage.

Louis, Meryl R. (1986) Sourcing workplace cultures: Why, when, and how. In Ralph H. Kilman *et al.* (eds), *Gaining Control of the Corporate Culture*. London, Jossey-Bass.
Lubatkin, M. (1987) Merger strategies and stockholder value. *Strategic Management Journal*, 8, 3. 39–53.
Mace, M. L., and Montgomery, G. (1962) *Management Problems of Corporate Acquisitions*. Cambridge, MA, Harvard University Press.
Marks, M. L. (1982) Merging human resources: A review of current research. *Mergers and Acquisitions*, Summer, 50–55.
Martin, Joanne and Meyerson, Debra (1988) Organizational cultures and the denial, channeling, and acknowledgment of ambiguity. In Louis R. Pondy, Richard J. Boland, Jr and Howard Thomas (eds), *Managing Ambiguity and Change*. New York, Wiley.
Martin, Joanne and Siehl, Caren (1983) Organizational culture and counterculture: An uneasy symbiosis. *Organizational Dynamics*, Autumn, 52–64.
Morgan, Gareth and Smircich, Linda (1980) The case for qualitative research. *Academy of Management Review*, 5, 4. 491–500.
Nahavandi, A. and Malekzadeh, A. (1988) Acculturation in mergers and acquisitions. *Academy of Management Review*, 13, 1. 79–90.
Nooter, E. J. and Peterse, H. J. (1989) *Besluitvorming bij fusies en acquisities door middelgrote Nederlandse ondernemingen* (*Decision making in mergers and acquisitions among middle-sized Dutch enterprises*). Thesis, Erasmus University, Rotterdam.
Peterson, Pete (1990) Comments during the Blackstone Group's corporate presentation, Wharton School, 25 October.
Reese, Jennifer (1991) General Electric as boot camp. *Fortune*, 8 April, p. 8.
Sales, A. L. and Mirvis, P. H. (1984) When cultures collide: Issues of acquisition. In J. R. Kimberly and R. E. Quinn (eds), *Managing Organizational Transition*. Homewood, IL., Irwin. pp. 107–133.
Sathe, Vijay (1985) *Culture and Related Corporate Realities*. Homewood, IL, Irwin.
Sathe, Vijay (1986) How to decipher and change corporate culture. In Ralph H. Kilman *et al.* (eds), *Gaining Control of the Corporate Culture*. London, Jossey-Bass.
Schall, Maryan S. (1983) A communication-rules approach to organizational culture. *Administrative Science Quarterly*, 28. 557–581.
Schein, Edgar H. (1984) Coming to a new awareness of organizational culture. *Sloan Management Review*, 25, 2. 3–16.
Schein, Edgar H. (1985) *Organizational Culture and Leadership*. San Francisco, Jossey-Bass.
Schein, Edgar H. (1986) How culture forms, develops, and changes. In Ralph H. Kilman *et al.* (eds), *Gaining Control of the Corporate Culture*. London, Jossey-Bass.
Scott, James C. (1985) *Weapons of the Weak: Everyday Forms of Peasant Resistance*. New Haven, CT, Yale University Press.
Shelton, L. M. (1988) Strategic business fits and corporate acquisition: Empirical evidence. *Strategic Management Journal*, 9. 279–288.
Shleifer, Andrei and Summers, Lawrence H. (1989) Breach of trust in hostile takeovers. In A. Auerbach (ed.), *Corporate Takeovers*. University of Chicago Press, pp. 33–67.
Shrivastava, P. (1985) Integrating strategy formulation with organizational culture. *Journal of Business Strategy*, 5, 3. 103–111.
Shrivastava, P. (1986) Postmerger integration. *Journal of Business Strategy*, 7, 1. 65–76.

Siehl, Caren (1984) Cultural sleight-of-hand: The illusion of consistency. Unpublished doctoral dissertation. Stanford University.

Sinatra, Allessandro, Singh, Harbir and Voukrogh, Georg (1992) *Managing Corporate Acquisitions*, New York, Macmillan.

Singh, Harbir and Montgomery, C. A. (1987) Corporate acquisitions and economic performance, *Strategic Management Journal*, 8, 4. 377–386.

Smircich, Linda (1983) Concepts of culture and organizational analysis. *Administrative Science Quarterly*, 28, 3. 339–358.

Terpstra, Vern and David, Kenneth (1991) *The Cultural Environment of International Business*, third edition. Cincinnati, OH, South-Western Publishing Co.

Trice, H. and Beyer, J. (1984) Studying organizational cultures through rites and ceremonials. *Academy of Management Review*, 9. 653–659.

Van Maanen, John and Schein, Edgar (1979) Toward a theory of organizational socialization. In Barry M. Staw and Larry L. Cummings (eds), *Research in Organizational Behavior*, vol. 1. Greenwich, CT., JAI Press, pp. 209–264.

Wall Street Journal (1990) U.S. Supreme Court term leaves billion dollar mark on economy. *Wall Street Journal Europe*, 29–30 June, p. 8.

Walter, Gordon A. (1985) Culture collisions in mergers and acquisitions. In Peter J. Frost *et al.* (eds), *Organizational Culture*, Beverly Hills, CA, Sage.

Weick, Karl E. (1985) The significance of corporate culture. In Peter J. Frost *et al.* (eds), *Organizational Culture*, Beverly Hills, CA, Sage.

Wilkins, Alan L. and Dyer, W. Gibb, Jr (1988) Toward culturally sensitive theories of culture change. *Academy of Management Review*, 13, 4. 522–533.

12

EFFECTIVE MANAGEMENT TRAINING AND DEVELOPMENT

D. E. Hussey

Managing Director, Harbridge Consulting Group Ltd

In recent years increasing attention has been given to the issue of trying to make management development and training more effective by tying it much closer to corporate objectives and strategies. Historically the link with corporate strategy has been somewhat tenuous, and although some companies have been changing emphasis, the majority in the UK (and I believe most of Europe) have treated training as an act of faith which somehow ought to, by some mystical means, do the company good. Not surprisingly, in times of economic difficulty, such training is one of the first expenses to be cut.

This paper will explore ideas through which development and training may become a more effective contributor to the corporate good, and more able to demonstrate that it serves the strategic aims of the organisation. For purposes of brevity, I will reduce the related but slightly different aspects of management development, training, and education to the one word training. However, I am really talking about all of these aspects, as this is where my experience lies, and where the researches referenced have mainly been focused. Inspiration is drawn from several sources. Since 1983 Harbridge Consulting Group has undertaken a continuing programme of research into management development in the UK. Work started at a time when little was available from other sources (Ascher, 1983, 1984; Airey and Goodman, 1986; Bateson, 1986; Baston, 1989; Tovey, 1991). There were also a number of unpublished research studies. There has been increasing attention to this issue from other researchers, and numerous research

International Review of Strategic Management, volume 4.
Edited by D. E. Hussey. Published 1993 by John Wiley & Sons Ltd

studies have been published (for example Peel, 1984; Mangham and Silver 1986; Constable and McCormick, 1987; Handy, Gordon, Gow and Randlesome, 1988. A useful body of knowledge has been built up. In the USA similar research information is available, such as Lusterman (1985) and the annual survey by the journal *Training*.

The research information is supplemented by case-history examples, from both published and unpublished sources. The final ingredient in the mix is my own practical and consulting experience in strategy and development.

Many of the arguments could also be applied to other aspects of human resource management, and there is in any case a relationship between training, manpower planning, succession planning, and appraisal systems. Their exclusion from this paper is on grounds of focus and space. Modern conditions make it essential that human resource considerations are treated in a more proactive way than is the case in many organisations. The pressures of the 1990s mean that the successful companies will be those which integrate HR issues into strategy formulation, as well as in strategy implementation. Some of the critical issues which make this an imperative are:

- Demographic profiles in many countries, which suggest a shortage of school leavers.
- The increased diversity in the workforce, because of the solutions to the expected labour shortages, the increased progression (and not before time) of women, and the cultural diversity from globalisation and the impact of European harmonisation.
- The massive change that faces most organisations as they meet intensified competition, respond to the needs to be more cost effective, and at the same time meet enhanced customer demands for service and quality. Almost every aspect of this change has a human dimension.

It is no longer appropriate for human resource strategies to be designed only as a response to corporate strategy, because the modern conditions of business require a more interactive role, with human resources influencing the overall strategy. This is part of the argument for drawing training strategy and the resultant actions much closer to the corporate strategy than is the case in many organisations.

The paper will first develop the argument for using training in a more strategic way. It will then present a model for achieving this, and indicate the sort of policy changes that spring from the use of the model. Attention will briefly be given to some of the instruments that enable the model to be converted to action.

STRATEGIC ORIENTATION OF TRAINING

The idea of using training to achieve organisational aims, as well as developing individuals, has been known for a long time by a minority of companies. However the research and observations about this approach are of recent origin. Lusterman (1985) found that there had been a significant increase in management training in the USA, and that in numerous cases programmes were being used in the implementation of new strategies. Putting bottom line objectives on to training programmes was becoming the norm rather than the exception. Bolt (1985) provided case examples from Motorola, Federated Department Stores, Xerox and General Foods, showing how implementation had become the focus of training programmes with measurable changes in corporate performance as the desired result. Hussey (1985) drew attention to case examples of companies that used training in this way, and contrasted them with research findings which showed that most British companies had no idea that training could be used for such a purpose. Ascher (1983) had found that only one-third of respondents believed that there should be a direct link between corporate objectives and training actions, and that many of these were interpreting the question in a somewhat abstract way, assuming that if training is good for the individual it must also contribute to corporate objectives. The number of UK companies using training in a proactive way at this time was very small. However, more recent research among a similar sample by Tovey (1991) showed more top management involvement, and a more thoughtful approach to management development. Slightly more than half the sample linked the management development and training activities to corporate objectives and strategy. This still left 46% who felt that the links were inadequate, and this sample was drawn from the larger UK companies who might be expected to be among the leaders in training thinking.

The introductions to the first two books on this theme were both dated January 1987, but the different publishing schedules meant that Nilsson (1987) appeared before Hussey (1988). Nilsson's book was largely based on experience in Hewlett-Packard. Hussy's drew from the Harbridge House research available at time of writing.

Tovey (1991) found in her survey that the management development people in the sample were generally aware of the major trends affecting business, what might be termed the forces of change. However, the implications were seen by most only at a superficial level. For example most companies had taken some action to 'delayer' the organisation and saw this as a strategic issue that found its way into company courses. Few had recognised that an impact of delayering is to change how managers have to manage.

Alexander (1985) researched the problems which American companies found when implementing strategy. About two-thirds of the sample reported that the capabilities of employees were inadequate for the new tasks. When key skills are lacking, they can only be obtained by recruitment or training, or by some form of strategic alliance. The value of using training to fill gaps so that implementation is facilitated is attractive and obvious. This is only one of the roles that training can fulfil in implementation. If Alexander's respondents had been aware in the beginning that there were shortfalls in skills and knowledge, no doubt they

Table 12.1 Ten most frequent strategy implementation problems as identified by Alexander (1985) (base 93 firms)

Problem	Percentage of firms	My comments
(1) Implementation took more time than originally allocated	76	This does not necessarily relate to training, but it can do. An appropriate initiative can cut down this time.
(2) Major problems surfaced during implementation which had not been identified beforehand	74	Again training is not the universal answer. However, the right sort of course can be used to identify and remove problems
(3) Coordination of implementation activities not effective enough	66	Do not rely on training to solve all of these problems, but do not neglect the power of an appropriate training initiative to enhance coordination
(4) Competing activities and crises distracted management from implementing this decision	64	Training initiatives can be used to ensure the priority of a policy or strategy
(5) Capabilities of employees involved were not sufficient	63	This may be a recruitment problem, but is more likely to be a training issue. It is dangerous to assume that everyone can cope with something new, without giving appropriate training
(6) Training and instruction given to lower-level employees were inadequate	62	A straight training problem
(7) Uncontrollable factors in the external environment had an adverse impact on implementation	60	
(8) Leadership and direction provided by departmental managers were not enough	59	Perhaps they did not know how to do it better!
(9) Key implementation tasks and activities were not defined in enough detail	56	A training initiative can often help this to improve
(10) Information systems used to monitor implementation were not adequate	56	

Source: From Hussey (1988), reproduced by permission.

would have taken action before this became a problem. The right sort of training programme can help identify the less obvious training needs as it builds understanding of the new strategy and its detailed implications. Understanding is vital for successful implementation, and is the first step to commitment. The right type of training initiative can help to build enthusiasm for the strategy and commitment to it. In addition, training can be used to help work out the many detailed tasks that have to be undertaken to convert the strategy into action. Training can thus be a very powerful tool in implementation, and it is significant that eight of the top ten problems identified in Alexander's research may have been reduced or removed by a training initiative (see Table 12.1).

There are at least six different sorts of implementation situation which may be aided by training:

- Implementing a new policy.
- Implementing a strategy.
- Effecting an organisational change.
- Changing the culture of an organisation.
- Meeting a major environmental change.
- Solving specific problems.

Implementing a New Policy

There is not a great deal of difference in concept between using a training initiative to implement either a policy or a strategy, and in some situations the distinction between the two terms may become blurred. One difference may be the degree of precision with which quantified corporate objectives can be set as the desired outcome of the training.

> One of the world's largest multinationals, always seen as one of the best managed, identified that more attention had to be placed on competitor analysis both at top level and in the development of marketing plans by each operating unit. This was after careful analysis had revealed that much of the company's recent growth was without profit, because of weaknesses in the market place where the competitors were proving more aggressive than the assumptions on which past plans had been based. Many companies would have issued a policy statement, in the form of an edict, that in future strategies should be formulated after more rigorous competitor analysis. Many would have failed to cause any change whatsoever because:
>
> - most people would be complacent about their own approach, while accepting that others needed to do better;
> - some would believe the issue was unimportant and only pay lip service to it;
> - others would not understand the policy;
> - a few might not receive or read the statement.
>
> Aware of these probable outcomes the chief executive of this multinational

> personally directed a world wide educational initiative to bring the new thinking to life. He led top managers in a week-long introduction to the theme of 'what about competition', and insisted that several hundred senior people should spend two weeks on a strategic planning workshop. He introduced an 8-hour audio-visual presentation to thousands more managers as a basis for discussion of, and commitment to, genuine strategic thinking. Many week-long implementation workshops have been held throughout the world, with practical training in competitor analysis which has led to the implementation of more realistic strategies.
>
> Not surprisingly, this policy change has been made to work, and is enthusiastically endorsed by thousands of managers who are now convinced of its practical value. (Hussey, 1988)

Implementing a Strategy

The right training initiatives can bring the understanding and commitment referred to earlier, and can ensure that the right skills are available so that implementation is possible. The three examples given below show what can be done.

Lorenz (1986a, b, c) described how ICL used management training as a major means of implementing its strategy. Some 2000 managers were put through a programme which was uniquely designed around the company and its industry to improve competitiveness against American and Japanese rivals. The training programme, which cascaded through all levels of management, was held to have '...done at least as much as the company's new range of products and systems to give ICL an unexpected chance of prospering in the threatening shadows of IBM, Digital Equipment, and the Japanese computer giants' (Lorenz, 1986a). There were several tiers of courses, launched at the same time. All senior managers went through the top-level course over an eighteen-month period. Courses focused on key strategic concepts and industry issues, and were designed after a careful study of the company.

Rose (1989) showed how management training was the key to the success of the strategic changes instituted in the retailers, Woolworths, in the UK. This lack-lustre group underwent a change of ownership and management, which among other things resulted in a change of the group name to Kingfisher. The Woolworth store strategy was considerably changed: indeed some critics felt that until this happened it actually had no strategy, which was one of the reasons for its poor performance. However, the new strategy involved much more delegation to local branch management, and at the time the strategy was formulated it was felt that branch management lacked the skills to operate in the way that was now essential for the success of the strategy. A training programme was developed for branch management, and was held to be a critical step in the implementation of the strategy.

From late 1988 until the present one of my assignments has been with the British subsidiary of an international insurance company. Part of the assignment was advice on the design and installation of a process of planning. The training workshops which were designed to launch the process were also used as the first in a series of strategy formulation meetings, when real issues were worked on. As an example, competitor analysis was not taught as an academic concept. Instead, dossiers were prepared on major competitors and used for real analysis by the planning teams who attended the workshops. Each workshop was attended by a team to whom one aspect of the planning task had been delegated. Much more work was done outside the workshop, before strategic plans were put by each strategic business to top management for agreement. In this case training was used at the formulation phase, integrated with all the other actions the company was taking, and linked to a modest consultancy input. A result was considerable enthusiasm for strategic change, and a completely different understanding of the competitive environment in which the company operated. Many immediate actions were implemented by the SBU managers, as not all of the actions identified were strategic. Even some of the research subsequently undertaken among brokers, as a result of a new appreciation of the information needs of the company, brought immediate benefits in an increase in requests for quotations by many brokers who had not realised the firm's involvement in certain types of insurance work.

Effecting an Organisational Change

In both policy and strategy implementation there is the possibility that an individual may feel threatened because of lack of skill or knowledge to meet a new situation or because his or her psychological contract has been changed. The concept of the psychological contract partly explains why changes are sometimes resisted. Although a person's salary or job title may not have altered, there may be a change in the unwritten expectations that the person has of the job. Perhaps previously certain decisions could be made without head office approval. Now the changes require that they be referred. This may take some of the job satisfaction away. The same thing may happen when authority is delegated to people whose psychological contract had included the comfort of a boss who has made all the real decisions. With an organisational change it is even more likely that 'people' problems will emerge during implementation, and that these will frustrate implementation unless they are addressed. Training offers one way of approaching these problems.

'Delayering' and 'downsizing' are a common response to strategic pressures, both to reduce cost but also to take decision-making closer to the customer. That at least is the theory, and many organisations have implemented it successfully. Some have achieved implementation merely by ripping out layers without changing individual jobs, or training people in the new skills needed. Scase and Goffee (1989) found in their research in the UK that many managers were frustrated by the extra pressures put on them, and were on a treadmill from which many could see no escape, and from which they obtained little job satisfaction.

Organisational change often accompanies a new strategy, and both can be frustrated unless implementation is effective. L'Oreal in the UK used a training approach to secure the implementation of a new organisational structure. A new strategy was devised to increase market share for hair care products in the retail market. Because in the past distribution had focused on certain major retail outlets through which L'Oreal already achieved a disproportionate outlet share, it was clear that the new objective could only be achieved if distribution were extended to outlets where at the time L'Oreal were not represented or had a poor outlet share. The sales and merchandising teams had been organised to meet the previous pattern of sales, and it was apparent to the management that the new strategy would only succeed if these teams were to be restructured to meet the changed distribution strategy. Originally the company thought of implementing the structural change through announcement at sales conferences and supported by normal management action. Although this may have been ultimately successful, the fear was that it would take too long, during which time the success of the new strategy would be in jeopardy.

The changes in structure had an impact on the job of every person in the sales and merchandising teams. For example, the two teams were being amalgamated, so that every person would handle both tasks in the future. Different types of outlet would be called on, and transfer orders on wholesalers would be taken from many retail chemists. Again this was to be a new activity. The concern was that changes to the psychological contract would be perceived in a hostile way and that the turnover of sales representatives, which was already high, would increase. There was also a fear that many of the people would not have the knowledge or skills to enable them to cope with the new job requirements.

The training initiative took the form of a two-day workshop which was repeated on a regional basis so that all persons affected by the change attended. The new structure was announced in advance, but was not implemented until after the workshops. In the workshops there was immediate agreement with the new market share objective. A case study was provided, based on real market research, which required participants to work out a distribution strategy to attain the agreed objective. It was clear to all that whatever strategy was decided, the target could not be met without changes in the types of outlet through which the company reached the consumer. It was also clear to everyone that a change of distribution policy would require a change of structure. The new organisational structure was explained in the context of this shared understanding. The rest of the workshop provided training in some of the new knowledge that would be needed by participants, and identified the further training that participants themselves felt would be essential for them to become fully effective. This identification was done on the basis of an informed understanding by participants. The training element of the workshop included bringing in different types of retailer so that they could explain their requirements for merchandising and sales support.

This approach was reviewed by L'Oreal a year later, when the firm claimed that the workshops had enabled it to achieve the market share objectives. An unexpected benefit was a reduction in the turnover of sales representatives, presumably because of the greater feeling of commitment to the firm which had been built up in the workshops and subsequent management actions. It is doubtful whether so much would have been achieved by more traditional approaches to implementation.

Changing the Culture of an Organisation

Culture has been increasingly recognised as a factor in strategic performance, popularised in particular by Peters and Waterman (1982). Many organisations devote a considerable amount of effort, including a great deal of training activity, to maintaining a particular culture. The Peters and Waterman research, and a film based on this, showed how Disney consistently used training to develop a consistent attitude to customers at Disneyworld.

There are also many occasions when a strategic change requires a change in company culture, and again a training initiative may be one of the most powerful tools that can be used. In this case the training programme must go hand in hand with the management process. Goshal, Lefèbure, Jorgensen and Staniforth (1988) described how the change of strategy at Scandinavian Airlines Systems after 1981 required a cultural revolution. This was led by the president Jan Carlzon and owed much to his personal energy. The needed change was from a bureaucratic organisation that referred all decisions upwards, to a customer-responsive entity where all reasonable decisions were taken by the person having point of contact with the customer. Management actions to change the process included 'junking' the procedures manuals. 'Education was considered necessary to reap the full benefits of the new organisation, and both managers and front line staff were sent to seminars' (Goshal *et al.*, 1988).

Training initiatives could also be used more than they are to aid implementation in acquisition strategy, particularly where full integration takes place, and it is desirable to get both parts of the new organisation working together and to a common philosophy.

Globalisation strategies are causing many US and European organisations to introduce common training across geographical frontiers, holding the same courses but running them in appropriate languages. One of the reasons may be to build a similar culture across units of the organisation which historically had been run as separate companies.

Meeting a Major Environmental Change

The implementation need may be to bring awareness of the change or the working out of detailed tasks in response to a change. Sometimes this sort of approach may also be used to formulate strategic actions.

Sometimes changes in the business environment can only be seen in the broadest of terms, yet the company has to begin to reposition itself to pressures that can only partly be foreseen.

> In the mid-1970s British Petroleum began to think about some of the organisational issues caused by the environment in which it operated. Until 1973 this had followed a predictable path. After the OPEC initiatives of that year the relative stability was succeeded by turbulence. It became clear that the world of the future was going to be very different from the past, and that one of the requirements would be for managers who could cope with changes, many of which could not even be visualised.
>
> At the same time BP was changing as a business, moving in new directions and becoming more diversified. This again overlaid a different pattern of managerial needs, making limited functional experience in one industry alone inadequate for the successful operation of the BP of the future. It was not that BP would overnight become unrecognisable, but that it could start to draw away from many of the experiences and characteristics that had made it successful in the past. In fact the pace of change has been fairly dramatic, and the BP of today has many significant differences with the BP of 1978 when I was first involved. It also has many cultural values and skills which were recognisable in the 'old' BP, and it is these which have played an important part in helping BP adapt to new circumstances.
>
> In thinking about these issues it was realised that modern managers in BP would have to be able to manage in a very different way from their predecessors, and that the pressures on them would intensify as BP underwent future changes. It was not just that the managers of 1977 faced a different situation from managers of 1973, but that the situation would change many times as their careers developed. It was in 1977 that BP began to look seriously at the management educational implications of the diagnosis, and whether an educational initiative could be used as a means of ensuring that the younger managers of the day would be in a position to manage effectively when they became the senior managers of the future. (Hussey, 1988)

Solving Specific Problems

Training works in the implementation situations described above. It is not surprising that it also works in some situations as a means of solving problems. For example, one multinational engineering company used a training mechanism as a means of improving profitability at branch level. After careful research, a course was designed which included all the skills needed to improve performance including planning, financial numeracy, marketing and team-building. A high level of project work was included, and many of the recommendations from the projects were subsequently implemented.

In another example a workshop was run for a unit of British Petroleum, which had been set up to supply high-technology products and services for large ships. Ten months after beginning operations, losses had reached £500 000 without a single sale. The workshop resulted in solutions, and incorporated enough educational input to enable the managers to apply them. In a short space of time after the event sales of £1.5 million were achieved.

Indirect Corporate Needs

Most of the examples quoted relate to direct initiatives, where there is some sort of overt need that organisations can solve through training. There are also less direct needs, such as the particular management competencies needed for success to achieve the strategy. These may be related to the critical skills factors that are relevant to the company, the strategies it is following and its overall vision. This use of competencies will be returned to later.

A STRATEGIC APPROACH TO MANAGEMENT DEVELOPMENT AND TRAINING

It is possible to approach management training in a more strategic way. Before I postulate a more systematic approach I should like to present a model of how management training operates in most British companies, and many that I have dealt with in many parts of the world. Management training is seen as an act of faith which has only indirect connections with corporate objectives. Ascher (1983) found in her survey of larger UK firms that in only about a third of the companies surveyed did the training staff see any need for a connection between training activity and corporate objectives. A large minority of about a fifth argued *against* such a connection. Of those that did see a link, it was apparent that many were taking a very general view of corporate objectives and that the actual number who carried the link through to management development plans were much fewer. As already mentioned there are likely to be a higher proportion of US firms which make this link (Lusterman, 1985); Tovey (1991) showed that the position has improved in the UK but still has a long way to go.

Typically management development needs are assessed from the bottom up, the majority of companies favouring some form of annual personal appraisal as the main source of information. A few companies use assessment centres, and some may undertake periodic assessments using either consultants or their own staff. From these sources alone the training plans are drawn up and programmes either run internally or selected from offerings of outside suppliers. The only interface with top management policy is on the size of the available budget. Because most activities are positioned as an act of faith, management development expenditure is seen as discretionary and is usually one of the first budgets to be slashed in times of business hardship.

Figure 12.1 shows this process in a diagrammatic way. Some note is usually taken of environmental forces, especially when there are legal requirements. Often this, in the UK at least, is a matter of prudence rather than a defined legal need, and would embrace such things as safety training, and of course the professional training given by accounting firms to enable their staff to qualify.

My argument is that a new philosophy for management training should put more emphasis on corporate needs. Figure 12.2 illustrates this, by including an extra element in the decision-making process. This is the top box in the diagram which illustrates the essential link with corporate strategy, policies and objectives.

In order to make this effective, those drawing up the management training plans and programmes must have an intimate knowledge of the corporate strategy, and the ability to get behind the strategy to the management development actions needed to support it. It is worth noting that few strategic plans that I have seen are explicit about people needs. This means that to develop a training strategy it is necessary to get behind the market/financial strategies which are probably the bulk of the formal document. This may require surveys among senior managers, additional analysis by human resource specialists who have an appreciation of the firm's strategy as well as a knowledge of their own craft, and a large supply of common sense. Management development and training people who expect to be able to find a company book with all the answers will be disappointed. It is they who have to be proactive and write the book!

My experience suggests that once a company begins to adopt this model, it will find that it also has to change how it assesses individual needs. One possibility is the use of company-relevant competencies, which can be used as a basis for assessing needs. These have value in many methods of assessment, including assessment centres. Some brief thoughts on the various approaches that might be

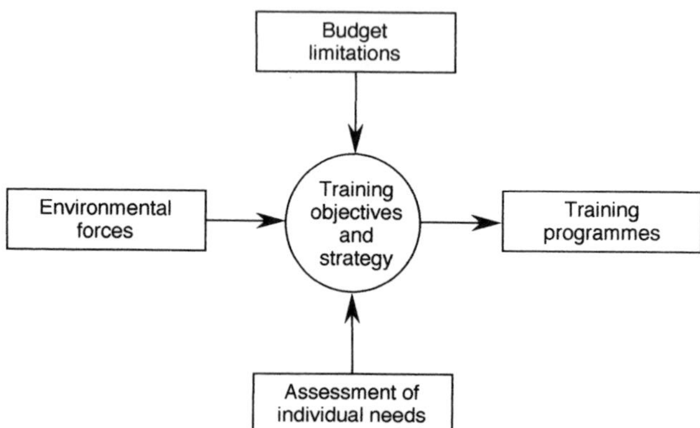

Figure 12.1 The traditional approach to training strategy

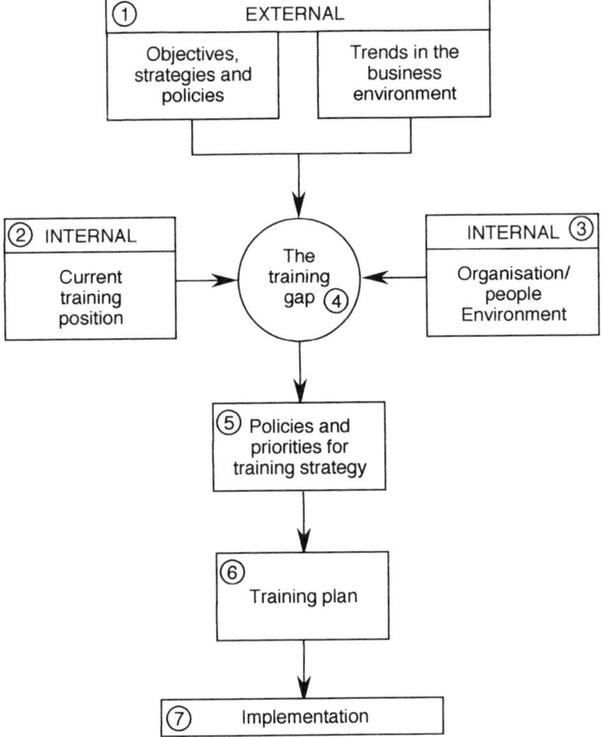

Figure 12.2 Strategic framework for training strategy

considered will be given later. The assessment of individuals remains an important element of the mix, but a strategic view may well lead to different ways of making that assessment.

Another new box on the diagram is the audit of current training provision. All our research suggests that cost benefit analysis is not a regular feature of training management, and that there is a tendency to hold on to programmes and the resources which teach them even when there is a high level of dissatisfaction.

Table 12.2 suggests a framework for auditing all current training activities. Many organisations find it surprisingly difficult to answer these simple questions, which suggests that the management of training has been less than professional.

Policy Implications of the New Approach

The integration of these various types of information in the approach shown in Figure 12.2 allows management training to be viewed in a business-oriented manner. Most organisations that work in this way change the priorities they had

Table 12.2 Audit of current training provision

For each initiative		
1. Aims	2. Results/Current plan	
• Objectives	• Number of events	
• Corporate goal, KSF or strategy supported	planned	1992
• Other rationale for initiative	actual	1991
• Target population	actual	1990
• How target population identified?	• Number of participants	1992
• How are people selected to attend?		1991
		1990
	• Participants as % of target groups	1992
		1991
		1990
	• When did the initiative start?	
	• How is it resourced?	
	• Breakdown of costs	
	• What were the course ratings?	
	• How are the benefits measured?	
	• How has the initiative contributed to the objectives?	

been following, and change many of their approaches to development and training. It also allows more initiatives which can be tied directly to bottom line results, thereby making it easier to demonstrate the value of training to the organisation.

Figure 12.3 suggests three groups of training needs that might be defined from such a study. Without trying to be dogmatic, because the decisions will vary by company, I have indicated on the diagram possible proportions of corporate effort that should be devoted to each group. Initially I should like to discuss each circle on the diagram as if it were a watertight entity, but later will try to show how initiatives that fall in the overlap areas of the circle may enhance the value of the initiatives, by killing two or more birds with one stone.

By direct priorities I mean initiatives that contribute directly to corporate aims and objectives, such as training events designed to implement a strategy or structural change, formulate strategy, deal with an issue from the business environment, implement a policy change, change culture to enable a strategy to succeed, or provide solutions to a specific problem or issue. By their nature these needs are likely to be met by initiatives that are action-oriented, have bottom line objectives, and have a high degree of urgency. In turn this affects the solutions, which may well be courses that cascade through several levels of an organisation, are entirely run in-company and have a high degree of tailoring. Only if they have

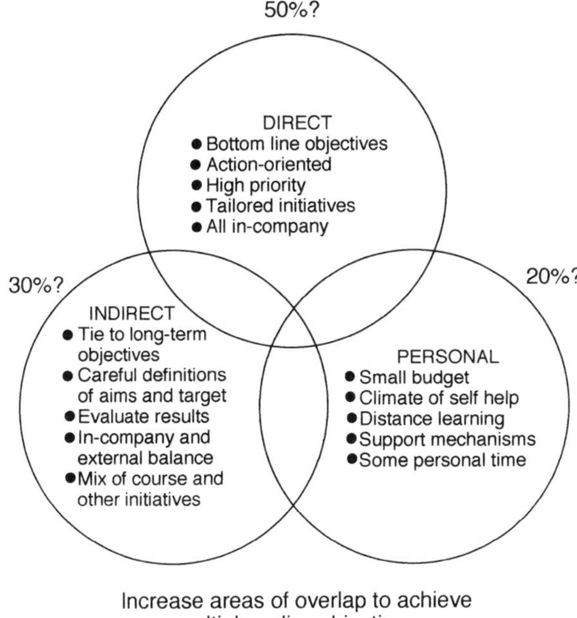

Figure 12.3 Some policy issues

these characteristics can these initiatives deal with the type of issue that is identified as a direct need.

Indirect priorities may be equally important for the company, and many of the initiatives will be more long-term both in their objectives, and in the time over which personnel are involved in an initiative. However, not all will be lengthy initiatives. Under this heading I include induction training, career development programmes, and actions to improve personal performance. I believe that the policy here should be to tie to long-term objectives where appropriate, to be very clear about the aims of and target population for the initiative. Here there may be a balance between in-company and external initiatives, and a mix of training and development actions. Many in-company courses under this category would benefit from being tailored, but the depth of tailoring may often be less than that for a course dealing with a corporate issue. The decision hangs on the learning objectives of the various components of a course or programme.

The final category is needs which are identified by individuals in discussion with their managers, but which are personal in that they do not have a high corporate priority. If people are motivated to develop themselves, there is likely to be value to the organisation in giving encouragement. What I believe is appropriate here is not company courses, but the creation of a climate of self help, and the provision of support. Under this heading I should consider giving financial support for distance learning, for example, and perhaps establishing a resource centre where self study can take place. In return for this support, I would expect individuals to give some personal time to the course of study.

Clarity emerges from such an analysis, but the benefits to the firm may be increased if deliberate attention is given to the overlap areas. For example, indirect needs can be tied closer to direct needs through the use of competencies as the standard against which the developmental and remedial needs of individuals are evaluated. The secret here is to define competencies which are in the context of the critical success factors of the business and which relate to it plans and long-term objectives. Except at the lowest levels of an organisation, the idea that there should be universal competencies that are the same regardless of the organisation is, in my opinion, completely barren. When I talk of competencies in this context, I mean the business and technical skills as well as the management and interpersonal skills, which immediately suggests that even within an organisation there are different clusters of competencies depending on functional and business differences. Competency assessment is a complex route, but one which can bring benefits.

A second way of adding value to 'indirect' initiatives is to build in some of the direct issues into the longer term development programmes, through teaching materials and project work.

Another example is of an initiative to help business units to develop sound strategies, which with modification can be used later for an indirect development need, to train less senior managers in business planning.

Creative thinking can help an organisation obtain much more from management development than the three-circle diagram may initially suggest, but the value of the planned approach cannot be over-stressed.

This approach does not mean that organisations should never do any training that can only be looked at as an act of faith. It is a question of balance. Just as it is poor management for the total management development strategy to be built from the bottom up, so it would be equally poor if it were to be totally built from the top down.

Designing a Training Initiative

A training initiative which is intended to achieve any of the above purposes has to be carefully designed, and in most cases should be specially tailored to the requirements of the company. Although this costs more than a standardised training initiative, the value to the company may be immense. Implementation of a strategy, if it is the right strategy, may be worth millions.

The tailored course may be a new concept to many readers. For this reason the three main approaches to the design of in-company training are first contrasted, following which the main steps in designing and developing a tailored course will be discussed.

The standard course

Although this may be delivered to a company audience, it is essentially the same course that the consultant will give to any other client. The client pays for delivery, and does not finance the development of the course. Often, when a course is put together by an in-house trainer, he or she will use various guest lecturers who employ standard material. Even if the course is completely delivered by internal trainers, it could equally well be given to another company, and includes nothing that is unique to the originating company. This is the cheapest type of course, and in the UK is one of the most common ways of approaching in-house training. It is unlikely to have any value in the sort of corporate change or implementation situations discussed here.

The slanted course

Here the provider uses what are basically standard materials, but spends some time trying to make the course more appropriate for the client. The activities undertaken may vary between merely learning the client's buzzwords to a genuine effort to make the course fit. When carefully matched to the overall objective, this approach may sometimes be appropriate for a particular change situation. Most UK suppliers who claim to offer tailored courses are in fact offering slanted courses.

The tailored course

This is a unique course built around the company situation. Concepts are translated into the context of the company, and a high proportion of the teaching material will be written especially for the situation. There are degrees of tailoring, but generally a course which is intended to implement a strategy, organisational change, or a new policy will be highly tailored.

It is possible for a company to design and develop its own tailored course with internal resources. Few organisations have the ability or objectivity to do this well, although sadly not all who try know this! Usually this sort of course will be better if designed and delivered by experienced outsiders. The reason for this becomes apparent when the main phases of work needed to develop a tailored course are considered.

Research

The length of this phase will be affected by the objectives of the course, the complexity of the organisation, and the quality of diagnostic work that has

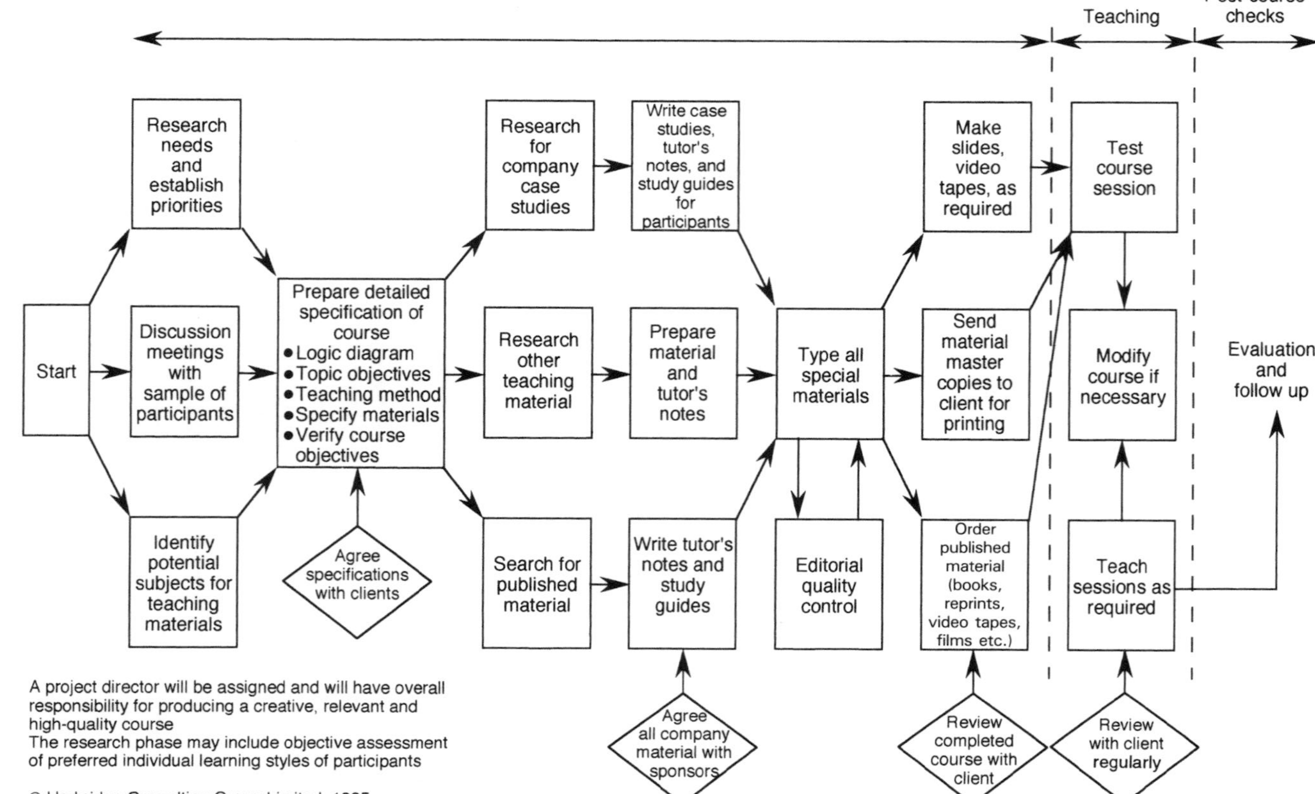

Figure 12.4 The Harbridge House general approach to developing tailored courses

already been undertaken. Whoever undertakes this task must be able to combine consultancy skills with a knowledge of what will work in a training situation. The purpose of this phase is to properly understand the issue around which the course is to be built, the priorities and weightings of the topics, the culture of the organisation, and the needs of participants. Thus it may involve a study of company material, interviews with key managers, group discussions with potential participants, and even surveys within the company.

Design and specification

After the research phase, the course can be specified in detail. This should result in a document for agreement with the sponsors showing the aims of the course, each topic included (with reasons), the teaching method, the materials to be developed, and the objectives for each topic. Agreement at this stage is essential if wasted effort is to be avoided. The key skill at this stage is in course design.

Development of the course

This is usually the most time-consuming phase, since often the situation faced by the company has to be mirrored in the course materials. These materials have to be researched, written, approved, and prepared for teaching. In addition to the appropriate functional, and often multifunctional, knowledge, a mixture of consulting, training and writing skills is needed.

Piloting

After a full review has been made of the developed course, it is desirable to run the first session of the course as a pilot. When the course is to be repeated many times, this is easy to organise. There are practical difficulties if the course is to be run only a few times in a short period, and a full pilot may not be possible. In these situations it is important to leave an interval between the first and second sessions of the course so that amendments can be made if these prove necessary. In cases where a pilot is possible, it should be followed by a careful review followed by any necessary modifications of the course.

Evaluation

As a rule little training in the UK is ever evaluated, apart from an end-of-course review which measures happiness more than it measures effectiveness. A course designed to achieve a corporate result is usually easier to evaluate, because in addition to personal learning objectives, there is a planned change of some sort in actions and results. Where there are only a few sessions of a course planned, the costs of evaluation may be more difficult to justify. If the course is intended to cascade through an entire organisation, then a break while an evaluation is made may be prudent.

A tailored course may be the most effective way of converting the intention to use training for implementation into concrete action. If done well, it carries little risk of failure and can bring enormous benefits. But whether the course is developed and delivered internally or by outsiders, a professional approach is vital for success.

What the balanced view suggested here does achieve is a means by which management development policies and plans can be prepared in a logical and cohesive manner. Many existing training activities of companies would fall away, to be replaced with results-oriented initiatives. The role of different training mechanisms can be more clearly determined and related to the aims of the initiative. For example, it may be desirable to use highly tailored courses and workshops, for corporate needs, and to use more standardised courses and distance learning for the purely individual needs.

In the underlying philosophy the switch should be from a purely cost-based decision on available options, to one of cost benefit analysis. It is common practice for training managers to take an out-of-pocket-expenses view of training initiatives. The cost of participants' time in attending training initiatives is rarely considered, and almost nobody considers the real economic factor, the opportunity cost of this time. As a result many current decisions on training matters are aimed at reducing the cost of the initiative, rather than increasing its benefits. This has led to many decisions which are wrong for the companies concerned.

A Different Slant to Assessing Individual Needs

It may be of interest to record that Tovey (1991) found that all of her sample of large UK companies used a performance appraisal method to establish needs, and for 40% it was the only method. Only 10% used competency assessment, and assessment centres, where used, were on a selective basis (which is sensible). Other methods such as surveys and assessments by training managers were used by the 60% that did not rely solely on appraisals.

The annual appraisal interview is a notoriously poor way of assessing development needs, as it depends on two levels of perception, the subordinate and boss, both of which could be erroneous. Greater use of the competency approach can ensure that the right questions are asked, but does not remove the bias.

We have found that bottom up assessment is particularly good at identifying needs that may have otherwise remained hidden, but this method can only be used for looking at management and interpersonal skills. On a confidential basis questionnaires are completed by the subject, and by at least three subordinates and/or peers. These are aggregated and the individual reports are not revealed to the subject. What is of value is the 'photograph' of management behaviour, which is often different from the self perception. This method can be used in a general way, although we also have approaches which are related to researched topics, such as the management of innovation, leadership, and organisation climate. The relationship with individual needs identified using the climate instrument has a direct relationship with the corporate needs.

Surveys can be a valuable periodic tool, and can be focused on the competencies that are important to the firm. We have found it useful to obtain ratings on perceived abilities and the perceived importance the person places on them. This is particularly useful in a change situation, when management sees the need for new skills, and this view of relevance is not shared by those below them.

The use of assessment centres is well known. What might be less well known is the way in which they can be designed to mirror the strategic requirements of the organisation, both in assuring the selection of the right people for a particular situation, and in identifying the strategically oriented training needs. Most experts in assessment centres come from the industrial psychology route and they give more emphasis to the individual than to the firm. Put a business orientation to assessment centre design and a very powerful tool is created. *HR Reporter* (1988) showed how Pratt and Whitney used an assessment centre approach to help restore their competitive position. Their response to being pushed out of the number one position in aero engines by GE was to break down a 21 000 person operation into 52 smaller business units. Managers had to be selected and trained to operate as small business managers, a move considered necessary to respond to the changed business situation.

CONCLUSIONS

The strategic view postulated here would improve the total approach to management development, allowing this function to add more value to the corporation, without necessarily spending more. At the same time it would provide a permanent mechanism for aiding the implementation of strategies, and remove many of the problems that currently occur, when the company finds that it has an implementation problem far too late. Bomona (1984) suggests that when a company finds that its strategy has not produced the right outcome, it is as likely to assume that the strategy is wrong, as it is to recognise that the problem may have been a failure to implement. This often leads to a change in a perfectly appropriate strategy. And this is hardly the way to effective management.

ACKNOWLEDGEMENTS

Parts of this paper have been published in Hussey, D. E. (ed.) (1991), Implementing strategy through management education and development. In *International Review of Strategic Management*, vol. 2.1, Chichester, Wiley.

Some parts have been drawn from papers by D. E. Hussey published in the

Management Training Update series by Harbridge Consulting Group Ltd, London and are used with permission.

Thanks are given to many colleagues in the UK and USA who have added to the development of the ideas in this paper.

REFERENCES

Airey, F. and Goodman, M. N. (1986) *A Survey of Distance Education in Industry Training*. London, Harbridge House.

Alexander, L. D. (1985) Successfully implementing strategic decisions. *Long Range Planning*, 18, No. 3. June.

Ansoff, H. I., Declerk, R. P. and Hayes, R. L. (eds) (1976) *Strategic Planning to Strategic Management*, Chichester, Wiley.

Ascher, K. (1983) *Management Training in Large UK Business Organisations*, London, Harbridge House.

Ascher, K. (1984) *Masters of Business: The MBA and British Industry*, London, Harbridge House.

Baston, R. (1989) *The Company Based MBA, A Study of In-Company and Consortium MBA Programmes in Great Britain*, London, Harbridge House.

Bateson, F. (1986) *Tailored Management Education: Myth or Reality*? London, Harbridge House.

Bolt, J. F. (1985) Tailor executive development to strategy. *Harvard Business Review*, November/December.

Bomona (1984) Making your marketing strategy work. *Harvard Business Review*, March/April.

Constable, J. and McCormick, R. (1987) *The Making of British Managers*, London, British Institute of Management.

Goshal, S., Lefèbure, R. B., Jorgensen, J. and Staniforth, D. (1988) *Scandinavian Airlines Systems (SAS) in 1988*. Case Clearing House of Great Britain and Ireland, Cranfield, No. 389-025-1N.

Handy, C., Gordon, C., Gow, I. and Randlesome, C. (1988) *Making Managers*. London, Pitman.

HR Reporter (1988) Training small business managers for a big business atmosphere, *HR Reporter*, Los Angeles, USA, V, Issue 3. March.

Hussey, D. E. (1985) Implementing corporate strategy: using management development and training. *Long Range Planning*, October.

Hussey, D. E. (1988) *Management Training and Corporate Strategy*. Oxford, Pergamon.

Lorenz, C. (1986a) ICL: Metamorphis of a European laggard. *Financial Times*, 12 May.

Lorenz, C. (1986b) ICL: A painful process of change. *Financial Times*, 14 May.

Lorenz, C. (1986c) ICL: The power of saturation training. *Financial Times*, 16 May.

Lusterman, S. (1985) *Trends in Corporate Education and Training*. Report No. 870, The Conference Board, USA.

Mangham, I. L. and Silver, M. S. (1986) *Management Training—Content and Practice*. London, Department of Trade and Industry.

Nilsson, W. P. (1987) *Achieving Strategic Goals Through Executive Development*. Reading, MA, Addison Wesley.

Peel, M. (1984) *Management Development and Training*. London, British Institute of Management/Professional Publishing Ltd.

Peters, T. J. and Waterman, R. H. (1982) *In Search of Excellence*, New York, Harper and Row.

Rose, D. (1989) Woolworth's drive for excellence. *Long Range Planning*, 21/1. February.

Scase, R. and Goffee, R. (1989) *Reluctant Managers: Their Work and Lifestyles*, London, Unwin Hyman.

Tovey, L. (1991) *Management Training and Development in Large UK Business Organisations*. London, Harbridge Consulting Group Ltd.

Training. An annual survey is published every October. *Training*, USA.

13

A COMPARATIVE ANALYSIS OF THE PERFORMANCE OF VENTURE CAPITAL FUNDS, STOCKS AND BONDS, AND OTHER INVESTMENT OPPORTUNITIES

W. Keith Schilit

College of Business Administration, University of South Florida

INTRODUCTION

The 1980s have witnessed the unprecedented performance level of large, publicly held investments, as measured by the Dow Jones Industrial Index (DJII). In addition, this period, which has seen the extraordinary growth of entrepreneurial companies, has been characterized by the remarkable performance of venture capital investments in small, privately held emerging companies.

Venture capital has had a significant impact on the success of thousands of small businesses. For example, researchers have found that the failure rate of businesses over their first five to seven years of existence was only 18% among companies funded by venture capitalists (Dorsey, 1977) and 8% among companies funded by a large bank's Small Business Investment Company (SBIC)

International Review of Strategic Management, volume 4.
Edited by D. E. Hussey.

(White, 1977). This compares quite favorably to the 50–80% failure rates generally associated with start-ups.

More recently, several researchers have begun to examine the financial performance of selected investment opportunities (see, for example, Bygrave, Fast, Khoylian, Vincent and Yue, 1988; Chiampou and Kallett, 1989; Ibbotson and Brinson, 1987; Young and Zaima, 1988). Despite the importance of this topic, however, there is still little empirical research that examines the comparative performance of such publicly held and privately held investments. Moreover, research is lacking on assessing the risk/return profiles of such investments. In other words, is a 20% return for a venture capital investment comparable to a 20% return for an investment in a portfolio of 'blue chip' stocks that comprise the Dow Jones Industrial Index, given their relative levels of risk?

According to research conducted by Venture Economics, Inc., approximately $4 billion is invested annually in privately held emerging growth businesses. How have such investments in privately held companies (as compared to investments in larger corporations) performed over the short term and over the long term? What returns have investors realized from these investments during this past decade? Is the performance of these investments commensurate with their levels of risk? What are the implications for public policy decisions? These questions are addressed in this study.

Research Questions

The purpose of this study is to track the financial performance of various investment vehicles over the past decade and to assess the riskiness of such investments, relative to their performance. In essence, this study examines the commonly held notion in finance of the relationship between risk and return by comparing the performance of privately held and publicly held investments. The hypotheses are:

H_1: The financial returns for privately held (i.e. venture capital) investments are greater than those for publicly held investments.
H_2: The risks (or variances in performance) for privately held investments are greater than those for publicly held investments.
H_3: There is a strong risk/return relationship in investment decisions.

REVIEW OF LITERATURE

Important Concepts in Financial Theory

Because venture capital involves investment decisions, financial theory has provided a solid foundation in this area (see Brophy, 1982, 1986; Carleton, 1986;

Carleton and Cooper, 1982; Cooper, 1977; Cooper and Carleton, 1979; Donahue, 1972; Hoban, 1981; Martin and Petty, 1983; Tyebjee and Bruno, 1984).

Risk and return

The basic notion of risk as it relates to return in terms of pricing of capital assets (see Sharpe, 1964) and as a measure of an investor's preference level—i.e. 'risk aversion'—(see Pratt, 1964) has been an important issue in financial management research. However, most of the research in this area has concentrated on publicly held investments.

Risk and return in venture capital financing decisions was first explored by Donahue (1972), who, by using Monte Carlo simulation, developed a generalized risk model and applied the model to large corporate ventures. The objective was to illustrate how formal risk analysis techniques can support intuitive techniques in the evaluation of venture opportunities.

Later research by Martin and Petty (1983) also addressed the risk-return notion that is so prevalent in the finance literature. These researchers reported that the level of risk is higher in venture capital investments than it is for mutual funds of publicly held companies as well as the Standard & Poor's (S&P) Index; furthermore, venture capital investments are preferred by risk-seeking investors.

Although we would expect early stage investments to produce better returns than later Stage investments—i.e. higher risks, associated with higher potential returns—there are conflicting results in the research literature. Hoban (1981) found that later stage investments produced better returns. Other researchers, however (see Charles River Associates, 1976; Poindexter, 1976), found that investments in venture capital firms (higher risk) had higher returns than did investments by mutual fund managers in publicly held companies (lower risk). (This is discussed in more detail in the section below on Performance of Investments.)

Market efficiency and the capital asset pricing model (CAPM)

As an extension of the notion of risk and return, there were a number of important studies that addressed the issue of market efficiency; that is, a capital market is considered 'efficient' if the returns are commensurate with the risks of the investment(s). Hoban (1976), in studying the characteristics of 50 entrepreneurial companies which received funding from four different venture capital funds, concluded that the market for venture capital financing appeared to be efficient with regard to observed risk/return relationships. Poindexter (1976) reported similar results to Hoban in terms of market efficiency in his comparative analysis of the performance of public equity markets and venture capital investments. Not surprisingly, the study was not able to produce results to modify the CAPM to fit the venture capital market; this was probably due to the fact that the CAPM itself was designed for 'efficient' *public* markets—i.e. markets with fully informed buyers and sellers, which is impossible in the 'private' equity markets—in equilibrium, in which more meaningful and objective valuations can be assessed.

The issue of market efficiency is later addressed in a study by Howat (1978), which examined the returns of small business investment companies (SBICs) which invested in entrepreneurial ventures. Howat found that the returns *were not* significant enough in light of the high risks associated with such investments.

Portfolio theory

Portfolio analysis theory is a normative approach for selecting portfolios on the basis of predictions about the performance of individual securities in that portfolio. This approach, which was developed by Markowitz (1952) and refined by several researchers (Fama, 1965, Markowitz, 1959, Sharpe, 1964; Treynor, 1965), enables us to examine the relative performance of diversified portfolios given varying levels of risk and expected return. Such an approach is the basis for selecting securities to be included in a mutual fund (see Meyer, 1977a, b). Interestingly, established venture capital firms manage a portfolio of investments in much the same way that a mutual fund manager manages a portfolio of securities. The key difference is that the venture capital portfolio is comprised of privately held, early to growth stage ventures, which are likely to require later rounds of financing, whereas the mutual fund portfolio is comprised of publicly held companies that tend to be more established. Despite the similarities, however, there is a lack of research applying the principles of portfolio theory to venture capital investments.

Performance of Venture Capital Investments

Several studies have explored the performance of publicly held investments (see Ibbotson, 1975; Ritter, 1984; Young and Zaima, 1988) as well as of venture capital investments (see Bygrave *et al.*, 1988; Hoban, 1981; Martin and Petty, 1983).

According to a recent study by the Joint Economic Committee (JEC), venture capital firms anticipated a minimum rate of return of 38% per year on an individual venture investment. Is that a reasonable expectation? Do individual investments perform at or above that level? What returns can be expected for a 'portfolio' of venture capital investments? In essence, do venture capitalists 'buy low and sell high'?

Performance of individual venture capital investments

There are numerous success stories of individual venture capital investments that give the appearance that venture capital funds, as a whole, perform remarkably well. For example, American Research and Development's (ARD) \$60 000–\$70 000 investment in Digital Equipment Corporation (DEC) grew to over \$1/2 billion in about 12 years (the actual numbers vary depending on whom you believe; see Kozmetsky, Gill and Smilor, 1984; Liles, 1977; Wells, 1974), which translates into a compounded annual rate of return of over 100%.

Of course, some venture capitalists have a way of overstating the performance of companies in their investment portfolio. As one venture capitalist has noted (see *Inc.*, August, 1989, p. 22):

What They Say	*What They Mean*
Product's 90% complete.	We've got a name for it.
Leading edge technology.	We can't make it work.
Limited downside.	Things can't get much worse.
Possibility of shortfall	We're 50% below plan.
Proven technology.	It nearly worked once before.
We're repositioning the company.	We're lost.
Upside potential.	It's stopped breathing.

Nonetheless, the performance of several venture deals, as illustrated below, is noteworthy (the examples are based on Schilit, 1991).

Kleiner Perkins Caufield & Byers. Thomas Perkins got into the venture capital industry in 1966 with a \$15 000 investment in University Laboratories, a Berkeley, California, based laser company. That investment grew to \$2 million. In 1972, Perkins became a co-founder of the prominent San Francisco based venture capital firm, Kleiner Perkins Caufield & Byers, which has invested in, among others, Genentech and Tandem Computer. Perkins has had an active involvement with his investments, having served as chairman of both Genentech and Tandem.

Sevin Rosen. Sevin Rosen Management, a venture capital firm founded by Benjamin M. Rosen, one of the most notable venture investors over the past 20 years, and L. J. Sevin, founder of Mostek, a semiconductor manufacturer, invested \$2.1 million in Lotus Development, a software manufacturer located in Cambridge, Massachusetts. That investment grew to \$70 million when Lotus went public in 1983. Sevin Rosen also invested \$2.5 million in Compaq Computer, a Houston based company whose first product was a portable computer. When Compaq went public in 1983, that investment was worth \$40 million.

Arthur Rock. Arthur Rock's investments as a venture capitalist include: Fairchild Semiconductor in 1957, a pioneer in silicon chips; Teledyne in 1960, a California conglomerate with sales today in excess of \$4 billion; Intel in 1968, a 'chipmaker', that is an outgrowth of Fairchild Semiconductor; and Apple in

1978, a pioneer in the field of personal computers. Rock's investment in Apple grew from $57 400 to $13.2 million (a 200-fold increase) when Apple went public in 1980.

Allen & Co. Allen & Company is best known for its investment in Syntex, a small pharmaceutical company, in the late 1950s. Within a decade, when Syntex became one of the leading manufacturers of birth control pills in the world, Allen's $800 000 investment grew to over $80 million. Allen & Company also invested in an early stage venture, Digital Switch, a developer of micro switching telecommunications equipment. This technology enabled MCI to become a major competitor of AT&T in the long distance telephone market.

Hambrecht & Quist. Hambrecht & Quist, a venture capital firm that also provides such services as investment banking and underwriting of stock issues, is responsible for a good deal of the growth of high-tech companies in Silicon Valley. Among the firm's notable investments are Apple Computer and VLSI Technology.

TA Associates. TA Associates was formed by Peter Brooke, as the venture capital arm of Tucker Anthony and RL Day, a Boston based investment banking firm. It eventually became an independent venture capital partnership and is now one of the largest venture capital firms in the country. TA Associates invested $1.7 million in Tandon Corp. between 1977 and 1980. By 1983, they had sold out their investment for $77 million. They also invested $171 000 in Biogen, a Boston based biotechnology company. They subsequently sold out of this investment with over a $10 million profit.

Some others. Several other venture capital firms have had similar success stories. Sequoia Capital, for example, a Silicon Valley venture capital firm specializing in high-tech ventures, has invested in Atari, Apple, Tandem, Tandon, Altos Computer, LSI Logic, and 3 Com Corp. Burr Egan Deleage & Co., a Boston based venture capital firm with $1/4 billion in paid-in capital, has invested in Triad, Tandon, Genentech, Tandem, Federal Express, and Chiron. The Mayfield Fund, a comparably sized Menlo Park, California, based venture capital firm, has invested in Amgen, Atari, Businessland, Compaq Computer, Genentech, and 3 Com Corp. And Institutional Venture Partners, also of Menlo Park, has invested a portion of its more than $200 million in committed capital to such companies as Borland International, Businessland, NBI, Seagate Technology, ROLM, Stratus Computer, and LSI Logic.

Failures. The most successful venture capital firms and venture capitalists have their share of failures. For example, in addition to its investments in Compaq Computer and Lotus Development, Sevin Rosen invested $400 000 in Osborne Computer Company, which later went bankrupt.

Franklin P. Johnson, who manages Asset Management Co., a Palo Alto,

California, based venture capital fund with approximately $100 million in paid-in capital, has realized tremendous returns from his early-stage investments in Amgen, Inc., a biotechnology firm based in Thousand Oaks, California, and Tandem Computer, of Cupertino, California. However, even for one of Silicon Valley's most successful venture capitalists, there are significant risks that go along with the high potential returns of early stage investments, as evidenced by his investment in VisiCorp, a San Jose, California, based software company that created the VisiCalc spreadsheet. Interestingly, it was VisiCorp (or Daniel Bricklin, the founder of VisiCorp—who has since taken on the role of venture capitalist), and not Lotus, that pioneered the concept of the spreadsheet, which shows that being *first* is not necessarily the surefire road to success.

Similarly, Fred Adler's investments in Data General, Daisy Systems, Life Technologies, and Advanced Technology Labs have made him a 'living legend' in venture capital circles. However, he was less successful in his investment in Tenet, a West Coast computer firm that ran into a major recession shortly after it started up in 1969.

Thus, even the best venture capital firms have had their share of failures. Osborne Computer, Fortune Systems, Pizza Time Theatre, Victor Technologies, Diasonics, etc., each had experienced, intelligent venture capitalists supporting them. Yet, all of those investments turned out to be losers for the venture capital firms which invested in them. The better venture capital firms try to limit their failures to one in ten—or, at worst, to two in ten. Their philosophy is that they cannot afford to have five or six losses that will be offset by one superstar performer.

Performance of venture capital portfolios

Sharpe's (1966) classic study of mutual fund performance is just one of several studies examining the portfolios of *publicly* held corporations. Venture capital investments, in a similar manner to publicly held investments, are managed by a fund manager. Consequently, in recent years, researchers have been concerned with the performance of *privately* held companies in the venture capitalist's portfolio as well as the overall performance of the venture capital industry (Bruno and Tyebjee, 1984; Bygrave *et al.*, 1988; Charles River Associates, 1976; Hoban, 1981, Huntsman and Hoban, 1980; Hutt and Thomas, 1985; Martin and Petty, 1983; Poindexter, 1976; Rotch, 1968; Timmons, Fast, and Bygrave, 1983).

It should be clear from the above discussion that investments in DEC, Apple, Tandem, Genentech, etc. are not at all indicative of venture capital portfolio performance as a whole. For example, even with DEC in its portfolio, ARD's annual rate of return from 1946 to 1966 was only 14% (Rotch, 1966). (Note: The investment in DEC had not reached its culmination by 1966. However, follow-up research, after DEC had been harvested, reports that ARD's return had fallen to below 10% by the late 1970s.)

Aside from ARD, studies have been made of the rates of return of the portfolios of other respected privately held and publicly held venture capital firms and SBICs in the 1960s and 1970s. The rates of return for these investments, after deducting management fees, ranged from approximately 12% to less than 20% (see Hoban, 1976; Huntsman and Hoban, 1980; Poindexter, 1976).

Given the fact that venture capitalists invest in ventures with high risk/return characteristics (see Carleton, 1986), we would assume that their portfolios would perform admirably. However, as Carleton notes, many of their investments have low or negative returns while few have substantial returns, thereby reducing the returns of the entire portfolio. This is consistent with Huntsman and Hoban's (1980) earlier research which reported that, in a portfolio of 110 venture capital investments over a 15-year period, the average annual rate of return was less than 19%. However, 18 of the investments (approximately 16%) were complete losses (Note: Similar findings were reported by DeHudy, Fast, and Pratt, 1981, and by Dorsey, 1977.) These percentages should not be alarming when you compare such low failure rates to the 70% or 80% failure rate that is typical of new ventures throughout our economy); 17 of the investments (or 15%) had rates of return of better than 40%; 4 (or 4%) might be considered 'superstars' since they had returns of greater than 80%; the highest return was 318%, which was for a \$200 000 investment (which is comparable to the average of \$228 000 for investments in this portfolio) that was held for only 8 months.

Some researchers have reported more positive results of the performance of venture capital firms. For example, Martin and Petty (1983) reported average rates of return of 27% for the stocks of publicly traded venture capital companies from 1974 to 1979. It should be noted, however, that these researchers studied the performance of the *stock prices* of the companies, rather than the performance of the ventures in which these firms had committed venture capital; the relationship of these two measures of performance is often misleading (see Wayne, 1988). Notwithstanding, a more recent study, using a similar methodology to Martin and Petty, reported that the average rate of return of publicly held venture capital companies from 1959 to 1985 was only 16% (Ibbotson and Brinson, 1987) and that venture capital firms had superior risk-adjusted returns that growth oriented mutual funds as well as the Standard and Poor's (S&P) 500 Index (Brophy and Guthner, 1988).

The popular notion is that venture capitalists generally strive for a 25–40% (or higher) return on their investments—i.e. an increase by at least 5-fold and, perhaps, up to 15-fold—(see Timmons, 1981). Such returns are certainly possible for any given investment. However, the research cited above suggests that the portfolios, as a whole, have not experienced such high returns.

Although the portfolio returns have not been as high as expected, there are situations in which certain venture capital funds have significantly outperformed others. Stevenson *et al.* (1987), found that higher returns resulted from longer holding periods, later stage funding of successful early stage investments, and attractive pricing of the deal. In addition, perhaps contrary to what might be expected, research by Chiampou and Kallett (1989) suggests that over the past 20 years, the more established funds had significantly outperformed the newer funds. It is worth noting that the weaker performers in a venture capital fund's portfolio often drop in the first three years. On the other hand, the better performers often take more than six years to reach their expectations. Therefore, even among venture capital investments, there are differences in their performance based on the maturity of the investment.

Comparative returns of venture capital investments over time

The returns of venture capital investments have varied somewhat over the last 20 years, both on an individual year basis and on a long-term (i.e. 10–15 year) basis. Returns—industrywide—have rarely been better than 20% in any given year.

Individual year returns

Between the late 1970s and the early 1980s, venture capital investments reached their all-time individual year highs in terms of annual returns for their investors—in excess of 30%. In the mid 1980s, returns were slightly above 20% per year. More recently (i.e. through the late 1980s), portfolio returns have declined further to their current level of somewhere between less than 10% to as high as 15–20%, for a given year, depending upon which data you believe.

Bygrave *et al.* (1988) analyzed the performance of venture capital funds from 1979 to 1985, as measured by their rates of return—or internal rate of return (IRR). They found that, although the average mean (i.e. mean)—IRR for one year—was over 30% in 1980, it was less than 10%—for one year—by the end of 1985, thereby indicating declining levels of performance of the funds. Jereski (1988) also reported that the returns of venture investments have declined substantially in recent years.

Long-term returns

How have venture capital portfolios performed over the long term? A comparative analysis of long-term portfolio performance, which was reported in *Venture* Magazine (in March, 1985), showed annual compounded returns for venture capital firms for the 10-to-15-year period from the early 1970s to the mid 1980s of anywhere from 20% to 25% as demonstrated below:

	Period of Study	*Compounded Annual Returns (%)*
First Chicago	1975–1984	24.5
Venture Economics	10 years	20–25
Harvard University	15 years	25
CIGNA	1970–1984	20+

Other analyses have reported that annual returns have been around 20% for the period from the late 1970s to the late 1980s, or slightly less than the results reported in *Venture* (see Chiampou and Kallett, 1989).

We should be cautioned, however, that anytime you have self-reports of the financial performance of privately held companies in a portfolio managed by privately held venture capital firms, there are bound to be discrepancies in the results from one study to another. Thus, the data just cited are meant to serve as approximate general ranges, rather than as absolute comparative measures of performance.

The performance of selected venture capital firms

The top venture capital firms have performed rather well. (Again, be cautious of self-reported data, however.) As a few examples, Sequoia Capital has averaged annual returns of better than 50% since its inception in 1973; and TA Associates has been averaging returns of approximately 40% over the past 12 years.

Of course, there is a lack of data available on the portfolio performance of most venture capital firms. Some venture capital firms will not provide data because their investments either are at too early a stage of development to reflect their performance or, simply, have not performed as well as expected; other venture capital firms will not provide data because, as privately held venture capital firms investing in privately held companies, it is their policy to keep that information confidential.

Comparative performance of investments

How does the performance of venture capital funds compare to that of publicly traded companies as a whole? The general perception is that venture capital investments have performed relatively well. About ten years ago, one of the leading venture capitalists in this country asserted that:

> there are enough performance records from the earliest venture pools to provide ten-year comparisons that suggest almost without exception, that venture capital investing has outperformed almost every other market—not to mention most managed funds. (Patricof, 1979, p. 125)

There is limited support for Patricof's claim. For example, Poindexter (1976), using data from 29 SBIC funds, reported a rate of return that was 63% higher than that of the S&P market index return. There was, however, much greater variability of the individual investments in this portfolio. This would suggest that the improved returns are offset by greater risks, which is indicative of an efficient market. Similar conclusions were reported by Charles River Associates (1976).

As might be expected, however, the empirical support for Patricof's claim has never been overwhelming. For example, Fast (1979) reported that a large percentage of venture capital funds that were formed within ten years prior to his study were no longer in existence.

More recent research has found that the average annual return for venture capital investments, which has been around 20% over the 10-year period from the late 1970s to the late 1980s, has been comparable to that of small stocks (i.e. a sample of small capitalization publicly held companies), but somewhat higher than that of the larger S&P 500 stocks and twice as high as the returns for corporate and government bonds (see Chiampou and Kallett, 1989). This provides some support for Patricof's earlier claim.

Have returns on investment been in line with investor expectations?

The popular notion (which is consistent with the JEC study cited earlier) is that venture capitalists strive for a 25–40% return—i.e. an increase of at least 5-fold and, perhaps, up to 15-fold—on their investments. Such returns are certainly possible for any given investment. However, the research cited above suggests that the portfolios, as a whole, have not experienced such high returns.

It is also important to recognize that as the venture capital funds have grown in size, and as their portfolios have become larger and more diversified, it becomes more difficult to realize the 30–40% returns that were prevalent over the late 1970s and the early 1980s.

The current situation regarding venture capital investments

It is getting tougher today to realize the traditional returns expected by venture capitalists. When Intel, currently a $5 billion company, was started in 1968, an initial investment of only $\$\frac{1}{2}$ million was all that was needed. Despite such a small investment, the returns to the investors were significant. Today, the situation is quite different. For example, in the mid 1980s, venture capitalists invested *$21 million* in Convex Computer, of Richardson, Texas. This is typical of high-tech start-ups; early-stage costs can often be $10–$50 million, with no guarantees of success. Convex was fortunate to have gone public in 1986 (before the stock market crash!), so we'll call it a success story. Despite the high risks involved with such a venture, the public offering brought some of the early investors only three times their original investment, despite a very strong IPO market. This is becoming more characteristic of the current venture capital market. It is becoming more and more difficult to expect a 10-fold return on an initial investment, let alone a 100-fold or more return, as was the case with such companies as Syntex, DEC, Genentech, Apple Computer, and Tandem Computer.

We can conclude that, although there are short run 'booms'—for example, in

1961, 1967–1969, 1972, 1980, 1983—in which venture capital funds may realize annual returns of approximately 30% or more, the overall rates of return for venture capital portfolios have been less than 20%. According to numerous studies cited in the finance literature, the returns for investments in public companies are somewhat lower. It is not surprising that these boom periods have coincided with favorable markets for IPOs since the new issues market allows for liquidation of (privately held) venture capital investments.

METHOD OF STUDY

As noted earlier, the purpose of this study was to measure the relative performance of selected investment vehicles and to assess the risk/return levels of those investments.

Variables Under Study

Independent variables

The independent variable in this study was the type of investment—i.e. the 'investment vehicle'. The investment vehicles that we examined, which can be anywhere on the spectrum from low-risk to medium-risk to high-risk, included:

- representative sample of select 'blue chip' industrial corporations (as measured by the Dow Jones Industrial Index);
- broader sample of large companies as measured by the Standard and Poor's (S&P) 500 and the Wilshire 5000;
- representative sample of smaller, 'over-the-counter' companies, as measured by the NASDAQ over-the-counter index;
- representative sample of companies having recently 'gone public' as measured by the IPO index;
- representative sample of companies on foreign stock exchanges (i.e. Japan, UK, France, West Germany, and Australia) as measured by individual company indexes and composite 'world' index;
- long-term government (i.e. Treasury, Municipal) bonds;
- long-term corporate (AA) bonds;
- short-term certificates of deposit (CD);
- short-term treasury bills (T-Bills);
- short term of money market accounts;
- precious metals (i.e. gold, silver); and
- representative sample of venture capital investments in privately held companies;

For comparative purposes, economic indicators (i.e. gross national product, consumer price index, residential real estate) were also obtained.

Dependent variables

The dependent measures in this study were:

- the short term (i.e. one year) performance of each investment vehicle;
- the long term (i.e. average over ten years) performance of each investment vehicle; and
- the relative risk of each investment vehicle over the short term and long term as measured by the dispersion (or the standard deviation) of the average returns for each type of investment.

Data Gathering and Analysis

Data were collected from a database which provided performance measures of privately held investments (see Chiampou and Kallett, 1989) as well as from several indices which provided information on the performance of publicly held investments. These data were collected over a ten-year period, beginning in 1978, to reflect 'up' and 'down' markets for stocks, bonds, and other investments.

We examined two types of venture capital investments, due to the relative differences in their risk levels (see Timmons, Smollen and Dingee, 1985):

- early stage venture capital investments (i.e. those venture capital funds that were 3–6 years old); and
- mature venture capital investments (i.e. those venture capital funds that were 6+ years old).

There were 20 early stage funds and 35 mature funds, each of which had approximately 25 investments in its portfolio. All venture capital funds were privately held, US-based partnerships. There was a cross-section of investments by these funds in early-stage, late-stage, and leveraged buyout (LBO) situations, as well as in high-tech, medium-tech, and low-tech companies.

This study made primary use of frequency counts and analysis of variance to determine the differential performance of the various investments opportunities and their associated risk (or variance). In addition, correlational data were gathered to analyze the risk/return relationship for these investments.

RESULTS

Table 13.1 describes the comparative results of the various investments over the ten-year period, along with the significant F values:

Table 13.1 Average annual returns and deviations of average returns

Type of investment	Average annual return (%)	Standard deviation of average returns (%)
Stocks:		
Dow Jones Industrial Index	11.4	13.9
Standard & Poor's 500 Index	13.9	13.8
Wilshire 5000 Index	12.1	11.0
NASDAQ Index	11.4	17.1
IPO Index	20.2	11.8
World Market Stock Exchanges:		
'World' index (avg. of 4 int'l mkts)	8.3	12.3
Japan	13.9	7.4
Britain	9.3	11.2
West Germany	1.9	28.0
Australia	7.3	22.9
Bonds:		
Long-term Treasury	11.7	14.0
Long-term AA Bonds	11.0	13.5
Municipal bonds	11.7	15.4
Five-Year Treasury note	10.8	15.1
Bank Instruments:		
3-month CD	10.9	3.4
Money Market Deposit Account	10.4	4.2
3-month T-Bills	9.0	2.6
Precious Metals:		
Gold (100 oz bar of bullion)	0.0	20.4
Silver (1000 oz bar of bullion)	4.5	43.3[b]
Venture Capital:		
3+ year-old funds	17.5	37.6
6+ year-old funds	24.4[a]	51.2[c]
Economic Indicators:		
Gross National Product	6.8	5.0
Consumer Price Index	6.5	3.0
Average New Single Family Home	3.9	4.0

[a] $F_{1,9} = 4.9$; significant at the 10% level.
[b] $F_{1,9} = 4.2$; significant at the 10% level.
[c] $F_{1,9} = 6.7$; significant at the 5% level.
All other F values not significant.

Total Returns and Variances

As demonstrated above, the highest average returns were realized by venture capital investments—24.4% for mature funds ($F_{0.10;\ 1,9} = 4.9$) and 17.5% for newer funds—whose returns were about twice those of publicly held stock. Venture capital investments, however, were also associated with the greatest risk, as measured by the standard deviation of the average returns—51.2% ($F_{0.05;\ 1,9} = 6.7$) and 37.6%, respectively—which was about triple the risk of common stocks. The IPO Index, which measures the performance of companies that have just gone public, had almost comparable returns (20.2%), but much less variance (11.8%), as the venture capital investments.

Securities of domestic companies traded on the major stock markets had returns of 11.4% to 13.9%, with variances of 11.0% to 13.9%. The smaller over-the-counter stocks had comparable returns (11.4%) to the larger, publicly held companies, but a somewhat higher variance (17.1%). Foreign stocks, on average, performed somewhat worse (an average of 8.3%) than did domestic stocks, but had a comparable variance (12.3%). It should be noted that stocks in two of the countries—West Germany and Australia—had much lower returns (1.9% and 7.3%, respectively), but had much higher variances (28.0% and 22.9%) than other stocks. The West German market, for example, lost 55% of its value in 1987 after appreciating by 45% in 1985.

Corporate and government bonds performed comparably (range of 10.8% to 11.7%) to domestic stocks, but had slightly higher variances (range of 13.5% to 15.1%). On the other hand, bank instruments (CDs, money markets, T-Bills), which are considered the least risky of the investments studied, performed almost as well as stocks (due to the high interest rates in the early 1980s), but had significantly lower variances (between 2.6% and 4.2%).

Precious metals were among the most erratic investments. Overall, returns were approximately 4.5% for silver and 0% for gold over the ten-year period. However, variances were very high—43.3% ($F_{0.10;\ 1,9} = 4.2$) and 20.4%, respectively. To illustrate, silver increased in value by 86% in 1980, but lost 49% of its value in the following year.

Individual Year Returns

As noted, individual year returns were somewhat variable, as illustrated by some representative investments below:

	1978	*1979*	*1980*	*1981*	*1982*	*1983*	*1984*	*1985*	*1986*	*1987*
DJII	−3.1	4.1	14.9	−9.4	19.6	20.3	1.4	33.6	27.3	5.7
World Index	8.3	1.7	3.1	−0.9	0.4	26.6	8.1	25.9	18.5	−11.4
AA Bonds	8.3	11.4	25.8	18.0	−2.3	−13.8	16.1	29.1	19.1	−1.4
T-Bill	7.2	10.1	11.5	14.1	10.7	8.6	9.5	7.5	6.0	5.8
GNP	4.4	2.3	8.9	11.7	3.7	7.6	10.8	6.4	5.6	6.8

In certain years—1982, 1983, 1985, and 1986—stocks performed quite well. Bonds, on the other hand, did particularly well in 1980, 1981, 1985, and 1986. Most of the investments lost value in *at least* one year over the ten-year period. The exception to this was the bank instruments—i.e, CDs, money market, T-Bills—which, as noted, were the investments with the least variance.

Default Rate

It would be expected that venture capital investments would have a high default rate. It is important to note, however, that although the default rate for early stage venture capital investments was 35.3%, the default rate for mature venture capital investments was 5.7%, or only slightly higher than the 4.5% rate for the S&P 500.

Risk and Return

The correlation, as measured by the Pearson product moment correlation coefficient, between the average annual returns for the investments and the variances (i.e. risk) associated with those investments was $r = 0.67$ which was highly significant ($t_{0.01;\,22} = 4.29$). As noted in Table 13.1, most of the best performing investments (i.e. the venture capital funds) had the highest standard deviations; in addition, some of the worst performing 'investments' (i.e. the economic indicators, which essentially measure how much we get for a dollar from year to year) had the lowest standard deviations. There were, however, low returns, but high variance (i.e. high risk) associated with the precious metals.

DISCUSSION

We have just examined the nature and performance of various investment opportunities, with a particular focus on venture capital investments. As noted, there are variances in the performance of such investments—for one individual investment vs another individual investment; for individual investments vs portfolios of investments; and for portfolios of investments over time.

The results provide some support for our earlier stated hypotheses. First, consistent with H_1, privately held (i.e. venture capital) investments outperformed publicly held investments. This was particularly true with the more mature venture capital funds, which had the highest average annual return of all investments examined. Moreover, the next highest returns were realized by the initial public offerings (IPOs), which had only recently made the transition from privately held to publicly held investments.

There was also support for H_2, which suggested that the risks for privately held investments were greater than for publicly held investments. The risks, as measured by variance—or standard deviation of the average returns—were greatest for the venture capital funds. Variances, however, were extremely high for the precious metals, particularly silver, which fluctuated wildly throughout the decade of the 1980s.

There was also support for H_3, suggesting that there is a risk/return relationship in investments. Correlational data confirmed that. We found that the highest returns were found in investments with the greatest variance (i.e. venture capital investments) and that low 'returns' were associated with the least variance (i.e. economic indicators). However, the investments with the lowest average performance (i.e. precious metals) had extremely high variances.

Of course, there were limitations with this study, especially with the information regarding venture capital investments. Because such investments are privately held, we have not been able to use publicly available data, which are generally more accurate and more reliable than self-reports which can be biased. Nonetheless, that is the only way to collect information on private investments.

It is essential that we evaluate the performance and the risk levels of the various investment opportunities to determine their appropriateness for investors. Moreover, it is critical that governmental policymakers (i.e. legislators, representatives from such agencies as the Department of Commerce and the SBA, officials from state governments, etc.) be aware of these results in order for them to make informed recommendations regarding investment opportunities. For example, in light of the high levels of performance of venture capital investments, what should be done to introduce legislation to encourage investments in emerging growth businesses? Can this be accomplished by maintaining a low rate for the maximum long-term capital gains tax, which according to Venture Economics, Inc., has been shown to be (negatively) correlated with venture capital commitments? What programs can be developed to assist the venture capital community and the entrepreneurial companies in which they invest?

Where do we go from here? Obviously, tremendous strides have been made in the area of venture capital research. However, there are numerous issues and approaches that need to be addressed. A significant amount of research has been done on the performance of the portfolios of venture capital firms. It is important to monitor the performance of those firms on a regular basis and to compare those results to the performance of other available investments. In addition, more attention needs to be devoted to the performance of leveraged buy outs (LBOs), which have taken on an increasingly greater portion of the portfolios of major venture capital firms.

Over the past few years, significant strides have been made in venture capital research. The field has benefitted from contributions from economics, finance, and several other disciplines. Empirical studies have provided us with an understanding of how venture funding decisions are made, how investments perform, who makes those investment decisions, and how public policy decisions affect the venture capital industry. Clearly, more research must be done to further our understanding of these issues and to better refine the field.

ACKNOWLEDGMENT

This work was supported, in part, by the University of South Florida Research and Creative Scholarship Program.

REFERENCES

Brophy, D. J. (1982) Venture capital research. In C. A. Kent, D. L. Sexton and K. H. Vesper (eds.), *Encyclopedia of Entrepreneurship*, Englewood Cliffs, NJ, Prentice-Hall, pp. 165–192.

Brophy, D. J. (1986) Venture capital research. In D. Sexton and R. W. Smilor (eds.), *The Art and Science of Entrepreneurship*, Cambridge, Ballinger, pp. 119–143.

Brophy, D. J. and Guthner, M. W. (1988) Publicly traded venture capital funds: Implications for insufficient 'Funds of Funds' investors. *Journal of Business Venturing*, 3. 187–206.

Bruno, A. V. and Tyebjee, T. T. (1984) *Venture Capital Allocation Decisions and Their Performance*, Santa Clara, Calif., University of Santa Clara.

Bygrave, W. D., Fast, N., Khoylian, R., Vincent, L. and Yue, W. (1988) Rates of return of venture capital investing: A study of 131 funds. Babson Entrepreneurship Research Conference, Calgary.

Carleton, W. R. (1986) Issues and questions involving venture capital. In G. D. Libecap (ed.), *Advances in the Study of Entrepreneurship, Innovation, and Economic Growth*. Greenwich, CT, JAI Press, vol. 1. 59–70.

Carleton, W. T. and Cooper, I. A. (1982) Venture capital investment. In R. T. Crum and F. G. Derkinderen (eds.), *Strategies of Corporate Investment*. Toronto, Canada, Pitman Publishing Co.

Charles River Associates (1976) An analysis of venture capital market imperfections. NTIS Report PB-254996, National Bureau of Standards, Washington D.C.

Chiampou, Gregory F. and Kallett, J. J. (1989) Risk/return profile of venture capital. *Journal of Business Venturing*, January, 1–10.

Cooper, I. A. (1977) A model of venture capital investment. Unpublished Ph.D. dissertation, University of North Carolina.

Cooper, I. A. and Carleton, W. T. (1979) Dynamics of borrower–lender interaction: Partitioning final payoff in venture capital finance. *Journal of Finance*, 34. 517–529.

DeHudy, T. D., Fast, N. D. and Pratt, S. E. (1981) *The Venture Capital Industry: Opportunities and Considerations for Investors*. Capital Publishing Corporation.

Donahue, T. W. (1972) An application of a generalized risk model to the analysis of major capital ventures. Ph.D. dissertation, University of Southern California.

Dorsey, T. K. (1977) The measurement and assessment of capital requirements, investment liquidity and risk for the management of venture capital funds. Unpublished doctoral dissertation, University of Texas, Austin.

Fama, E. F. (1965) Portfolio analysis in a stable Paretian market. *Management Science*, 11. 404–419.

Fast, N. D. (1979) A visit to the venture capital graveyard. *Research Management*, March, 22. 18–22.

Hoban, J. P. (1976) Characteristics of venture capital investments. Ph.D. dissertation, University of Utah, Provo.

Hoban, J. P. (1981) Characteristics of venture capital investments. *American Journal of Small Business*, 6 (2). 3–12.

Howat, J. D. (1978) An analysis of the investments of small business investment companies. Ph.D. dissertation, University of Illinois.

Huntsman, B. and Hoban, J. P. (1980) Investment in new enterprise: Some empirical observations on risk, return, and market structure. *Financial Management*, Summer, 9. 44–51.

Hutt, R. W. and Thomas, B. (1985) Venture capital in Arizona. *Proceedings: Babson Research Conference*, pp. 155–169.

Ibbotson, R. G. (1975) Price performance of common stock new issues. *Journal of Financial Economics*, 2. 235–272.

Ibbotson, R. G. and Brinson, G. P. (1987) *Investment Markets*. New York, McGraw-Hill.

Jereski, L. (1988) Too much money, too few deals. *Forbes*, 7 March, p. 144.

Kozmetsky, G., Gill, M. D. and Smilor, R. W. (1984) *Financing and Managing Fast-Growth Companies: The Venture Capital Process*. Lexington, MA, Lexington Books.

Liles, P. R. (1977) Sustaining the venture capital firm. Management Analysis Center, Inc., Cambridge, Mass.

Markowitz, H. (1952) Portfolio selection. *Journal of Finance*, 12. 71–91.

Markowitz, H. (1959) *Portfolio Selection, Efficient Diversification of Investments*. New York, John Wiley.

Martin, J. D. and Petty, J. W. (1983) An analysis of the performance of publicly traded venture capital companies. *Journal of Financial and Quantitative Analysis*, 18. 401–410.

Meyer, J. (1977a) Choice among distributions. *Journal of Economic Theory*, 14. 326–336.

Meyer, J. (1977b) Further applications of stochastic dominance to mutual fund performance. *Journal of Financial and Quantitative Analysis*, 12. 235–242.

Patricof, A. J. (1979) The new role of venture capital. *Institutional Investor*, December, 125–127.

Poindexter, J. B. (1976) The efficiency of financial markets: The venture capital case. Unpublished doctoral dissertation, New York University, New York.

Pratt, J. (1964) Risk aversion in the small and in the large. *Econometrica*, January–April, 32. 122–136.

Ritter, J. (1984) The 'Hot Issues' market of 1980. *Journal of Business*, 57. 215–240.

Rotch, W. (1968) The pattern of success in venture capital financing. *Financial Analysis Journal*, September–October, 24. 141–147.

Schilit, W. K. (1991) *Dream Makers and Deal Breakers: Inside the Venture Capital Industry*. Englewood Cliffs, NJ, Prentice-Hall.

Sharpe, W. F. (1964) Capital asset prices: A theory of market equilibrium under conditions of risk. *Journal of Finance*, 19. 425–442.

Sharpe, W. F. (1966) Mutual fund performance. *Journal of Business*, January, 39.

Stevenson, H., Muzyka, D. and Timmons, J. A. (1987) Venture capital in transition: A Monte Carlo simulation of changes in investment patterns. *Journal of Business Venturing*, 2. 103–121.

Timmons, J. A. (1981) Venture capital investors in the US: A survey of the most active investors. *Proceedings: Babson Research Conference* pp. 199–216.

Timmons, J. A., Fast, N. D. and Bygrave, W. D. (1983) The flow of venture capital to highly innovative technological ventures. *Proceedings: Babson Research Conference*, pp. 316–334.

Timmons, J. A., Smollen, L. E., and Dingee, A. L. M. (1985) *New Venture Creation*, 2nd edn. Homewood, Ill., Irwin.

Treynor, J. L. (1965) How to rate management of investment funds. *Harvard Business Review*, January–February, 43. 63–75.

Tyebjee, T. T. and Bruno, A. V. (1984) Venture capital: Investor and investee perspectives. *Technovation*, June, 1. 185–208.

Wayne, L. (1988) Management's tale. *New York Times Magazine*, 17 January, 42.

Wells, W. A. (1974) Venture capital decision making. Unpublished doctoral dissertation, Carnegie-Mellon University.

White, R. (1977) *The Entrepreneur's Manual*. Radnor, PA, Chilton.

Young, J. and Zaima, J. (1988) The aftermarket performance of small firm initial public offerings. *Journal of Business Venturing*, 3. 77–87.

MAILING ADDRESSES OF CONTRIBUTORS

Prof. H. I. Ansoff *Ansoff Associates, 10687 Arboretum Place, San Diego, CA 92131, USA*

Mr D. Asch *The Open University, School of Management, Walton Hall, Milton Keynes, MK7 6AA, UK*

Mr C. Carroll *College of Commerce and Business Administration, University of Illinois at Urbana, 350 Commerce Building West, 1206 South Sixth St, Champaign, IL 61820, USA*

Dr C. Coulson-Thomas *Chairman and Chief Executive, Adaptation Ltd, Rathgar House, 237 Baring Rd, Grove Park, London SE12 0BE, UK*

Prof. K. David *301 Kensington Road, East Lansing, MI 48823, USA*

Dr G. Hamel *London Business School, Sussex Place, Regent's Park, London, NW1 4SA, UK*

Mr D. E. Hussey *Managing Director, Harbridge Consulting Group Ltd, 3 Hanover Square, London W1R 9RD, UK*

Prof. Akira Ichikawa *Senior Managing Director, Japan Strategic Management Society, Room 604, Sunrise Meguro, 3-4-6 Shimomeguro, Meguro-ku, Tokyo 153, Japan*

Prof. Gen-Ichi Nakamura *SMI 21, 1-27-7 Naka-cho, Meguro-ku, Tokyo 153, Japan*

Dr F.-F. Neubauer *IMD, 23 Chemin de Bellerive, PO Box 915, CH-1001, Lausanne, Switzerland*

Dr J. Nicholls *The Old Rectory, Islip, Thrapston, Northamptonshire, NN14 3LQ, UK*

J. Pandian *University of St Andrews, St Andrews Management Institute, 3 St Mary's Place, St Andrews, Fife, KY16 9UY, Scotland, UK*

Dr J Parikh *IMD, 23 Chemin de Bellerive, PO Box 915, CH-1001, Lausanne, Switzerland*

Prof. C. K. Prahalad *Michigan State University, East Lansing, Michigan 48823, USA*

Dr W. Keith Schilit *Dept. of Management, College of Business Administration, University of South Florida, 4202 East Fowler Ave, BSN 3403, Tampa, Florida 33620-5500, USA*

Dr Harbir Singh *Associate Professor, Department of Management, University of Pennsylvania, 30 Westbury Drive, Cherry Hill, NJ 008003, USA*

Ms K.Soderberg *Harbridge House Inc., 11 Arlington Street, Boston, MA 02116, USA*

Prof. P. A. Sullivan *United States International University, School of Business and Management, 10455 Pomerado Road, San Diego, California 92131, USA*

Prof. H. Thomas *Dean of the College of Commerce and Business Administration, University of Illinois at Urbana-Champaign, 350 Commerce Building West, 1206 South Sixth St, Champaign, IL 61820, USA*

INDEX

Index compiled by Geoffrey C. Jones

CUMULATIVE CONTENTS LISTS TO THE SERIES*

CUMULATIVE CONTENTS BY TOPIC

State of the Art Reviews of Strategic Management

Role in the Planning Process

---

*Numbering scheme indicates **volume**(number): page range. For example **2**(1): 3–69 is Volume 2, Number 1, pages 3–69.

Systems in Planning

Process

Methods and Techniques

National/Regional Aspects

Organizational Situations

Functional Aspects

Other

CUMULATIVE CONTENTS BY CONTRIBUTOR

SUBSCRIPTION NOTICE

This Wiley product is updated annually to reflect important changes in the subject matter. If you purchased this copy directly from John Wiley & Sons, we will have already recorded your subscription and will inform you of new volumes.

If, however, you made your purchase from a bookseller and wish to be notified of future volumes, please complete the information opposite and return to Wiley (address printed overleaf).

INTERNATIONAL REVIEW OF STRATEGIC MANAGEMENT Volume 4

Please send me details of previous volumes:

❑ **Volume 1 1990**

❑ **Volume 2 1991**

❑ **Volume 3 1992**

For further details, or to place an order
Telephone: (0243) 770400
or Fax: (0243) 775878

Please complete details below:

NAME: ....

ADDRESS: ....

....

....

COUNTRY: ....

☎ ....

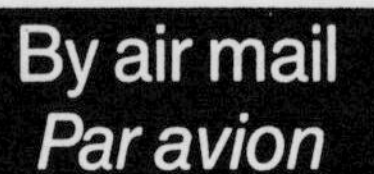

IBRS/CCRI NUMBER:
PHQ–D/1204/PO

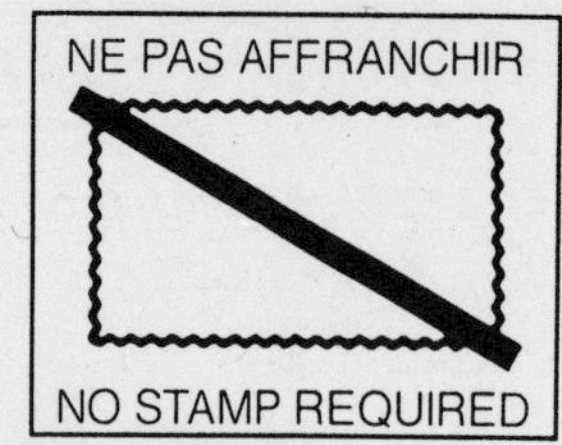

REPONSE PAYEE
GRANDE-BRETAGNE

Sarah Stevens (MARKETING)
John Wiley & Sons Ltd.
Baffins Lane
CHICHESTER
West Sussex
GREAT BRITAIN
PO19 1YN